Critical Engagement

Critical Engagement

Irish republicanism, memory politics and policing

Kevin Hearty

LIVERPOOL UNIVERSITY PRESS

First published 2017 by
Liverpool University Press
4 Cambridge Street
Liverpool
L69 7ZU

British Library Cataloguing-in-Publication data
A British Library CIP record is available

ISBN 978-1-78694-047-6

Typeset by Carnegie Book Production, Lancaster
Printed and bound by CPI Group (UK) Ltd, Croydon, CR0 4YY

Contents

Acknowledgements

This book has evolved from my PhD thesis that was undertaken at the Transitional Justice Institute, University of Ulster (TJI). When I moved to the University of Warwick in early 2015 as a post-doc, my plans to develop the book came with me too. It represents the culmination of approximately five years of research, reading and (re)writing, during which I often found the mere thought of re-reading some of my work again nauseating; yet, with the encouragement of many others, I persevered. Over the course of the book's lifespan I have accumulated enough debt of gratitude to last several lifetimes. As such, I wish to acknowledge the contribution that many people have made to help this book come to fruition.

An apposite starting point for reciting my long and ever-expanding list of thanks is with Liverpool University Press and Alison Welsby. Thanks to everyone, group aligned and independent republicans alike, who facilitated or participated in the interview process; 32 County Sovereignty Movement, Coiste na nIarchimi (and its local affiliate branches), Community Restorative Justice Ireland, Conflict Resolution Services Ireland, Éirígí, Expac, Irish Republican Socialist Party, Justice for the Craigavon 2, Republican Network for Unity, Republican Sinn Féin, Sinn Féin and Teach na Failte. Thanks also to the staff at the Northern Ireland Political Collection, Linenhall Library, Belfast for all their help and assistance during archival research. The collection is a magnificent resource whose worth is matched only by the helpfulness of those who staff it. I am also indebted to Daniel Holder of the Committee on the Administration of Justice for helpfully providing clarity on post-Historical Enquiries Team policing mechanisms for 'dealing with past'.

Many learned scholars have helped develop the critical thinking contained in this book. In particular, my PhD supervisory team of Kris Brown, Eilish Rooney and Bill Rolston will always have my gratitude for their wisdom, patience and humanity as they guided me through early academic development. Likewise, Kieran McEvoy and Fionnuala Ní Aolaín have always been generously forthcoming in their feedback and encouragement. Patricia Lundy helpfully offered words of encouragement and advice (as well as employment!) during my post-TJI and pre-Warwick days. Upon my arrival at Warwick, Jackie Hodgson and Alan Norrie kindly took me under their respective wings, giving me much needed encouragement to continue developing the book and my academic career. I am also indebted to Sharifah Sekalala whose unfailing humour and generosity as an office mate helped me settle in the early days at Warwick and educated me in the dos and don'ts of post-doc life. Colleagues at the TJI and the Criminal Justice Centre, Centre for Operational Police Research and Warwick Law School have also offered friendly encouragement and advice over the years.

Many other people have been instrumental in helping me develop the book, whether through commenting on early chapters, offering feedback on articles or seminar papers, directing me to useful literature, highlighting a particular news item, participating in and chatting at workshops or simply discussing matters addressed in the book over a coffee or the odd pint(s): Amaia Alvarez-Berastegi, Stephen Bartells, John Brewer, Anna Bryson, Henrique Carvalho, Anastasia Chemberlen, Phil Clark, Cheryl Lawther, Feargal Mac Ionnrachtaigh, Kirsten McConnachie, Phil Miller, Solange Mouthaan, Alice Panepinto, Sharda Ramdewor, Alison Riberio de Menezes, Fabienne Viala, Rachel Seoighe and Mark Simpson.

A very special word of thanks goes to Brian and Paris who distracted me with rugby (and tolerated my constant pointing out how much I loathe the sport itself!), pints and God knows what else as I slowly adapted to life away from the comfort of home. Your kindness in doing so will never be forgotten and continues to be much appreciated. Periodically cutting loose from the demands of work while in your presence has been immensely pleasurable and hugely cathartic! Brian Mór has never been short of words of encouragement and observant wisdom, and getting to chew the fat with him and Maureen has always been hugely enjoyable as well as informative. Since he moved to England shortly after me, Stephen has always been on hand to agonise over the trials and tribulations of the mighty Celtic FC – even though he reckons he is becoming a Sheffield Wednesday fan these days …

Finally, a few words of thanks will never truly do justice to the encouragement, love and support my family has shown me. In addition to keeping me cognisant of life beyond existence as a scholar, they are always willing to come to my assistance when or where it is needed. My sincerest thanks to our Brendan for enabling me to get the ball rolling. My brothers and sisters have always been hugely supportive, no doubt having to painfully feign interest in what I do in the process. Apologies for boring you endlessly when you'd rather just relax and enjoy life! My nieces and nephews are always a source of great entertainment and prevent me from taking myself too seriously. I'd like to finish by expressing my heartfelt gratitude to my parents for an incredible amount of love, support and effort they invested in me (and indeed my siblings) from an early age. Despite being the oldest and the first of a large working-class family to pursue university education, you never once burdened me with expectation. All you have ever asked is that I try my hardest and stay true to myself and where I've come from. With that in mind I hope this book reflects this (that is if you ever get around to reading it…).

I'd like to finish the acknowledgements by dedicating this book to my paternal grandfather Mick 'Wally' and my maternal grandmother Josie – two unique old-school characters who were never short of encouragement or words of wisdom yet who sadly never got to see this book come into print.

Figures and Tables

Abbreviations

32CSM	32 County Sovereignty Movement
AIA	Anglo-Irish Agreement
ANC	African National Congress
CAJ	Committee on the Administration of Justice
CHIS	Covert Human Intelligence Source
CRJ	Community Restorative Justice
DUP	Democratic Unionist Party
ETA	Euskadi Ta Askatasuna
FMNL	Farabundo Martí National Liberation Front
GAA	Gaelic Athletic Association
GFA	Good Friday Agreement
HET	Historical Enquiries Team
HIU	Historical Investigations Unit
HMIC	Her Majesty's Inspectorate of Constabulary
INLA	Irish National Liberation Army
IRA	Irish Republican Army
IRSP	Irish Republican Socialist Party
JSA	Justice and Security (Northern Ireland) Act 2007
MEP	Member of the European Parliament
MI5	Military Intelligence, Section 5
MLA	Member of the Legislative Assembly
MP	Member of Parliament
NCA	National Crime Agency
NIPB	Northern Ireland Policing Board
NIRPOA	Northern Ireland Retired Police Officers Association
OPONI	Office of the Police Ombudsman for Northern Ireland
PANI	Police Authority of Northern Ireland
PBP	People before Profit
PCSP	Police and Community Safety Partnerships
PLO	Palestinian Liberation Organisation

PSNI	Police Service of Northern Ireland
RAAD	Republican Action Against Drugs
RIC	Royal Irish Constabulary
RIPA	Regulation of Investigatory Powers Act 2000
RNU	Republican Network for Unity
RSF	Republican Sinn Féin
RUC GC	RUC George Cross Foundation
RUC	Royal Ulster Constabulary
SAS	Special Air Service
SDLP	Social Democratic and Labour Party
SHA	Stormont House Agreement
TACT	Terrorism Act
TD	Teachta Dála
UDR	Ulster Defence Regiment
UVF	Ulster Volunteer Force

Introduction

On Sunday 28 January 2007, at a specially convened Extraordinary *Ard Fheis* (party conference) Sinn Féin, the dominant political voice within modern Irish republicanism, voted in favour of endorsing the Police Service of Northern Ireland (PSNI). The party rank and file backed a leadership proposal to 'support the PSNI and criminal justice system' so that 'a civic policing service, accountable and representative of the community is delivered as quickly as possible'.[1] The motion was carried by a comfortable majority despite some internal disquiet. The Sinn Féin leadership had 'won' the debate and avoided the public walk out previously seen at pivotal *Ard Fheissana*.[2] The move marked a comprehensive redefinition of the relationship between the policing apparatus upholding the Northern Ireland state and Irish republicans with fundamental ideological opposition to that state. Sinn Féin's formal endorsement of policing was notable for both the historical relationship between Irish republicans and policing in the North of Ireland, and for the wider transitional backdrop against which it occurred.[3]

To grasp the magnitude of the move in terms of the former, one must first acknowledge that Irish republicans have traditionally had a fractious relationship with Northern Irish police forces – most notably the Royal Ulster Constabulary (RUC). This was characterised by violent opposition, mutual suspicion and political antagonism. Irish republicans and policing agents in Northern Ireland have been a source of violence, suffering and, on many occasions, death for one another. Given this fraught historical backdrop one

[1] 'Motion Passed by Sinn Féin at Extraordinary Ard Fheis on Policing, RDS, Dublin (28 January 2007)': www.cain.ulst.ac.uk/issues/politics/docs/sf/sf280107motion.htm (accessed 24 April 2012).

[2] Morrison, 2013.

[3] In reflecting the world-view of the research group, the author will use the terms Northern Ireland, the North of Ireland and the six counties interchangeably throughout the book.

may ask how a relationship of 'critical engagement' with those long considered the perennial 'other' was even possible. To understand 'critical engagement' in its proper context, one must not only remain cognisant of this historical relationship but also look *beyond* it to evaluate the move in accordance with political developments unfolding at the time.

If Sinn Féin endorsement of policing is to be truly understood, it must be necessarily viewed as a component of a choreographed process of political transition rather than an aberration that materialised in an apolitical vacuum. The veracity of this is borne out in the Ard Fheis motion itself, which stated that its implementation would occur 'only when the power-sharing institutions are established'.[4] While the move was seminal in its own right, it must nonetheless be viewed cumulatively with events that preceded and followed it. Although the 1998 Good Friday Agreement (GFA) significantly reduced political violence, the steady political progress it was expected to deliver remained elusive. Power-sharing institutions were established but they quickly became hostages to fortune of wider disagreement over decommissioning.[5] Following the 'Stormontgate' affair, the devolved institutions fell into prolonged suspension in October 2002. Direct rule from Westminster was reimposed in the absence of any solution to the political impasse, and even though political violence did not re-erupt the political process had stalled. Making continued and significant electoral gains but faced with an environment of political stagnation, Irish republicans exhibited a growing willingness to pursue ideological goals through exclusively peaceful means.

In the months prior to the policing debate, Irish republicanism had made tentative moves to commit irrevocably to conflict transformation. In July 2005, the Irish Republican Army (IRA) moved from a position of being on a permanent ceasefire to order a formal end to its armed campaign. IRA volunteers were instructed to 'assist the development of purely political and democratic programmes through exclusively peaceful means'.[6] After completing the protracted process of placing its weapons beyond use, the St Andrews Agreement set out a detailed series of proposals designed to resuscitate the power-sharing institutions via a compromise involving Sinn Féin and the hard-line Democratic Unionist Party (DUP). Accordingly, if Sinn Féin formally endorsed policing and

---

[4] 'Motion Passed by Sinn Féin at Extraordinary Ard Fheis on Policing, RDS, Dublin, 28 January 2007': http://cain.ulst.ac.uk/issues/politics/docs/sf/sf280107motion.htm (accessed 24 April 2012).

[5] Dixon, 2013.

[6] 'Text of Irish Republican Army (IRA) Statement on the Ending of the Armed Campaign (28 July 2005)': http://cain.ulst.ac.uk/othelem/organ/ira/ira280705.htm (accessed 10 March 2014).

criminal justice then the DUP would enter government with them. In furtherance of securing the return of the devolved institutions, Sinn Féin duly moved to instigate 'critical engagement' with policing. Consequent to this decision, the power-sharing institutions were re-established following elections in March 2007. Sinn Féin entered into government with the previously anti-power-sharing DUP as a lead partner that May. 'Critical engagement' was therefore the zenith of a protracted process whereby the Sinn Féin brand of Irish republicanism abandoned armed struggle, brought itself in from the political wilderness and pursued its goals by working the state from within. This, however, was not without internal opposition within the wider Irish republican constituency. Carrying on the unerring tradition of dividing over political compromise,[7] the policing debate not only gave renewed impetus to criticism of Sinn Féin by long-term detractors but it also hastened further departures. This birthed new political and militant groups to contest the field with the hitherto dominant Provisionals. It is worth briefly outlining the multifarious groups with whom Sinn Féin now competes for hegemony within the modern Irish republican constituency.

Republican Sinn Féin (RSF) are a traditionalist party with a purist approach to Irish republicanism. Rejecting every, and any, form of compromise, their loyalty is to a form of Irish republican doctrinarism that Kevin Bean labels 'the politics of faith'.[8] They split from the Provisionals in 1986, when the latter dropped their policy of abstentionism to Dáil Éireann (the Irish parliament). Their rejection of 'British policing' mirrors their rejection of any partitionist administration of 'British rule' in Ireland. The 32 County Sovereignty Movement (32CSM) split from Sinn Féin over pre-GFA acceptance of the Mitchell Principles of non-violence. They are hardline but less puritanical than RSF, having remained in the Provisional fold following the abstentionism policy change. Both these groups have been unapologetic in their support for continued armed struggle. They are generally regarded as the political wings of the Continuity IRA and Real IRA respectively.[9] The Real IRA subsequently merged with vigilante group Republican Action Against Drugs (RAAD) and non-aligned militant cells into the 'New IRA', while the Continuity IRA has factionalised into competing groups.[10] The Irish Republican Socialist Party (IRSP), the political wing of the Irish National Liberation Army (INLA), who formally ended their campaign in 2009,[11] also opposed the move. They are not,

[7] Morrison, 2013.

[8] Bean, 2007a, 181.

[9] Whiting, 2015.

[10] Morrison, 2013.

[11] '"Armed Struggle is Over" – INLA', BBC News, 11 October 2009: http://news.bbc.co.uk/1/hi/northern_ireland/8301241.stm (accessed 6 October 2015).

however, an offshoot of the Provisional movement. Having opted to stay with the Officials following the Official–Provisional split in 1970, they later split from the Officials in 1974.[12] Opposition was also forthcoming from socialist republican group Éirígí, which had been founded just prior to the policing debate amidst discontent with the changing direction of Sinn Féin policy. Focused on non-violent direct action to promote left-wing internationalism and anti-imperialism, the party has no formal links to militant 'spoiler' groups. IRSP and Éirígí criticism of Sinn Féin policy, not just on the matter of policing but on other social and economic issues addressed through the devolved assembly, has been decidedly leftist in nature and devoid of the hard-line militarism RSF and 32CSM relies on. More specifically, the move was opposed by a disaffected group of former prisoners who broke ranks during the debate. The group later morphed into the political party Republican Network for Unity (RNU). The RNU relationship with militant groups is more ambiguous, having expressed an affinity of sorts with Óglaigh na hÉireann.[13] RNU espouses criticism of Sinn Féin that is a hybrid of the hard-line militarism of RSF and the 32CSM, and the leftist critique of Éirígí and the IRSP. More recently the move has been opposed by the 1916 Societies which are a commemorative group with the policy of excluding those supportive of the PSNI from its membership.[14] The move was also opposed by a number of independent republicans – including some who were later elected to political office. In September 2016, Saoradh, an 'unashamed [*sic*] revolutionary party', was launched. The party was endorsed by New IRA-aligned prisoners, and presented itself as a radical republican socialist political alternative to post-GFA Sinn Féin. Outlining its opposition to current Sinn Féin strategy, chairman Davy Jordan rounded on the 'false prophets ... defeated and consumed by the very system they claim to oppose' and rejected devolved institutions for being 'designed to prevent the Irish people regaining their national sovereignty'.[15] How and if Saoradh can provide a greater electoral challenge to the Sinn Féin hegemony than Éirígí and RNU have (should they contest elections) is at the time of writing largely a matter of conjecture. Evidently, then, modern Irish republicanism is a densely populated political domain where contestation cannot be falsely reduced to the matter of being either for or against continued armed activity. Disagreement within

12 Hanley and Millar, 2010.

13 Frampton, 2011.

14 Hearty, 2017.

15 Connla Young, 'New "Revolutionary" Republican Party Saoradh Launched', *Irish News*, 26 September 2016: www.irishnews.com/news/politicalnews/2016/09/26/news/new-revolutionary-republican-party-saoradh-launched-708613/ (accessed 4 October 2016).

modern Irish republicanism is multivalent: something that a reduction of the matter to being for or against armed struggle, or being for or against Sinn Féin does not quite cover. Despite a false conflation of all those opposed to the 'mainstream' republicanism of Sinn Féin under the imprecise 'dissident' tag, arcane disagreement and competition exists among anti-policing militant and political groups.[16] That said, this book does not delve into this more nuanced disagreement in any particular depth, largely due to the fact that the memory politics of the policing debate falls neatly along fault lines of being either supportive of or against policing. That does not, however, deny or overlook the importance of division among anti-policing Irish republicanism itself – something alluded to in the interview process where members of certain groups were keen to distance themselves from other 'impure' or ideologically tainted groups.

Why this book?

Drawing on the historical, political and transitional contexts of the Irish republican policing debate, this book looks beyond sensationalist headlines and political soundbites trumpeting the historicity of the decision to interrogate the fundamental issues that lie behind 'critical engagement'. The formal acceptance of policing by Sinn Féin posed just as many quandaries as it remedied. Obvious questions arose: how did former combatants circle the square peg of policing with everything held as irrefutable during 30 years of conflict? How can a radical departure from physical force republicanism be reconciled with the sacrifices made by the Irish republican war dead? What of those unwilling to circle this most problematic of square pegs? How and where can they broadcast their opposition to policing? And what of those ideological purists who opposed the current Sinn Féin strategy from its very inception– where do they fit in during the policing debate?

This book addresses each of these quagmires by critically evaluating the role that memory plays in the continuing Irish republican debate on policing. It examines the interlocking questions of *what* role memory plays in the debate and *how* it performs this role. Specific emphasis is placed on the 'memory politics' of the debate: in other words, the process of selectively 'remembering' or 'forgetting' the past through the construction, maintenance and challenging of politically motivated discourses.[17] However, this book also recognises that

[16] Horgan, 2013.

[17] Hearty, 2016b.

the role of memory in the debate was not strictly confined to the internal politicking of competing Irish republican hegemons, but is evident in other ways and on other levels too. In particular, this book draws on the concept of the 'malleability of memory' – the ability to mould and remould memory in accordance with present needs[18] – to interrogate *how* and *why* memory is moulded by different actors, in different contexts and in different ways throughout the debate. To this end, the book examines how memory is used at the individual and collective level, how it is used at grassroots and at an elite level, and how it is used in contestation over the past *between* and *within* opposing ethno-nationalist blocs embarking on transition. The book uses the Irish republican policing debate as an empirical case study for providing an insight into the relationship between memory and elite agendas, the emergence of subaltern voices in transitional processes and the interaction and tension between individual and collective memory during periods of transition. As Frank Haldemann highlights, the term 'transitional justice' denotes a process of transition, which in turn raises the question of what society is transitioning from and what it is transitioning to. In answering his own question, Haldemann argues that in the North of Ireland this is transition from a 'conflicted democracy' beset by political violence to a post-conflict society of 'peace' narrowly defined as the absence of such violence.[19] It is worth briefly drawing out his point through further examination of the concept of transitional justice and the concept of transition within peace processes as relevant to the North of Ireland.

Jon Elster argues that, at its most based understanding, transitional justice represents movement from one political state to another.[20] Ruti Teitel goes further in her conceptualisation by arguing that transitional justice does not just include a process of political change but also includes processes to address past wrongdoing.[21] The paradigmatic understanding of transitional justice states is those that move from authoritarian rule to democracy while seeking to address the legacy of state repression during the previous era of dictatorship.[22] Latin American transitions like Chile are often cited as examples of this model. However, there are also non-paradigmatic transitions, characterised by the reform of states that were regarded as democratic and based on the rule of law but were nonetheless challenged by the political violence of non-state actors and defended through a combination of emergency provisions and low-level state

[18] Brown, 2009b.

[19] Haldemann, 2006.

[20] Elster, 2012.

[21] Teitel, 2000.

[22] McAuliffe, 2011.

violence.[23] This is the 'conflicted democracy' framework within which transitional justice academics like Haldemann have placed the North of Ireland. For Padraig McAuliffe, this means that the Northern Ireland transition has been movement from a state beset by political violence and human rights abuses into a reformed state built on consociational power sharing where political disagreement continues but the violence and abuses of the past are less likely to happen.[24] Accordingly, unlike other transitions, Northern Ireland has not witnessed a clean break with the past.[25] There has been no removal of an old dictatorial regime or military junta. Nor was there any decisive military victory for the state or non-state groups that had fought each other to stalemate. Rather, a negotiated settlement arose whereby under the GFA the systems of governance were reformed to allow those previously excluded and engaged in political violence to participate. In effect, those who resisted the pre-GFA state and those who presided over it now sit with each other in governance of the post-GFA state. However, while governing parties in the post-GFA state have committed to non-violence and power sharing, they have not decommissioned their irreconcilable ideological aspirations, nor have they repudiated their pasts. What has emerged from this peculiarity is fierce competition over how political violence in the pre-GFA state is now represented and interpreted. This has seen the past simultaneously framed by competing frameworks as a sectarian conflict, as a campaign of 'terrorism' and as a war. Ongoing debates over the past in the six counties speak to the magnitude in difference between the above interpretations in a region that might have moved on from the worst of the violence but has not yet effectively addressed its legacy. In the post-GFA state, the political and emotive energy previously expended physically fighting the conflict has now been channelled into defining what the conflict was about and how its legacy should be recorded.

The non-paradigmatic nature of the Northern Ireland transition and the lack of a clean break with the past also impacts on the perception of transition within peace processes, particularly among constituencies formerly engaged in or supportive of political violence. On the one hand, processes of political transition are seen as possessing potential to further advance ideological goals or revolutionary change.[26] On the other hand, a more sceptical reading sees them as processes that ultimately end up with the leadership of previously excluded groups being co-opted into the hegemonic project of the liberal

---

[23] Bell, Campbell and Ni Aolaín, 2004; Campbell and Ni Aolaín, 2005.

[24] McAuliffe, 2011.

[25] Bell, Campbell and Ni Aolaín, 2004.

[26] Elster, 2004, 60.

state.[27] Although these observations have been made about transitional justice processes in general, they have a significant relevance to post-GFA Irish republicanism, where views diverge over whether involvement in the transition equates with the continuation of armed struggle by other means or co-option into the Northern Ireland state that was previously opposed. This in turn has created differences of opinion concerning how the promotion of transition by former combatants has been played out within Irish republican communities. Depending on one's perspective of the GFA and transition, the driving of political transition by former combatants has been interpreted as a positive force of change that is advancing peace building or as post-conflict managerialism designed to ease Sinn Féin's party modernisation by reducing the ambit for dissent.[28] Disgruntlement like the latter mirrors the discontent seen in Algeria and South Africa when transition from conflict to politics failed to deliver on promises made by leaderships during conflict.[29]

Locating itself within the disciplinary spheres of memory studies and transitional justice, this book examines the continuing impact of memory in a political debate that is intrinsically linked to a wider transitional process. The overlap between memory studies and transitional justice that characterises this theoretical approach is symptomatic of the wider prevalence that memory studies is beginning to enjoy in the study of transitioning societies.[30] Scholars familiar with both fields will know that there is a common ground on which they naturally converge: the past. Memory studies examines collective pasts of conflict, suffering and violence, while transitional justice examines how various acts of past wrongdoing are addressed following transition from conflict. However, there is natural tension too. While memory studies concerns itself with the representation of the past from a particular perspective,[31] transitional justice, on the other hand, must grapple with notions of truth, justice, accountability and victimhood that extend beyond a particular group perspective. In locating itself within the realms of this inter-play, this book aims to contribute to a greater academic understanding of how memory can enhance or impede transitional justice processes by framing reform processes with assertions of change or continuity, by becoming an ideologised resource to mobilise in favour of or opposition to transitional processes, or by underpinning emerging demands for post-conflict human rights agendas and demands for truth. The book is nonetheless realistic about its aims and scope. It is, after all, an empirical

[27] Renner and Spencer, 2015.

[28] Shirlow and McEvoy, 2008; Hearty, 2016a; Hearty, 2016c; Whiting 2016.

[29] Fanon, 1967; Mattes, 2002.

[30] Hamber and Wilson, 2002; Brown, 2011.

[31] Wertsch, 2009, 127.

case study of how one collective in one transitioning society contests the past. That said, the empirical and theoretical basis of the book means that the observations made and conclusions reached herein may be extrapolated and applied to the study of how other collectives in other transitions are wrestling particular localised challenges of 'dealing with the past', police reform and 'spoiler' activity.

Following on from that latter point, it should be noted that this book is primarily an academic study of memory contestation *within* Irish republicanism. The main thrust of the book is to examine the much overlooked and under-researched *intra-communal* dimension to memory politics in Northern Ireland. This is not to deny that considerable *inter-communal* disagreement over the past remains – it evidently does. Nonetheless, the remit of this book is primarily to move the study of memory politics in Northern Ireland beyond a generic, yet flawed,[32] 'two tribes' approach. As such, it is not intended to be a narrative balancing act. It critically examines memory contestation beyond easily digestible Orange and Green master narratives to illustrate how other less visible binaries such as having 'moved on' or being 'left behind' by transition impacts on how transitional processes and the past are interpreted and represented. This approach has admittedly led to the exclusion of other memories of policing. Other studies have, however, provided a valuable insight from these perspectives; Cheryl Lawther provides insightful academic enquiry into Unionist and former RUC perspectives on the policing legacy,[33] Aoghan Mulcahy has produced a useful study on the organisational memory of the RUC[34] and Kirk Simpson has researched Unionist memories of the conflict.[35] These provide a fuller examination of divergent narratives not exhaustively covered in this book.

At this introductory juncture, a brief methodological note is warranted. Data for this book has been drawn from archival sources including the Conflict Archive on the Internet (CAIN) and the Northern Ireland Political Collection at the Linenhall Library, Belfast, from various Irish republican publications, including *An Phoblacht, Saoirse, Sovereign Nation* and the *Starry Plough*, from existing academic literature and from semi-structured interviews with 30 Irish republican former combatants, political activists and community activists. Interviewees were drawn from both genders, from different geographical locations, from different generations and from across the spectrum within modern Irish republicanism, including: those who actively participate in

32 Shirlow and McGovern, 1997.

33 Lawther, 2010; 2014.

34 Mulcahy, 2000.

35 Simpson, 2009.

'critical engagement', independent republicans, those from republican parties opposed to policing *and* to 'spoiler' violence, those imprisoned before and after the GFA, and those from political organisations with a close association with 'spoiler' groups. This book therefore represents, to borrow from Richard English in his study on Irish nationalism, a study of *Irish republicanisms* rather than Irish republicanism.[36] Given that the book addresses the legacy of conflict and continuing 'spoiler' violence in a post-conflict environment where some have not bought into transition and where the past has yet to be 'dealt with', it is perhaps advisable to offer a brief note on the perils of conflating the *researcher* with views espoused by the *researched*.

While conducting field research, this author adhered to the principles of 'research participant respect', which involves 'treating people with dignity when we do not condone their beliefs and actions', 'searching for their meanings and understanding their actions as they see them' and 'finding out how they view their worlds'.[37] Furthermore, John Morrison rightly points out that the rationale behind researching political violence is 'not to condemn or condone' it but to get 'closer to an understanding' of the phenomenon.[38] Failure to grasp this point has led to academics in Northern Ireland having to stave off reckless 'fellow traveller' claims,[39] claims of being 'one of them'[40] and 'guilt by association' claims.[41] With this in mind, it is worth clarifying, perhaps somewhat unnecessarily, that the aim of this book is *not* to offer justification or apology for past or current Irish republican political violence, nor is it designed to be a polemic in favour of or against 'critical engagement'. This book represents an academic study of the role memory played in the policing debate within Irish republicanism as told by those in the thick of the debate.

Overview

At this stage in the introduction, a brief synopsis of the chapters that follow is required. Chapter 1 sets out the historical context to the relationship between Irish republicanism and policing in Northern Ireland. It traces the development of divided-society policing in Ireland from the colonial policy of plantation that deliberately created a distinction between the privileged 'planter' and

36 English, 2006.

37 Charmaz, 2004.

38 Morrison, 2011, 18.

39 McEvoy and Shirlow, 2013.

40 Reed, 2012.

41 Sluka, 2012, 182.

the dispossessed 'native'. Cognisant of this historical backdrop, it critically evaluates how 'divided-society' policing impacted on relations between the minority Irish nationalist community and the Northern Ireland state after partition created a 'Protestant state for a Protestant people'. The chapter draws on archival sources and existing academic work to evaluate how the Irish republican approach to policing was ultimately responsive to their changing relationship with the Northern Ireland state and changing policing realities on the ground in Northern Ireland.

Although the primary aim of the book is to further the academic understanding of *intra-communal* memory contestation, there is an important *inter-communal* dimension to disagreement over the past in Northern Ireland that cannot be overlooked. Chapter 2 therefore highlights how, based on observations from Northern Ireland and elsewhere, the collective memory of violence and victimhood becomes 'war by another means' during transition. It examines the counter-memory function that Irish republican policing memory assumes in the continuing meta-conflict in Northern Ireland, where dominant Unionist, state and RUC narratives attempt to silence Irish republican experiences by monopolising victimhood and apportioning blame for the conflict exclusively to Irish republicans.

Chapter 3 provides an insight into the overarching ideological dimension to the policing debate by interrogating how competing views of where Irish republicanism is currently at during transition are construed through value-laden interpretations of where it has come from. As such, the chapter argues that 'critical engagement' is interpreted through long-held belief systems that frame the move in terms of congruence with or contradiction of past ideological positions. It posits that there are two contesting mnemonic-ideological models for understanding 'critical engagement': the 'progressive republican' model that interprets current Sinn Féin strategy as a change of *tactics* moving the pursuit of ideological goals from an armed struggle to a 'political struggle' and the 'constitutional nationalist' model that interprets Sinn Féin strategy as the abandonment of Irish republican *principles* in favour of a reformist working of the partitionist neoliberal Northern Ireland state. This chapter examines the interaction between individual and collective memory, as those who subscribe to the competing models use their own lived experience to locate their understanding within competing master narratives. It also assesses how these master narratives contribute to a wider hegemonic battle between the drivers and 'spoilers' of transition within modern Irish republicanism.

Drawing on theoretical and empirical observations on commemoration elsewhere, Chapter 4 critically evaluates the role that the collective memory of the Irish republican 'patriot dead' plays in the wider policing debate. The chapter examines how the patriot dead become a useful political resource for competing 'memory entrepreneurs'[42] – those seeking to appropriate and monopolise collective memory – to sanctify their current strategies during transition, as commemoration becomes a resource for mobilising in support of or opposition to transitional processes. It investigates the main components of the policing narrative proffered by each 'side' in relation to the patriot dead: the narrative of 'critical engagement' being the extension of the courage shown by the dead during armed struggle, and the counter-narrative that endorsement of policing represents a self-defeat of the goals for which the dead sacrificed themselves. It will also examine how the memory of past armed struggle frames competing discourses on continuing post-GFA 'spoiler' violence.

Chapter 5 interrogates the range of views within modern Irish republicanism on truth recovery, 'moving on' and 'dealing with the past'. It undertakes an examination of how the memory of human rights violations framed the policing debate, and how this shaped a master narrative of 'never again' whereby the value of 'remembering' past abuses lies in guarding against future repetition. The chapter examines how individuals 'move on' in the aftermath of such abuse to engage in a new 'working relationship' with former enemies. It probes the interaction between individual and collective memory, whereby individual memories of human rights violations are located within a narrative of collective human rights abuse and the tension that exists between individual and collective memory when 'moving on' at the individual level is a difficult process. Examination then turns to recent attempts at addressing the 'dealing with the past' impasse including the (now defunct) Historical Enquiries Team (HET), the Haas/O'Sullivan proposals and the Stormont House Agreement (SHA). This allows critical evaluation of how Irish republicans, as a principal party to the conflict, approach the difficult issue of 'dealing with the past' as both collective victims and perpetrators of human rights abuses.

Chapter 6 critically examines how police reform has interacted with individual and collective memory to fashion opposing narratives on community policing in Northern Ireland. Establishing the overarching context of post-conflict police reform within which opposing narratives are constructed, the chapter opens with an interrogation of changes in police symbolism, police composition and the nature of the core policing function of the PSNI. It establishes that there are currently two competing master narratives on community policing within modern Irish republicanism: the 'critical engagement' narrative constructed by those in favour of policing that uses the memory of past 'suspect community' policing to frame itself with assertions of newness, change and of the primary policing function now

[42] Jelin, 2007.

being to provide a policing service to local communities, and the anti-policing counter-narrative of 'cosmetic reform' that uses memory in a more ideologised manner to dismiss police reform as the normalisation of 'British' policing in Ireland. Critically evaluating the 'black-and-white' views proffered by these competing narratives, the chapter draws on the nuances of the overlapping 'grey' areas that define lived reality on the ground in republican communities. Viewing this lived reality through competing lenses of *continuity* and *rupture*, this chapter highlights where aspects of reform have successfully cultivated a new image of the PSNI within Irish republican communities and areas where reform has been less successful.

Establishing the overarching context of institutional crossover within which competing policing narratives are fashioned, Chapter 7 conducts a thematic examination of opposing narratives on political policing. The chapter interrogates how those supportive of 'critical engagement' have constructed a narrative that is premised on a notion of *rupture* seeking to differentiate the PSNI from the RUC. In doing so, this narrative will be shown to have drawn on thematic tropes including pragmatism and negotiation in a post-conflict environment, disaggregating the policing monolith into 'good' policing and 'bad' policing, proactively fighting the 'roll back' of change, and of police reform as a component of an ongoing process of wider equality-based transformation of the 'Orange state'. The chapter will contrast this with the anti-policing narrative that is conversely predicated on drawing a line of *continuity* between the RUC and the 'PSNI/RUC'. It will interrogate how themes like the continued abuse of 'anti-terror' legislation, the retention of RUC 'political policing' methods and the refined targeting of Irish republicans by the PSNI frame this narrative. It will illuminate how this latter narrative is constructed through ideological appeals with a basis in deeper cultural memory that is more conducive to its narrative end point, but also how, in a post-9/11 context, it has adopted a wider human rights discourse to frame itself within more prevalent global concerns of the human rights implications of 'anti-terror' provisions and the ongoing 'war on terror'.

Establishing a theoretical framework

Having outlined the context to the Irish republican policing debate, the rationale for this book and what each chapter covers, attention now turns to providing a theoretical overview that will contextualise the arguments made throughout this book. This overview has four strands: the construction of collective memory, the role of collective memory during conflict, memory contestation during transitional processes and how this all applies to modern

Irish republicanism. Each of these strands is vital in their own right, yet they also form part of a necessarily collective overview. If the arguments made throughout this book are to be truly understood, it is necessary to appreciate the cumulative theoretical underpinnings to them. The phenomenon of memory itself must be grasped before its application can be robustly critiqued. Any adequate understanding of the role that memory played within the Irish republican policing debate must be preceded by a sufficient awareness of the dynamics that lie behind memory construction. Likewise, familiarity with the dynamics that underline collective memory during conflict and the changing dimensions transition out of conflict brings to this, are prerequisites to appreciating fully the particularities of memory contestation within contemporary Irish republicanism. In essence, this overview represents a theoretical skeleton that is fleshed out with empirical data and further original argument throughout the chapters of this book.

The construction of memory

Memory is not a pre-existent entity that neatly defines our past experiences or validates our own historical perception of who and what we are. It does not exist in this sense. Memory, rather, is constructed through cultural and social processes. These processes incorporate commemoration, memorialisation and narration as building blocks to define who we are, where we have come from and, more often than not, where we are headed. For Pierre Nora, 'memory is life, borne by living societies founded in its name. It remains in permanent evolution, open to the dialectic of remembering and forgetting, unconscious of its successive deformations, vulnerable to manipulation and susceptible to being long dormant and periodically revised'.[43] Memory, then, is formed through the dualities of 'remembering' and 'forgetting', with an understanding of 'remembering' premised on a mutual understanding of 'forgetting'.[44] Thus memory comprises the positive (that which we actively 'remember', narrate and commemorate) and the negative (that which we 'forget', silence and erase). The intrinsic importance of 'forgetting' to the mnemonic process means that 'full memory' is an illusion.[45] In transitioning societies where there is a need to 'construct collective memory',[46] the fallacy of 'full memory' is particularly jarring.[47]

---

43 Nora, 1989.

44 Connerton, 2009.

45 Jelin, 2003, 16.

46 Teitel, 2000, 116.

47 Osiel, 1997.

To appreciate fully the dialectics of 'remembering' and 'forgetting', it is imperative to acknowledge that the primary function of memory is to provide a 'usable' past – that being 'an account of events and actors that can be harnessed for some purpose in the present'.[48] Thus we 'remember' all that is required for a 'usable' past and 'forget' that which has no place in this preferred account. 'Structural amnesia' expunges that which has no currency in present interests.[49] Memory becomes favourable to who we regard ourselves to be in the present, whether this entails selective 'remembering' or wholesale 'forgetting'. The practical applicability of this to the memory politicking of competing hegemons in an ever-changing political landscape such as Northern Ireland cannot be overstated.

But, if memory is constructed for present consumption through the processes of 'remembering' and 'forgetting', who then determines what to 'remember' and what to 'forget'? One school of thought argues that the only 'genuine memory' is the memory of the individual, as groups do not have a common mind capable of direct memory.[50] By this reading, collective memory can be seen as the means through which the collective – or those at its apex – coaxes the individual into distorting, revising and changing their individual memories to adhere to the collective master narrative. Collective memory can, after all, make individuals 'remember' events they have no experience of and 'forget' others they have direct experience of.[51] In subscribing to collective memory the individual commits to 'complex negotiations about what is acceptable and what is to be silenced, what can and cannot be said in the disjunctions between private narratives and public discourses'.[52] However, it must be acknowledged that group membership is dependent on the individual giving assent – they can of course withhold this.[53] If the individual finds that their individual memory is so overwhelmingly incongruous with the collective master narrative, they can step 'outside' the group and create counter-memory. Options beyond mere acceptance of the dominant master narrative of the group do exist. Furthermore, willingness to articulate personal experience through, and marry it with, collective memory can exist. Rather than being a process of competition and displacement, the process can be seen as one of interaction between the individual and the collective.[54] This suggests a mutual interaction

[48] Wertsch, 2002, 31.

[49] Tota, 2001.

[50] Khazanov and Payne, 2008.

[51] Olick, 1999.

[52] Jelin, 2003, 16.

[53] Gook, 2011.

[54] Crane, 1997.

premised on a give–take relationship paradigm where memory is constructed pluralistically through social processes. This is reflective of the worldly reality that it is virtually impossible to live life in total solitude; meaning that when we 'remember' we must therefore recall in some form other people and factors external to our being that have featured in or shaped our past experiences. Those external to our being will also inevitably recall these events and experiences too. This is the embryonic basis upon which a wider, more substantial collective memory is formed.

This line of reasoning is famously evinced by Maurice Halbwachs, the most notable exponent of collective memory. Halbwachs contends that while memory may reside within the individual 'it is in society that people normally acquire their memories. It is also in society that they recall, recognise and localise their memories'.[55] Paul Connerton has expanded on this to emphasise the role that the collective can play in helping individuals 'remember'. He argues: 'if I recall something that is because others incite me to recall it, because their memory comes to the aid of mine and mine finds support in theirs'.[56] No matter how individualistically personal a recollection may seem, then, it is still influenced by external social factors such as date, place and others present. The role of the collective in helping flesh out the memory of the individual is evidenced in the remarks of one interviewee who alluded to discussions they had with family and friends about the past:

> When we're in our own gang of friends from the past – 'Do you remember that night such and such happened'. Incidents with UDR and RUC, you know. I'd remember most of the names and I certainly remember all of the faces because they were so horrible – you'll always remember that! I'll never forget them. But you know other things – maybe some of the where you were going, 'do you remember when you were going to such and such a disco?' and I'm thinking, 'Jesus I forgot all about that'.[57]

Moreover, individuals belong to 'mnemonic communities'.[58] When individuals 'remember' they do so not solely as an individual but as a member of a particular social class, national collective, generation, family etc. As such, collective memory can assume a communicative value whereby it proffers a common denominator understanding of the past that binds individuals in these collectives. This common denominator is shaped by external social factors,

[55] Halbwachs and Coser, 1992, 38.

[56] Connerton, 1989, 36.

[57] AB, critic of Sinn Féin policy, interview, October 2013.

[58] Kansteiner, 2002.

cultural factors and collective needs It invests symbols, myths and memories with a sense of commonality that deflects from internal variance by creating a sense of togetherness among those identifying with the shared past they engender, and a sense of hostility towards those foreign to this shared past.[59] Subscription to this shared past underpins the personal, familial, communal, ethnic or national identities individuals simultaneously possess.[60]

By dint of membership of 'mnemonic communities', we come to possess 'the ability to experience events that happened to groups and communities to which we belong long before we joined them'.[61] The collective past, whether personally experienced or not, becomes part of the individual's identity as an indistinguishable component of their own past. This is particularly relevant in relation to collective memories of historical injury and injustice. Holocaust memory, for example, continues to impact heavily on the identity of secular Western Jews with no personal connection to the horrors of Nazism, even decades after the original horror.[62] More specifically to Northern Ireland, not every Nationalist witnessed, has first-hand experience of or was personally affected by Bloody Sunday, yet, through social interaction with the wider milieu and the dynamics of identity politics, they collectively 'remember' it as part of a 'community of memory'.[63] Collective memory of this nature can also be used to give political meaning to and contextualise the exigencies of the present. Collectives come to view the struggles, dangers and enemies of today through the prism of the struggles, dangers and enemies of yesterday. For example, a culture of resistance and suffering has informed Palestinian narratives of struggle from the Nakba to the first intifada through to the present conflict.[64] The other side of this coin is that the ancient siege of Masada continues to inform modern Israeli narratives of defence against a foreign enemy.[65] When one moves beyond the cultural and social dimensions of memory and into the purely politicised domain of memory politics, this becomes incredibly potent – especially in contexts where collectives are emerging from political violence and grappling with the new challenges transition poses. When faced with the demands of transition, the urge to frame these challenges with reference to the collective past of struggle and sacrifice is irresistible. In seeking to marry their current positions, strategies and self-image during the transitional period

---

[59] Smith, 1996.

[60] Green, 2001, 21.

[61] Zerubavel, 1996.

[62] Olick, 2008.

[63] Conway, 2003.

[64] Khalili, 2007.

[65] Schwartz, Zerubavel and Barnett, 1986.

with those held during the conflict, political elites become extremely adept at mastering the processes of 'remembering' and 'forgetting'.

Collective memory during conflict

Collective memory underpins communal identity during ethno-nationalist conflict – something particularly relevant in Northern Ireland as 'the archetype of a society deeply divided by collective identity conflict'.[66] Ties of kinship and common experience become magnified in the face of the threat from the 'other'. For Irish republicans, the threat from the 'other' was bifurcated: that from the internal six counties ethno-nationalist 'other' (the Protestant/Unionist/Loyalist constituency) and from the external occupying 'other' (the British Army). The harsh realities of ethno-nationalist conflict create the context whereby communities lead their lives within polarised confines. This polarisation means that life is, by necessity, conducted on the basis of cognitive maps of 'safe' and 'unsafe' places.[67] The divisive premise of 'safe' and 'unsafe' survives by dint of the fact that education, housing, employment and socialisation occur along these defined lines. The conflict is understood through 'us/them' binaries, meaning that the importance of knowing who a person is and what 'side' they belong to becomes exponentially heightened. In the North of Ireland, this gave rise to the curious process of 'telling'; using name, place of residence, phonetics and (somewhat bizarrely) physical appearance to determine to which community a person belongs.[68] To know who you stand with is then to know where you stand. Leading life in the midst of the 'in group', being educated, housed and, in a way, developed with those of our own ilk, cocoons us from the potential harms of the 'out group'. The benefit may be communal safety but at the price of almost total exclusion from the 'other'. This exclusion conditions how we interpret the conflict and its origins, causes and consequences.

Within such destructive environs, you will identify with your group and view harm against the 'other' as a form of self-defence. Collectives adopt an inward-looking view of injury inflicted during the conflict, as the 'collective self' becomes the victim of the 'collective other'.[69] The 'genealogy of the dead' collectivises death and suffering because the individual victim killed by 'them' is tied to place, community, narrative and group, making the harm a

---

[66] Aiken, 2013.

[67] Shirlow, 2003b.

[68] Burton, 1978, 37.

[69] Shirlow, 2003a.

'collective act of defilement'.[70] Perceptions of collective guilt allow the violent events of the conflict to be viewed through the axis of the 'abuser' and the 'abused'.[71] This notion of the 'abuser' and the 'abused' enables happenings to be linked together, even where no causal link exists. As Spillman and Conway highlight, the memory of Bloody Sunday is 'widespread and powerful', with the event now being placed in protracted conflict narratives that link it to other events like Bloody Friday.[72] No direct causal link exists per se, but in the intricate weaving together of communal narratives of the conflict a link can nonetheless be fabricated to lay the blame at the door of the 'other'. The implication of this is that collectives selectively construct a master narrative of the conflict that locates fault and blame with the 'other'. These master narratives of the conflict relate 'the causes for its outbreak, the reason for its lack of resolution, the major events that shaped the conflict, particularly malevolent acts perpetrated by the adversary and the sacrifices that the in group incurred during the conflict, including its heroes' sacrifices. These beliefs are one-sided and selective'.[73] Whilst, as Bruce acknowledges, narratives of 'they started it' seem infantile, they nonetheless serve 'to make people feel better about their own sins'.[74] In facilitating selective finger-pointing and clouded moral judgement of the 'other', collective memory functions to exonerate the 'in group' as the 'abused' because they are, after all, 'us' and 'safe', and to condemn the 'other' for their role in the conflict as they are the 'abuser', 'them' and 'unsafe'.

In an 'us versus them' environment, communal solidarity embeds itself into the wider collective, amplifying the commonality of shared past experience. In the face of threat from the 'other', this commonality of background, past experiences and culture transforms the community into 'a source of collective organisation and survival'.[75] External threats push the 'in group' closer together, allowing any internal heterogeneity to be overlooked through magnifying difference from the 'other'. This is not confined to the North of Ireland. Merridale, for example, highlights how the violent excesses of Nazism 'united' the Soviet people in a 'common cause' during the 'Great Patriotic War'.[76] The threat of the 'other' largely precludes any intra-communal questioning of

---

[70] Feldman, 1991, 64.

[71] Shirlow, 2008.

[72] Spillman and Conway, 2007.

[73] Bar-Tal, 2003, 87.

[74] Bruce, 1994, 6.

[75] Rolston, 2010.

[76] Merridale, 2000.

master narratives as 'guilt transfer' and 'group think' prevail.[77] The narrative as related by 'us', who share the same communal experience, is accepted and repeated unquestioningly, whilst that told by 'them' is dismissed, contested and repudiated. In the North of Ireland, this meant that during the zenith of conflict there was what equated to wholesale internal acceptance of master narratives. Shanahan ventures as far as to argue that the Irish republican narrative on the outbreak of conflict 'has been repeated so often that it goes largely unquestioned, especially by working class Catholics, the republican movement's main audience'.[78]

Collective memory during transition

When the shackles of conflict loosen and the perceived threat of the 'other' is no longer as pressing, scope opens to 'remember' differently than during the highly strung 'us versus them' environment of conflict. Suspicion of the 'other' does of course remain – they are, as Karstedt notes, 'still enemies'.[79] In Northern Ireland, this has been most notable in post-conflict politicking over perceived attempts by the 'other' to deny 'us' communal identity, cultural recognition or acknowledgement of victimhood. High-profile instances of this have caused a hasty retreat from the 'middle ground' back into polarised trenches at certain key junctures. Consequently, divisive issues like flags, parading, symbols and victimhood become re-politicised during transition as dominant ethno-nationalist elites use them to set 'the limits to compromise'.[80]

Post-conflict contextual change, nonetheless, develops new critical narrative space. Whilst contestation naturally continues in some vein on an inter-communal basis, a new intra-communal questioning of collective memories and master narratives also surfaces. When the threat of the 'other' subsides, 'us' no longer retains the same value, meaning that hitherto masked heterogeneities emerge and mature. The commonality of past experience, rather than being a unifying factor, now becomes a battleground for hegemons intent on using the collective past to legitimise their current position. In South Africa, the collective memory of the black liberation struggle is contested by a number of schools who accuse the African National Congress (ANC) of using it to strengthen their hegemony.[81] In transitioning Argentina, the human rights movement had to reflect on its own internal cleavages, resulting in differences

[77] Alonso, 2007, 168.

[78] Shanahan, 2009, 21.

[79] Karstedt, 2013, 36.

[80] Hayward and Komarova, 2014.

[81] Hlongwane, 2008.

that had previously been contained eventually forcing a split in Las Madres de la Plaza de Mayo.[82] Internal division surfaced among Greek-Cypriots following inter-ethnic conflict, with hegemonic rivals in Dimokratikos Synagermos and Anorthotikó Kómma Ergazómenou Laoú proffering their own narrative of the conflict.[83] Observations like the above are easily extrapolated to post-conflict Northern Ireland, where there has been an unprecedented fragmentation of previously tight knit collectives. In addition to the previously outlined unparalleled fissuring identified within modern Irish republicanism, contemporary Unionism and post-conflict loyalism have witnessed continuing division, splitting and internal feuding.[84] The growth of intra-communal division during transitional periods is symptomatic of the fact that 'during an armed conflict we need to know where we stand, who is the enemy, who is the ally. Now that the period of armed conflict is drawing to a close, we... move beyond such black and white thinking'.[85]

Transition out of political violence allows reflection on the violence inflicted by 'us' not only on 'them' but on those within the 'in group' too. In Northern Ireland, the Ardoyne Commemorative Project asked tough questions about intra-communal violence, as well as that committed by the state and 'other'.[86] A dimension opens up for deep probing questions previously gagged by communal loyalty to now be asked. New victims and voices emerge to pose difficult unanswered questions about the conflict.[87] These voices come from within the 'in group', where periods of gestation and reflection facilitate a deeper examination than the unthinking reaction typical during the conflict. When we reflect on events post-conflict, we are no longer blinded by the threat of the 'other' and can take a different reading of taken-for-granted versions of the past. Even narratives once considered unassailable, such as the Irish republican master narrative on the 1981 hunger strike, are prone to internal challenge.[88] This creates 'increased struggle over the meaning of the past', reflecting the friction between reluctance to abandon old beliefs and values and the necessity to 'refashion' memories for 'new interpretations' in a 'new era'.[89] There will inevitably be a degree of tension between the old, traditional meanings and interpretations that were prominently held during the conflict and these new

---

[82] Jelin, 2003, 16.

[83] Papadakis, 1998.

[84] McAuley, 2003.

[85] Breen-Smyth, 1999.

[86] Lundy and McGovern, 2006.

[87] Simpson, 2007.

[88] O'Rawe, 2005.

[89] Rolston, 2010.

interpretations more apposite to a post-conflict environment. This tension is channelled into dichotomous positions adopted by competing hegemons who use the past to justify their current position and to simultaneously undermine that of their rivals.

Intra-communal memory contestation is not limited to the memory politicking of elites vying for hegemonic influence within their collective. It can also manifest itself at grassroots level where victims may oppose what they perceive to be attempts to 'forget' and move on. In post-conflict societies 'the hardening of feelings of revenge and anger may be seen as one method of keeping faith with the dead in not allowing the injury to be forgotten or trivialised'.[90] Reconciling these feelings with transitional 'moving on' agendas is a mammoth task. Where the task falters, contestation over the past thrives, complicated further by the fact that those in political power (invariably those driving 'moving on' agendas) allow those voices that strike the same chord as 'moving on' agendas to have the loudest hearing. In tandem with this, there is an attempt to suppress subaltern voices opposing 'moving on' agendas or new interpretations of the past. However, memory remains an outlet to challenge this hegemonic activity. Where hegemons fail to silence dissenting voices, memory becomes a tool of resistance for those 'left behind' by transition to challenge transitional 'moving on' processes and hegemonic accounts of the past.[91]

Mnemonic contestation within modern Irish republicanism

These observations are highly relevant to contemporary Irish republicanism. Transition in the North of Ireland has witnessed the majority of Irish republicans abandoning armed struggle (or at least supporting abandonment moves) and embracing purely political means. There is nonetheless a significant, and growing, minority – both violent and non-violent – within the constituency who have been 'left behind' by transition. They have not bought into Sinn Féin's political project, have not engaged with transitional processes and have sought to tear up the 'moving on' script in Northern Ireland. The emergence of an ideological rearguard opposed to transition has fuelled a whirlwind of mnemonic contestation within modern Irish republicanism. Given the extent of division evident in the earlier examination of the multifarious groups now in existence, it seems impossible to argue with meaningful conviction that any Irish republican master narrative can adequately represent the cacophony of

[90] McLernon, Cairns, Hewstone and Smith, 2004.

[91] Rigney, 2008.

multitudinous Irish republican voices shouting to be heard in the twenty-first century.

This disagreement is problematic, least not due to the fact that 'republicans have often been described as having their own insular ... worldview that brooks no dissent from within and recognises as valid no critique from without'.[92] Compounding this is the fact that the Provisional narrative has, from the earliest stages of the conflict, been synonymous with 'a fervent rejection of any other political group's ability to represent the Nationalist community'.[93] Despite having to contend with the Officials and latterly the IRSP, the Provisional movement managed to attain relative hegemony within republican communities. Despite this hegemony, Jon Tonge argues that the Irish republican constituency has traditionally been 'an eclectic, non-cohesive body', giving it a heterogeneity that invariably leaves it susceptible to splitting on major policy issues when the prospect of 'compromise' arises.[94] It is this historical curse of compromise that fuels mnemonic contestation because the various anti-policing schools of Irish republicanism deride the Sinn Féin leadership for defaulting on past ideological positions. The further Sinn Féin travels down the path of post-conflict transition, the heavier condemnation becomes – whether that be from militant 'spoilers' or from those with leftist political opposition. Policy changes during transition are viewed with one eye turned towards the past, and although the Sinn Féin leadership has kept most of its supporters on board there have been significant departures at crucial junctures during the transitional process. Foremost among these was the decision to endorse policing and the criminal justice system in the North of Ireland – a decision that fostered division even within Irish republican families on the matter.[95]

It is within these broader theoretical parameters that this book will examine the memory politics of the Irish republican debate on policing. It will employ the theoretical framework outlined in this introduction to determine *how* and *why* mnemonic contestation continues to define political disagreement over the transition within the wider Irish republican constituency today.

92 Shanahan, 2009, 41.

93 Wright, 1991, 126.

94 Tonge, 2004.

95 Rolston, 2011.

Chapter 1

Understanding a Fraught Historical Relationship

Introduction

This chapter traces the historical development of the changing relationship between Irish republicans and the various police forces that have upheld the rule of law in the North of Ireland. Accepting that there is an inherent link between state legitimacy and police legitimacy, it traces how changing relations with policing mirrored changing relations with the state. Views of policing are, after all, shaped within broader 'value systems' that include perceptions of state institutions and the political system that decrees the rule of law that the police force enforces.[1] Building on that observation, this chapter will critically examine how the Irish republican position on the legitimacy of policing evolved in tandem with a changing political world view of the Northern Ireland state. Many of the issues later examined in greater detail are initially established herein; an understanding of that examination relies on grasping the trajectory of a wider changing relationship identified in this chapter. Rather than being an immediate or exhaustive exploration of those issues, this chapter sets out a framework that draws on the development of divided-society policing in Northern Ireland *and* the Sinn Féin process of buying into the post-GFA Northern Ireland state in order to contextualise the arguments made later in this book.

'Planters and natives'

To truly comprehend the fraught historical relationship between Irish republicanism and policing, it is necessary to begin with the seventeenth-century British colonial policy of plantation: that of dispossessing and displacing the

[1] Albrecht and Green, 1977.

hostile Irish Catholic native and redistributing their land to imported loyal Protestants of English and Scottish extraction. Ross notes that early narratives about plantation were constructed along obvious fault lines, notably a narrative of civilisation and advancement, and a competing narrative of displacement and dispossession.[2] Consequently, competing ethno-nationalist narratives have across generations corresponded to diametrically opposed frameworks. For Unionist descendants of the 'planter' it is one of providential delivery from the repeated threat of Catholic rebellion, while for Nationalist descendants of the 'native' it has been a redemptive one to atone for centuries of heroic defeats.[3] These recurring motifs of repelled assaults while under siege and avenging historical defeats created narrative friction that persists today.[4] The privileging of the 'planter' over the 'native' heightened religious and political tension, giving subsequent conflict an unmistakeable ethno-nationalist flavour. Although often erroneously portrayed in simple sectarian terms, political violence in the six counties was ethno-nationalist in nature; religion is the most pointed to fault line of division (particularly by external observers subscribing to the British state narrative) even though competing claims to self-determination, competing national allegiances and competing narratives of persecution also underpinned disharmony. O'Leary and McGarry argue that plantation created a context whereby three different nationalities (Irish, Scottish and English), three different religions (Catholic, Presbyterian and Anglican) and three different cultures collided in the 'ethnic frontier' of Ulster.[5] Within time this division manifested itself around competing national (Irish and British) and religious (Catholic and Protestant) identities, setting in motion a trend that would see conflict-era Northern Ireland become 'a site of twin nation-building failures' and a 'site of two competing sovereignty claims, each of which is morally problematic and legally contestable'.[6] However, while they recognise the *colonial origins* of the conflict, they have also rejected the colonial framing of *later conflict*. This is premised on a 'moral statute of limitations' that prevents later generations being held responsible for the conquests of their ancestors.[7] Of course, while the descendants of the original 'planters' cannot be charged with creating the systems of inequality they inherited, it is not irrational either to argue that they did little to address the inequality inherent in these systems when they were gifted control of the Northern Ireland state.

2 Ross, 2007, 99.

3 McBride, 2001, 16.

4 McDonagh, 1983.

5 O'Leary and McGarry, 1993, 83.

6 McGarry and O'Leary, 1995, 348.

7 McGarry and O'Leary, 1996.

If anything, they moved to entrench their inherited dominance more deeply. O'Leary and McGarry argue further that the doctrines of Irish Nationalism and Ulster Unionism that defined later political disagreement and shaped competing national identities, were not even conceived at the time of the Ulster plantation.[8] In rejecting a colonial framing of later conflict, they have offered some thoughtful insights into other interpretations, including one that sees the conflict as one of competing nationalities fought between Ireland and Britain in the Northern 'ethnic frontier' that ended in failed state-building projects for both the British and Irish.[9] Notwithstanding this, insider researchers like Mac Ionnrachtaigh, and critical leftists like Scraton, have sympathy with neo-colonial interpretations of the conflict.[10] This is, of course, an entirely legitimate academic position to adopt and it is not one that this author seeks to challenge.

On one level, the plantation policy was reflective of the macro-level infighting among contenders to British imperial power. On another level, it had particular strategic relevance in Ulster because it was the last centre of Irish resistance to English rule.[11] Deliberately privileging the 'planter' created the context whereby:

> A relation of mutual dependence developed between Britain, who needed Protestant support to secure its own control, and Protestants, who needed British support to maintain their position. To hold Ireland for the Crown, Protestants had to be accorded power in Ireland; thus British dominance over Ireland was further reflected in Protestant dominance within Ireland.[12]

The heavy concentration of the plantation policy in Ulster meant that, by 1705, 93 per cent of land in eight of the nine Ulster counties was in 'planter' hands.[13] The fact that the dominant 'planter' was instructed to remain detached from the disloyal 'native' population inculcated a siege mentality that set the two peoples and their respective world-views on a collision course. This siege mentality, along with the rhetorical myth of the dangerous 'native', became the basis on which the 'planter' would arm themselves to protect, at all cost, the preponderance of their interests over those of the dispossessed 'native'.[14]

[8] O'Leary and McGarry, 1993, 55.

[9] McGarry and O'Leary, 1995, 352.

[10] Mac Ionnrachtaigh, 2013.

[11] Smith, 2011, 27.

[12] Ruane and Todd, 1996, 12.

[13] Smith, 2011, 27.

[14] McIntosh, 1999, 16.

This arming of the 'planter' was accompanied by the systematic use of the rule of law to formally privilege the settler over the indigenous. It was within this environment that the 'planter', and subsequent generations of their descendants, would find affinity with and maintain ownership over militias and police forces tasked with upholding laws that enshrined their privilege over the 'native' into the established order.

In addition to enforcing 'planter' privilege, these early-style militias also became the bulwark of a drastic state response to even the merest stirrings of rebellion in Ireland. Dermot Walsh observes that police forces in Ireland were 'always armed and always ready to respond to any hint of rebellion' by the disaffected 'native' population.[15] Differentiating the early development of policing in Ireland from that in Britain, Jessie Blackbourn further notes:

> Policing in Ireland was used to crack down on political dissent, principally to prevent any attempt by nationalists in Ireland to secede from the Union. Policing was therefore used to retain Ireland's status as a colony of Britain. In contrast, there was no such violent threat in Britain; the police were engaged to investigate and prevent ordinary crime.[16]

By the nineteenth century, the British government would invoke what would later transpire to be their principal *modus operandi* of using the guise of 'special disturbances' to saturate certain areas with military and police.[17] In consequence, sporadic episodes of Fenian and Young Irelander violence were followed by expansive emergency provisions that effectively penalised the 'native' population in its entirety.

The Act of Union 1800 statutorily entrenched Britain's colonial domain over Ireland, and, with this, further sustained 'planter' privilege. The political lexicon in Ireland duly altered as the terms 'Unionist' and 'Nationalist' came to supplant 'planter' and 'native'. When the Union came under threat, so too did Protestant interests. Unionist dominance in the North East of the country was sustained by holding political and economic clout in this highly industrialised region – a region decidedly more advanced than the rest of the country.[18] Unionists in Ulster also had an affinity with one another that they did not have with those of 'planter' stock elsewhere.[19] Thus it was in Ulster that Unionists exhibited the greatest willingness to arm themselves in defence of the Union.

---

15 Walsh, 1998, 6.

16 Blackbourn, 2015, 124.

17 Breathnach, 1974, 24.

18 Smith, 2011, 27.

19 Ruane and Todd, 1996, 49.

As early as the mid-nineteenth century, Unionists could muster 125,000 men in Ulster willing to defend their interests.[20] This would intensify during the 'Home Rule crisis' of the early twentieth century, when Unionist mobilisation reached its zenith with the signing of the Ulster Covenant and establishment of the Ulster Volunteer Force (UVF) militia. The 'Home Rule crisis' temporarily abetted when war broke out on the continent – that was until a group of rebels launched an attack against the British presence in Ireland during Easter 1916. Although a spectacular military failure, the event would spark a renewal of Nationalist fervour. Sinn Féin stormed to electoral success in the 1918 general election. Refusing to participate in a British parliament, they convened the revolutionary Dáil Éireann as the legitimate government of Ireland in anticipation of an intensive guerrilla campaign by the IRA. The increase in such violence in the years immediately preceding partition witnessed renewed Unionist mobilisation. The UVF were resurrected in 1919, due partly to the fact that Unionists in Ulster believed the Royal Irish Constabulary (RIC) and British Army were incapable of protecting Protestant Ulster from the levels of IRA violence seen elsewhere.[21] Acutely aware of the imperative to protect their self-interests, Unionists in Ulster sought to take as much security and political power away from Dublin Castle and silo it in the more favourable climes of Belfast, where it was better placed for such a purpose.[22] A somewhat paradoxical relationship existed between Unionists in Ulster and the RIC; although innately suspicious of the mainly Catholic force (and of Dublin Castle officials whom it was believed would have no qualms about selling out Ulster's interests for political expediency), those members of the force based in Ulster tended to share Unionist sympathies.[23] Shared sympathies meant there was no RIC intervention against, or opposition to, the reorganisation, training and arming of the UVF.[24] This was matched by a reluctance to use emergency provisions to intercede against the sectarian violence and intimidation increasingly exercised by Unionist mobs in Belfast.

Although far from an exhaustive account of the development of policing and the rule of law in pre-partition Ireland, this overview nonetheless points to the emergence of early trends: ownership of policing and the rule of law being concentrated in Unionist hands, a penchant for reflecting this through misapplication of emergency provisions against those deemed subversive by the state, and willingness to use legal and, if deemed necessary, extra-legal means

[20] Rose, 1971, 79.

[21] Hezlet, 1973, 11.

[22] Farrell, 1983, 36.

[23] Farrell, 1983, 18.

[24] Breathnach, 1974, 65.

to uphold self-interests. These trends would become more apparent following partition and the creation of 'a Protestant state for a Protestant people' in Northern Ireland.

The Protestant state

The Government of Ireland Act 1920 created two regional parliaments: one in Dublin and one in Belfast for the six North Eastern counties later to become the Northern Ireland state.[25] The Anglo-Irish treaty of December 1921, between the IRA and British, superseded the 1920 Act by creating an Irish Free State, but with a provision that allowed the predominantly Unionist Northern parliament to opt out. Partition was, as Ruane and Todd note, 'an attempt to accommodate, rather than to transcend or resolve, the historic conflicts on the island'.[26] Mac Ionnrachtaigh views partition as a colonial intervention that created 'the northern settler-colonial statelet' bordering a Free State that 'continued neo-colonial administrative rule in indigenous form'.[27] The treaty was a source of division among Irish republicans, who split along the lines of pragmatic acceptance of the Free State on offer and ideological rejection due to the exclusion of the six Northern counties. A bitter civil war ensued, ending in victory for the pro-treaty Free State forces. The IRA's capacity and organisational strength sharply declined as increasing numbers subsequently broke away to engage in constitutional politics and the political life of the Free State.[28]

Partition left Irish republicans in a political vortex. Two states now existed on the island of Ireland, neither of which they deemed legitimate; one presided over by traitorous former comrades, the other by Unionists. Viewing the Free State (which became a *de facto* republic following the 1937 constitution and was *officially declared* a republic under the Republic of Ireland Act 1948 but was (and is) pejoratively still referred to as the Free State by Irish republicans) as partitionist, and therefore illegitimate, Irish republicans withheld formal participation in the state. The Free State, for its part, showed little tolerance for this 'internal subversion'.[29] It enacted emergency legislation like the Offences against the State Act and the Unlawful Organisations Order to intern, jail and ultimately execute Irish republicans.[30] Subtle differences in rejection of

[25] Smith, 2011, 30.

[26] Ruane and Todd, 1996, 48.

[27] Mac Ionnrachtaigh, 2013, 30.

[28] Bowyer Bell, 1997.

[29] Walsh, 1998, 7.

[30] Ó Broin, 2009, 196.

the Free State and the Northern Ireland state are nonetheless detectible; IRA orders eventually prohibited the use of force against the Free State, Sinn Féin had their first meaningful tryst with constitutional politics here by dropping abstentionism in 1986, and they built an alliance with the Dublin Government in the pan-Nationalist front of the 1990s. By the time of the IRA's 'Border Campaign' (1956–62), it was apparent that any military activity by the IRA would be directed at targets in the Northern state.[31]

For Unionists, partition brought long-term hegemony and political ascendancy in the new state. The inbuilt demographic Protestant majority was used simultaneously to uphold pre-existing Unionist privilege and to subjugate the 'disloyal' Catholic minority community. Commenting on the unassailable position partition afforded Unionists, Breathnach argues that 'the new parliament gradually showed the tyrannical potential inherent in its peculiar two-against-one democracy. Through nepotism, jobbery, local representation, the civil service, education, housing, the trade unions and the cultural and economic spheres, the Catholic minority was gradually ghettoised'.[32] James Whyte is more measured on the matter, arguing that claims ranged from 'the deepest black' Nationalist assertions that discrimination was the bedrock of the state to the 'purest white' Unionist denials.[33] Although Whyte refused to endorse Nationalist claims of systemic discrimination in *every* sphere of governance, he nonetheless accepted that discrimination *did* occur – the issue of contention for him was to what extent it could wholly or partly explain Catholic disadvantage. Institutional exclusion left Catholics – whether Irish republican or Nationalist (or neither) – in a precarious position. It is perhaps useful to draw out slightly the differences between Irish republicans and Nationalists at this point. Although both largely emanate from among the Catholic community, that constituency is not a homogenous political bloc. Dixon's differentiation is that 'the term "nationalist" is often used to describe someone who aspires to a united Ireland but is opposed to the use of violence to achieve it, while a "republican" often shares much of the analysis of the "nationalist" but is prepared to use violence'.[34] Although there is broad agreement on the 'national question', arcane differences developed due to Nationalists accepting tacitly the principle of majority consent, seeing Unionist objection to Irish unity as grounded in real fear and viewing British government policy towards Ireland as neutral, while Irish republicans held more purist views of self-determination, saw Unionists as the dupes of British colonialism and regarded British policy

[31] Sanders, 2011, 10.

[32] Breathnach, 1974, 101.

[33] Whyte, 1983, 29.

[34] Dixon, 2008, 6.

as strategic and imperialist.[35] These differences became more apparent with the emergence of various power-sharing and joint authority initiatives.

The Irish republican view of policing in Northern Ireland, at this point, is intrinsically shaped by their wider view of the Northern Ireland state. The state was regarded as a colonial product 'brought about by the violence and brute force of the British Empire and its Orange-Unionist henchmen in "Northern Ireland" between 1920/22'.[36] The IRA subsequently began to articulate its political rejection of this colonial entity through sporadic political violence, although even their most concerted effort, the 'Border Campaign', never remotely threatened the life of the Northern Ireland state.[37] While episodic and poorly organised, this violence nonetheless provided the Unionist regime with the opportunity to unleash draconian legislation and a formidable security apparatus on anyone dissenting from the Protestant supremacy that epitomised the state. The Stormont administration afforded itself more draconian legislation to face down this violence than the British had equipped themselves with when facing pre-partition IRA violence.[38] Even when violence waned, the Stormont administration froze emergency provisions into the normal legal structure rather than revoking them. Walsh observes that while IRA violence never posed 'any real threat', it ineluctably drew an 'invariably severe and militarily orientated' state response.[39] Emergency legislation was quickly used to curtail any semblance of political affinity with or support for Irish republicanism – violent or otherwise. Commemorative parades celebrating 1916 were outlawed by the Stormont regime under the Special Powers Act,[40] a law reported to be the envy of the Apartheid regime in South Africa. Any legitimate political activity of a republican hue fell foul of emergency legislation via the outlawing of seditious publications, the prohibition on the flying of the Irish national flag and the use of public order provisions to ban assemblies and gatherings.[41]

Remarking on the sheer breadth of the Special Powers Act, Guelke observes that it 'contained Orwellian provisions that listed offences against the maintenance of law and order and then provided that any other acts that undermined law and order, but were not listed, were also offences under the legislation'.[42] For Whyte, the act was so naturally conducive to abuse and bias that one did

---

35 Ruane and Todd, 1996, 72.

36 'Quislings Publicly Thanked', *Republican News,* 27 June 1973.

37 Hanley and Miller, 2010.

38 Farrell, 1976, 50.

39 Walsh, 1983, 9.

40 Anderson, 2002, 46.

41 Farrell, 1976, 94.

42 Guelke, 2012, 61.

not have to rely on Nationalist grievances to criticise it as profoundly undemocratic.[43] The thrust of the act extended beyond the political suppression of Irish republicanism to enable the cultural suppression of Irish Nationalism more generally. Rather than simply maintaining law and order, legislation was premised on maintaining Protestant supremacy through guaranteeing only overt assertions of Britishness within the state. The Flags and Emblems Act (1954), for example, outlawed any overt signs of Irishness.[44] Expressions of Irish identity or culture, much less any assertion of violent or non-violent political opposition to the state, drew the rigours of emergency legislation.[45] The minority community in its entirety became a 'suspect community' as the rule of law and policing in the North of Ireland predicated itself more towards keeping 'order' (i.e. the socio-political order of Protestant supremacy) than fighting 'normal' crime.[46] Unionists would defend this approach on the grounds of having an 'enemy within'.[47] The mistreatment of the minority community was no doubt further driven by a siege mentality arising from having an aggressively Catholic conservative Free State that bordered it (and laid claim to it) *and* by the need to prevent any class split within Unionism that might aid the 'enemy within'. But, as Patterson notes, this only *explains* rather than *excuses* the actions of the Stormont administration.[48] In the face of this, Nationalists quickly withdrew from state life and found themselves resident in a state that regarded them *not* as model citizens but as the 'enemy'.

If the Unionist regime had at its disposal discriminatory legislation to uphold Protestant supremacy, it could similarly rely on the RUC to enthusiastically enforce it. Mulcahy notes:

> From the outset, the Northern Irish government conceived of the RUC as a paramilitary police force that would play a direct role in the maintenance of the state and its unionist character. In addition to the RUC, an auxiliary police force called the Ulster Special Constabulary (USC, or 'B-Specials') was set up.[49]

From the foundation of the state, then, policing in the six counties was markedly disparate from that seen in most liberal democracies. The RUC was

---

43 Whyte, 1983, 25.
44 McIntosh, 1999, 125.
45 Hassan, 2005.
46 Hillyard, 1988.
47 Dixon, 2008, 56.
48 Patterson, 2006, 12.
49 Mulcahy, 2013, 8.

not bound by traditions of minimum force, policing by consent or an arm's length relationship with the Unionist government.[50] McGarry highlights the reality of the RUC's function thus:

> It was armed and paramilitary in character, unlike police forces in Britain, or even the new police in the Irish Free State ... to assist it in its paramilitary role, it was equipped with some of the most draconian police powers ever passed in a liberal democracy ... the RUC contravened the standard norm in liberal democracies that the police exercise a semi-autonomous or arm's length relationship with civil and political authorities. Its senior officers were subordinate in practice to the political direction of the Northern Ireland government ... this government was always Unionist, and with the exception of one cabinet minister appointed towards the end, always Protestant.[51]

Even prior to conflict in 1969, the RUC exhibited demonstrable signs of divided-society policing; it showed systematic bias in law enforcement, carried out a politicised policing function, enjoyed special powers, was monopolised by the dominant group and had a dual purpose of internal security and 'ordinary' law and order.[52] The implication this had for police ownership in Northern Ireland reflects a broader phenomenon highlighted by Brewer and Magee whereby 'subordinate groups view the police as agents of oppression or occupation and show a minimal commitment to them, while the dominant community tend to look on the police as its own and the guarantor of its position'.[53]

Compounding difficulties in relation to the function of the RUC was the massive imbalance in the force's composition. Although it was initially envisaged that one-third of the force would be Catholic, recruitment figures never came close to this,[54] leaving it as Protestant and Unionist in personnel as it was in function and ethos. Beyond the mere religious imbalance, there was also the fact that the most ardent anti-Catholic elements in pre-partition Ulster had been subsumed into the security apparatus of the state. This security apparatus comprised 'thousands of Protestants ... who had gained experience in the hard school of civil war from 1916 to 1922'.[55] Their absorption into the state security apparatus saw the underlying function of the previously paramilitary UVF

[50] McGarry and O'Leary, 1999, 28.

[51] McGarry, 2000.

[52] Weitzer, 1995, 5.

[53] Brewer and Magee, 1991, 260.

[54] Ellison and Smyth, 2000.

[55] Rose, 1971, 91.

'legitimised'.[56] The crossover between the UVF and the security apparatus of the Northern Ireland state is best examined through the paramilitary police reserve the 'B-Specials'. Even after the imposition of partition, the 'B' division of the USC were retained as a part-time reserve to help combat prospective IRA violence. The 'B-Specials' were to batten on 'emergency situations'.[57] That such emergencies seldom arose did not alter this one iota. The USC drew its membership from the ranks of the UVF and the Ulster Imperial Guards – both mired in intense anti-Catholic sentiment and violence.[58] This tactic of channelling potential Unionist discontent away from challenging the state by merging armed organisations into the state security apparatus became a 'perennial security arrangement in Northern Ireland'.[59] Founded by Unionist politicians to protect Unionist interests, the USC adopted a world view that Protestants were 'loyal' and Catholics were 'disloyal'.[60] As a consequence, the force became the natural home for Protestant extremists and a cold house for Catholics. Unionists attributed religious imbalance to the Roman Catholic hierarchy and the Ancient Order of Hibernian (AOH) instructing their followers not to engage with the force.[61] A much greater likelihood is, however, that the pro-Unionist outlook of the force and its tenuous origins meant the minority community, in the words of Nationalist MP Joe Devlin, 'would not touch your special constabulary with a 40-foot pole'.[62]

It is within this divided-society policing climate that not just Irish republican but more general minority community disconnect from policing must be viewed. Mirroring the relationship between state legitimacy and police legitimacy, those on the outside of the state found themselves on the outside of policing, having little input into, control over or affinity with either. They were given little reason to identify with or align themselves to the state or police. Rather, the minority community found itself at the mercy of laws formulated and administered by Unionist politicians who had been integral in the formation of the UVF and had spent years inculcating the mentality that Catholics were a 'disloyal' threat to Protestant interests. Moreover, the enforcement of this legislation was delegated to those who had previously shown no hesitation in foisting violence and intimidation on the minority community. The links between the state and the security apparatus, and the

56 Boyle, Hadden and Hillyard, 1980, 32.

57 Breathnach, 1974.

58 Bowman, 2012.

59 Dixon, 2008, 107.

60 Farrell, 1983, 19.

61 Hezlet, 1973, 26.

62 Quoted in Farrell, 1983, 49.

sense of Protestant supremacy that underpinned this, meant that any change was not of function, but the fact that those indulgent in sectarian exclusion now had legislative power and loyal followers in state uniform to back it up. It is therefore unsurprising that from the very establishment of the RUC Catholics refused to get 'involved' with policing.[63]

Into the conflict

The outbreak of conflict in 1969 was preceded by two significant developments: increased leftist politicisation of the IRA and the Northern Ireland Civil Rights Association (NICRA) campaign of peaceful protest. The public-apathy-induced collapse of the Border Campaign demonstrated IRA failure to garner sympathy or strength from the populous. An internal IRA newssheet argued:

> There are many lessons to be learned from the last campaign, the most notable being that it is not enough to have men with guns in their hands ... We must have men who are capable of teaching the people what is wrong in this country of ours. We must have men who are capable of working with and for the people.[64]

As a result, the IRA began to align itself with those 'fighting social injustice' in order to broaden its sphere of influence.[65] Class-based political agitation, particularly in the Free State, would be the method of translating this broad front approach into practice. As Morrison notes, however, introducing a stronger political emphasis is a prelude to Irish republican splitting.[66] Even prior to the 1970 Official–Provisional split, the *Saor Éire* breakaway faction derided the IRA leadership for degenerating from a 'radical movement' into 'parliamentary reformists'.[67] Underlying tension persisted to eventually manifest itself in the 1970 split. Although the reasons behind the split are manifold and complex, as exhaustively examined by others,[68] for the brevity of this overview they will be reduced to leadership attempts to politicise the republican strategy by dropping abstentionism and avoiding where possible military action in the North so class-based solidarity with the Protestant working class could

63 Walker, 2004, 57.
64 'Editorial', *An tÓglách*, 3 (December 1967).
65 'Tasks', *An tÓglách*, 1 (1967).
66 Morrison, 2013, 4.
67 'Open Letter to Republicans', *Peoples Voice*, December 1968.
68 Hanley and Miller, 2010; Rekawek, 2011; Sanders 2011; Morrison, 2013.

be built. Coincidentally, the NICRA campaign was seen as the appropriate vehicle for building a broad front approach capable of incorporating inter-communal class-based solidarity. Irish republicans were openly supportive of and active participants in the NICRA campaign.[69] It should, however, be cautioned against taking this tactical alliance as evidence of IRA control over the NICRA or NICRA sympathy for the IRA. The demands of the NICRA were not ostensibly Irish republican; they wanted reform of the Northern Ireland state not its complete destruction; they sought 'British rights for British citizens' not Irish reunification, and they had a number of Protestants among their membership. Henry Patterson argues that the earliest permutations of the civil rights movement did not seek a British withdrawal but rather a new form of British intervention to tackle discrimination.[70] He also points out that during the NICRA era the Dublin-based IRA leadership was more concerned with agitating against the Free State, and that the then IRA would not have had the capacity to mobilise on the scale that the civil rights movement did.[71] The civil rights movement was therefore a 'new way of conceptualising an old problem' because Nationalist demands for an end to discrimination were being articulated outside the traditional framework of calling for resolution through settlement of the national question.[72] Paisleyite vilification would nonetheless condemn it as an IRA front, thus invoking a ferocious Unionist backlash. Bob Purdie has argued that the outbreak of this violence demonstrates the failure of the NICRA to successfully channel the tension created into compelling Stormont to concede demands rather than allowing this tension to be released through violence.[73] He further argues that the decision to turn to street demonstration tactics was a misguided one that allowed old fault lines about the national question to emerge and subsequently dominate the campaign.[74] This, he concludes, reduced the scope the Unionist government had for making concessions without upsetting the populism it relied on.[75]

Reactionary police violence towards peaceful NICRA marches dispelled any lingering pretence of police neutrality. There was official acknowledgement of this in the Scarman Report, which conceded that violent RUC misconduct left the impression that 'the police would be used as a partisan force to suppress

[69] 'Where Were the Republicans', *United Irishman*, October 1969; 'Whither Civil Rights?', *United Irishman*, December 1969.

[70] Patterson, 2006, 194.

[71] Patterson, 2006, 199.

[72] Purdie, 1990, 1–2.

[73] Purdie, 1990, 3.

[74] Purdie, 1990, 244.

[75] Purdie, 1990, 248.

... those opposed to the Northern Ireland government'.[76] More tellingly, it recognised 'the fateful split between the Catholic community and the police'.[77] Accordingly, complaints about discrimination soon became complaints about policing.[78] This reflected the growing police tendency to participate in, rather than curtail, violence directed at NICRA marches.[79] As this violence escalated, the notion of police complicity became central to Irish republican depictions of the police as the violent guardians of a corrupt 'Orange state'. The outbreak of violence in Derry in August 1969 following clashes between Catholics and Paisleyite mobs was narrated along the lines that '[the] RUC immediately attacked Nationalists with batons, wearing helmets and shields. The inevitable had happened and the fight was on. The rest is history'.[80] Similarly, the Belfast pogroms were orchestrated by 'the combined UVF, RUC and B-Specials forces'.[81] Irish republicans drew on the sectarian origins of the 'B-Specials' to frame its current activity with reference to this past: 'recent events in Derry, Belfast and elsewhere have shown they have not changed their colours one whit since 1920. They have not lost their addiction to violence nor their strictly sectarian character'.[82]

In foregrounding the police role in violently marginalising the minority community, 'boundary work' establishing defined categories of 'us' and 'them' continued to condition Irish republican attitudes to policing.[83] This drew on the historical origins of the 'Orange state' and the divided-society policing model it was sustained through, to communicate the message that the failed state that had privileged 'them' by disadvantaging 'us' was beyond reform. This countered the impact of the belated, yet tokenistic, concessions by the Stormont administration to NICRA demands, and the Hunt Report attempt to salvage the police reputation. An 'injustice frame' recognising violent police defence of the exclusionary 'Orange state' as a 'political wrong' soon gained traction.[84] Usefully, this gave meaningful articulation to traditional Irish republican opposition to the very existence of the Northern Ireland state. Peaceful demands for the reform of the 'Orange state' had only succeeded in incurring the wrath of the security apparatus of that very state. The argument

[76] Scarman, 1972, 1.4.
[77] Scarman, 1972, 3.6.
[78] Ellison and Martin, 2000.
[79] Rose, 1971, 105.
[80] 'Derry's Story', *United Irishman*, November 1969.
[81] 'How Belfast Fought', *United Irishman*, September 1969.
[82] 'B-Specials No Change', *United Irishman*, October 1969.
[83] Hunt and Benford, 2004, 443.
[84] Polletta, 1998.

that 'a tyranny that is maintained by force can ultimately be only overthrown by force' seemed increasingly plausible.[85]

The deployment of British troops in August 1969 saw Irish republicans retain their colonial interpretation of the turmoil in the North of Ireland. Refusing to countenance that the British Army was a neutral peacekeeping force, they evinced traditionalist interpretations of British involvement in Ireland: 'the fact is Britain is not unwilling to have a civil war so that she can arrive again as a "saviour", abolish Stormont, and have the anti-Unionist population delighted to be fully absorbed in the United Kingdom'.[86] The Lower Falls curfew in July 1970 and internment in August 1971 provided succour on the ground to those questioning the role of British troops in Nationalist areas.[87] As British Army visibility increased, it was met by the violent outworkings of the fledgling Provisional IRA's escalation policy of moving from a defensive to an offensive position, engaging British troops and bringing down the 'Orange state' in the process.[88] When the British government prorogued Stormont in 1972, a colonial framing of the conflict was adjusted to replace rhetoric about the 'Orange state' with that of 'occupation'. By this stage, the Provisionals had 'changed the terms of the debate' in the six counties.[89] From a republican viewpoint, instead of facing the British occupier's colonial dupes, they were now pitted against the British occupier itself. Political resentment of the predominantly Unionist police force protecting Protestant supremacy in order to prop up the colonial statelet now became political resentment of foreign troops who were enforcing military occupation directly on the ground in the North of Ireland. The narrative of occupation became integral to Provisional rejection of the electoral and political process in the post-1972 state:

> Elections are not free when armed troops with cameras are posted inside and outside polling booths, when ballot boxes are held overnight in the custody of enemy soldiers, when the major opposition party Sinn Fein is not allowed to put up candidates, when opposition areas are saturated with troops, and candidates are liable to internment, in short a state of police and military dictatorship.[90]

---

[85] 'Blame Britain', *United Irishman*, September 1969.

[86] 'Civil War Britain's Aim', *United Irishman*, October 1969.

[87] Campbell and Connolly, 2003; McCleery, 2015.

[88] MacStiofáin, 1975.

[89] Purdie, 1990, 250.

[90] 'Ten-Point Summary: Spoil Your Vote and Spoil It Early', *Republican News*, 27 June 1973.

Strident in their opposition to any political settlement that guaranteed the existence of a Northern Ireland state, the Provisionals made appeals to Unionists to 'accept the hand of friendship' and reject the 'cancer of sectarianism which a foreign power through its agents has inoculated into our people'.[91] Similarly, they presented their rejection of the 1974 Sunningdale Agreement as being premised on the fact it was a 'life belt for the Protestant and Catholic upper and middle classes' who were enriched by the colonial divide-and-conquer policy. Behind this rhetorical appeal to working-class Unionists, there was, of course, fundamental ideological opposition to Sunningdale's partitionist power-sharing assembly too. This ideological purity was also reflected in the IRA leadership's public line that the prerequisite for any political settlement in Northern Ireland was a British declaration of intent to withdraw:

> Only a solution arrived at by Irishmen and women, in light of an English declaration of withdrawal, will achieve a lasting peace for this province of Ulster, and indeed, for the whole of Ireland ... Only then, acting in concert with each other, free from any outside interference, can we come to an honourable agreement.[92]

'Ulsterisation'

By the mid-1970s, it was clear that there would be no quick victory for either side in the conflict. British government policy and IRA strategy adapted to this reality. Dropping the rhetoric of impending victory, a restructured IRA adopted a 'long war' strategy.[93] The British government's 'The way ahead' security policy adopted a three-track approach of 'Ulsterisation', normalisation and criminalisation. 'Ulsterisation' was designed to starve the IRA of propagandistic oxygen by relying primarily on the RUC to combat IRA violence. Pitting British soldiers against the native Irish gave credence to the IRA assertion it was waging a legitimate war of national liberation. 'Ulsterisation' was premised on the calculation that 'it would be more difficult for the IRA to depict the British as occupiers if it was confronted with a local police rather than a "foreign" army'.[94] The criminalisation policy meant that IRA and INLA violence would be treated as 'normal' crime and dealt with by the police, rather

91 'Call to Ulster Protestants', *Republican News,* 13 July 1974.

92 'Let us Make an Honourable Agreement', *Republican News,* 13 July 1974.

93 Bowyer Bell, 1997.

94 McGarry, 2000.

than the military. The policy coincided with a dipping in morale within Irish republican communities as 'war weariness' crept in.[95] The government wrongfully surmised that deflecting away from the political nature of Irish republican violence and depicting it as normal crime would lessen support for it.[96] Instead, the policy popularised the republican cause during the 1981 hunger strike and laid the foundations for unprecedented support for Sinn Féin. Normalisation tried to create a facade of normality during the conflict, with the intention being to use a 'normal' police force to fight 'normal' crime.

'Ulsterisation' gave the RUC the lead role in counter-insurgency operations, making it responsible for undertaking the more contentious activities in Nationalist districts. Upon taking up this role, the RUC 'encountered some of the same difficulties which the Army has long faced in carrying out an effective policing operation without being drawn into the kind of confrontations and incidents which are likely to cause an escalation in communal antagonism'.[97] The policy eradicated any salvageable relationship the RUC may have still had with the Nationalist community on two accounts. First, it placed the RUC inconspicuously in the firing line of republicans, and secondly, it meant the RUC would now be performing tasks that had led to Nationalist discontent with the military. As McGarry and O'Leary note, the policy 'reduced the likelihood of a gentle policing touch in predominantly Nationalist areas'.[98] The RUC was seen not as a 'normal' police force but as the extension of the British military apparatus in the six counties.[99] This became a central tenet of the Irish republican narrative, as it provided justification for violence directed at the supposedly 'normal' police force.

Counter-insurgency policing is militarised, aggressive and intrusive in nature. Giving the RUC such a function in the midst of political violence created an environment on the ground conducive to claims that Nationalist districts were under militarised occupation. Heavily fortified police stations, armed police officers jointly patrolling with armed British soldiers and widespread checkpoints pointed to no other conclusion. Just as the RUC had violently defended the 'Orange state', so too in the aftermath of 'Ulsterisation' would it be charged with enforcing British occupation in the six counties. This was again framed as a political wrong, again framed in terms of the force's innate enmity towards Nationalists, and again premised on trying to justify violence directed at the force. Using the reality on the ground that 'Ulsterisation' had

---

95 Ross, 2006.

96 Boyle, Hadden and Hillyard, 1980, 31.

97 Boyle, Hadden and Hillyard, 1980, 33.

98 McGarry and O'Leary, 1999, 103.

99 'On the War Front', *Volunteer*, 19 September 1976.

created, republicans argued, 'it is us, the Nationalist people ... who daily bear the brunt of the now naked sectarian RUC. All pretence at playing community policing has gone being replaced by the ruthless and calculating systematic harassment of this community'.[100]

This not only portrayed the RUC as the front line of occupation, but also drew on historical tropes of RUC collaboration with loyalists. Initially, this involved claims of 'collaboration of the RUC by neglect'.[101] Essentially, this argument maintained that while the RUC took a hard line on Irish republican violence it was at very best negligently indifferent towards loyalist violence. Following a murder by the infamous loyalist 'Shankill Butchers', republicans protested that 'the RUC remain indifferent towards the plight of innocent Catholics ... these gangs of loyalists remain intact simply because the RUC allows them to'.[102] To this end, it was argued that 'the RUC are not a police body' but 'an extension of the loyalist paramilitary groups'.[103] By the late 1980s, a more sinister proactive policy of RUC collusion with loyalist paramilitaries became the more pressing issue. Loyalist attacks were labelled 'semi-official killings'.[104] The lack of proper investigation into these killings, the public dismissal of concerns on the matter and the vilification of the dead and their relatives strengthened, rather than assuaged, suspicions within the Nationalist community.[105]

Collusion was not the only concern with RUC counter-insurgency policing that began leaving an indelible mark on Nationalist communities by the 1990s. Cases of shoot-to-kill and plastic bullet deaths – and the associated impunity – began to generate concern outside the Irish republican constituency.[106] Such blatant wrongdoing, and the complete lack of accountability for it, became the 'moral shocks'[107] that would make the issue of counter-insurgency policing one much wider than a mere Irish republican one. Collusion, shoot-to-kill and the killing of civilians by plastic bullets expanded the counter-insurgency policing issue beyond the Irish republican constituency by sufficiently concerning human rights activists, academia and more moderate Nationalist elements perturbed by events on the ground.

---

[100] 'The Road to Peace, Freedom and Justice', *Waterside Republican Newssheet*, 3 (April 1989).

[101] Faul and Murray, 1975, 88.

[102] 'Murder', *Freedom Fighter*, 7 (1977).

[103] 'Join the RUC and See the Next World', *Freedom Fighter*, 5 (1976).

[104] 'The Overtime Killings', *Iris*, 10 (July 1985).

[105] Relatives for Justice, 1993.

[106] Rolston, 2000; Ni Aolaín, 2000.

[107] Jasper and Poulsen, 1995.

External condemnation of the RUC was invaluable in what Dixon refers to as 'the propaganda war' that ran in parallel with the physical war.[108] The relevance of this was heightened following the 1985 Anglo-Irish Agreement (AIA). O'Malley argues that the AIA was a governmental, and to a lesser degree SDLP, response to the nascent electoral threat posed by Sinn Féin in the aftermath of the hunger strikes.[109] By providing an 'Irish dimension' to proposed political settlement of the conflict, it was hoped that support for Sinn Féin and for the IRA campaign would wane. The AIA also heralded closer security co-operation between the British and Irish states in tackling IRA activity. In accordance with a changing security context, Irish republicans had to ensure that the RUC remained 'othered' from the Nationalist community. To this end, Irish republicans maintained that the RUC was still sectarian, still unacceptable and still the coercive arm of the British occupying state. This fuelled opposition to attempts at rehabilitating the image of the RUC following the AIA.[110] To Irish republicans, the RUC remained 'another section of Britain's military forces'.[111] The implication of this, then, was that the force, contrary to the normalisation policy, was an integral component of the British 'war machine' in Ireland and as such prone to attack. Despite the AIA appeasement of the SDLP, the RUC remained 'legitimate targets'.[112] This discourse was vital in cultivating continued rejection of the RUC, continued rejection of moderate supported internal settlements and continued justification for the IRA campaign. As conflict lessened and talk of peace emerged, Irish republican discourse would again change to mirror their changing relationship with the Northern Ireland state.

Patten politicking

The preceding pages evidence how the Irish republican attitude towards policing is ultimately conditioned by the contemporaneous state of play in the wider political environment. Until the mid-1990s, that environment was defined by divided-society policing in the throes of political violence. The tentative emergence of the peace process and the advent of the ceasefires altered this dynamic. Even if the IRA ceasefire did not remove political contestation

---

108 Dixon, 2008.

109 O'Malley, 1991, 221.

110 Robbie Smith, 'The not so Irish News', *Iris*, 10 (July 1985).

111 'Comment', *Sceal*, 8 (7 August 1986).

112 'Forums', *Iris*, 10 (July 1985).

over policing, it nonetheless enabled a protracted debate to take root.[113] Irish republicans and the RUC began posturing around dichotomous positions; one pushing for complete disbandment of the RUC on historical and political grounds, and the other railing for minimal reform given the force's apparent increase in professionalisation and normalised function.[114]

The changed political climate birthed a narrative moving beyond the RUC being 'legitimate targets' to argue instead that policing reform required the complete disbandment of the RUC.[115] Most notably, this saw the lexicon of international human rights displace ideological rhetoric in the Sinn Féin policing discourse.[116] Moving beyond crude depictions of an 'Orange' force, the RUC was now presented as an obstacle to lasting peace in the North of Ireland. Refuting a 'Hans Christian Anderson' RUC self-narrative,[117] Irish republicans refused to countenance any notion of RUC involvement in the political or social life of post-conflict Northern Ireland. Simple ideological rejection became redundant, as police reform seemingly became a prerequisite to any lasting political settlement on human rights, political and historical grounds.

Violent eruptions over contentious Orange Order marches ignited the human rights dimension to calls for RUC disbandment. RUC conduct at Drumcree, the Ormeau Road and in Derry provided plentiful sustenance for Irish republican grievances. RUC heavy-handedness and their discharging of thousands of plastic bullets at Nationalist residents, was criticised and contrasted with the restraint it had previously shown towards loyalists.[118] A 'Disband the RUC' campaign involving letter writing, a poster campaign and co-ordinated pickets soon followed. Violent public order policing had a resonance with all too familiar past problems, thus RUC short-sightedness in forcing the Orange march down the Garvaghy Road inadvertently strengthened the Irish republican argument. Moreover, scenes of RUC violence were hardly doing the force's assertions of heightened professionalism and increased normalisation any favours. Mulcahy places this into the perspective of the pre-Patten debate: 'the impact of Drumcree was profound. Not only did it implicate the RUC in familiar troubles and controversies surrounding public order, excessive force and use of plastic bullets, but it re-immersed it in debates on its respective relationships with the communities in Northern Ireland'.[119]

113 Mulcahy, 2000.
114 Murphy, 2013.
115 Sinn Féin, 1995.
116 Sinn Féin, 2000.
117 Maskey, 1996.
118 Pat Finucane Centre, 1995, 5; Sinn Féin, 1996a.
119 Mulcahy, 2013, 143.

Amidst this chaos, political negotiations edged towards the GFA. Given the inherent link between state legitimacy and police legitimacy, it became evident that Nationalist acceptance of reformed policing could only be precipitated by their acceptance of any proposed political settlement.[120] Both Nationalist parties accepted the GFA – albeit with division within Sinn Féin on acceptance of the sacrilegious 'principle of consent'.[121] The GFA, however, barely addressed the issue of policing directly. While it recognised that a 'new beginning' for policing was required, it delegated out resolution of the issue to the Independent Commission on Policing for Northern Ireland (commonly known as the Patten Commission). Such a move, as Christine Bell notes,[122] typifies the political choreographing that had seen consensus for the GFA achieved by removing the most divisive issues from negotiations via delegating them to separate commissions. This meant that while a peace agreement had been brokered, and power-sharing institutions established, policing remained a yet to be resolved issue that would be dealt with somewhat paradoxically as separate from, yet also relevant to, the rest of the political process.

As part of its remit, the Patten Commission instigated a wide-ranging consultation process to gather policing experiences from across the North of Ireland. Localised meetings that allowed people to relate at first hand their individual and communal experiences were an integral component of this process. It also entailed receiving written submissions from various interested parties across the political and social spectrum. Sinn Féin engaged with this consultation process, and articulated their opposition to the RUC. Several other interested groups within the wider Nationalist community did likewise. When the Patten Commission finished this process, it produced an official report on policing that contained a voluminous catalogue of proposals for reform. Although cautiously welcoming the Patten proposals, Sinn Féin was nonetheless reticent about prematurely calling for support for policing.[123] That, it seemed, hinged on how the proposals translated into practice. When the Policing Act diluted the Patten proposals beyond recognition, the scope for Sinn Féin acceptance of reformed policing dissipated. Sinn Féin remained opposed to the PSNI and refused to become involved with the Northern Ireland Policing Board (NIPB) unless reform was brought into line with Patten.[124] The SDLP, who had initially been sceptical about the Policing Act, later accepted it following the Weston Park talks. There was now an evident split within the

[120] McGarry, 2000.

[121] Bean, 2007a.

[122] Bell, 2003.

[123] 'Sinn Féin Responds to Patten', *An Phoblacht*, 2 December 1999.

[124] Sinn Féin, 2001.

Nationalist constituency on the matter: Sinn Féin continuing to disengage from reformed policing and the SDLP promoting it. Political jostling between the parties on the matter naturally ensued.[125]

Although the disconnect from policing remained, by this stage it had a decidedly less absolutist flavour. This reflects Sinn Féin's acceptance of the de facto existence of the Northern Ireland state as laid out in the GFA – after all, how could they reject policing on an ideological fundamentalist basis if they had endorsed the GFA and were active participants in the power-sharing government established thereafter. An increasingly pragmatic and less ideological approach to policing became discernible. The gradual navigation from a position as 'outsiders' in the Northern Ireland state to post-GFA political 'insiders' led to less fundamental opposition to 'British policing' and greater political interrogation of the post-conflict reform process. Moving away from ideological absolutism, there was, for example, acknowledgement that a post-conflict state would need a police service, that Nationalist communities were suffering in the absence of any such force, and that any reformed policing body would inevitably see some element of RUC crossover.[126] These considerations would later come to frame debates in the prelude to formal Sinn Féin endorsement of policing.[127] In retrospect, it seems that in light of accepting the GFA and departing from ideological absolutism it was, at this point, not a matter of if Sinn Féin would come to endorse policing but how it would choreograph the process of doing so, and what exactly was required to secure formal engagement.

'Critical engagement' and beyond

Continued Sinn Féin participation in the power-sharing institutions exposed the increasing peculiarity of its position; legislating laws in the post-GFA state but withholding support for the police force enforcing these laws. Excising ideological fundamentalism, their opposition to policing was now presented, not as opposition to policing per se, but opposition to 'political policing' by the 'securocrats' who had crossed over from the RUC Special Branch into the PSNI.[128] The collapse of the power-sharing institutions amidst the 'Stormontgate' affair in October 2002, provoked outrage from Sinn Féin, who claimed it had been concocted by 'securocrats' to damage the peace process. The 'securocrats' were using 'political policing' in an attempt to defeat

[125] Murphy, 2013.
[126] Gibney, 1996.
[127] Sinn Féin, 2007.
[128] Sinn Féin, 2002.

republicanism, having failed to defeat it militarily during the conflict.[129] Having already relinquished ideological absolutism by tacitly accepting the need for a police force in the post-GFA state, Sinn Féin discourse after 'Stormontgate' was not about ideology, but whether policing could be 'depoliticised' as a means of furthering political goals.[130] 'Stormontgate' was evidence that if approached 'strategically', engagement with policing would thwart those who 'do not want a Shinner about the place'.[131] Adopting a discourse of advancing the 'republican agenda' from within,[132] Sinn Féin orientated its support base towards formal acceptance of the PSNI.

As the formal policing debate commenced, Sinn Féin rebranded policing as a site of Irish republican struggle. This resonated more generally with their discourse on equality-based change of the Northern Ireland state. To this end, Adams asserted that Sinn Féin wanted 'a service for citizens who are nationalists, republicans, unionists, of different racial or ethnic backgrounds. We don't have it at the moment but we have the ability to get it, and that's what Sinn Féin is about'.[133] Although indubitably 'an emotive issue', delegates at the Ard Fheis were urged to view engagement with post-Patten policing 'strategically' and for the political benefits in the present, rather than the historical baggage of the past.[134] The increased political strength of Sinn Féin, it was argued, meant that the time was ripe to cash in the chips accumulated through disengagement to maximise change and advance the overarching ideological agenda.[135] Engagement with policing became essential to the process of accruing greater political strength; if republicans engaged with policing they would be empowered and opponents of republicanism disempowered. To continue disengaging, this logic suggested, was to forfeit this site of struggle to those anathema to the aspirations of Irish republicanism. Strategy, accountability, transformation and empowerment became the staple diet of 'political speak' enunciated by the Sinn Féin leadership, as it secured the necessary support from within its constituency.

The decision to endorse policing was inescapably a political decision by the Sinn Féin leadership and its persuasion of grassroots activists inescapably a political sell. Yet the fact remains that this was only possible when it freed itself

---

[129] Sinn Féin, 2003.

[130] Adams, 2003.

[131] Kelly, 2006.

[132] Anderson, 2006.

[133] 'CIRA Says No to Adams Invitation', BBC News, 26 January 2007: http://news.bbc.co.uk/1/hi/northern_ireland/6301051.stm (accessed 23 April 2012).

[134] Murray, 2007.

[135] McDonald, 2007.

from the encumbering ideological absolutism it had previously subscribed to by embracing the mantra of pragmatism and the *realpolitik*. Only then was it possible to frame policing as a site of struggle and as a process leading to ideological goals, rather than an end dropping short of them. It had on occasions previous to this shown a willingness to favour *realpolitik* pragmatism over ideological absolutism. The atavistic rejection of the application of 'British law' in Ireland had given way to the pragmatic realisation that tactical engagement with 'British law' could create political and material capital.[136] Contempt for the supine collaborators in Dublin and the SDLP had also come to pass when the opportunity to engage them as 'fellow travellers' in a pan-Nationalist front arose.[137] Likewise, the changed relationship with policing has been followed by further removal from ideological absolutism. Most notably, this has seen increased Sinn Féin engagement with the British Royal Family being couched in the language of redefining the relationship between those of the Irish republican tradition and those who represent the imperial and military tradition of the British state.[138] A colonial interpretation has been displaced by one that engorges talk of peace and reconciliation and speaks of Britain and Ireland sharing a special relationship as geographical neighbours. This has also seen Sinn Féin representatives officially attending Remembrance Day commemorations – previously seen as the valorising of Britain's imperialist war dead – as an act of outreach to Unionists.[139] According to Garry and Matthews, such moves have been forced by the need to popularise Sinn Féin's electoral appeal beyond its traditional support base.[140] If it was guided by ideological purity in the past, Sinn Féin is led today by 'electoral logic'.[141]

When located within this wider post-GFA political geography, the formal acceptance of policing is not an isolated move, but one that must be viewed in terms of an ongoing continuum away from ideological absolutism and into constitutionalism. Increased involvement in the post-GFA state came at the price of being led by the diktats of *realpolitik* pragmatism, rather than relying on

[136] McEvoy, 2000.

[137] O'Donnell, 2008, 49.

[138] D. Kearney, 'The Two Significant Sinn Féin and Royal Meetings Will Promote Reconciliation and Healing', *An Phoblacht*, 22 May 2015: www.anphoblacht.com/contents/25006 (accessed 4 September 2015).

[139] 'Historic Day as Sinn Féin Mayor Attends Armistice Day Ceremony in Belfast', *Belfast Telegraph*, 11 November 2013: www.belfasttelegraph.co.uk/news/northern-ireland/historic-day-as-sinn-fein-mayor-attends-armistice-day-ceremony-in-belfast-29743016.html (accessed 4 September 2013).

[140] Garry and Matthews, 2015.

[141] Whiting, 2015.

the comforts of unerring ideological purity. Standing on the outside is straightforward, the argument is easily digestible and every course of oppositional action can be reduced to ideological absolutism. For all that, it is hardly progressive. Becoming a political 'insider' ill affords the luxury of simple purist rhetoric, and relies instead on rhetoric about strategy and tactics. As Sanders argues,[142] the fact that the route to political power lies within government rather than a protesting position outside it, removes the option of ideological rigidity from Irish republicans who engage in electoralism. Formal engagement with state structures through electoral intervention may be tentative and minimalist to begin with, but once the initial act occurs further engagement is a natural consequence. Tonge, for example, argues that Sinn Féin engagement with the Northern Ireland state can be traced back to its first engagements with local council committees after realising the administrative power that lies within such bodies.[143] Over time, this engagement evolved into the creation of what Bean calls the 'Sinn Féin state' in Nationalist communities.[144] Evidently, then, Irish republicans who engage with the state adapt their position accordingly, meaning that aspects once considered imperative for a political settlement (e.g. British withdrawal) become long-term aspirational goals instead.[145] In tandem with this, the language of self-determination is also downgraded to the language of co-determination that more accurately reflects the reality of their post-GFA position.[146]

The *realpolitik* knife, however, cuts both ways. Presenting policing as a progressive site of struggle is premised on the assumption that it can be utilised as such. Political speak of accountability and transformation is rhetorically powerful but practicably impotent if this assumption proves to be a fundamental miscalculation. The logic of strategic interaction essentially becomes hoist by its own petard:

> Policing will not be sold to the faithful as a maintaining of the status quo, or a toll to protect the state but rather a 'site of struggle', a means by which to hollow out the union and bring down the state of 'Northern Ireland' from within. The British state in Ireland is comfortable with this knowing that they have given the Provisionals no latitude to do this and knowing that they have no intention of pulling down the power structure anyway.[147]

---

142 Sanders, 2011, 9.

143 Tonge, 2006.

144 Bean, 2007a.

145 Whiting, 2015.

146 Tonge, 2009, 170.

147 'An Open Debate, and a Principled Stance', *Sovereign Nation*, January/February 2007.

This challenges the principal precepts of the Sinn Féin argument by locating the matter within pre-existing structural boundaries. Essentially, it suggests that Sinn Féin cannot dictate the state of play but has to function within current power relations that preclude any realisation of a transformative project like the one they propose. This argument mirrors critiques found in critical criminology whereby the enactment and enforcement of law are inseparable from wider power relations that legitimise and protect the status quo.[148] Within the confines of such an argument, the police force, rather than being a tool capable of challenging the prevailing status quo, represents the 'repressive state apparatus' that works in tandem with the 'ideological state apparatus' to protect dominant interests.[149] This link between state and police legitimacy has birthed a polyvalent problematic; the post-GFA state, as a partitionist institution, remains propagated by 'British' policing, the consociationalism at the heart of the GFA has institutionalised sectarianism, and the post-GFA state remains driven by neoliberal interests. Accordingly, there is a greater sophistication in criticism of the Sinn Féin position that draws on these observations and infuses them with Marxist understandings to move the debate beyond simplistic rejection of 'British' policing:

> It was a stupid thing for politicians to say in the first place. I mean, your initial assumption runs through every state in the world – I don't care what the politics and ideology of it are – and that is the purpose – the first purpose – of a state police force is to protect the state. That invariably means protecting property, but it also means protecting significant individuals so putting manners on a police force is basically changing the state and the Good Friday Agreement never mentioned the constitutional change of the state. Quite the opposite.[150]

This allows the notion of changing policing in the six counties from within to be critiqued in class terms:

> I certainly wouldn't buy into that and I think anybody with any cop on doesn't. Like you don't go in and join, for want of a better word, your enemy – your class enemy, your national enemy – by going and treatising with them. Changing things from within – I can't speak for Sinn Féin, but that was something that they were actually preaching against for quite a

148 Hepburn, 1977.

149 Brogden, 1982, 12.

150 Y, critic of Sinn Féin policy, interview, October 2013.

> long time. You know, 'You can't become involved in the various assemblies that was set up, it was irreformable'. And the very fact that the RUC are irreformable, a cosmetic name change to PSNI – they're still irreformable as a police force. They are still protecting a sectarian state which is based on a sectarian head count, you know. And that would be the republican view. A wider Marxist view would be that if a united Ireland was declared tomorrow and the PSNI were all called the Gardaí, they would still be class enemies, really you know. They would be anti-working class. You see it in England, you see it in Germany, France, wherever. The police are no friend of working-class people.[151]

In drawing on long-standing critical observations of the power relations that underpin policing, some critics offer a more nuanced analysis of policing that transcends the Northern Ireland context. Many referred to how the miners' strikes in the UK were policed to substantiate their argument. By doing so, they have mirrored previous criticisms made by Phil Scraton.[152] Moreover, criminological literature has long ruminated over how effective external oversight bodies can actually be when forced to operate within these structural confines.[153] Again, this allows critics to assess the Sinn Féin line of reasoning in view of how policing elsewhere operates:

> All police services throughout the world spy, use informers, infiltrate political parties, plant agents in the media, recruit academics in the universities, stitch up so-called subversives and use any and other means necessary to maintain specific structures of oppression. It is entirely illusory to imagine that the PSNI in Northern Ireland would ever be some kind, beneficial or helping-hand institution. It will always be an instrument of oppression.[154]

But what happens, then, to those who engage the apparatus of the state with transformatory intent? Critiques offered in critical criminology and neo-colonial literature suggest that the reality of how the state–police power relation manifests itself means that the edge of this transformative intent smoothes over time as the would-be reformers adapt to the prevailing surroundings they find themselves in. This, as Scraton argues, sees the state neutralising the threat

---

[151] J, critic of Sinn Féin, interview, June 2013.

[152] Scraton, 1985.

[153] Marenin, 1982.

[154] Gerry Ruddy, 'Ireland: Some Thoughts on the Policing Issue', *Plough*, 3:40 (12 December 2006).

of would-be reformers by slowly involving them in its hegemonic project.[155] Harris, drawing on the example of Latin America, similarly suggests that would-be reformers can be lured away from their counter-hegemonic position over time through protracted processes of 'co-option' or 'corruption'.[156] This often thrives on the would-be reformer's ignorance of the machinations of the system they seek to reform, meaning that by the time the facade of state benevolence wears off it is too late to retreat. Critics who frame their rejection of the Sinn Féin position in this wider critical landscape thus conclude:

> What is happening is we're looking at a situation where the Sinn Féin party – and you know admittedly with the best will in the world, the best intentions in the world – is being drawn into giving support to the establishment willy-nilly. Whether they actually see it as such, but it actually does and at that stage then your argument is with the local police rather than with the system of policing, and you may well then find that the local police will say, 'Well, fine, a little tweak here, a little tweak there', but the system doesn't change, the legislation doesn't change and I think that's where the argument has to be ... policing ultimately can't be better than the legislation and/or the state, and if we have problems with the legislation and/or the state then we are going to have problems with policing and at best you're asking for the coercive arm of that state to pretty its act up but not to fundamentally change it.[157]

Inasmuch as the *realpolitik* can cocoon Sinn Féin's policy of 'critical engagement' from detractors citing absolutist ideological interpretations of Irish republicanism, it can nonetheless leave it exposed to the observed wisdom of leftist critiques proffered by others.

Conclusion

The historical backdrop to the relationship between Irish republicanism and policing in the North of Ireland cannot be critically examined without adequate consideration of the political choreographing that birthed measured changes in this relationship. Successfully grasping the magnitude of the changes in the Irish republican relationship with policing is predicated on firstly grasping the magnitude of its changing relationship with the Northern Ireland state.

155 Scraton, 2007, 220.
156 Harris, 2007.
157 Q, critic of Sinn Féin policy, interview, July 2013.

Rejection of the state led to rejection of the police. Tentative engagement with the structures and processes of the state led to tentative engagement with police reform and a less ideologically purist view of policing. Acceptance of the Northern Ireland state with a long-term view of equality-based reform led to similar acceptance of post-Patten policing. 'Critical engagement' with policing was the totality of a process of adaptation by the 'native', the 'other' and the 'outsider' to the changing political environment they were faced with. Externally, the process of engagement was driven by the demands of the *realpolitik* that a post-conflict climate threw up for Irish republicanism. Internally, however, it would be the very process of engagement itself that would prove divisive, not only due to the legacy of generations of divided-society policing but also because of the present and future political implications that continued movement away from ideological absolutism would herald. The remainder of this book uses this chapter as a framework for interpreting and critically evaluating how the politics of memory condition current disagreement on the issue of policing within the wider Irish republican constituency.

Chapter 2

Irish Republican Memory as Counter-Memory

Introduction

The previous chapter established how policing lay at the heart of the conflict in Northern Ireland. Unsurprisingly, the legacy of policing remains contested during post-conflict transition. This is symptomatic of the general fact that all transitioning societies witness contestation between parties to the conflict who are determined to broadcast their own narrative. More specifically, it reflects how views of policing in the North of Ireland were/are inextricably linked to differing political perspectives. During the conflict, this was played out through the 'legitimacy politics' of police and state legitimacy, but in transition contestation – between even if not within opposing ethno-nationalist blocs – is played out through the memory politics of what policing was, rather than what policing is.[1] The memory politics of policing gravitate around competing narratives that are either favourable to or condemnatory of the RUC. These narratives are hardly apolitical; they are engineered through deliberately selective 'forgetting' and 'remembering', articulated with present political needs in mind and endowed with post-conflict political functionality. To grasp the veracity of this, it is necessary to evaluate the interplay between 'narrative substance' – what the narrative says – and 'narrative context' – why it says this – that defines memory politics in Northern Ireland.

Substantively, opposing narratives articulate the 'remembered past' rather than the 'actual past'. Unlike the 'actual past', which is susceptible to natural processes of forgetting, the 'remembered past' is manipulated through selective 'remembering' and 'forgetting' processes that feed into collective memory, political identity and group boundaries. As such, the 'remembered past' is integral to engendering feelings of injustice, a sense of victimisation and the

1 Hearty, 2014.

apportioning of blame to the 'other'.[2] The 'remembered past' can then be used to apportion blame in accordance with the thrust of master narratives proffered by various parties to the conflict; Unionists can blame Irish republicans (and to a lesser extent Nationalists) for attempting to overthrow the state by subterfuge through the NICRA campaign, the British state can blame warring sectarian factions (conveniently excising itself from the post-conflict blame game) and Irish republicans can blame the British for creating the discriminatory 'Orange state' before subsequently laying siege to the six counties through military occupation when that state was brought to the point of collapse. Contextually, this is incredibly useful in a transitional setting where an end to the violent manifestations of political disagreement rarely heralds an end to political disagreement itself. Parties formerly locked in physical conflict are unlikely to relinquish their previously held world view and subscribe to that articulated by the 'other' simply because physical violence has given way to non-violent politics. Nor are they likely to repudiate their past, even if the means of the past are no longer practised. With the exception, perhaps, of acknowledging certain occasional deviations from the accepted norms of conflict, they will continue to assert the legitimacy of their past actions and the illegitimacy of those of their opponents. In transition, memory politics becomes 'the continuation of war by other means'.[3] Its value is heightened in transitions, like Northern Ireland, that have yet to comprehensively 'deal with the past'. In the absence of consensus over the past, memory politics underpins the meta-conflict over who caused the conflict and who suffered most because of it. Indeed, the genesis of the meta-conflict lies in the divergent interpretations of its very status; a subversive campaign of Irish republican 'terrorism' (Unionists), a sectarian conflict between opposing factions (British state) or a war of national liberation against British occupation (Irish republicans).

Memory politics and the meta-conflict

Contestation over the what, the when, the how and the why of the conflict is directly correlative to contestation over the what, the when, the how and the why of policing. For all that they disagree, opposing narratives similarly reduce the causes and consequences of the conflict to an easily digestible morality play. Common to opposing narratives is a simplistic, yet emotional, tale of 'good versus evil'. Each narrative is resplendent with victims of violence

[2] Brewer and Hayes, 2015.

[3] Olick, 2013.

and of the heroics of those who fearlessly defended the community from an omnipresent evil. The major divergence, though, is that while sharing the same 'good versus evil' plot, opposing narratives cast different actors in the roles of 'good' and 'evil'. Commensurability with easily digestible morality plays and binary caricatures of 'good' and 'evil' lies not in their absolute truth, but in the fact that these correspond to differing lived experiences of political violence.[4] The RUC, then, can simultaneously be seen as the heroic, much suffering 'good' character in the Unionist morality play *and* the violent, sectarian 'evil' character in the Irish republican morality play. Uncoincidentally, the British state morality play is broadly analogous to that of Unionists. As the self-proclaimed neutral arbitrator of the conflict, it constructs a morality play where the RUC, supported by their colleagues in the British Army, upheld the 'good' inherent in the democratic rule of law by combating the 'evil' of 'terrorism'.[5] The common trait is what Assmann calls 'the memory of perpetrators' whereby 'as easy as it is to remember the guilt of others, it is difficult to remember one's own guilt'.[6] Meta-conflict memory politics therefore 'remembers' the violence of the conflict in accordance with morality play interpretations of the past; we 'remember' the violence of 'them' and 'forget' the violence of 'us'.

The fallout from violence exercised by the RUC and that directed against it can be easily situated in communal narratives on the conflict; for the Unionist community from which the RUC was drawn there is a predilection for viewing the RUC as a victim, and for the Nationalist community subjected to the violent manifestations of public order and counter-insurgency policing, there is a tendency to see the force as a perpetrator. The dynamic that more generally underpins narratives on in-group and out-group violence in post-conflict societies enjoys increased traction in contestation over the policing legacy. Using the co-constitutive processes of 'remembering' and 'forgetting', these narratives pre-determine that 'our' past transgressions are overlooked but 'our' suffering, endurance and dead are 'remembered'.[7] Admittedly, this is not unique to Northern Ireland; it is evident in Turkish narratives on the Armenian genocide,[8] belated assertions of victimhood among the Argentine right[9] and in memory contestation in Bosnia.[10] It is not difficult to apply these observations to the substance of opposing policing narratives. Lawther identifies glaring

[4] Hearty, 2014.

[5] Hearty, 2016a.

[6] Assmann, 2008, 219.

[7] Paez and Liu, 2009.

[8] Demirici, 2013, 26.

[9] Salvi, 2011.

[10] Moll, 2013.

silences of RUC wrongdoing, their active role in the conflict and Nationalist victimhood in the Unionist narrative.[11] Likewise, it is necessary to acknowledge that the impact political violence had on the RUC and the fact that this was often construed – rightly or wrongly – as sectarian by the Unionist community from which the force was largely recruited, are silenced in the Irish republican policing counter-narrative.[12] The British state narrative is defined by the wholesale silencing of security force complicity in the conflict, usefully leveraging support for its neutral referee self-image from the Unionist narrative.

Some illustrative examples may suffice. The protectors of RUC organisational memory promote a narrative of a heavily victimised force that withstood a 'terrorist onslaught' for over 30 years in defence of the people of Northern Ireland.[13] This narrative accentuates the 'enormous cost in terms of death and injury' that the RUC collectively paid during the conflict, rather than their active 'perpetratorship' in it.[14] Contrast this with the following accounts drawn from interview data:

> I don't think they [the RUC] done themselves any favours. I can honestly say I didn't shed any tears if I ever heard that, you know, one was blown up or killed and that, and you'd hear on the news, because my own experience of them was that they were bad. Very bad. And, as I said at the start of that question, I never met a good one – never.[15]

> Some people did it [joined the RUC] for the financial benefit, which was great. Also, that hidden hatred of Catholics and a chance to get a good kick into them and a lovely lifestyle. The downside of that was then there was a cost to pay for that, and that was with their lives, and then you had the whole uproar from the Unionist community and stuff, but if a man is putting on a uniform and putting a gun on his hip and getting plenty of money for it ... he knows what he's going out to face, and I can never understand all the crying and whinging about it when it happened.[16]

Disparity between the accounts is clear. Discernible, however, is a common reliance on the 'memory of perpetrators'. Moreover, both chime with differential lived experiences and communal conflict narratives.

11 Lawther, 2014.
12 Hearty, 2014.
13 Police Federation for Northern Ireland, 1999.
14 Patterson, 2006.
15 AB, critic of Sinn Féin policy, interview, October 2013.
16 P, critic of Sinn Féin policy, interview, June 2013.

Constructing counter-memory

Irish republican policing memory must be looked at in terms of its role as counter-memory to official discourses on policing. The 'official' memory of policing is characterised by the denial of state wrongdoing and the 'invisibilisation' of Irish republican victimhood.[17] This is attributable to the mnemonic censuring of critics of the RUC[18] and to the fact that 'official' memory seeks to present an authoritative account of the conflict that silences discordant voices.[19] Memory, as Gallagher asserts,[20] is 'activated by contest'. As such, those denied voice and recognition will articulate a counter-memory challenging the exclusion of their experiences from official discourses. Irish republican policing counter-memory therefore counters the silences of 'official' memory. What is often pejoratively dismissed as a 'rewriting' of the past, may simply be *the writing* of experiences never acknowledged in 'official' memory. This was the view of Sinn Féin's Jim Gibney, who argued during the debate that republican experiences of policing were 'an unacknowledged history, ignored in the main and dismissed by those who knew and remained silent'.[21] The debate on policing therefore provided an important platform for Irish republicans to broadcast their (counter)memories of policing. The fact that the debate was taking place at every conceivable level within the homes, social spheres and daily lives of republicans, effectively debarred those who have constructed official discourses from wielding any stranglehold over the mnemonic process. In challenging the very fibre of state, Unionist and RUC narratives, Irish republican policing memory assumed the 'counter-hegemonic purpose' that Irish republican conflict narratives have traditionally held.[22] It is worth noting, however, that it is not just Irish republicans who feel their experiences have been excluded from official discourse on the past. In the aftermath of the Belfast flags dispute, it has become apparent that working-class loyalists feel their experiences have been underappreciated too.[23]

Interviewees exhibited an acute awareness of the value of Irish republican memory as counter-memory. One tied its importance to the fact that Unionist narratives continue to misrepresent the past:

---

[17] Lawther, 2014.

[18] Mulcahy and Ellison, 2001.

[19] Rolston, 2010.

[20] Gallagher, 1999.

[21] Jim Gibney, 'First Step to Accountable Policing is Support', *Irish News*, 25 January 2007.

[22] Hackett and Rolston, 2009.

[23] Mulvenna, 2015.

> You've these people who are still in denial that there was discrimination went on in this country. They are still in denial that the RUC were a bunch of bastards, to the extent that 'no, no they were good' and all this here crap ... there's a lot of denial going on within Unionism, so I don't expect them to agree with my analysis at all of anything to do with policing.[24]

Others, however, found alternative value in Irish republican memory as counter-memory. A counter-hegemonic broadcasting of the Irish republican experience became essential to a process of recognising the experience of the 'other'. Elaborating on the importance of this more generally, one republican stated, 'there is no agreed narrative about what actually happened here. There's no agreement about what happened, why it happened'.[25] In the absence of this, the interviewee asserted, it was imperative that Irish republicans engaged with former RUC officers *not* to perpetuate disagreement but to provide them with an alternative insight into the causes and consequences of the conflict. While questioning how far outside the republican community the counter-narrative actually resonated, another republican noted that a post-conflict questioning within Unionism and within policing itself on the role of RUC Special Branch in lethal intelligence wars was emerging. Assessing whether this meant Unionists now accepted the Irish republican counter-narrative, the interviewee concluded:

> I would doubt it, you know, but I think what you got was a shift in their sort of simplistic 'We're right, the RUC is right, everything done was right'. I think there's that bit of grey area now for a lot of Unionists who you know in the past might have heard things from republicans and they would have just immediately dismissed and now they wouldn't be as quick to.[26]

The same interviewee noted that after 'good conversations' with former RUC members, there was a change in their own attitude. Elaborating on how they have come to realise that there was a tradition of 'policing families' within Unionism, the interviewee admitted, 'it was a step for me at one time to accept that not everybody in the RUC was there to smash Fenian skulls'. Similarly, another interviewee noted that after an initially fractious first encounter with former RUC personnel they had come to a mutual position of being 'willing to listen'. This exchange left the interviewee 'surprised by some of the stuff they

[24] K, critic of Sinn Féin policy, interview, June 2013.

[25] A, supporter of Sinn Féin policy, interview, April 2013.

[26] M, supporter of Sinn Féin policy, interview, June 2013.

were coming off with. How they felt let down, and how they felt sort of sold down the Suwannee and all the rest'.[27]

Notwithstanding incipient recognition of the 'other', the extended republican debate on policing became an arena of memory politics in which Irish republicans could attest to their past experiences and challenge prevailing state and Unionist policing narratives. This chapter now engages in a critique of Unionist, state and RUC narratives through the lens of Irish republican counter-memory. This is *not* to suggest, misleadingly, that the Irish republican policing narrative itself is not afflicted by its own particular silences. As a conflict narrative, it is as selectively constructed by 'the memory of perpetrators' as the narratives it seeks to counter. Unionists and former RUC officers are unlikely to identify with it. However, in accepting this, it must also be recognised that it is legitimate for Irish republicans to articulate their own conflict experiences and it is also legitimate to use these experiences to critique dominant narratives.[28]

The Unionist narrative

The Unionist policing narrative cannot be divorced from the relationship Unionists had with the Northern Ireland state and the RUC. As the dominant group in a state that operated a divided society model of policing, Unionists had a natural affinity with the criminal justice system and the police force perceived to be the protectors of their material advantage. Such is the strength of this historical relationship that Ellison and Martin refer to Unionists and the RUC enjoying 'a shared history'.[29] Many of the narrative planks in the Unionist narrative can also be found in the narrative proffered by the guardians of RUC organisational memory, like the RUC George Cross Foundation (RUC GC) and the Northern Ireland Retired Police Officers Association (NIRPOA).[30] Both have core notions of 'policing by consent', selfless sacrifice by RUC officers and the rejection of moral equivalence between 'those who set out on a daily basis to save life and those who set out on a daily basis to take it'.[31]

As a consequence, the Unionist narrative has been built on a central plank of pre-conflict 'policing by consent' in an ideal pre-conflict state, sustained by

[27] G, supporter of Sinn Féin policy, interview, May 2013.

[28] McIntyre, 2012, 182.

[29] Ellison and Martin, 2000.

[30] RUC GC Foundation, 2003; Northern Ireland Retired Police Officers Association, 2013.

[31] Northern Ireland Retired Police Officers Association, 2013.

the erroneous supposition that policing problems emerged only in response to Irish republican violence. This portrayal of a pre-conflict 'golden age' is symptomatic of a general tendency among formerly privileged groups to idealise the pre-conflict past. In South Africa, for example, problems with white supremacy may have been brought into sharp focus with the introduction of apartheid in 1948 but they long preceded this.[32] In Rwanda, the post-genocide discourse of harmonious living between Tutsis and Hutus prior to the genocide of the 1990s has selectively 'forgotten' episodes of genocide in previous decades.[33] In the North of Ireland, a narrative of the 1960s being a period of cross-community tranquillity is 'rather superficial' given the tension that surrounded the 50th anniversaries of the Battle of the Somme and the Easter Rising, the Divis Street riots of 1964, mobilisation by Paisleyites and the reformation of the UVF in 1966.[34] The Unionist narrative therefore views the pre-conflict state through 'rose-tinted spectacles'.[35] What gets lost in adopting such a lens, is the historical context of divided-society policing. Rather than latently becoming an issue in 1969, policing was integral to the polarisation of society in the North of Ireland from the foundation of the state. It was a *key* issue in dividing society along ethno-nationalist lines rather than belatedly coming to reflect this division once events turned violent. The ability to exert such a divisive influence is derived from the fact that where divided-society policing is practised the issue is not just what the police do but what they represent.[36]

Police legitimacy and state legitimacy

What is more pertinent than acknowledging that these observations apply to pre-conflict Northern Ireland, is establishing why they apply. There must be some reason why Nationalists could not view the RUC in the same favourable light as Unionists. The only explanation otherwise would be that Nationalists were simply antagonistic to notions of law and order – a claim without foundation that is impossible to substantiate. Rather than being a product of innate antagonism towards law and order, the differential relationship arises from the alienation caused by exclusivist state structures.[37] Their fractious relationship with the state conditioned their relationship with the police force upholding the state. As outlined in the preceding chapter,

[32] Guelke, 2012, 70.

[33] Buckley-Zistel, 2012, 81.

[34] Dixon, 2008, 70.

[35] Ellison and Smyth, 2000, 35.

[36] Hasisi and Weitzer, 2007.

[37] Bew and Patterson, 1985.

from the foundation of the Northern Ireland state the Nationalist minority found themselves occupying a precarious position in a state dominated by the ethno-nationalist 'other'. The exclusion inherent in state structures meant that the minority community withdrew from Unionist dominated state life rather than integrating themselves into it. The cumulative effect of this was that the minority community felt merely 'resident in the territory which Northern Protestants had marked out as their own'.[38] If one cannot identify with the state, it is only logical that one will not identify with the police force upholding that state. If the state is perceived purely as a Protestant state for a Protestant people, it is also foreseeable that Protestants will endeavour to take ownership of the police force constituted with protecting that state. Thus, notions of privilege on the one hand and marginalisation on the other determined how different communities interpreted the operation of the state and its policing apparatus. Police legitimacy is ultimately reduced to state legitimacy. What transpires is that 'the security forces of a state established for Protestants, a state by and large supported by Protestants and by and large not supported by Catholics has utterly different relationships with these two communities'.[39]

A narrative of pre-conflict 'policing by consent' fails to marry with the more general policing reality on the ground in pre-conflict Northern Ireland. Divorced from the Unionist viewpoint, the reality emerges that the RUC only delivered 'normal' policing pre-conflict where it was compatible with and coincidental to their key function of suppressing Nationalist dissent and upholding the Unionist state.[40] The very *raison d'être* of the force from its outset was to uphold Unionist rule and suppress any dissent to this. In times of relative peace, the performance of this task may have masqueraded as 'normal' policing, but the key underlying function was always the same. Normality operated only in so far as this key function could be carried out in a manner that vaguely resembled 'normal' policing. The overt aggression of counter-insurgency policing later seen during the conflict is admittedly absent, but this should not be fallaciously taken as indicative that pre-conflict policing was 'normal'. As Raimundo and Costa Pinto note, using the example of Salazarist Portugal, policing does not have to be overtly violent to be repressive but can be highly 'judicialised' by relying on emergency provisions rather than assassination and torture to silence opponents.[41] The misuse of emergency legislation identified in the previous chapter certainly suggests that the pre-conflict Northern Ireland state adopted this modus operandi. The reality of pre-conflict policing, then, is that 'everyday

[38] Ruane and Todd, 1996, 95.

[39] O'Dochartaigh, 1997, 316.

[40] Ellison and Smyth, 2000, 42.

[41] Raimundo and Costa Pinto, 2014, 176.

policing was as much, if not more so, directed towards the cultural and social subordination of Nationalists as it was towards the prevention and detection of "normal" crime'.[42] Seeking middle ground, Whyte argues that the 'fairest summary' of policing in the Northern Ireland state is that it 'teeter[ed] uncertainly between impartiality and partisanship'. While he certainly tempers the seriousness of claims about the Northern Ireland state, he also recognises that aspects of policing were problematic because it failed to apply the law evenly to 'unionist and anti-unionist alike'.[43] Unionists were exempt from the adverse effects of this two-tiered policing, thus a narrative of pre-conflict 'policing by consent' chimes with their lived experience. For the minority community, however, the pre-conflict state of play involved being policed by the 'other'.

The veracity of such observations can be found in strong interviewee assertions that policing was *always* far removed from 'normal' policing. One interviewee, who rather unusually had a neighbour in the RUC, recalled that 'you were always very aware even as a child that the policemen were something different from us ... they weren't to be trusted, they weren't our people'.[44] Another revealed the flaws in the Unionist narrative by noting that even though they had no personal reason to feel detached from pre-conflict policing they nonetheless 'would've had a concept they [the RUC] were not Dixon of Dock Green'. Conceding that 'I didn't have any personal run-ins with the RUC prior to the conflict', the interviewee was nevertheless 'aware of what they represented' and endeavoured to 'stay as far away as possible'.[45] This sentiment was corroborated by another republican who opined:

> I do remember policemen in the past and in the 1960s when I would have been a teenager, policemen in [area]. They were not necessarily dangerous or brutal. We knew them and they were about, but there was always a clear understanding that despite how affable they might be on the surface, that their primary responsibility was maintaining the state, and the state to me was a deeply flawed state. It was discriminatory against me and the community I come from and the police were there to uphold the legislation that was discriminatory. So that's the way I looked at policing then.[46]

Irish republican counter-memory, as articulated above, evidences how those who were *the policed* in the pre-conflict state and those who *policed* the

[42] Smyth, 2002.
[43] Whyte, 1983, 29.
[44] G, supporter of Sinn Féin policy, interview, May 2013.
[45] H, supporter of Sinn Féin policy, interview, May 2013.
[46] Q, critic of Sinn Féin policy, interview, July 2013.

pre-conflict state have markedly different narratives. Interviewees – *the policed* – used their identity as the 'other' in a discriminatory state to explain their attitudes to pre-conflict policing. The exclusivity bred by structural discrimination thus seeped into their understanding of policing from an early age. Policing pre-1969 seemed premised less on the notion of normalised consent and more on a subconscious understanding that it entailed whatever degree of coercion necessary to maintain the status quo of Unionist privilege and Nationalist marginalisation.

'Tasks of a paramilitary nature'

A further challenge to the Unionist 'policing by consent' narrative is the fact that in Northern Ireland policing was *always* in a semi-permanent counter-insurgency mode. This is completely irreconcilable with the notion of 'normal' policing. The RUC was equipped with 'emergency' legislation to enforce internal security of the state long before 1969. If Unionist policing memory does not accommodate this fact, the governmental zeitgeist at the time does. The Hunt Report, for example, spoke of 'the special difficulties' for policing in Northern Ireland and 'those tasks of a paramilitary nature which the Royal Ulster Constabulary has shouldered since its inception'.[47] That the report felt it necessary to mention such 'special difficulties' is itself indicative that pre-conflict policing was not 'normal'. Moreover, paramilitary policing is anathema to any semblance of 'normal' policing. This governmental report very clearly states that the RUC was *always* engaged in paramilitary policing. If this is taken to be the official governmental line at the time, then the Unionist narrative is contradictory even to this. The reality was that the RUC had at its disposal wide-ranging emergency legislation, a vast array of armoury and an armed part-time militia (the 'B-Specials'). While Whyte argues labelling Northern Ireland a 'police state' is an exaggeration,[48] at the same time it is hardly unreasonable to argue that none of this fits with a narrative of 'policing by consent'. The reality on the ground can be more accurately gauged through one republican's 'first real sort of memory' of policing:

> I remember in 1966, believe it or not, there was an Easter parade … it was the 50th anniversary of the [Easter] Rising, but that didn't mean anything to me. I remember the sight then of all the cops everywhere, carrying

[47] 'Report of the Advisory Committee on Police in Northern Ireland' (Hunt Report) (1969), [8–10].

[48] Whyte, 1983, 23.

> machine guns, you know they had these Sten guns and that was a fairly sort of intimidating image walking through them to get to the parade.[49]

Little seems consensual about this type of policing. The presence of heavily armed police officers is by its very nature coercive because it communicates what the cost is of stepping outside the permitted boundaries. This is heightened when the specific context of this memory – a republican commemorative event – is taken into consideration. Of course, it could be argued that this memory is typical of the republican tendency to 'remember' the *what* of pre-conflict policing while 'forgetting' the *why*.[50] Such activity could only reinforce, rather than assuage, the Unionist siege mentality identified in the previous chapter.

Perpetuating the myth

How Unionism portrays pre-conflict policing corresponds with their portrayal of a harmonious pre-conflict Northern Ireland being unceremoniously wrecked by Irish republican violence. Ellison and Smyth dismiss this as 'mythical Eden folklore', arguing:

> The tendency to look back at the two decades between the end of the Second World War and the beginning of the civil rights agitation as a period of peace and communal harmony is at variance with the facts. The police managed to keep the simmering discontent of Nationalists under control by a combination of repressive legislation and blanket surveillance, assisted to no little extent by the tactical and strategic ineffectiveness of both the IRA and constitutional Nationalism.[51]

Rather than simply accepting that the Unionist narrative is premised on a myth, it is important to identify why this myth is perpetuated today.

On one level, the Unionist narrative is reflective of their lived experience in the pre-conflict state; the state was *theirs*, the RUC was *theirs*, the writ of law being enforced sustained a hegemony that was *theirs*. Policing was indubitably 'policing by consent' from such a perspective. On a more complex level, attuned to the jostling of meta-conflict memory politics, the reason for perpetuating a narrative inconsistent with fact is patently obvious. Having been the

[49] A, supporter of Sinn Féin policy, interview, April 2013.

[50] Hearty, 2014.

[51] Ellison and Smyth, 2000, 46.

group in the ascendancy, any admission by Unionists of the shortcomings of the pre-conflict state is essentially an admission of their own wrongdoing. As Ruane and Todd have noted, even if some Unionists did feel uneasy about certain aspects of the discriminatory state, 'no Unionist saw good reason to integrate Nationalists into the institutions of the state'.[52] If they concede that this was in fact the case, they provide mnemonic ammunition to Irish republicans. Republicans could then point to Unionist recognition of the exclusionary nature of the Northern Ireland state which would effectively vindicate their violent opposition to it. Although the Unionist stance has recently softened a little – for example, a dying Ian Paisley's concession that discrimination was 'no way to run a country' and Mike Nesbitt's admission that discrimination made Northern Ireland a 'cold house' for Catholics[53] – they nonetheless maintain that a subversive NICRA campaign or violent IRA campaign were not measured responses to whatever discrimination existed. In making only a minimalist admission of discrimination, Unionism has adroitly avoided giving republicans the advantage in memory politics. It is by virtue of necessity and the demands of meta-conflict memory politics that the narrative persists. There is therefore a favourable juxtaposition of the 'order' of pre-conflict Northern Ireland with the 'disorder' of the conflict.[54] The narrative is unambiguous, even if fallacious; there was order, peace and harmony in Northern Ireland until the IRA plunged the place into disorder, bloodshed and sectarianism. This 'mythology of a prelapsarian Ulster' allows Unionists to blame the outbreak of conflict on Nationalist demagogues and the IRA.[55] The detached out of focus 'remembering' exhibited in this narrative is demonstrative that memory will, much to the cost of historical accuracy, only accommodate the facts that suit it.[56] Unionist memories of policing overlook the underlying problems with policing since the inception of the state, shoring up their position on the moral high ground, to buttress them from criticism about state discrimination. This then leaves the blame for the outbreak of conflict and the resulting decades of devastation at the door of

[52] Ruane and Todd, 1996, 91.

[53] 'Ian Paisley Criticised Over Dublin-Monaghan Bombs Comment', BBC News, 10 January 2014: www.bbc.co.uk/news/uk-northern-ireland-25673999 (accessed 28 September 2015); Gerry Moriarty, 'Ian Paisley: Power House Unionist Who Eventually Shook Hands with Nationalists', *Irish Times*, 31 December 2014: www.irishtimes.com/news/politics/ian-paisley-powerhouse-unionist-who-eventually-shook-hands-with-nationalists-1.2051277 (accessed 7 October 2016).

[54] RUC GC, 2003.

[55] Patterson, 2008, 151.

[56] Nora, 1989.

Irish republicanism. 'Forgotten' amidst the clamour for the meta-conflict moral high ground, however, is the fact that policing problems were not a by-product of the conflict but 'part of the problem'.[57]

The British state narrative

The British state has perpetuated a 'two tribes' narrative that reduces conflict in the six counties to inevitable clashes between opposing sectarian factions. This is characteristic of British state refusal to acknowledge its role in the conflict.[58] Such a narrative, as Faligot asserts, distorted events on the ground by 'projecting the irrational image of a war of religion' through 'concealing the real causes and consequences of the Anglo-Irish conflict'.[59] In any event, it disguised asymmetries of power. Had the 'two tribes' theory any vestige of accuracy – highly questionable at best – it overlooked how one 'tribe' was marginalised in the Northern Ireland state, while the other 'tribe' dictated social, political and economic matters. If there were indeed 'two tribes' battling each other, it was not on an even keel. The role of successive British administrations in creating and subsequently sustaining this inequality is similarly neglected. A 'two tribes' misconception could perhaps be rhetorically applied to externally drawn British Army members. However, it could hardly apply to the Ulster Defence Regiment (UDR) or RUC. After all, these were indigenous forces heavily drawn from one 'tribe'. The facade of being neutral arbitrators in a supposedly sectarian conflict would be difficult to sustain – especially when 'Ulsterisation' gave them the lead counter-insurgency role. Normalisation and criminalisation would solve this propagandistic quandary. Accordingly, the British state narrative proclaimed that the conflict was not a 'war' between British and Irish parties, but criminal violence undertaken by opposing sectarian factions that sparked a public emergency to be dealt with professionally by the indigenous RUC supported primarily by the indigenous UDR, with other British Army regiments acting as further backup. Britain used its position as a liberal Western democracy to shield its role in the conflict from international scrutiny, thus allowing the erroneous 'two tribes' narrative to prevail internationally.[60]

---

57 Ellison, 2007.

58 Lundy, 2010.

59 Faligot, 1983, 43.

60 Bell, Campbell and Ni Aolaín, 2004.

'Ulsterisation'

'Ulsterisation' was something of an enigma; narratively it withheld the propagandistic advantage from republicans by reinforcing the 'two tribes' narrative but practicably it reified historical hostility towards the RUC by implicating them in contentious counter-insurgency activities. The wisdom of believing that Nationalists would buy into the narrative of a professional and even-handed indigenous police force when reality on the ground saw that same force use counter-insurgency policing disproportionately against them must be questioned. The disconnect between the rhetoric and the practice of the policy generated republican claims that it was enacted to make occupation 'seem more acceptable'.[61] The veracity of this is evident in the following recollection of the RUC's increased counter-insurgency function:

> I suppose the earliest memories were constant raids on the family home by the British Army. Then you seen a sort of change then that raiding parties were being led by the RUC and then really the British Army phased out as such and it was then just pure RUC that were raiding and, believe it or not, found that to be more sectarian, more vicious in its approach. Where the squaddies were coming in and sort of probably creating more damage to the home – not abusing physically or verbally anybody – just coming in and wrecking the home and leaving, where the RUC were more ruthless, more premeditated in what they did.[62]

Similarly, when reflecting on police primacy, the Sinn Féin motion to the Extraordinary *Ard Fheis* condemned the RUC as 'a partisan, Unionist militia which engaged in harassment, torture, assassination, shoot-to-kill and collusion with death squads'.[63]

Evidently, then, 'Ulsterisation' further nurtured an already established view that the RUC was a Unionist force. The reasoning behind the policy was to deny the IRA propagandistic oxygen by using a home-grown force against it. However, the force was not an inherent part of the community per se, only an inherent part of the Unionist community. To the minority community there could only be suspicions of bias. The RUC was, after all, overwhelmingly

61 'Comment', *Sceal*, 8 (7 August 1896).

62 P, critic of Sinn Féin policy, interview, June 2013.

63 'Motion Passed by Sinn Féin at Extraordinary Ard Fheis on Policing, RDS, Dublin (28 January 2007)': www.cain.ulst.ac.uk/issues/politics/docs/sf/sf280107motion.htm (accessed 24 April 2012).

Protestant, yet its victims were overwhelmingly Catholic.[64] This may well have been the case before the policy and even prior to the conflict, but 'Ulsterisation' fuelled rather than ameliorated matters. If RUC conduct towards the NICRA led Nationalists to feel that 'the police were their enemy',[65] then surely the more robust targeting of Nationalist areas as a result of 'Ulsterisation' could only have a similar effect. The salience of this is magnified by O'Dochartaigh's concession that the RUC 'did not treat these two communities equally – whether it be equally harshly or equally gently'.[66] 'Vicarious punishment' of the entire Nationalist community in response to IRA and INLA activity produced a disproportionate counter-insurgency impact on that community.[67] As the community at the rough end of this, it was merely natural that Nationalists would develop antipathy towards the RUC. Hostility to the RUC was not a result of 'bias or hatred' but 'bitter experience of the RUC's brutality and sectarianism'.[68] Of course, one could argue that Irish republicans posed the greatest threat to the state and security forces, thus counter-insurgency policing would be foreseeably calibrated to reflect this.[69]

Notwithstanding this, 'Ulsterisation' was clearly problematic in the 'divided society' environment of the North of Ireland. Having failed to coerce republicans into subscribing to state normalisation and criminalisation narratives, the policy simply hardened their resolve towards the RUC and widened the gulf between the RUC and Nationalists. Not only was policing seen as highly militarised, it was also seen as highly sectarian. The impact that 'Ulsterisation' had in instilling such an outlook can be seen in how interviewees 'remember' in a way that juxtaposes their own lived experience of the policy with that of their Unionist neighbours. One interviewee who grew up in a predominantly Unionist town, alluding to their familial experiences, said:

> We would have experienced harassment by the likes of the UDR, the RUC quite regularly ... the impression the police gave us verbally and by their behaviour was that they were most certainly a Unionist force to protect the Unionist people. They weren't in the business of protecting people like ourselves.[70]

---

64 Lundy and McGovern, 2001.

65 Scarman Report, 1972, [2.4].

66 O'Dochartaigh, 1997, 316.

67 Weitzer, 1995.

68 McAuley, 1988, 1.

69 McGarry, 2000.

70 J, critic of Sinn Féin policy, interview, June 2013.

Another spoke of being singled out for 'special treatment' at road blocks. This 'special treatment' was reserved solely for Nationalists and was not foisted upon the local Unionist population from which the security forces were drawn.[71]

These memories challenge the 'Ulsterisation' portrayal of the RUC as an even-handed indigenous police force. The policy failed to gain any meaningful contemporaneous traction. Little has changed in the intervening years. Irish republicans today – including those who have embraced police reform and had meaningful engagements with ex-RUC personnel on the past – continue to 'remember' the RUC as a Unionist counter-insurgency police force rather than an impartial normalised police service.

Normalisation

Normalisation depicted the RUC's counter-insurgency function as a simple extension of its professional job fighting 'normal' crime. Unlike other combatants, where loyalists died in defence of Ulster against republican attack and republicans died waging a war of national liberation against occupational forces, slain RUC personnel were normal police officers having died for the entire community. Their blood was shed not in waging war on the 'other', but in an attempt to keep peace, restore normality and prevent civil war.[72] Were it not for the force diligently discharging its duties the North of Ireland would seemingly have descended into 'an abyss of the kind seen in Bosnia, Rwanda and Kosovo'.[73] The force represented 'the thin green line standing between bloody anarchy and the rule of law'.[74] Apparently, then, the only thing distinguishing them from other police forces was the environment of heightened danger they had to function within – circumstances that were 'very difficult' incurring 'considerable sacrifice'.[75] The cumulative effect of this was a morality play portrayal of the RUC as the quintessential 'good guys' fighting against the evil 'terrorist' on both sides of the political divide. Even if some Unionists have deviated slightly from the normalisation script by acknowledging that some aspects of policing were abnormal, as Lawther highlights,[76] they have continued portraying it as a necessary response to republican violence.

---

71 AB, critic of Sinn Féin policy, interview, October 2013.

72 O'Connor, 1999.

73 'Save the RUC', *Daily Telegraph*, 28 September 1999.

74 Lord Tebbit, quoted in G. Jones, 'Tebbit Launches Bitter Attack on Patten's Proposals for RUC', *Daily Telegraph*, 6 October 1999.

75 Her Majesty's Government, 'Principles for Policing in Northern Ireland: A Discussion Paper Prepared by Her Majesty's Government' (1998).

76 Lawther, 2014.

The shortcomings of this narrative are obvious. Primarily, it relates a past that is depoliticised and ahistorical; it outlines the RUC's historical role in tackling crime and in upholding security of the state and it acknowledges the losses of its members but it offers no contextualisation of why they were killed or why the force had to assume a dual policing role.[77] Like the 'Ulsterisation' narrative, this hinges on the dissonance between the policy in terms of narrative and application on the ground:

> The intent behind this [normalisation] at least as far as the use of the RUC was concerned, was to create an image of normality on the ground. The theory was that a uniformed policeman was much less likely to attract as much attention or to provoke a hostile reaction as a fully equipped soldier. No steps were taken, however, to disarm them or put them back on beat patrol instead of patrolling in the military type Land Rover.[78]

Furthermore, while the underlying intention of the policy was to give the impression of normality, what were apparently 'ordinary crimes' were dealt with through the Northern Ireland (Emergency Provisions) Act and the Prevention of Terrorism Act rather than through 'normal' legislation.[79] Although the normalisation narrative serves the memory politics needs of the state, it also discards certain rudimentary truths about conflict policing more generally. Most notably, there is a lack of recognition that 'in most, if not all, war-torn societies (from intra-state conflicts) the police were prior to and/or during the conflict period, politically biased, militarised, corrupt, ethnically (or group) divided, disrespectful of human rights and inefficient at ensuring the security of all citizens'.[80] There is similar non-recognition that police forces become active participants in – or at the very least contributors to – internal conflict through spying, torture and the use of proxy death squads.[81] To assert that the RUC was somehow an aberration is either naivety or mnemonic cherry-picking. The voluminous criticism of the force from human rights groups outside the republican community demonstrates as much.[82] Although criticism from within republican communities was dismissed as propaganda,[83] external criticism was

---

[77] Mulcahy, 2000.

[78] Walsh, 1983, 13.

[79] Boyle, Hadden and Hillyard, 1980, 32.

[80] Celador, 2005.

[81] Nelid, 2001.

[82] Amnesty International, 1994; Human Rights Watch, 1992; International Lawyers Inquiry, 1985.

[83] Compton, 1971, [6]; 'Report of the Committee of Inquiry into Police Interrogation

more problematic. It eventually birthed a 'bad apple' narrative whereby the transgressions of a few officers should not undermine the integrity and sacrifice of the RUC as a whole.[84]

Favourable narratives highlighting the RUC's human cost thrive on the 'memory of perpetrators'. Whilst the RUC did indeed shoulder considerable death and misery from IRA and INLA violence – something admittedly silenced by the 'memory of perpetrators' in the Irish republican counter-narrative – it similarly inflicted much death and misery too. Not only were they implicated in conflict-related death but they were also responsible for other less obvious harms like systematic harassment of target groups at vehicle check points and through 'stop and search' operations. Ellison maintains that 'although the RUC did not cause the conflict that emerged in the late 1960s it was nevertheless a key factor in prolonging it'.[85] This is a compelling assertion that completely undermines the state normalisation narrative. The basis for this argument is that 'the RUC itself could be a catalyst for conflict'.[86] Indeed, when one considers the lived experience of the RUC reflected in Irish republican policing counter-memory it is difficult to reach a conclusion that differs from Ellison. The logic of this, then, is that it appears misguided to argue that a force that contributes to, periodically aggravates and in some cases prolongs the conflict is in any guise a 'normal' police force. To all intents and purposes, the most rational conclusion to make is that any such police force is an active party to the conflict whether official discourse concedes this or not.

Inasmuch as the 'memory of perpetrators' can be a silencing tactic from the pro-state perspective, it can also be a counter-memory tactic frontloading RUC wrongdoing from a victim-centric Irish republican perspective. Commentary during the policing debate highlighted how 'the history of policing in Ireland is one of oppression and tyranny ... it is a record of police forces rather than police services'.[87] Gerry Adams refuted the normalisation narrative in his opening remarks to the Extraordinary *Ard Fheis*, arguing that 'we who live in the North have never had proper policing. The old RUC and all of its associated militia served the Union, upheld the Orange state and repressed everyone else'.[88] Likewise, interview data reflected how the 'suspect community' at the

---

Procedures in Northern Ireland' (1979).

[84] Lawther, 2014.

[85] Ellison, 2007.

[86] Ellison and Mulcahy, 2001.

[87] 'Ógra Shinn Féin National Congress Opposes SF Policing Motion', *Ogra Shinn Féin*, 22 January 2007: www.ograshinnfein.blogspot.co.uk/2007/01/gra-shinn-fin-national-congress.html (accessed 24 April 2012).

[88] 'Opening Address by Gerry Adams, then President of Sinn Féin (SF), to the Sinn

sharp edge of RUC counter-insurgency 'remember' experiences of policing as far removed from 'normal' policing as is imaginable. One interviewee from an area that bore the brunt of 'suspect community' policing remembered feeling that:

> It was very much a 'them and us', and I suppose looking back on it it's easy to understand as far as they were concerned: everybody, no matter what age you were, was the enemy and they expressed that at every opportunity ... they definitely were not a police service in [area]. They were a police force who were, if you like, sent in to put manners on the people of [area].[89]

Another recalled growing up in a different republican district, where the consensus was:

> While there was this mistrust towards policing it wasn't about policing per se, it was about the RUC. It was about the political nature and existence of that body and what that body represented ... I always remember growing up that it wasn't a lawless society. People did need policing but recognised that the RUC wasn't it. So republicans that I grew up with and republicans in my family in particular weren't against policing. They were against the RUC.[90]

In a further snapshot of this reality on the ground, one interviewee summarised their experiences of policing as being either 'negative' or 'huge periods of nothing because to me for a lot of my life the police when it came to protection and the rule of law were irrelevant'.[91] These autobiographical narratives no doubt reflect lived reality from the perspective of these individual interviewees. However, on the collective level, there is a silence in relation to how some moderate, usually middle-class, Nationalists *did* engage with the RUC on matters of 'normal' crime.[92] This could be reflective of differential experience of the application of normalisation on the ground. In 'mixed' middle-class neighbourhoods, where conflict-related activity was minimal, counter-insurgency policing easily passed under the guise of 'normal' policing.[93] In predominantly

---

Féin Extraordinary Ard Fheis on Policing, RDS, Dublin (28 January 2007)': http://cain.ulst.ac.uk/issues/politics/docs/sf/ga280107a.htm (accessed 10 May 2012).

89 I, supporter of Sinn Féin policy, interview, May 2013.

90 B, supporter of Sinn Féin policy, interview, April 2013.

91 T, supporter of Sinn Féin policy, interview, August 2013.

92 Pickering, 2002.

93 Brewer and Magee, 1991, 267.

republican working-class areas it did not. Even though the state was trying to roll out normality and police primacy, the RUC still relied on military backup when patrolling republican districts. These communities became a clearly defined 'target group' for militarised 'over-policing'.[94] For those unfortunate enough to fall within this 'suspect community' population, everyday policing was experienced through a system predicated on 'policing people' rather than 'policing crime'.[95]

Unsurprisingly, republicans at the time did not buy into the normalisation narrative. Retrospective post-conflict reflection has not changed this. Interviewees related a plethora of negative 'suspect community' policing memories yet *no* positive memories of 'normal' policing. The overwhelming effect of the RUC's counter-insurgency role, as gleaned from the memories of interviewees, was a clear identification of the force with the British Army. This made the force 'the enemy' by precluding any distinction between their counter-insurgency role and their 'normal' policing function:

> My experience with the RUC was they were flown in from other areas to fortified barracks. Their function or their role within [area] was very much a counter-insurgency role ... like most of the Nationalists and republicans I'd say ... they were a militia but they certainly weren't what we would see in a normal democratic society as a police force ... they would have been people from Unionist backgrounds, Unionist areas coming into a strongly republican/Nationalist area ... they came in armed, they were trained and they were financed by Britain to play a particular role and that's what they did.[96]

The recurrence of such a world view throughout the interview process shows that it transcended temporal and geographical barriers, which suggests this was the collective Irish republican policing experience. Irish republican policing counter-memory can be usefully viewed through Kalmanowiecki's argument that counter-insurgency policing blurs the distinction between the military and the police because both become tasked with protecting the state from internal and external threat. Rather than viewing the two institutions as separate they should instead be viewed along 'a continuum from military to police'.[97] The overwhelming identification of the RUC with the military and the centrality of

---

[94] Hillyard, 1988, 197.

[95] Hillyard and Percy-Smith, 1988, 270.

[96] AD, supporter of Sinn Féin policy, interview, July 2013.

[97] Kalmanowiecki, 2000.

its counter-insurgency function in Irish republican policing counter-memory offer empirical sustenance to the continuum model.

Irish republican policing counter-memory, fashioned by the 'memory of perpetrators', is wholly irreconcilable with the state normalisation narrative. Articulated by those at the rough edge of conflict-style policing, it is constructed and sustained by feelings of victimisation and vulnerability. As such, it has adopted narratives put forward by human rights groups outside the constituency. Although such a blatant assertion is not explicitly made in the counter-narrative itself, the memories proffered by interviewees and the narrative gleaned from archival sources exhibit considerable correlation with concerns about collusion, misuse of 'emergency' provisions and police brutality previously raised by human rights groups. As a consequence, human rights groups have rather misguidedly been accused of peddling a republican agenda.[98] This victimhood is precisely what is silenced in the state narrative. The British state, for its part, has a vested interest in failing to recognise republican victimhood. Were it to accept the reality of the 'suspect community' policing it fostered, it would effectively entangle itself in a web of systematic human rights abuse. Instead, it continues to push the demonstrably false line that it was a bystander in the conflict, thus conveniently overlooking how their actions and misuse of long-standing 'emergency' legislation contributed to, exacerbated and prolonged political violence.[99] Britain is not unique in this regard. Indonesia, for example, continues to peddle a similar line in relation to their involvement in the conflict in Timor-Leste.[100] This narrative may deny republicans any belated justification for their violence but, as Rolston argues,[101] it is somewhat self-contradictory given that subsequent police reform represents implicit acceptance that policing was not 'normal' during the conflict.

The RUC narrative

RUC organisational memory regales 'narratives of public acceptability, political neutrality, impartiality and a primary concern with enforcing ordinary criminal law rather than exceptional security measures'.[102] In line with this, it suggests that although it appeared the force had no support within the Nationalist

98 Cochrane, 2013.

99 Bell, Campbell and Ni Aoláin, 2004.

100 Stanley, 2008, 175.

101 Rolston, 2006b.

102 Lawther, 2011.

community it actually enjoyed considerable 'behind closed doors support'.[103] The absence of an open manifestation of this support was attributed to IRA threats and violence against anyone seen co-operating with the force. This narrative propagated the legitimacy of the force by insulating it from republican accusations of sectarianism. It was a decidedly clever narrative to adopt in the midst of the 'propaganda war'. Republicans could not, even if they used a reality on the ground suggesting otherwise, *definitively* disprove this narrative. They could fundamentally question it to the nth degree. They could stretch the fibres of its credibility for sure. But they could not unequivocally disprove it. How does one prove or disprove what happens privately behind closed doors anyway? On the other hand, the RUC could laud even the most negligible applicability as evidence that the narrative was true, thus engineering a sense of legitimacy for itself in the face of visible legitimacy problems in Nationalist communities. It extended beyond mere insulation of the RUC position, however, to effectively cast aspersions about the amount of support the IRA had among working-class Nationalists by questioning whether the IRA were their *protectors* or *tormentors*. Two principal methods became apparent: use of official survey data and magnification of displeasure with IRA internal policing. It is worth interrogating these further.

Dissecting hidden support claims

The RUC narrative of cross-community support lacks validation by credible empirical evidence.[104] Data from attitudinal surveys specifically designed to dismiss claims of policing bias is its only supportive 'evidence'.[105] The findings of such surveys did indeed suggest that the RUC enjoyed cross-community support at an initial glance, but on further examination their worth becomes questionable. An argument has long persisted that they were cynically manipulated to exaggerate moderate opinion at the expense of accuracy.[106] The socio-economic orientation of the surveys often helped produce findings favourable to the RUC. Survey sample pools usually comprised middle-class professionals rather than lower-class manual workers. Given that the former were normally supportive of the cross-community Alliance Party and moderate SDLP while the latter were more sympathetic to republican groups, findings naturally gravitated towards less critical conclusions. Those included in the surveys were middle-class people living in middle-class neighbourhoods

[103] Mulcahy, 2000.

[104] Ellison, 2000.

[105] Northern Ireland Office, 1996.

[106] Ellison and Smyth, 2000, 35.

– essentially those least effected by the conflict and those least effected by counter-insurgency policing. Those at the counter-insurgency policing coalface were effectively debarred from surveys. Surveys essentially became a process of asking those most likely to concur with the government line their thoughts on policing while excluding any possibly dissenting voices. Findings are therefore tainted at best and entirely self-serving at worst, leaving their worth in measuring the accuracy of 'hidden support' claims severely diminished.

Similarly, pointing to disquiet about how the IRA internally policed its own community through 'rough justice' as evidence of wide-scale intimidation is also problematic. The process was undeniably brutal and no doubt alienated the friends and families of its victims.[107] To suggest otherwise is to stretch credulity. Beating and kneecapping those deemed to have transgressed communal norms invited foreseeable claims of intimidation. However, by focusing on the *what* of internal policing there is a convenient elision of the *why*. 'Rough justice' may have repulsed certain sections of the Nationalist population but at the same time it also appeased the demands of other sections of that community for criminality to be dealt with.[108] One can infer from the very existence of these demands that a legitimacy-deficit-induced policing vacuum existed in working-class Nationalist communities. 'Rough justice' was a product of the 'supply/demand' conundrum this caused. Blackbourn argues that the emergence of the phenomenon is not only indicative of a failure of policing but is symptomatic of the more general failure of the entire criminal justice system to inspire confidence among or support from the Nationalist community.[109] The symbiotic relationship between state illegitimacy and IRA legitimacy in the Nationalist psyche naturally invited the IRA to plug this vacuum. Their response to criticism of 'rough justice' was that it was not intimidating the community but rather protecting it in the absence of a 'normal' police force. This challenged the state normalisation narrative and bolstered their communal defender self-image in the 'propaganda war'. The IRA would, it asserted, protect the community from the 'oppression' of the occupier, the 'other' and petty criminals.[110] In Ardoyne it thanked the local community for 'their wholehearted support and assistance' in enabling them to punish local criminality.[111] The argument that 'rough justice' was symptomatic of the RUC's own shortcomings permeated the synopsis of one interviewee who contextualised it as follows:

---

[107] Knox, 2002.

[108] McEvoy and Mika, 2001.

[109] Blackbourn, 2015, 122.

[110] 'Crime and Punishment', *Strabane Republican*, 1972.

[111] 'Thanks for Support', *Freedom Fighter*, 5 (January 1977).

> You couldn't go to a police station and report the theft of your car because they would try and turn you into an informer. So people just went to republicans if there was a house break-in or someone was at anti-social behaviour and that's what really created that sort of atmosphere, but it was one where you could leave your door open. There was no drugs on the street or knife crime.[112]

Although this account contextualises internal policing it also idealises the practice. There is little recognition of the human rights abuse that the inarguably brutal process entailed. If the 'memory of perpetrators' fails to recognise the violence of 'us' on 'them', it also neglects the internal policing violence of 'us' on 'us'. 'Rough justice' is simultaneously sanitised by republicans to legitimate it but divorced from its context by the RUC in order to reduce it to crude intimidation. The posturing around competing viewpoints on the matter is reflective of how discourses on the practice were intricately linked to competing narratives on normalisation that underpinned the 'propaganda war'. As such, two dichotomous frameworks for presenting the practice emerged: *exaggeration* to give any semblance of communal disapproval hyper visibility and *minimisation* that silenced the adverse impact of the practice at the intra-communal level through legitimacy claims gleaned from a communal demand and/or need.

The 'hidden support' narrative is built on an exclusivist premise that completely discounts other factors that may have deterred Nationalists from openly supporting the RUC. Intimidation is presented as the only obstacle to open co-operation.[113] Such a narrative, while serving the legitimacy purposes of the RUC, ignores how 'the strength of Nationalist opposition to the police suggests that while intimidation is a factor ... it is not the only and perhaps not the most important factor – it may be more a symptom than a root cause'.[114] Perhaps the lack of open support was due (drawing on O'Faolean's analogous critique of the UDR)[115] to the predominantly Protestant membership and ethos of the force, its dubious historical roots and their role in the conflict. Then there is the historical and traditional loathing of informers in Ireland.[116] Lack of open support can be equally attributable to some unwritten communal code about not collaborating with the security forces, meaning that historical consciousness and the possibility of wider communal ostracism also prevented

[112] P, critic of Sinn Féin policy, interview, June 2013.

[113] Ellison and Smyth, 2000, 35.

[114] McGarry and O'Leary, 1999, 22.

[115] O'Faolean, 2015.

[116] Dudai, 2012.

open support for the RUC. This wider societal stigma led Ryder to concede that republicans 'rarely needed to resort to threats'.[117] That someone as sympathetic to the RUC as Ryder should acknowledge this speaks volumes about the exaggerated claims on which the 'hidden support' narrative is premised. There is also the questionable manner in which the RUC sought to secure Nationalist 'co-operation'. Resorting to blackmailing drink-drivers into informing on republicans is hardly supportive of claims of 'hidden support'.[118] Rather, it seemingly 'exposes the lack of support Nationalists have for the RUC when they have to arrest Nationalists and intimidate them into gathering low level intelligence on local republicans'.[119] Moreover, the 'hidden support' narrative completely disregards the adverse effect that 'over-policing' had on Nationalist districts. In the 'see-saw' relationship the Nationalist community had with the IRA, any digression by the IRA from 'acceptable' conduct led to reduced communal support.[120] Yet this was also surely the case in relation to attitudes towards the RUC. When the RUC was targeting Nationalist communities via 'Ulsterisation' the 'see-saw' tipped against the RUC, either towards indifference or towards tacit support for the IRA. With Nationalists having only confrontational experiences of policing, the 'see-saw' was more often than not tipped against the RUC. While this did not invariably translate into hardened support for the IRA it did militate against the RUC nonetheless. Republicans could certainly tap into a reservoir of RUC misdeeds to 'turn' Nationalists against the RUC via the 'propaganda war'. Given this, one must question to what extent the IRA even needed to resort to the crude intimidation alleged by the RUC.

Multitudinous factors may have impeded open support for the RUC in Nationalist areas, yet the force continued to counsel that IRA intimidation was the lone determinant. A governmental declaration that 'the aims of the IRA are to intimidate the population by brutal terrorism and so to prevent any co-operation with the government, the police and the courts of law' reinforced this.[121] That the IRA tried its utmost to prevent the RUC getting a foothold in Nationalist communities is incontestable. That it actively discouraged Nationalist communities from co-operating with the RUC is also incontestable. They were, after all, at war with the RUC and were unlikely to passively tolerate the enemy encroaching on its territory and poaching its wider support base. These efforts undoubtedly involved the exertion of a certain level and type of pressure but hardly by the wholesale, crude intimidation the RUC claimed.

---

117 Ryder, 1989, 147.

118 'Local Man Reveals RUC Blackmail Attempt', *Sceal*, 58 (3 September 1987).

119 'Attempts to Recruit an Informer', *Sceal*, 87 (31 March 1988).

120 Burton, 1978, 85.

121 Compton, 1971, [6].

Policing 'hearts and minds'

Historically, the IRA response to informing has been unambiguous – the death sentence. From 1969 to 2001, the IRA shot dead 59 people as alleged informers.[122] These included IRA volunteers, republican sympathisers and civilians who had passed on information on IRA activity to the security forces. The policy has featured in all IRA campaigns since the Tan War in the 1920s.[123] It was justified by the IRA, both at the time and ever since, as a form of 'necessary evil' spawned by the harsh realities of war. To this end, those fraternising with the security forces were advised to desist or be 'dealt with'.[124] But it was not enough, in either the physical war or the 'propaganda war', to retrospectively punish this conventional informing through death. The RUC had to be actively 'othered' from the Nationalist community on every level to prevent it getting into Nationalist communities to win 'hearts and minds'. This required a greater effort than simply shooting informers. One aspect of this was a conscious tactic of targeting businesses that served RUC members. Fitting into a wider strategy of economic sabotage, if the IRA were to blow up businesses it would channel its ire towards those engaged in the RUC's 'hearts and minds' games. The intent was clearly to stop the RUC from capitalising on a charm offensive of using local businesses while also inflicting the necessary damage on the local economy so as to make occupation economically unviable – admittedly the wider implications of this strategy have been excised from the Irish republican narrative by the 'memory of perpetrators'. In Lurgan, for example, the IRA bombed a number of businesses for 'their refusal to stop serving the security forces', warning further: 'your shop could be next – STOP SERVING THE SECURITY FORCES NOW'.[125] In Newry, businesses with a 'policy of collaboration with crown forces' were issued with a 'final warning'.[126] The campaign continued into the late 1980s, extending to a business that was bombed for placing an advertisement in an RUC magazine.[127] In response to the increased militarisation of republican areas following the AIA, the IRA began targeting 'contractors supplying and maintaining Britain's war machine'.[128] This led some firms to subsequently withdraw their services.[129]

---

[122] Sutton, 2001.

[123] Hanley, 2010, 17.

[124] 'Fraternisers Beware', *Armalite*, 3 (9 June 1973).

[125] 'War News', *Volunteer*, 19 September 1976.

[126] 'Final Warning', *Sceal*, 81 (18 February 1988).

[127] 'Collaborators', *Sceal*, 28 (15 January 1987).

[128] 'Sustained Guerrilla Campaign', *Iris*, 5 (Easter 1991).

[129] 'Forkhill Barracks Mortared', *An Phoblacht*, 20 November 1986.

This type of discouragement, however, does not mean that the IRA had its community in a vice-like grip, where the community was too afraid to speak out against the IRA. Open criticism of the IRA from the SDLP, community groups and the Catholic clergy in particular, was part and parcel of everyday internal politicking within the Nationalist community. For example, an open letter from Catholic bishops read to every Catholic congregation in Ireland following the Enniskillen bombing stated that it was 'sinful to join organisations committed to violence or to remain in them. It is sinful to support such organisations or to call on others to support them'.[130] It is difficult to envisage how castigation of the IRA could be any more open or categorical. Certainly, it is difficult to reconcile the many instances of this public criticism with the thrust of the 'hidden support' narrative. Rather than demonstrating that the IRA demanded acquiescence via iron-fist tactics, it shows the complex internal 'hearts and minds' games that republicans and more moderate elements had become enmeshed in. The IRA was not hesitant in returning derision to its critics. It lambasted the 'political collaborators, compromisers, beggars and crawlers' that had aligned with the British to 'discredit the republican movement'.[131] These exchanges are not evidence of intimidation nor could they be conceived to be. Whatever the virulence of the republican retort above, it was ultimately responsive to similar virulence directed at the IRA from its detractors. That republicans chose to engage in such exchanges is symptomatic of the 'hearts and minds' game at play within Nationalist communities. This is important for two reasons: first, it shows that there were those prepared to publicly challenge the IRA, and secondly, the fact that this provoked a republican response evidences implicit recognition within the IRA that some within its own community did not support them. This reality is in clear discord with the underlying tenet of the 'hidden support' narrative.

The IRA and community support

The 'hidden support' narrative is predicated on the assumption that the IRA enjoyed no support given willingly by the Nationalist community. Notwithstanding the fact that some Nationalists clearly opposed the IRA, empirical and documentary evidence is nonetheless indicative that the IRA enjoyed sizeable communal support in certain districts.[132] In the 'propaganda war' this became a shield against claims of intimidation; the IRA enjoyed a popular support the RUC did not, but this was given not demanded. High levels

---

[130] Cited in O'Malley, 1990, 253.

[131] 'Brits Out', *Freedom Fighter*, 4 (December 1976).

[132] Burton, 1978; Sluka, 1989; De Baroid, 2000; McKearney, 2011.

of community support had apparently raised IRA morale to 'an all-time high' during testing periods.[133] Gerry Adams, in a characteristic defence, classified the IRA as 'a people's army' that was:

> Closely knit with the Nationalist community, it was made up of the sons and daughters of ordinary people, its members indistinguishable to any outside observer from the rest of the community. Whether people in the Nationalist areas agreed or disagreed with the IRA and all of its actions they recognised it as their army, knew for the most part which of their neighbours were members, and referred to it as simply the 'ra'.[134]

Kevin Bean has previously touched on the relevance of this, noting that 'given the numbers of people who have passed through the IRA and their wider family and communal links, it would be an unusual family in the nationalist areas that had no links, no matter how tenuous, with the Republican Movement'.[135] One former combatant illustrated the centrality of this argument to the Irish republican counter-narrative by arguing that 'we were respected and admired by the populous', noting further that 'bullies are feared but they are never respected'.[136] This reflects how the 'language of community' was central to republican self-legitimation.[137] The IRA, for example, defended its bombing campaign through reference to the popular support afforded to volunteers active on the ground: 'behind those bombers, is massive structure based on streets and districts, whose existence is dependent upon the active support and mandate of the people'.[138] Indeed, private assessments of the calibre, capacity and support for the IRA contained in internal British Army documents failed to match the official position taken during the 'propaganda war'.[139]

There is a simple logic to the Irish republican counter-narrative that feeds off the illogicality of suggesting that the IRA only garnered community support through intimidation. How could you possibly intimidate a grassroots support base your survival is reliant upon into giving this necessary support? Sluka characterised the IRA and INLA as 'community-based' organisations that relied on popular support for their survival, elaborating further that 'they

---

133 'The Barricades are Down – but the People Have Risen', *Tatler*, 25 (1971).

134 Adams, 1986, 40.

135 Bean, 2007a, 66.

136 H, supporter of Sinn Féin policy, interview, May 2013.

137 Bean, 2007a, 53.

138 'The Nature of Strategy, Politics, Revolution and British Withdrawal', *Republican News*, 27 March 1976.

139 D. Campbell, 'The Army's Secret Opinion', *New Statesman*, 13 July 1979.

cannot maintain that support through intimidation'.[140] Far from being a convoluted argument, this assertion is based on a certain level of common sense. Surely the intimidation alleged by the RUC could only prove fatalistic for republicans. It would have turned Nationalists against the IRA and pushed them to co-operate with the RUC. That this did not ostensibly occur calls the 'hidden support' narrative further into question. One interviewee used this to argue that the 'hidden support' narrative was 'disingenuous' because if it was true then the RUC was 'incompetent' for failing to capitalise on alleged ill-feeling to defeat the IRA.[141] It seems then that the IRA sustained its campaign 'by dint of its popularity' rather than crude intimidation.[142]

The 'hidden support' narrative espouses a simplistic 'black-and-white' approach to communal support that overlooks existent 'grey' areas. The chief flaw in this 'black-and-white' thinking is a perplexing insinuation that not supporting the IRA somehow equates with supporting the RUC – if you are not with the IRA you are unfailingly against it and with the RUC. Participant observation in Nationalist districts of Belfast by Burton and Sluka comprehensively dispelled this. Two types of community support were observed: 'hard' support from activists and a support network prepared to offer shelter, intelligence and auxiliary support, and a more common 'soft' support that was not material or active but empathetic.[143] Although the 'soft' support base did not actively assist the IRA it did not hinder them either. The IRA no doubt enjoyed considerably more 'soft' support than 'hard' support, yet the 'hidden support' narrative is devoid of recognition that 'soft' support even existed. The ebb and flow of 'soft' support that defined the 'see-saw' relationship between the IRA and Nationalist community was often most noticeable at IRA funerals. The underlying sense of self-sacrifice for a noble cause mobilised Nationalists who may not have been hardened IRA sympathisers yet felt compelled to express solidarity with the deceased – who were also, in many cases, friends, relations and neighbours too. The most notable manifestation of this was during the 1981 hunger strike when funerals attracted up to 100,000 people, not all of whom were 'hard' supporters. Referring to the complexity of the IRA relationship with the Nationalist community, O'Malley has previously argued that these funerals revealed:

> The complicated nature of the relationship between the IRA and its community, a love–hate relationship that would always resolve itself on the side of love, especially in the matter of death, where the quarrels are always

---

140 Sluka, 1989, 166.

141 U, supporter of Sinn Féin policy, interview, August 2013.

142 Rolston, 2002, 64.

143 Burton, 1978; Sluka, 1989.

> internal – almost like family rows – and always misunderstood by outsiders who mistook occasional disapproval for disavowal.[144]

Even Nationalist critics of republican violence like O'Doherty readily concede that even if people did not support the IRA they did not co-operate with the RUC in relation to what they knew about IRA activity, and that while they frowned upon political violence in general they were acceptant of republican violence towards the RUC.[145] In totality then, the IRA may have enjoyed the 'hard' support of only a 'minority within a minority' in Northern Ireland but they nonetheless garnered more 'soft' support within the wider Nationalist community.[146] In accepting such an actuality, Danny Morrison asserts that the IRA 'never claimed to represent the majority of the nationalist community' but it did claim to represent those in the 'ghettos' and 'poor rural areas' who supported its armed campaign and subsequently voted for Sinn Féin in the six counties.[147]

Conclusion

The use of memory in the Irish republican policing debate became integral to transforming the 'legitimacy politics' of the conflict into post-conflict memory politics. Narratives selectively constructed during the 'propaganda war' were transplanted into the policing legacy where the 'memory of perpetrators' holds political currency. Irish republicans used their policing counter-memory to challenge dominant Unionist, state and RUC narratives. It contests notions of 'normal' pre-conflict 'policing by consent', of the RUC being a neutral force in a sectarian conflict between 'two tribes' and of 'hidden support' for the RUC among the Nationalist community. As counter-memory, Irish republican policing memory seeks to dispel official narratives that discount their policing experiences from the very inception of the Northern Ireland state. It is in essence the memory of the 'suspect community' at the sharp edge of counter-insurgency policing – essentially the *policed* – and it stands in contrast to the narrative of the police. The acceptance of policing by Sinn Féin has moved the matter from 'legitimacy politics' to memory politics at the inter-communal level where contestation is about what policing was rather than what policing is, yet at the intra-communal level policing remains mired in 'legitimacy politics'. It is to this that the next chapter now turns.

---

144 O'Malley, 1991, 158.

145 O'Doherty, 1998.

146 Tonge, 2012.

147 Morrison, 2016a.

Chapter 3

Ideology and Policing

Introduction

The policing debate was not the starting point of ideological contestation within modern Irish republicanism. As such, it must be mapped onto a bigger picture of contestation over the past within contemporary Irish republicanism. This chapter therefore interrogates how competing views of where Irish republicanism is currently at in transition and where it is believed to be heading are construed through value-laden interpretations of where it has come from. Locating the policing debate within this wider ideological context, two contesting ideological models of the current Sinn Féin strategy in Northern Ireland are proffered: the 'progressive republican' model and the 'constitutional nationalist' model. Irreconcilability between these models has generated intense ideological debate over what constitutes principles and what constitutes tactics, as well as disagreement over what represents continuity with traditional ideology and what is a rupture from it. Before delving deeper into this ideological debate, it is necessary to outline briefly the historical development of Irish republicanism. An exhaustive historical review is beyond the parameters of this book, yet it is nonetheless necessary to provide some historical context in order to allow present ideological debate within Irish republicanism to be understood.

Historical development

Irish republicanism is invariably traced back to Theobald Wolfe Tone and the Society of United Irishmen. This lineage itself arguably contains an element of myth because the Society of United Irishmen was initially a political club aimed at political reform that only opted for conspiratorial revolution in line with developments in France.[1] Their initial aim was the unity of the Irish people

[1] Comerford, 2003, 10.

via equality rather than through the ending of English occupation.[2] By 1798, however, their aim had become to 'break the connection with England'.[3] This formed the basis of a narrative that has been handed down through successive generations within the 'republican tradition'.[4] Ensnared in the third wave of major international revolt during the closing stages of 1848, the Young Ireland movement tried to resurrect the United Irishmen's aim of breaking the English connection through violent revolt.[5] Young Ireland rebellion solidified the concept of using physical force, which by the Fenian era was a well-established concept in Irish republican ideology. English notes that 'the Fenians were not asking for what England might give, but were demanding what was rightfully theirs, and were prepared to take it by force'.[6]

The 1916 Rising brought a departure from the initial Sinn Féin position of seeking a dual monarchy affording Ireland political and economic autonomy to an Irish republicanism premised on national self-determination. This allowed armed struggle and blood sacrifice to take root within a vaguely defined Irish republican ideology.[7] Armed struggle was firmly ensconced within the ideology when the Second Dáil Éireann vested its authority in the IRA as the de facto 'Government of the Republic'.[8] Whilst several members of the Second Dáil would later accept the Anglo-Irish treaty and renounce armed struggle – and more would do likewise upon the later establishment of Fianna Fail – seven members of the body later re-vested this legitimacy into a floundering IRA.[9] This spawned an ideological interpretation that the IRA, drawing on the democratic mandate of the Second Dáil, held authority as representatives of the people of Ireland and not those governing the two partitioned states – a view still propagated by some purist ideological readings today.

Whilst the above clearly shows that Irish republican ideology has consistently revolved around 'breaking the connection with England' and using armed force to achieve this, historically there has been little expansion beyond these base components. To this end, McGarry contends that Irish republicanism is afflicted by an 'ideological vagueness' that has defined it less like the republican principles of the French or American revolutions and

---

2 Smyth, 2005.

3 Ó Broin, 2009, 27.

4 McIntyre, 2012, 170.

5 Hobsbawm, 1962, 122.

6 English, 2006, 188.

7 Alonso, 2001.

8 Maillot, 2004.

9 Bowyer Bell, 1997, 154.

more as a form of 'insurrectionist anti-British nationalism'.[10] The consistent failure to venture far beyond the national question has led Irish republicanism to lack political or intellectual continuity in any ideological sense. For example, Wolfe Tone's Irish republicanism largely rejected the Catholicism and romantic cultural Nationalism that Pearse's republicanism embodied.[11] An ideological ambiguity therefore lies at the heart of Irish republicanism. It has differed from what has gone before but has paradoxically remained the same in terms of base values. This ambiguity reflects how Irish republicanism has been cultivated by 'a complex and diverse range of intellectual and ideological antecedents, many of which are often not merely competing but contradictory'.[12] Thus, despite contemporary elites attempting to draw ideological *continuity* with those espousing past versions of the ideology, the reality may in fact be, as McGovern notes, that as a loosely defined ideology differing from one historical stage to the next Irish republicanism is 'characterised by discontinuity'.[13]

On one level McGovern's assertion may seem anomalous. How can an enduring political tradition be epitomised by discontinuity? The answer to this lies in how Irish republicanism has not been definitively derived from any one singular ideological source. By this, the argument is that no *one* single source can be realistically argued to define neatly what Irish republicanism ideologically is or was. Hence, on the one hand, there may be the historical discontinuity that McGovern alludes to, yet, on the other hand, there has always been adherence to minimalist base principles of national self-determination and a right to use armed force to achieve this. This in itself becomes problematic. Whilst paradigmatic documents like the 1916 proclamation and the 1919 Declaration of the First Dáil enshrined the right to national self-determination and the right to use force against foreign 'occupation' into Irish republican ideology, apart from brief allusions to 'equality', little else of substance was nailed down. Apart from an end goal, namely national self-determination, and apart from a right to use force to achieve this, little else can be seen to evidence fully what the ideology embodies. Furthermore, whilst the right to use force may be enshrined into the ideology, there is a failure to clarify whether this 'right' should be regarded as a principle or a tactic. Clearly, that armed force *can* be used in pursuit of the end goal is outlined, but whether it has to be is open to interpretation. This ambiguity over what constitutes tactics and what constitutes principles is evident in ideological contestation within contemporary Irish republicanism.

---

[10] McGarry, 2003, 4.

[11] Garvin, 2008.

[12] McGovern, 2000.

[13] McGovern, 2000.

Such ambiguity has given Irish republicanism an ideological malleability that has allowed it to continue changing as wider political events change. This malleability means that:

> Republicanism is discursive in that it offers an internally differentiated series of ideological possibilities. It contains within it a range of exemplary models, memories, stories and rational political arguments that can be interpreted and re-interpreted through time. The 'republican tradition' may therefore be conceived as a discursively constituted, culturally and politically specific collective resource by which power is contested at the level of the idea.[14]

The historical failure to establish consensus on what Irish republicanism 'is' beyond an end goal and the right to use armed force has somewhat cocooned its contemporary form from fuller ideological development. The ramification of this has been Irish republicanism assuming forms that were not only historically anomalous but also ideologically irreconcilable: 'Twentieth century republican organisations have been radical and conservative, bigoted and non-sectarian, left and right wing, supporters of the Soviet Union and Nazi Germany, inclusive and xenophobic, intransigent and supinely flexible. The more successful and enduring of them ... accommodate the most disparate interests and outlooks'.[15] The only commonality amongst these otherwise irreconcilable positions has been adherence to the historical end goal of independence and the belief in the right to use force to achieve it. The subordination of internal differences to the 'national struggle' has the dual effect of placating, yet not actually resolving, internal contradictions prone to conflagrate at key political junctures and of affording considerable ideological flexibility to embrace or shun particularist positions as political needs dictate.[16]

In one sense, then, contemporary Irish republicanism is a 'catch-all' ideology enabling those with varying socio-economic views to coalesce around the base values of self-determination and a right to use armed force. The cohesive quality of a loosely based ideology becomes further apparent upon examination of those within the Provisionals who are generally regarded as the archetypal contemporary Irish republicans. Many within the founding Provisional leadership aspired to the grand ideals of 1916 and 1919.[17] For others, activism was stimulated by reaction rather than ideology. Motivation

---

[14] McGovern, 2000.

[15] McGarry, 2003, 5.

[16] Patterson, 1989.

[17] Tonge, 2008.

was tempered by a protectionist mentality of defending their community from the violence they witnessed around them rather than ideological devotion to a United Ireland.[18] For Bean, this meant 'the ashes of Bombay Street were more important in shaping the outlook of the young volunteers who flocked into the ranks of the IRA than the faintly glowing embers of the GPO'.[19] This was further echoed in the following account of reactionary involvement in republican activism:

> It wasn't for a 32-county socialist republic. Jesus, I don't even know if I could've spelt socialist in those days. I joined the movement because of what I witnessed as a child personally on the streets and I knew somebody had to do something about it ... it was only through maturity and later on that I became more aware, if you like, about all of those other things of republicanism. You know, I wouldn't have known what a republican was in those days.[20]

The narrative of communal self-defence has been complemented by the collective remembrance of events built around this notion.[21] As a result, the discourse of communal defence has been interwoven with ideological discourses in the Irish republican conflict narrative.[22]

This supports the argument that the contemporary IRA was an umbrella group of 'situationists and ideologues', consisting of older traditional republicans, those who 'inherited' their republicanism and those who reacted to the violence unfolding around them.[23] What bound this broad church together was the use of armed force, whether that was to achieve long-held ideological goals or in defence of the violence of the 'other'. This reflects Fanon's argument that armed struggle brings the collective together against the external enemy because 'it throws them in one way and in one direction'.[24] The logical consequence of this was that Irish republicanism was able to build a 'thick' consensus around the use of armed struggle – yet still eschew whether it was a principle or tactic – which left 'thin' consensus around everything else. In hindsight,

---

18 Morrison, 2011, 25.

19 Bean, 2007a, 56.

20 W, critic of Sinn Féin policy, interview, September 2013.

21 'Remembering the Burning of Bombay Street', *An Phoblacht*, 19 August 2004; 'Belfast's "Battle of St Matthew's" Remembered', *An Phoblacht*, 1 July 2014: www.anphoblacht.com/contents/24150 (accessed 7 August 2014).

22 Brown and Viggiani, 2010, 227.

23 Shirlow, Tonge, McAuley and McGlynn, 2010, 95.

24 Fanon, 1967, 73.

whilst this may have accommodated a broad church of opinion, it also bred the conditions for contestation, as the finer ideological points of purists and the left-wing critique of those 'left behind' by transition now demonstrate. The reality that the Provisionals consisted of 'situationists and ideologues' and the inherent ideological tension of such disparity grew discernible as the older 'ideologues' became marginalised by a new generation of 'situationists' who had developed a different ideological interpretation whilst in jail.[25]

Contemporary Irish republicanism

By the mid-1970s, a new ideological understanding gravitating towards a 'long war' involving political mobilisation rather than inevitable military victory for the 'government in waiting' emerged within the jails.[26] Studying struggles elsewhere, republican prisoners resolved to raise the collective political consciousness by bringing localised radicalism into everyday lives within their communities.[27] Increased mobilisation during and electoral success following the hunger strike heralded a realisation of the potential for mobilising popular support via Sinn Féin.[28] Whilst still adhering to a militarist 'Brits out' agenda, Irish republicans nonetheless began building a community-based movement to push for their ideological end goal. This began a departure from the 'elitist, conspiratorial assumptions of the armed struggle'.[29] This departure was aided by the fact that ideological lightness in a conventional sense allowed Sinn Féin to implement strategic change to move beyond the politics of *Eiré Nua,* whilst support for the 'armed tradition' meant it could retain its identity as an Irish republican party.[30] *Éire Nua,* which had been Provisional policy until 1982, was the brainchild of the Southern-based leadership duo of Dáithi Ó'Conaill and Ruairi Ó'Bradaigh.[31] It reflected the 'Ireland united Gaelic and free' outlook of the Provisional movement's first leadership. Highly critical of the Free State, British occupation, European institutions and foreign multinationals, the 'core value' of the document was to build a republic based on

[25] Moloney, 2011.

[26] Shirlow, Tonge, McAuley and McGlynn, 2010, 95.

[27] Mac Ionnrachtaigh, 2013.

[28] English, 2006, 380.

[29] Bean, 1995.

[30] Maillot, 2004, 4.

[31] When the pair resigned from Sinn Féin after abstentionism was dropped at the 1986 Ard Fheis they founded RSF who adopted the policy. RSF still advocate a modernised version of the policy today.

the ideals of the 1916 proclamation that would give 'power to the people'.[32] Rejecting any notion of simply subsuming the six counties into the existing arrangements of a corrupt Free State, the document advocated a secular decentralised system of federal, provincial and local governance based on Ireland's four provinces – crucially with the sweetener that Unionists would hold the balance of power in *Dáil Uladh* (regional parliament for a nine-county Ulster).[33] The policy was dismissed by Northern critics like Danny Morrison as being premised on a fundamental miscalculation of the world views of Northern Unionists and most people in the Free State, and was seen as a traditionalist comfort blanket that was becoming an impediment to further growth.[34] Discarding *Éire Nua* was the harbinger that the takeover of the republican movement by politically minded and ambitious Northerners was complete. Now that the excoriation of the Free State institutions was jettisoned, the path towards a more involved electoral intervention there soon emerged. Dropping abstentionism to Dáil Éireann in 1986 signalled a further departure whereby Sinn Féin would now seek an electoral mandate from the people rather than portraying the IRA as a 'government in waiting'.[35] At this juncture, Mulholland identifies a strategic change to build Sinn Féin as a political party rather than as a radical mass movement. To achieve this, armed struggle – increasingly limited to ingenuity rather than intensity – would be 'downgraded to extinction' with time.[36]

The increasingly politicised dimension to Irish republicanism led to a rethink on the overlap between electoralism and armed struggle. Sinn Féin moved from being a peripheral actor to become a central partner in a community-based approach that comprised electoralism and armed struggle. Post-hunger strike 'community politics' duly intertwined social agitation by a now electable Sinn Féin with continued support for the armed struggle.[37] Although politics had by no means replaced armed struggle at this juncture, it had at least come to complement it. McAllister notes that the 'Armalite and ballot box' strategy reflected the 'classic method of Irish republicanism' of using 'any means necessary' to achieve its goals.[38] While this may have allowed Irish

[32] Sean O'Bradaigh, '40 Years of Éire Nua', *Republican Sinn Féin:* https://republicansinnfein.org/miscellaneous/rsfposition/40-years-of-eire-nua-by-sean-o-bradaigh/ (accessed 3 October 2016).

[33] Sinn Féin, 1971, 55–56.

[34] Morrison, 2016a.

[35] Tonge, 2008, 60.

[36] Mulholland, 2007.

[37] Tonge, 2009, 167.

[38] McAllister, 2004.

republicans ideological and tactical flexibility, it nonetheless became as much a weakness as it was a strength. Having armed struggle running contemporaneously with electoralism may have allowed Irish republicans to garner a certain level of popular support without sacrificing the cutting edge that kept its end goal in constant focus, yet it was never a viable long-term strategy to have both coexisting. Sooner or later one would have to make way for the other.[39] After all, the greatest threat to those trying to build popular political support for their cause is that their violent actions generate higher cost than benefit. Fanon noted this in his 'threefold concern', arguing that the deaths of 'possibly innocent victims', preventing a 'false picture' of the conflict and trying not to isolate popular democratic opinion both domestically and internationally must come to bear on how conflict is conducted.[40]

The applicability of Fanon's analysis to 1980s Irish republicanism is obvious. Deaths of civilians at Enniskillen and elsewhere came dangerously close to giving succour to a state narrative of 'sectarian terrorism' that would undermine electoral advancement. Moreover, it also had the potential to strangle the development of a pan-Nationalist front by making Sinn Féin politically toxic. Within this wider context, the drawbacks IRA violence had for a dual strategy forced Irish republicans to confront long-eclipsed 'political realities'.[41] Continuing violence would stifle political advancement and risk wasting electoral gains, as had happened during the 1950s amidst the violence of the Border Campaign.[42]

To this end, electoralism began to replace militarism. On an ideological reading this suggests that armed struggle is a tactic rather than a principle. The principle would appear to be the end goal of independence, whereas components such as abstentionism and armed struggle could be relegated to the status of tactic. If the goal is to be reached by 'any means necessary', then armed struggle simply becomes one tactic that gives way to another tactic of electoralism. The ideological flexibility of Irish republicanism enabled Sinn Féin not only to label armed struggle a tactic but to change tactics throughout the conflict as needs dictated.[43] This latter-day 'republican pragmatism' not only existed due to, but was strengthened by, the lack of an ideologically 'developed theoretical framework'.[44] Thus, even if the principle (i.e. end goal) remained the same, the argument began to formulate that if it were to be realisable tactical flexibility

39 Van Tengen Page and Smith, 2000.

40 Fanon, 1970, 41.

41 English, 2006, 380.

42 Ó Broin, 2009, 199.

43 Tonge, Shirlow and McAuley, 2011.

44 Bean, 1995.

was required. In the spirit of using 'any means necessary', Irish republicanism, under the Adams leadership, became governed by the 'principle of success'.[45] This new principle meant that, as conflict reached stalemate, armed struggle and abstentionism would be remodelled as tactics and sacrificed on the altar of the 'principle of success'. This ideological reading is suggestive that at the most base level the foremost principle of Irish republicanism is the end goal of self-determination, with a further secondary principle of doing whatever it takes to achieve that aim. Such a view epitomised the analysis of one interviewee, who argued:

> Brian Keenan coined a phrase that 'wish lists are for Christmas', and they are, because you don't live in the real world if you think by talking something the way it should be it's going to happen ... This phase of our struggle has learnt very clearly that sometimes you need to be more practical than principled because principles don't bring about the changes needed.[46]

A sceptical synopsis from McIntyre contends, however, that an inherent reformism within Provisionalism emanating from its evolution in response to British strategy inevitably doomed it to 'pull up short of its stated goals'. Rather than 'switching tactics', the Provisional strategy was 'ceding the goal' of a British withdrawal, which he attributes not to 'farsighted and intelligent thinking' but to 'following the line of least pressure'.[47]

If one subscribes to the 'principle of success' then something that may at one time have seemed anathema to Irish republicanism – endorsing the policing apparatus that upholds Northern Ireland's constitutional status quo – can now appear to be in furtherance of the ideological end goal. The inference being that it represents not the culmination of Irish republican struggle but yet another step in a protracted process working towards the end goal. This was certainly the message broadcast by Sinn Féin during the policing debate. Republicans were told that even though they were debating policing they should 'keep [their] eye firmly on the big prize ... of unity and independence'.[48] Moreover, the Sinn Féin leadership reaffirmed to their grassroots support that 'although this very crucial debate today is on policing and justice let us be clear that all our debates, all our activity is about achieving our primary goal of a free, independent and united Ireland'.[49] Although it may differ radically from past

[45] Rafter, 2005, 5.

[46] B, supporter of Sinn Féin policy, interview, April 2013.

[47] McIntyre, 1995.

[48] 'Seamus Harvey 30th Anniversary', *An Phoblacht*, 25 January 2007.

[49] 'Speech by Gerry Kelly, then Sinn Féin Justice and Policing Spokesperson (SF),

tactics such as armed struggle and abstentionism, the logic forwarded seems to be that it is nonetheless ideologically sound as it adheres to the 'principle of success' by doing 'whatever it takes' to obtain the end goal. Moreover, Dickson and Osborne observe that police composition was increasingly addressed by Sinn Féin within a framework of equality.[50] With notions of equality-based transformation embedding themselves in the Sinn Féin brand of Irish republicanism,[51] turning an unrepresentative police force that 'upheld the Orange state and repressed everyone else' into a more representative police service that will 'deliver accountable, civic, non-partisan policing for ... all of our people',[52] may arguably further a republican equality agenda. That it remains a police force protecting the constitutional status of Northern Ireland is nonetheless ideologically problematic.

Ideological contestation

Within Irish republicanism division has traditionally been not on what is wanted but on how to get it. In pursuit of the end goal what are tactics for some become indistinguishable from ideology for others, making them principles. Ideological contestation then occurs on different levels. It may be contestation over 'operative ideology', that being the means by which the aims of 'fundamental ideology' are achieved.[53] Essentially, it becomes a debate over tactics:

> A lot of this comes down to a disagreement over tactics, over strategy ... when Sinn Féin says, 'this is furthering the struggle', I'm not questioning their integrity or I'm not questioning their bona fides or their honest belief that this is it, and I can see a lot of reasons we had to bring the armed conflict to an end ... there's no question about that. So, therefore then we had to sit down. If we are to advance how do we advance? And Sinn Féin

---

Delivering the Policing Report to the Sinn Féin Extraordinary Ard Fheis on Policing, RDS, Dublin (28 January 2007)': http://cain.ulst.ac.uk/issues/politics/docs/sf/gk280107.htm (accessed 10 May 2012).

[50] Dickson and Osborne, 2007, 157.

[51] McEvoy, 2000; McGovern, 2004; Bean, 2007a.

[52] 'Opening Address by Gerry Adams, then President of Sinn Féin (SF), to the Sinn Féin Extraordinary Ard Fheis on Policing, RDS, Dublin (28 January 2007)': http://cain.ulst.ac.uk/issues/politics/docs/sf/ga280107a.htm (accessed 10 May 2012).

[53] Seliger, 1970.

> put forward the proposal, which, I mean, I can understand some of the arguments; it's just that I disagree with them.[54]

For others, contestation relates to 'fundamental ideology' (principles) rather than 'operative ideology' (tactics). This reflects a traditionalist ideological reading that views armed struggle and abstentionism as principles rather than tactics. This is symptomatic of a reluctance to divert from the 'established script' to the point that defeat is preferable to compromise.[55] For these republicans, endorsing policing is not a change of tactics but rather a departure from 'certain fundamentals' at the heart of Irish republican ideology.[56] Moreover, the debate on 'fundamental ideology' goes beyond whether armed struggle is a principle or tactic. It also includes a leftist critique of the current Sinn Féin position. Several interviewees articulated left-wing opposition to policing, reflective more broadly of the left-wing criticism those 'left behind' make of the wider transitional process that Sinn Féin are involved in.[57] For example, Éirígí has been critical of the veneer of post-conflict betterment that masks how areas like West Belfast remain defined by a reality where 'unemployment is rife. Mental illness is endemic. Lack of housing and overcrowding as the Stormont government artificially inflates house-prices via underinvestment and lack of new-builds for social housing. This is the real Belfast, kept hidden in the back streets and alley ways of a broken city'.[58] Colin Coulter has noted the disturbing veracity of criticism that the 'peace dividend' has bypassed working-class communities in spite of

---

[54] Q, critic of Sinn Féin policy, interview, July 2013.

[55] Frampton, 2011, 79.

[56] AA, critic of Sinn Féin policy, interview, October 2013.

[57] Republican Network for Unity, *Standing Outside the 'Peace Process': A Revolutionary Republican Analysis of the Irish Pacification Process by the Republican Network for Unity* (Belfast: Republican Network for Unity, 2010); Republican Network for Unity, *Revolutionary Republicanism: National Liberation, Socialism, International Solidarity* (Belfast: Republican Network for Unity, 2013); 'Imperialism – Ireland and Britain', Éirígí, 2007: https://web.archive.org/web/20140826184807/www.eirigi.org/campaigns/imperialism_paper.html (originally accessed 12 December 2013); Irish Republican Socialist Party, *Perspectives on the Future of Republican Socialism in Ireland* (Belfast: Irish Republican Socialist Party, 2010); Irish Republican Socialist Party, *Perspectives on the Future of Republican Socialism in Ireland* (Belfast: Irish Republican Socialist Party, 2010).

[58] 'Welcome to West Belfast, Poverty Capital of the Six Counties', *Éirígí*, 15 September 2015: https://web.archive.org/web/20160312145124/http://eirigi.org/2015/09/15/welcome-to-west-belfast-poverty-capital-of-the-six-counties/ (originally accessed 14 December 2015).

an official image of a 'better' Belfast.[59] It is worth noting too that the Stormont executive was recently found to have breached its statutory duty to adopt an anti-poverty strategy.[60]

This leftist critique has grown in recent years as the *realpolitik* of austerity forced Sinn Féin to address the spectre of welfare reform. The 'two card trick', as Rafter termed it,[61] of opposing government cuts in the 26 counties while sitting in a government that imposed them in the six counties finally played itself out. Sinn Féin initially agreed to welfare reform under the SHA before later backtracking. However, under the 'A Fresh Start' agreement they agreed that the Conservative government could implement cuts they themselves were not willing to impose by temporarily handing back fiscal power to Westminster. The move drew considerable derision from leftist opponents – not least because Sinn Féin had only secured marginal financial protection in a deal that also paved the way for a lowering of corporation tax and allocated additional resources to policing paramilitarism. Martin McGuinness defended the deal, arguing that Sinn Féin had won extra concessions from the Tories, that lowering corporation tax would boost job creation and that it was ultimately the best deal that could be secured in difficult circumstances:

> Of course, no one is saying the agreement is perfect or that it shouldn't be scrutinised. But it also needs to be seen in the context from which it emerged – a backdrop of economic and political crisis created by Tory austerity policies, electoral competition within unionism, and the failure of the British and Irish governments to live up to commitments made in previous agreements. That is the scenario in which we entered the negotiations and, like all the other parties, Sinn Féin faced a choice. We could either work to do the best deal possible for the people we represent, or we could walk away and content ourselves with sniping from the sidelines. We chose to do the former because that's what responsible parties do.[62]

This held little currency with leftist critics. The IRSP savaged the 'former revolutionaries of Sinn Féin' for inflicting 'a wave of cruel and vicious attacks on working class families':

---

[59] Coulter, 2014.

[60] 'Northern Ireland Executive Breached Duty Over Anti-Poverty Strategy', BBC News, 30 June 2015: www.bbc.co.uk/news/uk-northern-ireland-33326631 (accessed 30 June 2015).

[61] Rafter, 2005.

[62] 'Martin McGuinness Opinion Piece on Deal', *Derry Sinn Féin*, 4 December 2015: www.derrysinnfein.ie/news/3530/ (accessed 14 December 2015).

> SF may argue that in the circumstances they had no choice but to swallow the pill which the Tories were forcing down their throats. This being the case, the IRSP in turn poses the question, what is the point in the Sinn Féin project? The Sinn Féin project has not forwarded the concept or prospect of Irish Unity. It has not ended (merely repackaged) the oppressive features of the British State in Ireland. And now it has been seen to accommodate the worst ravages of Tory Social planning, leaving the business class the winners and the working class the losers.[63]

For RNU, the lowering of corporation tax and the increased resources allocated to policing meant the only beneficiaries of this 'ideological assault on the working class' were 'big business, dole touts and unaccountable securocrats'.[64] The synopsis of veteran socialist campaigner Bernadette Devlin-McAliskey was that working-class communities had 'gained nothing from the struggle despite giving so much', having been consigned to a post-GFA reality that had brought them 'continued [reliance on] welfare, poor education and now austerity'.[65] Seemingly, then, critics subscribe to Bryce's conclusion that Sinn Féin has effectively followed others in embracing the bourgeois democracy it set out to destroy.[66] In addition to this politicised leftist criticism, there has also been some unfamiliar, yet hardly unjustified, criticism of certain decisions taken by Sinn Féin ministers from within its own constituency.[67]

Despite such observations, the reality remains that Sinn Féin does possess a significant electoral mandate. In various elections held in 2016, Sinn Féin accumulated 462,104 votes on the island of Ireland, bringing their presence in political office to 4 Members of the European Parliament (MEP), 4 Members of Parliament (MP) at Westminster, 7 Oireachtas Senators, 23 Teachta Dála (TD), 28 Members of the Legislative Assembly (MLA) at Stormont and 264 local councillors. Opponents did not deny the existence of such a sizeable mandate but chose instead to question where this growing mandate has come

---

[63] 'Make Sinn Féin's Betrayal the Catalyst for a Real People's Alternative!', *IRSP*, 18 November 2015: www.irsp.ie/news/?p=2039 (accessed 14 December 2015).

[64] '"Fresh Start" Represents the State's History of Failure', Republican Network for Unity, 19 November 2015: https://web.archive.org/web/20151123225626/www.republicanunity.org/fresh-start-represents-six-countys-history-of-failure/ (originally accessed 14 December 2015).

[65] Bernadette Devlin-McAliskey, 'Left Behind by Good Friday', *Jacobin*, 21 (2016): https://www.jacobinmag.com/2016/04/bernadette-devlin-interview-derry-civil-rights-troubles-good-friday/ (accessed 2 May 2016).

[66] Bryce, 2013.

[67] Mac Ionnrachtaigh, 2013, 213–14.

from, with many opining that it was largely a middle-class vote poached from the SDLP. The salience of this point can be seen through the results of the 2016 assembly elections. While Sinn Féin increased their vote in the middle-class former SDLP strongholds of South Down and South Belfast, their electoral ambitions in Foyle and West Belfast (two of the most deprived regions in the North of Ireland) were laid low by the election of anti-austerity People before Profit (PBP) candidates and a reduced share of the vote.[68] Such an outcome had indeed been forecast by Devlin-McAliskey who noted that in 'moving further and further' to accommodate Stormont's austerity policies Sinn Féin were:

> Losing the trust and the support of the people who once voted for them, the Catholic working class. Those people have been replaced by the Catholic middle class which most benefited from the peace process. These are former SDLP voters. They have a vested interest in stability and participation in the state, so they now support Sinn Féin.[69]

This echoes Brian Kelly's argument that trying to balance an electoral appeal to middle-class Catholic voters and upwardly mobile Nationalists with the traditional appeal to its working-class base has become increasingly unsustainable for a Sinn Féin that sits as partners in a post-GFA administration so fond of neoliberalism.[70] This wider criticism proves that those who do not necessarily advocate continued violence can also draw on the memory of previous ideological positions grounded in republican socialism to attack current Sinn Féin policy for rupturing with these. Ideological contestation is multifaceted, stretching beyond a simple 'black-and-white' contestation over the use of armed struggle, and cannot therefore be reduced to a peaceniks versus hawks understanding.

The breadth of such contestation coupled with the change in Provisional strategy has meant their project is incapable of being encapsulated by a single narrative. Fundamental changes to 'Provisional ideology' created new critical counter-narratives of Sinn Féin's rise to political power.[71] Questions relating to the motives and integrity of 'the leadership' are now being asked by those

---

[68] 'NI Assembly Election: DUP Remains Largest as Assembly Count Ends', BBC News, 7 May 2016: www.bbc.co.uk/news/election-2016-northern-ireland-36234717 (accessed 12 May 2016).

[69] Devlin-Mc Aliskey, 'Left Behind by Good Friday'.

[70] Kelly, 2012.

[71] Bean, 2007a, 138.

previously viewed as 'loyal lieutenants'.[72] From this, a critical counter-narrative of republican involvement in the transition of Northern Ireland has developed. This provides what Olick refers to as 'mnemonic resistance' to the Sinn Féin master narrative.[73] The counter-narrative contends that the 'mutually hurting stalemate' was transferred into the political arena by the Provisional leadership, where they were ignominiously defeated but continue presenting this defeat as impending victory.[74]

This counter-narrative has derived sustenance from how the Sinn Féin leadership has sought to rearticulate 'the meaning of republicanism'.[75] This modern – or, perhaps more aptly, moderate – republicanism has not only culled armed struggle and abstentionism but also seen radical socialism 'expelled and expunged'.[76] The erosion of radical socialism has seen 'equality' emerge as the new republican buzzword.[77] The irony of course being that whilst this may seem out of synch with Sinn Féin's previous leftist anti-imperialism it is arguably closer to the egalitarian permutation of the ideology professed by Wolfe Tone. Bean has labelled the Sinn Féin strategy of pursuing their goals via transformational equality-based politics from within as a 'post-republican' position beyond 'Brits out'.[78] This constitutive change means that aspects like a rights agenda, that had initially been considered 'partitionist', are now a 'defining characteristic' of post-conflict republicanism.[79] For a republican critic like McIntyre, however, the frank synopsis is that the political project of the Provisionals 'began as Brits out and ended as Paisley in'.[80]

Irish republicanism is now comprised of 'establishment republicanism', espoused by those who pursue the ideal within parliamentary forums, and 'dissident republicanism', adhered to by those outside such forums.[81] Contestation between these strands is attributable to natural hegemonic rivalry. Both strands use the same 'political vocabulary' but invest their own meanings into it.[82] What is 'republican' depends on which hegemon one is listening to because republicanism cannot belong to a 'sell out' or a 'dissident'.

72 Frampton, 2009, 191.
73 Olick, 2013, 139.
74 Frampton, 2011, 231.
75 McGovern, 2004.
76 McIntyre, 2008c, 115.
77 Smyth, 2005.
78 Bean, 2007b.
79 McEvoy, 2000.
80 McIntyre, 2008a.
81 Honohan, 2008, 12.
82 Honohan, 2008, 14.

Figure 3.1 Progressive republican model

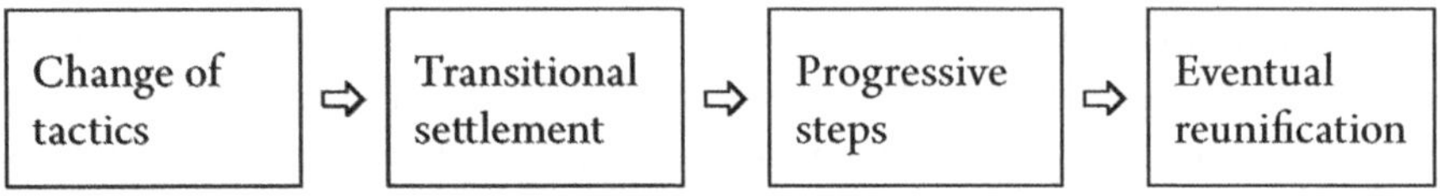

Figure 3.2 Constitutional nationalist model

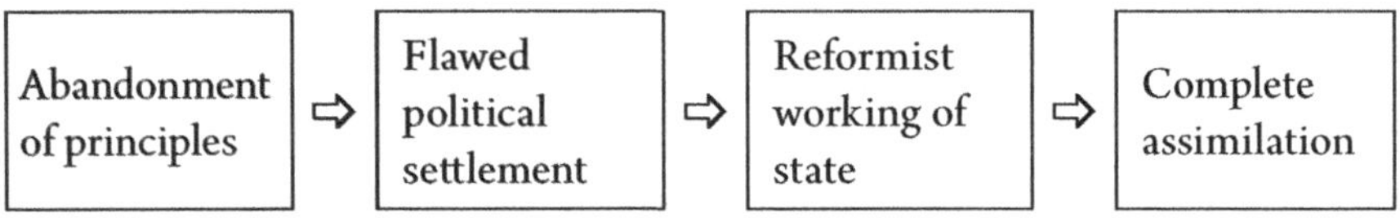

This has birthed two broad ideological models of interpreting the transition in Northern Ireland. The first model can be termed the 'progressive republican' model (Figure 3.1). It interprets Sinn Féin involvement in the transitional process as a tactical change which necessitated acceptance of a transitional political agreement in the form of the GFA. The transitional nature of the GFA has given rise to the endorsement of policing which is interpreted as a progressive step towards the ideological end goal of unity. The 'constitutional nationalist' model (Figure 3.2) reads the Sinn Féin strategy as an abandonment of republican principles which culminated in acceptance of a flawed political settlement. The out-workings of accepting such a settlement has been working the partitionist state from within followed by complete assimilation into the state, as evidenced by the acceptance of the policing apparatus that upholds the constitutional status quo in Northern Ireland. By necessity, then, the models are mutually exclusive, relying on the process of 'narrative closure' to preclude any alternative meanings to their preferred interpretation emerging.[83]

What follows is a critical examination of the interface between memory and ideology to determine how individuals 'remember' in accordance with whichever ideological model they subscribe to. Malešević's argument that correlation with master narratives requires the past to be reinterpreted in a 'particular ideological light' is key to understanding this evaluation.[84]

[83] Cobb, 1994, 54.

[84] Malešević, 2006, 150.

Progressive republicanism

Change of tactics

Those subscribing to the 'progressive republican' model see no contradiction between Irish republican ideology and endorsing policing. This is despite the fact that endorsing policing means accepting the state monopoly of the right to use force. An inherent tension exists around this issue given that many of those who now endorse policing once opposed it militarily. Ideological accommodation of accepting the state monopoly of the use of force with former combatant activism rests on reading armed struggle as a tactic rather than a principle. Movement away from armed struggle becomes a tactical shift rather than defaulting of principle. Just as the dropping of abstentionism represented a tactical shift that was 'opening up a new front',[85] policing was similarly a tactical manoeuvre into 'another area of struggle'.[86] This is attuned to a wider narrative depicting Sinn Féin's strategy as a tactical shift that will enable 'participatory republicanism', rather than militant republicanism, to realise ideological goals.[87] Despite movement away from a traditional militant understanding of republican ideology, the ideological end goal nevertheless remains unchanged. The 'progressive republican' reading has been sustained by leadership claims that republicans are winning the peace.[88]

Former combatants subscribing to the 'progressive republican' model recalled having a simplistic understanding of the conflict when they were younger. This understanding mirrors the belief within the IRA at the time that military victory was inevitable. However, political maturity brought the realisation that victory will not be attained via armed struggle but through a protracted political settlement. Recalling their earlier interpretation of the conflict, one interviewee noted:

> When we were kids we watched the Yanks being driven from South East Asia ... we were sitting in jail watching this and saying, 'this is right; I can't wait to get out of jail and we're gonna drive the British into the sea just like that'. But it's only whenever you get older and you realise, just because of the nature of this place, that the IRA were never going to have the capacity to inflict that type of military victory over the British Army ... So how does

---

85 Gerry Adams, 1986 Ard Fheis, quoted in Ó Broin, 2009, 254.

86 'Adams Seeks Police Stance Backing', BBC News, 20 January 2007: http://news.bbc.co.uk/1/hi/northern_ireland/6281805.stm (accessed 23 May 2017).

87 Tonge, 2008, 59.

88 McGovern, 2004.

> conflict end? If you understand that you cannot achieve a military victory over your opponent – and you understand also that your opponent isn't able to defeat you … once you arrive at that understanding the only way the conflict can end is at the negotiating table.[89]

A similar reappraisal came from another interviewee who recalled:

> Whenever I was younger and in the IRA and then in jail and reading the whole revolutionary stuff, you know, and you see yourself driving into City Hall in Belfast with an AK47, the same as Fidel and Che, did you know, and then it gets to the point where you realise it's not going to happen that way.[90]

Reaching the realisation that goals would not be met through armed struggle was 'part of the revolutionary process' of moving beyond being a 'rebel' to progressively state 'what we are for' and to positively pursue that rather than remaining 'negative'.[91] In being revolutionary there seemingly comes an ability to look at tactics beyond armed struggle and to pursue them if circumstances are favourable. This meant that another former combatant – who defined their activism as 'more revolutionary than militant' – had no 'major difficulty' with the policing move because being revolutionary:

> Is about negotiation, it is about compromise, it is about steps of trying to get where you want to go. And it's never about, you know, 'I was fully committed to armed struggle' … there was a time during the struggle – and this struggle is still going on – that I believed that was the only way forward, and that was the only way to bring this to some type of negotiation, but it was brought to a negotiation, you know, and that's where we have to move on.[92]

The former combatants above have subscribed to the new 'principle of success' and in being 'revolutionary' have reached the conclusion that ideological goals must be pursued by 'whatever it takes', and in a transitional context this means politics. Although they did not repudiate the armed struggle or their own role in it, they nonetheless 'remembered' in a way favourable to a 'progressive republican' reading of the past. Reading armed struggle simply as a tactic allows these individuals to place their lived experience within

---

89 A, supporter of Sinn Féin policy, interview, April 2013.

90 M, supporter of Sinn Féin policy, interview, May 2013.

91 M, supporter of Sinn Féin policy, interview, May 2013.

92 AD, supporter of Sinn Féin policy, interview, July 2013.

the confines of the 'progressive republican' master narrative. As individual activists, they have neatly located their own past within their interpretation of the master narrative of the collective past. What may have been 'forgotten' in doing this at the individual level, however, is the criticism that had been made of tactical changes by others in the past. What this demonstrates is the ability to 'remember' the past as a different person than the person who experienced the events at the time.[93] This means 'life scripts' become inextricably linked to the context that the person narrating the experience today finds themselves in rather than the circumstance of the person who lived that experience at the time.[94] The wise 'revolutionary' that now accepts policing displaces the naive 'rebel' who believed in inevitable military victory as the narrator of past activism. While this allows a different reading of the past, the ideological motivation remains the same. Continuity is therefore drawn between their armed struggle using 'old' tactics in the past and their political struggle using 'new' tactics today. In addition to providing an insight into how individuals 'remember' in accordance with master narratives, narratives of transition from 'rebel' to 'revolutionary' are also reflective of the fuller contribution former prisoners have made to the Northern Ireland transition and the ideological debate within Irish republicanism. Using the status obtained through imprisonment to support narratives of continuing the struggle by 'other means',[95] former prisoners have lent ideological credibility to the 'progressive republican' argument through visible involvement in policing bodies.[96] A somewhat bizarre echoing of the 'rebel' to 'revolutionary' master narrative also came from the unlikely source of PSNI Chief Constable George Hamilton following the killing of Kevin McGuigan in August 2015. Although Sinn Féin rejected media speculation of IRA involvement on the basis that the organisation had stood down in July 2005,[97] Hamilton argued that the IRA infrastructure remained 'broadly in place' but now had a 'radically changed' purpose as a control mechanism for guiding republicans through transition.[98]

---

[93] Pinkerton, 2012.

[94] Bernsten and Bohn, 2009, 66.

[95] McEvoy and Shirlow, 2009.

[96] 'SF Policing Board Nominees Named', BBC News, 23 April 2007: http://news.bbc.co.uk/1/hi/northern_ireland/6581857.stm (accessed 7 August 2014).

[97] 'Kevin McGuigan: Reaction to PSNI's Assessment on Murder', BBC News, 20 August 2015: www.bbc.co.uk/news/uk-northern-ireland-34011551 (accessed 23 August 2015).

[98] 'Kevin McGuigan Murder: Provisional IRA Still Exists, says PSNI Chief', BBC News, 22 August 2015: www.bbc.co.uk/news/uk-northern-ireland-34026678 (accessed 24 August 2015).

Transitional settlement

Acceptance of the 'progressive republican' model is predicated on acceptance of the GFA not as a final political settlement but as a transitional political arrangement endowed with an ability to further the republican agenda. Such a reading reflects the 'constructive ambiguity' that defines the GFA whereby different parties can take whichever reading of the deal they prefer.[99] For 'progressive republicans' this means that while the GFA may indeed enshrine the 'principle of consent' it also contains a provision for a future vote on Irish unity that can then be subsequently re-held on a recurring seven-year basis. The authority to convene such a poll, however, rests with the British Secretary of State. As a transitional arrangement, the GFA then represents a building block on which a process culminating in reunification can be initiated. The 'progressive republican' task is to create the conditions for a border poll to first be called and then eventually won. Patterson, however, argues that it was 'inevitable' that the new dispensation would be tied to a narrative depicting political institutions in the North as a stepping stone to the big prize of unity.[100] The transition, then, represents 'not a united Ireland' but something bringing that ideological goal 'nearer' than armed struggle ever could.[101] Acceptance of the GFA thus becomes not acceptance of it per se but acceptance of its potential as a 'work in progress' that can get to the goal of reunification. Adhering to the 'progressive republican' model, one interviewee maintained that the GFA did not represent 'the end' for Irish republicans. Rather, the transitional nature of the GFA made it 'a foundation' and 'an opportunity to move things forward'.[102] If policing is viewed through such a lens, it becomes a progressive step towards ideological goals rather than a step away from them. Moreover, for those subscribing to such a view it is not only a progressive step, but it is one in the absence of any viable alternative. This fact, interviewees argued, had not yet dawned on the traditionalist or leftist critics of the Sinn Féin strategy.

Dismantling the state

In this context, policing becomes one component in a process of 'dealing in the round' with how Irish republicans 'move forward'.[103] The ability to adopt such a reading of 'critical engagement' requires republicans to think about the

[99] Mitchell, 2009.

[100] Patterson, 2008, 148.

[101] English, 2006, 410.

[102] B, supporter of Sinn Féin policy, interview, April 2013.

[103] H, supporter of Sinn Féin policy, interview, May 2013.

issue 'strategically' rather than individualising it. The ability to 'put your heart to one side' allowed one interviewee to get 'around' their personal difficulty with policing. Although the interviewee still had reservations that were natural on any individual level, the prevalence of 'strategic' thinking made the issue 'easier'. Revealing the thought process behind buying into the 'progressive republican' narrative the interviewee elaborated:

> To look at policing as an individual issue isolated – that's not the way I looked at it. I looked at it as part of the overall strategy of going in and in my opinion the only way you can change anything is to go in and work at it from within and challenge it and not let the mistakes of the past happen. So strategically it was the right thing to do.[104]

If 'critical engagement' is evaluated in combination with other transitional processes rather than simply as acceptance of policing for the mere sake of acceptance, it would appear from the argument above that it is ideologically sound because it is 'strategically' right and it is progressive. In accepting the need to be progressive interviewees argued that republicans did not have the luxury of ignoring policing until attaining reunification. Rather, as a matter of political reality, the issue needed to be addressed in advance of securing the 'big prize'. The ability to look upon policing as a pro-active process fits neatly with the argument of Sinn Féin that 'critical engagement' would effectively take control of policing 'off' their political enemies.[105] Accepting this premise enables republicans to take a long-term view of the transition, meaning that when it comes to the issue of endorsing policing they will be 'comfortable enough with it'.[106] Such individual rationalising not only exhibits remarkable resonance with Sinn Féin's master narrative of 'change from within' but also indicates the ability of memory to become intertwined with strategy. Ideological goals have not changed even if the means of attaining them have. Continuity is to be found not in tactics but in principles whereby what was sought in the past and what is currently being sought in a transitional setting are the same.

For those supportive of 'critical engagement', ideological vindication is discernible through dividends paid out already. Martin McGuinness declared six months after the policing Ard Fheis that republican involvement in policing was 'dismantling the hold that Unionist policemen and strategists had on

[104] I, supporter of Sinn Féin policy, interview, May 2013.

[105] C. Ní Dhonnabhaín, 'Motion Passed by Huge Majority', *An Phoblacht*, 1 February 2007; E. O'Dwyer, 'Speakers Exude Confidence and Stress Need for Unity', *An Phoblacht*, 1 February 2007.

[106] A, supporter of Sinn Féin policy, interview, April 2013.

policing in the North'.[107] The analysis proffered by Mc Guinness gained notable traction amongst interviewees who argued that republicans had 'wrecked the Orange state', 'devastated' the policing institutions[108] and 'dismantled' the RUC.[109] The acceptance of policing for these republicans would appear to be strategic acceptance geared towards long-term ideological goals rather than carte blanche acceptance. To this end, interviewees drew on past experiences of engaging with the 'enemy' by depicting 'critical engagement' as another step in the post-conflict re-unification process just like engagements with the prison administration following the hunger strike, engagements with the British Government in the run up to and the aftermath of the GFA, the more general political engagement with Unionism and grassroots engagement with former loyalist combatants. Irish republicans who have accepted policing have nonetheless avoided 'ideological ditching' and have come to an accommodation with the 'enemy' that is 'pragmatic not ideological'.[110]

Although ideological goals remain wed to self-determination, there has nonetheless been an evolution from seeking a 'revolutionary reconquest of Ireland'[111] to building 'an Ireland of equals'.[112] This has seen Sinn Féin pursue what McCrudden terms the 'two equality agendas' of the GFA.[113] The consociationalism of the GFA enables 'progressive republicanism' to portray itself as the defender of particularistic political rights for Nationalists while wider equality provisions allow Sinn Féin to assume the mantle of championing universalistic rights.[114] While the former accounts for the use of equality discourse to champion GFA provisions with considerable relevance to its own constituency, the latter has seen attempts to utilise equality measures in section 75 of the Northern Ireland Act 1998 to support wider equality-based

---

[107] M. McGuinness, 'Republican Strategy Now the Route Map to Irish Unity', *Iris* (summer 2007), 2.

[108] B, supporter of Sinn Féin policy, interview, April 2013.

[109] H, supporter of Sinn Féin policy, interview, May 2013.

[110] Shirlow, Tonge, McAuley and McGlynn, 2010, 138.

[111] 'Extract from Presidential Address by Gerry Adams, then President of Sinn Féin, on the Issue of Abstentionism (Resolution 162), Sinn Féin Ard Fheis, Dublin (1 November 1986)': www.cain.ulst.ac.uk/issues/politics/docs/sf/ga011186.htm (accessed 7 August 2014).

[112] '"We are Determined to Create an Ireland of Equals" – South Armagh Annual Volunteers Day 2014', *Newry Armagh Sinn Féin*, 23 June 2014: http://newryarmaghsinnfein.com/determined-create-ireland-equals-south-armagh-annual-volunteers-day-2014/ (accessed 7 August 2014).

[113] McCrudden, 1999, 106.

[114] McGovern, 2004.

transformation of the Northern Ireland state. This has seen the pursuit of 'an Ireland of equals' beyond traditional interpretations of smashing the 'Orange state' by supporting same-sex marriage, gender equality and ethnic minority rights. The pervasiveness of such a notion in current Sinn Féin discourse is evident in Gerry Adams controversially telling an internal party conference, in reference to religious fundamentalists in the DUP, that equality is the way to 'break these bastards'.[115] Pursuing strategic, ideologically tainted and equality-based reform of policing seemingly mirrors a wider strategy of orchestrating equality-orientated destruction of the 'Orange state' that will progress towards self-determination and 'an Ireland of equals'. A significant parliamentary presence in both jurisdictions continues to underpin the stages rhetoric of their narrative on equality-based reform of the Orange state.[116]

'Mild sceptics'

Thinking 'strategically' may have made the collective decision easier, yet at the individual level acceptance remained difficult for some. Those labelled 'mild sceptics'[117] – supporters of the Sinn Féin strategy who struggle with certain elements of it on a personal level – revealed individual difficulty with policing. One former combatant highlighted the tension between the individual and the collective by revealing:

> I never contemplated leaving the movement or leaving the struggle over it because you know things like this take time and I appreciate that too … it's a struggle a day for to make change as some of the politicians said … and I suppose in that concept the same can be said for an overall change of the way I thought … I just got it very hard to contemplate how former activists just went with the change so fast. I was one of the ones that just couldn't handle that.[118]

Another interviewee recalled:

> I didn't see the bigger picture right away to be truthful. I was just 'you know, these have been our enemies for so long and now we are going to engage' …

---

[115] M. Moloney, 'Gerry Adams Clarifies "Bastards" Comment – About Bigots, Homophobes and Racists', *An Phoblacht*, 25 November 2014: www.anphoblacht.com/contents/24570 (accessed 16 December 2015).

[116] Bean, 2014.

[117] Shirlow, Tonge, McAuley and McGlynn, 2010, 111.

[118] L, supporter of Sinn Féin policy, interview, June 2013.

> After healthy debates that we had, you know, within Sinn Féin, I could see the bigger picture then and I knew it was the way to go. I mean certainly it stuck in your throat a lot of times.[119]

Despite the personal difficulty evident in the above accounts, a belief that at a collective level the Sinn Féin strategy is paying dividends is nonetheless discernible. This tension is worked through via an internal cost–benefit analysis. The cost of individual unease at the policing move is offset against the strategic gain at the collective level. What can be deducted from this is that a leadership-constructed discourse of strategic thinking can prove rhetorically valuable but it can also frame individual rationalising of the move for those with a natural reluctance to accepting policing. So, while strategic-thinking pleas correlate seamlessly with a master narrative of changing tactics for the new mode of struggle that provides rhetorical soundbites in Ard Feis and commemorative speeches, they nonetheless have a real impact on how the individual at grassroots evaluates the move in terms of their past activism. Individual difficulty is duly subordinated to the perceived needs of the collective good. This is evidenced by how 'mild sceptics' who have tacitly endorsed policing against their initial feelings do not regard themselves as any less republican for having made the decision. The perfect illustration of this is the latter interviewee's assertion that 'I don't regret one minute of my past – I regret getting caught – but you know I've no regrets and I'm very proud of my past, but I'm also very proud of where we are now, you know, in the political situation'.[120]

That the interviewee remains 'very proud' not only of the past but also of the transitional process Irish republicans are embarking on suggests that the principles have certainly not changed for those like the interviewee even if the tactics have. The result of this is that they feel secure enough in their ideological conviction and in the current strategy they support to endorse the policing apparatus of the state and simultaneously regard themselves as Irish republicans just as they did when opposing the RUC during the conflict.

---

[119] F, supporter of Sinn Féin policy, interview, May 2013.

[120] F, supporter of Sinn Féin policy, interview, May 2013.

Constitutional nationalism

Abandonment of principles

Those who adhere to a 'constitutional nationalist' model believe that current Sinn Féin strategy is borne out of a defaulting of principles rather than a tactical change. Finding fault with the wider transitional process, they believe that 'critical engagement' represents movement away from reunification rather than towards it. For these republicans, 'policing cannot be detached from the constitutional issue,'[121] meaning that endorsing policing in the absence of settling the 'national question' is legitimising the British occupation of Ireland.[122] From this perspective, policing represents something of an ideological malaise as it equates acceptance of the existence of the Northern Ireland state and the monopoly of the police force to use force within that state.[123] Why policing represents a breach of principles to those who take such a view is axiomatic; accepting Northern Ireland's constitutional status quo flies in the face of the principle of self-determination whilst acknowledging the state monopoly of the use of force removes the right to use armed force.

Central to this ideological view is the structuralist argument that policing and the state are two inseparable sides of the one coin. If there is an ideological flaw with the state – and for Irish republicans of all hues there is as the partitioned state is standing in the way of their end goal – then that flaw will be replicated in the policing apparatus defending the state. The logical follow on from this is that accepting 'British policing' is accepting 'British rule' in Ireland – something anathema to Irish republicanism. One interviewee articulated such an argument, noting that 'we can't separate the police force from the state. The state is ultimately a British state; the police force ergo is a British police force'. Elaborating further on this analysis, they argued that to think that policing could be solved outside of any 'radical transformation' of what was for them an 'irreformable' state would be 'illogical' and a case of 'putting the cart before the horse'.[124] Another argued that the ideological argument could not be divorced from the wider role of the police in protecting the state. In believing that they could undermine the state and advance a republican agenda 'by supporting the organs of the state that prevent all of that', Sinn

---

[121] 'The Necessity of Policing and the Necessity for Constitutional Change', 32 County Sovereignty Movement: www.32csm.net/p/32csm-policy-documents.html (accessed 24 April 2012).

[122] 'Disband the RUC/PSNI', *Saoirse*, 238 (February 2007).

[123] Frampton, 2011, 206.

[124] AA, critic of Sinn Féin policy, interview, October 2013.

Féin was making a 'profound mistake' that the interviewee disagreed with 'tactically and strategically'.[125] The sentiment of those who cannot see merit in the 'progressive republican' model is that accepting policing equates co-option into the very state that Irish republicans seek to dismantle. This structuralist argument is attuned to Tonge's synopsis that accepting policing represents 'the culmination of working rather than removing the state'.[126]

Flawed agreement

The policing decision – just as in the 'progressive republican' reading – cannot be detached from its wider context for those opposed to the move. Central to the reading of policing as anathema to Irish republican ideology is a similarly dim view of the GFA. Most notable in the anti-policing critique is the fact that the GFA enshrines the 'principle of consent'. For one critic, this made the GFA not simply a 'non-republican' settlement but rather an 'anti-republican' settlement.[127] Rather than buying into the narrative that the GFA represents the banking of concessions won thus far as a foundation for making further advances, it is rejected on the basis that it accepts an outcome that not only falls short of but actually contradicts the principle of national self-determination. Instead of focusing on the transitional potential of the GFA, critics 'remember' how similar political settlements were rejected as heresy in the past – something that those buying into a 'progressive republican' reading 'forget'. McIntyre argues that in accepting the GFA the Sinn Féin leadership have implicitly acknowledged that what was on offer to Irish republicans via Sunningdale is as 'good as it gets', thus posing the awkward question of why the 'war' was waged until the mid-1990s.[128] Interviewees who engaged in a wider memory politics reading of the transition also posed the question of why something that was seemingly anathema to republicanism in 1974 became acceptable in 1998:

> The Good Friday Agreement, if you read it properly, you know in it you have exactly the same things that you had in 1974. Exactly, except you didn't have to decommission and all prisoners were getting out of jail and there was going to be an amnesty for all prisoners. They were getting the same things in '74. None of them can answer the question, 'but why was it not accepted in '74?'[129]

125 Q, critic of Sinn Féin policy, interview, July 2013.
126 Tonge, 2011.
127 Y, critic of Sinn Féin policy, interview, October 2013.
128 McIntyre, 2008a.
129 N, critic of Sinn Féin policy, interview, June 2013.

Given the centrality of this 'Sunningdale for slow learners' argument to republican criticism of the GFA, it is worth drawing it out slightly. While there is a certain merit to the substance of this argument, what it overlooks is an important contextual difference.[130] Sunningdale was rejected against a backdrop of republican belief in an inevitable declaration of British withdrawal and against a wider global backdrop of post-colonial national liberation struggles – as evidenced by the remarks of former combatants in previous sections and by the approach taken by the IRA leadership during negotiations with the British. As Wolff notes, by the turn of the millennium most of these other conflicts had concluded or evolved into protracted political settlements.[131] By the time the GFA emerged, a 'mutually hurting stalemate' in the six counties, the ending of the Cold War and movement out of political violence elsewhere had significantly altered the political landscape. Accordingly, what was rejected 25 years previously in the misguided anticipation of inevitable victory was later re-evaluated as a foundation for further strategic advancement. Where the 'Sunningdale for slow learners' argument falters is not on the substantive likeness of the two agreements but on their considerable contextual difference. If the latter-day revolutionaries 'forget' their past criticism of others to justify their current positions, then those espousing a 'Sunningdale for slow learners' argument similarly 'forget' an important contextual disparity to support theirs.

Nevertheless, the identification of an ideological flaw in the GFA – that being that any internal settlement short of self-determination copper fastens partition – prevents these republicans from accepting the 'progressive republican' premise of the transition being a series of progressive steps building towards the goal of unity. The 'constitutional nationalist' premise is, rather, that if the GFA is ideologically flawed then every step emanating from that becomes part of a process that is fundamentally flawed and built on an erroneous supposition that it is progressive. Rather than removing the state, it results in assimilation into the state and a venture out of Irish republicanism into constitutional Nationalism to contest that field with the SDLP. The reality would then appear to be that the GFA 'constitutes an uncomfortable reality for anyone who claims to be a republican' as the actual outworkings do not live up to the Sinn Féin stages rhetoric.[132]

[130] Tonge 2014b, 115.

[131] Wolff, 2006, 5.

[132] Bean and Hayes, 2009.

Reformist working of the state

What opponents see in the Sinn Féin strategy is not progressive steps towards unity but desperation to do 'whatever it takes' – including sacrificing principles – to wield power within Northern Ireland's political institutions. The IRSP, for example, accused Sinn Féin of signing up to 'A Fresh Start' 'for the sake of maintaining positions of power and relevance, along with the perks and privileges that come with the posts of career politicians'.[133] For critics, the Sinn Féin aim has ceased to be the republican goal of self-determination to now become assuming the mantle of power as the dominant force within constitutional Nationalism. In contextualising this, one interviewee offered the following frank assessment of the Sinn Féin position:

> If someone said to me, 'look listen, after 37 years, I was knackered and I'm taking the money and to hell with everybody', I respect that man or woman because they are telling the truth. My next thing would be, 'Well then, don't call yourself a republican. You're a constitutional Nationalist, which is what the SDLP were. You wanted their prime position and you worked long and hard and choreographed yourself very well, and fair play to you. You got where you wanted to go. All your nights of study and all your nights of manoeuvring, handshaking and back rubbing has paid off. You're in government. Sín é. Now, tell the truth because you can't be a republican who is administering British rule in this country'.[134]

From this analysis, endorsing 'British policing' in Ireland is a natural consequence of a willingness to administer 'British rule' in Ireland:

> The notion that policing represents a Rubicon for the Provisional movement to cross is a distortion of their true political and constitutional predicament. Accepting policing is the logical consequence of accepting the legitimacy of British parliamentary activity in Ireland. That Rubicon was publicly crossed in 1998 and if the Humes/Adams document was to see the light of day a private crossing could be acknowledged from an earlier date.[135]

---

133 'Make Sinn Féin's Betrayal the Catalyst for a Real People's Alternative!', *IRSP*, 18 November 2015: www.irsp.ie/news/?p=2039 (accessed 14 December 2015).

134 P, critic of Sinn Féin policy, interview, June 2013.

135 'No Other Law: The Politics of Policing in Occupied Ireland', 32 County Sovereignty Movement, 15 January 2007: http://indiamond6.ulib.iupui.edu:81/32CSM210107.html (accessed 17 May 2017).

One critic argued that endorsing policing was 'the price of admission' that Sinn Féin had to pay to get into 'the political institutions of the six counties'. Recalling the wider political context prevalent at the time, the interviewee argued:

> We remember the November deadline of 2006. They simply had no choice. If they wanted to continue along the political path that they'd chosen then they had to swallow British policing ... they were forced into accepting the political anomaly ... they have to gloss up the reality of it by using terminology such as 'changing from within', 'putting manners on them' in the words of Martin McGuinness, but they are living a lie.[136]

It is worth noting that the St Andrews Agreement, intricately linked to the choreography of 'critical engagement', made positions in the power-sharing executive dependent on ministerial pledges of support for the rule of law. 'A Fresh Start' later extended this to all members of the assembly.[137] To that end, the argument above may not be entirely without foundation. Indeed, it is given further credence by Hayes' argument that what forced the policing move was essentially 'political pressure' rather than ideological commitment.[138] Nor is Hayes alone in this analysis. Wilford and Wilson argue that the change in policing policy occurred against a backdrop of threats that elections to the local assembly would not take place without this.[139]

Frampton notes that Sinn Féin has been able to fend off criticism on the basis that other groups have yet to offer an alternative.[140] Whiting goes further in her analysis, concluding that while Sinn Féin's detractors may have policy documents that can in themselves act as a rebuttal to claims of having no strategy, the policies outlined in them hardly represent a viable alternative.[141] Those who supported policing were keen to point this out when interviewed. Although there is considerable merit in this point, what it fundamentally overlooks is that, unlike the *realpolitik*, in the realm of memory politics absence of a progressive alternative is essentially a non-issue. Memory politics favours critics in the regard that they simply have to state that they are continuing to do what Irish republicans always did – whether that be mounting military

---

136 O, critic of Sinn Féin policy, interview, June 2013.

137 'A Fresh Start: The Stormont Agreement and Implementation Plan' (London: HMSO, 2015), Section A 2.6–2.7.

138 Hayes, 2010, 66.

139 Wilford and Wilson, 2007.

140 Frampton, 2011, 224.

141 Whiting, 2015.

campaigns, politically opposing 'partitionist' internal settlements and resisting 'British policing' – and then point to the criticism the Provisionals made of other 'reformists' in the past. This was certainly not lost on interviewees when the Sinn Féin argument that there was 'no alternative' was put to them. One interviewee responded that even a 'slight analysis' of such an argument exposed its shortcomings:

> I could use all the arguments they used against the SDLP. I could use all the arguments they used against the pro-treaty people in the early '20s about buying into the system, about becoming part of the system ... If you look at the '70s and '80s, when the SDLP were basically legitimising the British presence in Ireland because they were the largest Nationalist party and they were co-operating fully with the British state, they were heavily criticised by the Provies. Now the Provies are doing the exact same thing that the SDLP were doing in the '70s, '80s and '90s. Yet they don't see the hypocrisy in what they're saying. Is the only difference because they are talking to us now, so that makes it okay?[142]

For another interviewee, the mere suggestion that there could be an Irish republican 'alternative' short of self-determination was in itself ideologically flawed. It was held that 'people talk about republican alternatives. There is no alternative to the republic ... We can't have a Northern and a Southern assembly. We can't have any kind of concessions or anything other than the republic'. Taking exception to the suggestion that such a stance was 'backward'-looking rather than progressive, the interviewee defended their position:

> Really and truly, everything has been tried. We've had Direct Rule. We've had partition. We've had devolution. We've had internment. They have tried to kill us. They have tried to lock us up. They have done everything. The one thing that they haven't tried to secure peace in Ireland is full independence, and to me that is the only thing that will work. So, while they keep banging their head off a brick wall, I think they are looking backwards. They're looking for a solution, an alternative in Ireland that isn't ever going to work.[143]

Implicit in this argument is a rebuke of the 'progressive republican' 'no alternative' argument whereby instead of there being no alternative to the Sinn

[142] K, critic of Sinn Féin policy, interview, June 2013.

[143] AC, critic of Sinn Féin policy, interview, November 2013.

Féin strategy it is held that there is 'no alternative' to self-determination. Adopting this view means that any settlement falling short of self-determination is ideologically flawed. 'Equality agenda' republicanism may afford Nationalists increased political power in a reformed Northern Ireland state but that is not self-determination. Sustenance for this argument may be found in MacGinty's analysis that Sinn Féin participation in the transition has blurred constitutional options, with the effect that many Nationalists are feeling they can accept devolution and a place within a reformed Northern Ireland state rather than clinging to the historical aim of a united Ireland.[144] Interestingly, Evans and Tonge note that support for the GFA is strongest among Sinn Féin supporters.[145] One reading can attribute this to their belief in the transformative capacity of the GFA to deliver self-determination. Another can, however, attribute it to the fact that 'equality-agenda' republicanism has succeeded in placating them via equal status in the Northern Ireland state meaning that self-determination is no longer regarded as sacrosanct.

Assimilation

A belief that the Sinn Féin strategy has its antecedents in failed policies of the past has been at the heart of criticism proffered by their opponents. The fallibility of the 'reform from within' theory behind the 'progressive republican' model is the fact that an unrealised practical implementation of it is a 'recurring theme of Irish history'.[146] For opponents, the onus is on the Sinn Féin leadership to differentiate between their current strategy and that of 'all those it had previously labelled traitors'.[147] This task becomes arduous in a memory politics environment where opponents are only too willing to draw such parallels. Morrison notes that this has led to considerable correlation between the past narrative of the Provisionals as the 'original republican dissidents' and that forwarded by those challenging their position today.[148] Critics argue that Sinn Féin has adopted Official IRA policies they once 'vehemently opposed'.[149] This is both politically and mnemonically charged and it shows the growing dimensions of the hegemonic contestation within modern Irish

---

[144] MacGinty, 2006.

[145] Evans and Tonge, 2013.

[146] S. McGowan, 'Republicanism and Policing – A Historical Context', Irish Republican Socialist Party, 13 February 2007: www.irsp.ie/Background/theory/republicanismandpolicing.html (accessed 24 April 2012).

[147] McIntyre, 2008b, 122.

[148] Morrison, 2011, 20.

[149] 'Total Collaboration with British Rule', *Soairse*, 238 (February 2007).

republicanism. It is also reflective, more generally, of how Irish republicans tie their views of the transition in the North of Ireland to how they view the past and, more importantly, to how they seek to represent that past.[150] The ability to draw parallels with past failed reformist programmes, is demonstrative that Irish republicans adhere to what Wertsch terms a 'narrative template' that acts as a 'gist of what happened', wherein specific actors, dates and times may change but the plotline remains constant throughout.[151] Where it was Fine Gael in the 1920s, Fianna Fail in the 1930s and the Officials in 1969, today the Provisionals become the 'reformist' villains of the narrative.[152] Compounding this further is the ability of critics to see vindication in what they had argued when they initially opposed the Sinn Féin 'progressive republican' project at its inception.[153] Rejection back then was broadcast as an 'apocalyptic history' that 'writes the future as pre-ordained';[154] dropping abstentionism would lead to the de-escalation of the armed campaign, which in turn would allow a partitionist internal settlement to eventually enmesh republicans in the system that protects the constitutional status of the Northern Ireland state. 'Critical engagement' represents the latter-day fulfilment of that prophecy. Interviewees noted, however, that the ideological drawbacks of this vindication meant that they took little solace in being proven 'right'. The ideological implication of this being that Irish republicanism had to come through 'its weakest point probably – if not ever – since the 30s or 40s',[155] meaning that self-determination 'is further away than it has ever been'.[156] In a damning assessment of where Sinn Féin has brought Irish republicanism to today, one interviewee concluded:

> See, when big Ian [Paisley] walked away, people thought, fuck all of it. But there was something very, very important about that and they missed it all. Paisley knew – a sectarian bigot, you better believe it, responsible for hundreds of deaths, you better believe it. Stupid? Not a chance. He knew. He knew he had them right where he wanted them. They couldn't go anywhere in a political cul de sac. They couldn't go anywhere. They couldn't renege on stuff. And he had them and he says, 'Well, go ahead young Peter [Robinson]. You take the reins now and I'll keep a wee eye over you. Just

---

150 McGrattan, 2010, 10.

151 Wertsch, 2009, 131.

152 Hearty, 2016b.

153 'RSF: Leading the Struggle', *Saoirse*, 237 (January 2007); 'Easter Statement from Republican POW's Maghaberry Jail', *Saoirse*, 241 (May 2012).

154 Bryant, 2012, 171.

155 V, critic of Sinn Féin policy, interview, September 2013.

156 AC, critic of Sinn Féin policy, interview, November 2013.

> keep them in that corner and throw them an old bone now and again'. And Peter's doing that.[157]

The picture of the ideological consequences painted by the 'constitutional nationalist' model therefore stands in stark contrast to the 'progressive republican' model that depicts Irish unity as the inevitable conclusion to the current Sinn Féin strategy.

Conclusion

To be understood in wider ideological terms, 'critical engagement' cannot be divorced from its transitional context or the internal Irish republican politicking that conditions competing views of the transition. Ideology and memory intertwine to allow long-held belief systems to frame current policy choices through comparisons with past positions. For those subscribing to a 'progressive republican' model, memory centres on *continuity*; it provides continuity between the ideological goals sought using current strategy in the political struggle and those sought under past strategy during the armed struggle. In drawing this continuity, policing becomes a component of a wider strategy that has seen Irish republicanism adopt a tactical shift in order to meet the needs of the 'principle of success'. This has witnessed the evolution of 'progressive republicans' from 'rebel' to 'revolutionary'. Continuity offering ideological assurance is grounded in the retention of the goal being sought if not in the tactics being used to seek it. Others subscribe to a 'constitutional nationalist' reading of the transition that is premised on the gradual yet irreversible abandonment of Irish republican principles by those prepared to administer 'British rule' and endorse 'British policing'. 'Critical engagement' becomes the latest phase in a process that has consistently subverted republican principles. Memory enables the Sinn Féin strategy to be seen from this perspective in terms of rupture and continuity; as a rupturing with the ideological principles of Irish republicanism and the continuity of failed 'reform from within' strategies that have historically plagued Irish republicanism. Contestation has been fuelled by the historical failure of Irish republicanism to succinctly adopt a rigid ideological framework capable of ascertaining what is tactic and what is principle. This wider debate over principles and tactics has also allowed notions of continuity and rupture to frame contestation over the legacy of the dead who sacrificed themselves in the pursuit of ideological goals during the armed struggle.

[157] P, critic of Sinn Féin policy, interview, June 2013.

Competing hegemons who are vying for the same political space within Irish republicanism have sought to use the legacy of the armed struggle to legitimise their own reading of the transition in Northern Ireland and undermine that of their rivals. It is to a fuller exploration of this that the next chapter now turns.

Chapter 4

The Patriot Dead

Introduction

This chapter examines the curious case of how the memory of those killed by policing agents could later be used to advocate support for policing in the North of Ireland. Leading on from examination of ideological contestation on policing to which the dead are inextricably linked, it interrogates contending narratives on whether 'critical engagement' is in furtherance of or a contradiction of the ideological goals for which the Irish republican patriot dead sacrificed themselves. It investigates the main components of the policing narrative proffered by each side of the debate; 'critical engagement' being the extension of the courage shown by the patriot dead during armed struggle, or whether endorsement of policing represents a self-inflicted defeat of the goals for which the patriot dead sacrificed themselves. This is followed by an examination of the political utility of the patriot dead to competing 'memory entrepreneurs' that critically evaluates why each side attaches so much worth to the patriot dead and why they go to considerable lengths to distance them from intra-communal rivals.

Irish republican martyrology

Firmly ensconced in 'Irish republican theology',[1] the patriot dead are embedded in 'the language of sacred soil and the cult of the dead'.[2] The 'historical determinism' within Irish republicanism has seen the patriot dead provide a mandate to various Irish republican groupings, even if a mandate from the living evades them.[3] One can say without exaggeration that the patriot

[1] Arthur, 2007.

[2] Bean, 2012.

[3] Tonge, 2012.

dead are omnipresent in the memory politics of modern Irish republicanism. The 'cult of the dead' is, however, hardly exclusive to Irish republicanism. It has been indulged in by political actors the world over. Before turning attention to the Irish republican case study, it is pertinent to outline why the 'cult of the dead' has such a strong appeal.

Christ's position as the ultimate martyr who died for a greater 'cause' projects a latent divinity onto those who give themselves in furtherance of a political cause couched in Christian traditions of self-sacrifice.[4] Even those who die whilst engaging in violence bathe in this divinity that places them beyond reproach. Narratives of those killed in political conflict revolve around the selflessness of their sacrifice made for the greater good of the cause.[5] It is the selflessness of this sacrifice that sanctifies and legitimises their very cause.[6] The mere virtue of death places the fallen on a higher moral plain, thus purifying the cause they died for. In Irish republicanism, this manifests itself in collectively celebrated Pearsian ideals of self-sacrifice by the 'children of the nation' in the name of 'mother Ireland'. However, it is not only those who meet a violent end on the battlefield that hold importance to their constituencies. The value of Martin Luther King to African American 'memory entrepreneurs' demonstrates that even pacifists who die 'political' deaths become revered.[7] The mere fact that a death is political endows it with an inherent sense of 'commemorability' which 'memory entrepreneurs' with the requisite 'mnemonic capacity' can turn into collective memory.[8]

Death in the service of one's country 'assumes a moral grandeur' that little else can rival.[9] This generated a culture of 'martyrology' within Irish republicanism that has been used by republican elites to obtain sympathy for the republican cause within wider Nationalism.[10] It is the inherent ability of commemoration to construct collective identity through teaching the lessons of the past by using ritualism and symbolism that makes it so useful.[11] Collective identity can be fostered around the dead as they enable 'memory entrepreneurs' to tie local events and local martyrs to larger national events and the collective dead. The dead may be from a particular locality and community, yet at the same time they belong to a larger national collective. As such, they

4 O'Shaughnessy, 2004.

5 Cromer, 2004.

6 Grant, 2005.

7 Alderman, 2003.

8 Armstrong and Crage, 2006.

9 Anderson, 2006, 141.

10 Alonso, 2007, 81.

11 Fitzpatrick, 2001, 186.

transcend temporal barriers by continuing the struggle of past martyrs and showing the way for future martyrs.[12] The prevalence of the memory of Adem Jashari, 'The Legendary Commander' in Kosovo, is a case outside of the North of Ireland that demonstrates these points. Jashari's memory has been projected beyond the confines of the Prekaz region where he was killed into the collective Kosovar Albanian memory that ties him seamlessly with past Albanian heroes.[13] Likewise, muralisation of the dead in Gaza has served a similar purpose for Palestinians,[14] while competing ethno-nationalist master narratives in Bosnia link the local dead of recent conflicts to the memory of the antifascist Partisans and the collective memory of the Ottoman era.[15] Instructive examples from within Irish republicanism are the 'Loughgall Martyrs'[16] and the 1981 hunger strikers.[17]

The considerable value the dead hold for elites is indicated by how 'acts of blood sacrifice have their greatest significance through a kind of hidden "moral causation" that eventuates in the desired political outcome'.[18] That gunmen could have hidden moral value is indeed baffling on one level. However, within Irish republicanism the reality is, as Devine-Wright highlights, 'the status of historic figures as soldiers or freedom fighters idealise aggression and fighting, thus providing important legitimacy for those who are fighting in the present'.[19] This legitimating function takes on added significance because the dead 'can speak only through the tongues of present day interpreters'.[20] Though essentially casualties of a past conflict, the dead take on the role of inspiration, guiding and directing those pursuing the same objectives today. Nowhere has this been more obvious than in modern Irish republicanism. The ability of the dead to 'lead the way' is demonstrated through the assertion that 'republicans will always remember and honour those who struggled in the past to achieve our shared objectives. We do so not merely out of respect and admiration but also to learn about the present and to plan for the future'.[21] The importance of the patriot dead to the wider Irish republican constituency and rival hegemons within

---

[12] Di Lellio and Schwander-Sievers, 2006.

[13] Obucina, 2011.

[14] Rolston, 2014a.

[15] Moll, 2013.

[16] Hearty, 2017.

[17] Brown and Viggiani, 2010.

[18] Shanahan, 2009, 48.

[19] Devine-Wright, 2003, 22.

[20] Liu and Hilton, 2005.

[21] S. Mac Brádaigh, 'Remembering the Past, Looking to the Future', *Iris* (summer 2007).

that constituency cannot be underestimated. The patriot dead provide moral justification of the armed struggle, are useful in garnering political support, can help establish and solidify collective identities and, most importantly, they can be seen to posthumously endorse present strategies.[22] When present strategies differ within a single constituency contestation intensifies, making the memory of the dead a potent and deployable resource for competing elites.

The traditional dominance of the Provisional movement within Irish republicanism birthed 'a fervent rejection of any other political group's ability to represent the Nationalist community'.[23] As a consequence, they came to dominate commemoration of the patriot dead. Commemoration and 'Provisional politics' are infused, meaning that commemoration is as much orientated towards 'Provisional politics' as 'Provisional politics' is towards commemoration.[24] The centrality of commemorative rites to Sinn Féin's post-conflict memory politics is evident through their widespread use of murals, monuments, commemorative lectures and commemorative booklets to keep the memory of the dead 'alive' amongst their grassroots support. This feeds into the point made by Graham and Whelan that whilst commemoration acts as a reminder of the sacrifice of the fallen it 'is concerned too, with the need to establish Sinn Féin as the rightful heir to the legacy of Irish nationalism'.[25] The strength of the bonds between the memory of the patriot dead and Sinn Féin's political project has led McDowell to conclude that they are 'inexorably linked'.[26] Commemoration of the patriot dead has a political value whereby the 'performed memory of violence and sacrifice underlines a transformed politics' thus conveying to the republican support base that 'Provisional Republicanism is aware of its roots and remains true to them'.[27] The practical outworking of this can be seen in the following extract from a social media advertisement for a commemorative event for IRA volunteer Francis Jordan in South Armagh: 'People like Francis Jordan are the reason we all enjoy the rights we have today and it was their sacrifice that allows us to carry on the struggle for freedom peacefully and democratically. They went to war so later generations did not have to'.[28] Provisional commemorative dominance, however, stops just short of a monopoly of the patriot dead. Members of other groups died too

---

22 Hearty, 2017.

23 Wright, 1991, 126.

24 Brown and Viggiani, 2010, 225.

25 Graham and Whelan, 2007.

26 McDowell, 2007.

27 Brown and Viggiani, 2010, 229.

28 This advertisement appeared on the Newry Armagh Sinn Féin Twitter account in the run up to Jordan's 40th anniversary in June 2015.

and are commemorated by their organisations. Moreover, these groups also commemorate older collective heroes. For example, Belfast once hosted seven different Easter commemorations by multifarious Irish republican organisations.[29] During the centenary year, this mnemonic free-for-all became more apparent as 'memory entrepreneurs' of every hue staked their claim to the 1916 legacy. Commemorative events ranged from a hard-line commemoration in Coalisland, Co. Tyrone that called for the completion of the 'unfinished revolution' to state-sponsored events in Dublin attended by the President and Taoiseach.[30]

There is a distinct difference in how the memory of the dead features in narratives when a war has been 'won' and when it has not been 'won'.[31] In victory, the dead are hailed as the champions of a cause that was proved righteous only through their blood sacrifice. The victory enjoyed by the living is the eternal debt they owe to the dead. In defeat, the death of martyrs is a 'chosen trauma' that spurs future generations on to avenge the injustice of their deaths.[32] The inapplicability of either observation to the patriot dead speaks to the peculiarities of the position modern Irish republicanism finds itself in, being caught somewhere between victory and defeat depending on which perspective of the Northern Ireland transition one wishes to take. Neither militarily defeated nor militarily victorious when Irish republicans discontinued armed struggle, the dead of the most recent phase of conflict remain in a limbo-like state; their deaths facilitated a political process that has politically empowered Irish republicanism yet by the same token their military efforts did not drive the British Army into boats swiftly departing Belfast docks as initially thought.

It is from this very matter that the contestation inherent in post-conflict Irish republican memory politics stems. 'Progressive republicans' argue that Irish republicans are only in a strengthened political position today due to the sacrifices made by the dead during the armed struggle.[33] They argue that as republicans move forward politically they continue to be guided by the sacrifices of the patriot dead. They are working towards the goal that sacrifice was made in pursuit of, albeit in a different manner. For others, this new means has essentially become an 'end' rather than a 'means'. This 'end' falls short of that

[29] Bryce, 2013.

[30] 'The Main Easter Commemorations', *Irish Republican News*, 26 March 2016: http://republican-news.org/current/news/2016/03/the_main_easter_commemorations.html#.VxSPNzArLIU (accessed 18 April 2016).

[31] Nelson, 2003.

[32] Volkan, 1997.

[33] McLaughlin and Arthur, 2001.

which the patriot dead pursued. These groups who oppose policing – with the exception of the IRSP, whose members were keen to point out during interviews that unlike other Irish republican groupings they had no 'shared past' with the Provisional movement – are 'contesting a shared past' with Sinn Féin.[34] They invoke the memory of the same armed struggle and the same martyred dead to sanctify their opposition to Sinn Féin's current strategy. By contrast, the IRSP utilise the memory of the INLA dead rather than contesting the memory of IRA dead. They have, however, taken issue with the apparent expropriation of the INLA hunger strikers by Sinn Féin.[35] Rivalry of this nature reflects that seen in South Africa over who can legitimately claim the memory of Steve Biko and the Sharpeville massacre.[36] What was effectively an 'official memory' of the 1981 hunger strike, as ordained by Sinn Féin, has recently come under unprecedented internal challenge from a range of 'memory entrepreneurs' with varying agendas.[37]

With increasing division within Irish republicanism comes increased contestation over the memory of the patriot dead. No longer is there the unquestioning assumption that the dead actually died for what Sinn Féin say they died for. Those in disagreement with Sinn Féin are able to offer a different explanation of what the patriot dead died for and what their sacrifice means within contemporary Irish republicanism. Competing hegemons endeavour to carve a political genealogy that heralds these 'struggle heroes' as their ideological ancestors.[38] This tendency to latch on to 'struggle heroes' was also noted by Laleh Khalili in Palestine when she observed that hegemons vying over the memory of Izz al-Din al-Qassam:

> Chose to remember the martyr as it befitted their agenda and their ideology, analogizing the martyr's strategies with those of the current period and drawing conclusions on the basis of this analogy ... which legitimated the claims of the commemorating institution ... the organizations instrumentalized the martyr and the practice of remembering him.[39]

The 'malleability of memory' gives it an uncanny adaptability, meaning that 'struggle heroes' 'are evoked at various historical moments, places and contexts,

---

[34] Bean, 2012.

[35] 'New Patsy O'Hara Hunger Strike Mural Unveiled in Belfast', *IRSP*, 18 November 2013: www.irsp.ie/news/?p=1335 (accessed 6 August 2014).

[36] Marschall, 2006.

[37] Hopkins, 2014.

[38] Marschall, 2006.

[39] Khalili, 2007, 132.

by interested agents as reverential and referential models of a communicable past; they can be used both for and against the same institutions against which the martyr once struggled'.[40] In this context, the patriot dead become invaluable to both sides in the policing debate. What follows is an in-depth examination of their respective narratives; a narrative of continuity depicting policing as an extension of the sacrifice of the patriot dead and a narrative of rupture portraying it as the defeat of the goal for which the patriot dead gave their lives.

The extension of struggle

The greatest difficulty for those supporting policing lay in reconciling support for the PSNI with the sacrifice made by republicans fighting the police in the past. How, after all, can one pledge support for the same forces that comrades died fighting against a short time ago? This involved walking a mnemonic tightrope that required extreme dexterity lest a plunge to political suicide would result. This balancing act was not made easier by the natural apprehension over the move in areas that had suffered most at the hands of the security forces. Asking these families and communities to 'move on' and embrace policing as part of a larger strategy was a monumental task. The families of the patriot dead have always been important to the Irish republican collective. They have been central to republican commemoration as not only do they 'remember' the sacrifice as members of the Irish republican collective but they are also remembering members of their family.[41] They embody the interface between republican collective memory of suffering at losing a member of the wider collective and the individual memory of loss stemming from losing a loved one. Sinn Féin therefore engaged with the families of the dead in an effort to get them 'on board' with policing. In areas where the issue was particularly problematic, special meetings were convened for families to air their concerns and provisions made for them to attend the Ard Fheis.[42] At the Ard Fheis, special mention was made of the families of the patriot dead and the difficulty the move represented for them.[43] That such effort was expended by Sinn Féin indicates just how important a constituency the families are within Irish republicanism. They were likely to be the most hesitant group within the

---

40 DeSoucey, Pozner, Fields, Dobransky and Fine, 2008.

41 Dolan, 2003; Brown, 2011.

42 'SF to Meet with Families of "Fallen Comrades"', *Derry Journal*, 19 January 2007.

43 Opening Address by Gerry Adams, then President of Sinn Féin (SF), to the Sinn Féin Extraordinary Ard Fheis on Policing, RDS, Dublin (28 January 2007)'.

constituency and if they came 'on board' it was likely to persuade others to do so. Perhaps there was also an implied assumption that if the families came 'on board' this de facto meant that the patriot dead were 'on board' too.

The dead are immeasurably useful to elites in times of 'system transformation'.[44] They become a resource for reassuring doubters at grassroots levels and for anchoring the new direction of the present to the struggle of the past. The need for this on the policing issue is obvious. The move represented such a departure from the militant republicanism the dead had known that a link with this past was what 'the leadership' proposal would stand or fall on. Accordingly, the patriot dead were depicted as leading the way for the new political developments that were unfolding. These developments became the continuation of the war waged by the dead but by different means. This reflects how the Sinn Féin leadership habitually invokes the dead to 'sanctify current strategies' in a post-conflict setting.[45] The irony of this is, as Rolston notes, that the party and its current strategy are 'very different' from that which the patriot dead would have known.[46] Despite this, 'the dead are woven into an advancing and evolving narrative of struggle where the "chosen destination" of past IRA volunteers and a republicanism now embarked on a peace strategy are the same'.[47] In this context, memory becomes more than simply commemorating the dead. Rather, it involves placing them in a 'meaningful' post-conflict narrative.[48] There is a distinct difference between 'remembering' and narration in this sense. While individuals can 'remember', it is only political elites that can place these memories in carefully constructed collective narratives. The patriot dead subsequently became actors in a protracted conflict narrative that led to the political project of Sinn Féin.

Constructing the narrative

The opportunity to write the patriot dead into this master narrative arose in the weeks prior to the Extraordinary Ard Fheis, first at the annual commemoration of two republican icons killed in a Border Campaign assault on Brookeborough RUC barracks and then at a commemorative event in Crossmaglen.[49] At the first event, Gerry Adams acknowledged the quagmire that policing represented,

44 Brown, 2009a.

45 Patterson, 2011, 81.

46 Rolston, 2010.

47 Brown, 2009a.

48 Zaretsky, 2009.

49 'Policing: Transfer of Powers Would be Advance for Struggle', *An Phoblacht*, 4 January 2007; 'Seamus Harvey 30th Anniversary', *An Phoblacht*, 25 January 2007.

noting that republicans were 'very aware of the irony' of commemorating those killed in an attack on an RUC barracks in the middle of a debate on accepting policing. There was, however, 'no contradiction' in promoting republican acceptance of policing while honouring those who died physically resisting the RUC.[50] For Adams, there was 'no contradiction' because he intertwined the narrative of the Brookeborough raid with that of the 'political struggle' Sinn Féin was currently engaged in; both were risky, both moved the republican cause forward and both were necessary. To this end, Adams exhorted: 'like all republican initiatives, it is risky. The Brookeborough raid was risky. Struggle of any kind is risky. We should remember that those who want to maximise change, must be prepared to take the greatest risks'.[51] Confronting policing in the new 'political struggle' was depicted as a bold move that required the same courage and tenacity that those who died had shown when taking up arms. Failure to confront policing would be a grave disservice to the sacrifice that the fallen had made:

> Republicans have never lacked courage. The courage to take up arms like Séan and Fergal in their time, and countless other men and women in our own time. The courage to confront injustice and discrimination. The courage to seize an opportunity for peace. The courage to take risks and at all times to move forward.[52]

Policing therefore represented an extension not a repudiation of past armed struggle. It was the means through which the ideals of those who died during the conflict would come to be realisable. This point was reinforced by Adams in Crossmaglen when he told republicans that while strategy changed their objectives remained the same as those of the fallen:

> The policing debate is the most challenging and difficult we have yet faced. But ... let us also keep our eye firmly fixed on the big prize – the prize of unity and independence. Because everything we do is about taking us one step closer to that goal ... I believe if we advance together, united behind

[50] Quoted in Chris Thornton, 'Adams Backs PSNI as he Honours IRA Men', *Belfast Telegraph*, 2 January 2007.

[51] 'Speech by Gerry Adams, then President of Sinn Féin, at an Event to Commemorate Seán Sabhat and Feargal Ó hAnnluain, County Fermanagh, 1 January 2007': http://cain.ulst.ac.uk/issues/politics/docs/sf/ga010107.htm (accessed 10 May 2012).

[52] 'Speech by Gerry Adams, then President of Sinn Féin, at an Event to Commemorate Seán Sabhat and Feargal Ó hAnnluain, County Fermanagh, 1 January 2007'.

> our republican goals, we will win our freedom and build the united Ireland for which Seamus Harvey and his comrades gave their lives.[53]

It is important to bear in mind McEvoy and Conway's point that 'an act of commemoration is more than a straightforward process of remembrance'.[54] Indeed, the commemorative events helped reinforce 'the leadership' position as much as paying homage to those being commemorated. These commemorations were the platform on which Adams' performances reinforced the pro-policing position, reassured doubters at grassroots level and issued a rallying call for togetherness during a time of difficulty. They laid the foundations for a narrative bestowing the courage of the dead onto those who were now continuing past struggle politically, thus using the dead to tie two markedly different strategies to a common end goal.

The extension of struggle narrative was further constructed by the prevalence of the patriot dead in the consultation process Sinn Féin rolled out across the six counties. Constructing a pro-policing narrative around the sacrifice and courage of the dead was an 'important tactic' during this process.[55] Like countless other political elites elsewhere,[56] the Sinn Féin leadership used the dead for the purposes of 'clarification' and 'inspiration'. This was necessitated by open recognition from Martin McGuinness that some republicans had difficulty in understanding what accepting policing would 'mean' for the republican dead. In response to criticism for 'selling out' the patriot dead, he argued, 'I could have been one of the republican dead in the past. Many of my friends are the republican dead ... but I don't call them to support my case'.[57] If others relied on 'knowing' how the dead would view policing, then the former IRA commander in Derry was not prepared to do the same. This reflects how Sinn Féin avoided specifically stating that the dead would have accepted policing, instead preferring to depict the move as an extension of the armed struggle they had waged. What opponents stated with absolute clarity in support of their case, Sinn Féin implied through constructing a narrative that depicted policing as an extension of past struggle. It would be incredibly difficult, after all, to assert with utmost certainty that someone who died firing a gun at the RUC would some years later come to endorse the successor force of the same RUC. Linking current strategy with past strategy via an overarching master

---

53 'Seamus Harvey 30th Anniversary', *An Phoblacht*, 25 January 2007.

54 McEvoy and Conway, 2004.

55 Brown, 2009a.

56 Schwartz, 1996.

57 Quoted in W. Graham, 'McGuinness Admits Sinn Féin is Playing for "Big Stakes" on Policing', *Irish News*, 16 January 2007.

narrative cleverly implied as much without making such a bold public assertion of support from the patriot dead. This reflects how political elites will use memory to reduce opposition to proposed political changes by making the changes appear consistent with the activities of their forebears.[58]

In contextualising this reality, one interviewee drew on their personal circumstances to argue:

> I've family members; one of them was the patriot dead. I don't know what he would think if he was alive. I don't know if he would have supported it or wouldn't have supported it so I can't say that he would support it. But when he died, he died as an IRA volunteer and it's the same IRA constitutionally that have moved onto the ground that we are on.[59]

Others picked up on the point that the IRA that the patriot dead belonged to had moved as an overall organisation to support the current Sinn Féin strategy:

> Well, the problem with all that is that all those comrades are dead and you can't really second guess – it's impossible to second guess what anyone would do. All that I can say is that the vast majority of the guys who were active at the period ... they have stayed on the path and have stayed true to the republican leadership.[60]

This line of reasoning adopts a 'weight of numbers' argument to provide a neat corporate transfer of past armed struggle into current political struggle.[61] The logic of this is that there is an implicit belief that the patriot dead would support policing. This enables former combatants to not only 'keep the faith' with the dead but also buffers them from the criticism of intra-communal rivals that allege a 'sell out' of the patriot dead.

The counter-narrative of self-inflicted defeat

While Sinn Féin busied themselves convincing their support base that the move was not injurious to the integrity of the patriot dead, those opposed began countering this argument. They were, of course, in the much easier position of being able to rely on the fact that republicans had always militarily opposed

---

[58] Bodnar, 1992, 247.

[59] B, supporter of Sinn Féin policy, interview, April 2013.

[60] A, supporter of Sinn Féin policy, interview, April 2013.

[61] Hearty, 2016b.

rather than endorsed policing. No 'outside the box' thinking was required to convey the merits of their argument. Simply put, the republican position on policing had to, if the sacrifice of the dead was not to be dishonoured, remain the same as it was when that sacrifice was made. This counter-narrative defined 'critical engagement' not as the extension of the patriot dead's armed struggle but rather as the self-inflicted defeat of it.

The thrust of the counter-narrative was that endorsing a Northern Irish police force as part of a political settlement was not what the patriot dead had sacrificed themselves for. It was argued that those sacrifices were being wilfully, yet treacherously, traded by Sinn Féin for something falling drastically short of the republican objectives they were made in pursuit of. Adhering to a traditional ideological standpoint, these republicans asserted that policing and a political settlement were not what motivated Irish women and men to take up arms. Their ultimate prize was reunification to be gained through violent resistance not governing in Stormont or overseeing policing reform. This recurring criticism appeared at many crucial junctures throughout the peace process. For example, Bernadette Sands-McKevitt once famously proclaimed that, 'Bobby [Sands] did not die for cross-border bodies with executive powers. He did not die for Nationalists to be equal citizens within the Northern Ireland state'.[62] One anti-policing republican invoked the same counter-narrative when resigning from Sinn Féin on the policing issue: 'people did not die, they did not take up arms for equality. They did so for Irish freedom ... it should be remembered that, as republicans, we were committed to fight on until Britain made a declaration of intent to withdraw from Ireland'.[63] This has remarkable resonance with the analysis of one interviewee who dismissed the Sinn Féin 'extension of struggle' narrative by asserting:

> If that's the level of depth of their analysis then the people who have died in the last 30 years fighting in the IRA and upholding the sovereignty of the nation were led to believe they were fighting for something then they must have been used by that leadership that have accepted much less.[64]

These republicans are correct when they state that the patriot dead did not die with these outcomes in mind. What their counter-narrative fails to acknowledge, however, is that these outcomes were virtually unthinkable during the conflict. The vastly changed political landscape of contemporary

---

[62] Quoted in Tonge, 2004.

[63] Brian Arthurs, quoted in S. McKay, 'People Did Not Die or Take Up Arms for Equality: They Did So for Freedom', *Tribune*, 24 October 2010.

[64] R, critic of Sinn Féin policy, interview, July 2013.

Northern Ireland made these events possible, with the effect that many who had fought alongside the patriot dead have come to accept, encourage and endorse these moves. Simplistically arguing that 'this is not what the dead died for' conveniently overlooks this crucially important contextual matter.

Constructing the counter-narrative

Like Sinn Féin, the anti-policing lobby utilised republican commemorative culture to their advantage. RSF used the anniversary of the Brookeborough raid to reinforce their position on policing and in the process, dismiss as perfidious treachery that of Sinn Féin. The event was used to construct the counter-narrative by highlighting the obvious differences in armed resistance to policing agents and political endorsement of the same agents. Sinn Féin's use of the event to promote policing was criticised on the basis that 'Sean South did not die to reform the RUC nor to take part in overseeing the police. He died in the cause of Irish freedom ... the latest moves by Martin McGuinness and those around him to recognise the police is akin to siding with the force that killed Sean South'.[65] Further scathing criticism dismissed Sinn Féin's commemoration of the men as 'nothing more than an act of defilement to the memory of these men'. If Adams could not see any contradiction in voicing support for the PSNI while commemorating the patriot dead, this outraged republican could, venting 'not only is there massive contradiction but there is hypocrisy, treachery, deceit and downright brass neck'.[66] Another noted that having fallen in action against the RUC it was difficult to conceive of the men 'joining the ranks of the enemy – donning a peeler's coat – and siding with them in the inevitable confrontation with former comrades'.[67] This commemorative event provided a platform for the counter-narrative to argue that policing was not an extension of the armed struggle of the dead as the two men did not die endorsing policing but attacking the RUC. If anything, the counter-narrative contends, those endorsing policing are aiding the defeat of the goals of the patriot dead through contrived betrayal of the principles on which past armed struggle was fought. The counter-narrative, as fashioned above, moved beyond merely placing distance between the patriot dead and Sinn Féin by

[65] Des Long, quoted in S. Breen, 'Sinn Féin Told to Stay Away from South's Grave', *Sunday Tribune*, 31 December 2006.

[66] Mick McManus, quoted in 'Sean Sabhat 50th Anniversary Marked in Limerick', *Saoirse*, 237 (January 2007).

[67] Ruairi O' Bradaigh, quoted in 'Neither Ó hAnluain or Sabhat Would Follow "A Path of Deceit, Duplicity and Treachery over 20 Years"', *Saoirse*, 238 (February 2007).

implying that endorsing policing was more than just dishonouring the patriot dead; it became a process of siding with those who killed them.

In a bid to further strengthen their counter-narrative, anti-policing republicans used their public meetings to put as much distance as they could between the patriot dead and the proposals of the Sinn Féin leadership. Supporters were told that accepting policing was a 'sell out' that could not be dressed up as an ideological advancement of the aspirations of the patriot dead. Addressing the obvious ideological quandary of supporting the police when republicans had suffered and died at the hands of such a force, one critic told supporters that accepting policing would have the effect of retrospectively 'dishonouring and criminalising' those who died for Irish freedom.[68] Given the reverence the patriot dead are afforded by Irish republicans, such a claim generated foreseeable unease with and distaste for the move.

As the mnemonic debate over the patriot dead intensified, some families bought into the counter-narrative by openly questioning whether their loved ones would have supported the move. In Derry, a number of families broke ranks publicly to oppose the move.[69] One family stated their opposition was grounded in the belief that 'if Sinn Féin support the RUC/PSNI then not only will the ideals of our volunteers remain unfulfilled they will be reversed'.[70] The mother of one of the iconic hunger strikers went so far as to state that Sinn Féin had 'sold out' to the establishment. In a damning indictment of the Sinn Féin proposal she asserted that 'if they [the hunger strikers] had known that the struggle would end in support of the police they would not have thought it worthwhile'.[71] It became evident that the families of the patriot dead were just as divided on the matter as other sections of the republican constituency. Anti-policing republicans were just as able – and willing – to call on the support of certain families to bolster their position as Sinn Féin was. The brother of Fergal O'Hanlon, for instance, aligned with critics, arguing that the acceptance of policing was 'a betrayal' of the cause for which his brother had died.[72] There

---

[68] Francie Mackey, quoted in 'Dissidents Roar "No, No, No" to SF Policing Plans', *Derry Journal*, 19 January 2007.

[69] 'IRA Man's Family Accuse SF Leaders of "Dishonesty"', *Derry Journal*, 16 January 2007.

[70] McBrearty family statement, cited in 'IRA Man's Family Accuse SF Leaders of "Dishonesty"'.

[71] Peggy O'Hara, quoted in O. Bowcott, 'The 76-Year-Old Dissident Taking on Sinn Féin', *Guardian*, 1 March 2007: www.theguardian.com/politics/2007/mar/01/uk.northernireland1 (accessed 17 May 2017).

[72] Quoted in 'Neither Ó hAnluain or Sabhat Would Follow "A Path of Deceit, Duplicity and Treachery over 20 Years"'.

was no unanimity on the matter amongst the O'Hanlon family. O'Hanlon's sister and cousin were prominent members of Sinn Féin who had been present at the Sinn Féin event some days earlier.[73] This indicates just how divisive the policing issue actually was. As a consequence of familial division, not only can no one state categorically how the dead would have viewed events but little clarity can be gleaned from the considerable disagreement amongst their closest relatives who have taken opposing sides in the debate.

A growing gulf between Sinn Féin and families opposed to the move came to public prominence. Despite engaging with the families of the patriot dead during the consultation process, some families felt that they were not properly briefed on the matter by the Sinn Féin leadership.[74] Matters came to a head following one peculiar exchange at a public meeting in Galbally, Co. Tyrone. In a bizarre outburst, Gerry Adams attacked a rival by asking him if the dead had contacted him through a Ouija board to express their disapproval on the policing matter. The remarks created a media furore and were criticised by families in Derry, causing Adams to make a rather ignominious climbdown on the verge of the Ard Fheis to apologise for the remarks.[75] Several points are noteworthy about this. Primarily, its shows the raw emotion involved in the debate. Secondly, that the families forced someone of Adams' prominence into a public retreat speaks volumes about just how powerful a constituency they are. To slight the families is akin to dishonouring the patriot dead. Such a constituency are invaluable to competing 'memory entrepreneurs' when onside and a formidable foe when in opposition. An acute awareness of this probably contributed to Adams' decision to apologise.

The disconnect between Sinn Féin and certain families has grown in recent years, with interviewees highlighting the case of families withdrawing their support from Sinn Féin in East Tyrone. As a consequence, 'independent republican' commemorations convened by the 1916 societies in conjunction with the families now compete with Sinn Féin commemorations in the area. In the aftermath of mass resignations from Sinn Féin, the 1916 societies emerged as the localised guardians of the memory of the patriot dead in East Tyrone that would prevent the Sinn Féin leadership from misusing it.[76] According to interviewees, these independent republican events have come to dwarf those of Sinn Féin. In contrasting the sizeable Sinn Féin vote in the area with the

[73] 'Policing: Transfer of Powers Would be Advance for Struggle', *An Phoblacht*, 4 January 2007.

[74] 'IRA Man's Family Accuse SF Leaders of "Dishonesty"', *Derry Journal*, 16 January 2007.

[75] 'Adams Apologises to Volunteer's Families', *Derry Journal*, 26 January 2007.

[76] Hearty, 2017.

dwindling attendance at their commemorations, one interviewee argued that it evidences how 'those currently voting for Sinn Féin are not republican, they never supported the IRA or the armed struggle and as witnessed at the Sinn Féin commemorations they don't support its legacy'.[77] This analysis, in suggesting that there is irreconcilable difference between the current Sinn Féin strategy and the armed struggle of the past, challenges the very foundation of the 'extension of struggle' narrative.

Contestation continues

Mnemonic contestation of the patriot dead rumbled on following the Extraordinary Ard Fheis. With assembly elections called as a result of the decision, Sinn Féin faced anti-policing candidates that included relatives of the patriot dead.[78] As it transpired, Sinn Féin easily saw off this anti-policing challenge in the March 2007 elections, going on to entrench its position further as the largest Nationalist party in the North of Ireland. The results of these elections led to the restoration of devolved institutions in May 2007, coinciding with the twentieth anniversary of eight IRA members killed by the Special Air Service (SAS) at Loughgall. This further fuelled mnemonic contestation. For critics, it demonstrated just how far removed Sinn Féin was from the 'Loughgall martyrs', but for Sinn Féin, they were continuing the Loughgall fight via different means.[79] Sinn Féin re-entering Stormont at such a time was derided as a 'shameful act', and further criticised as 'akin to the Provo's dancing on the coffins of dead men. In fact their pathway to political power is littered with dead bodies of men and women who believed in the unity of Ireland and the all-Ireland republic proclaimed in 1916'.[80] Mnemonic contestation along this vein continued to simmer in the background before reaching fever pitch following successful attacks by anti-policing militarists against the British Army and PSNI in March 2009.[81] Two British Army sappers were killed in a Real IRA gun attack on Massereene Army Barracks in Co. Antrim on 7 March, before PSNI officer Stephen Carroll was shot dead by the Continuity IRA in Craigavon, Co. Armagh two days later. Having unstintingly supported armed struggle in the past and having many senior members that had formerly engaged

[77] Z, critic of Sinn Féin policy, interview, October 2013.

[78] Bowcott, 'The 76-Year-Old Dissident Taking on Sinn Féin'.

[79] Hearty, 2017.

[80] 'Sharing Power with DUP a "Shameful Act"', *Saoirse*, 240 (April 2007).

[81] Michael Lea and Sam Greenhill, 'Fury as Adams says British Special Forces Provided Pizza Delivery Murders of Unarmed Soldiers', *Daily Mail*, 9 March 2009.

in such activity, the attacks threw up a quagmire for Sinn Féin. Condemnation would present the difficulty of having to distinguish between past violence and current violence. Nonetheless, the Sinn Féin position was to argue that past acts were different from current attacks. This allowed them to protect the integrity of past armed struggle on the one hand, whilst condemning current activity by militant rivals on the other hand. This has been their default position on the matter ever since.

Rupture or continuity

A narrative depicting armed attacks as a *rupture* with the IRA of the past was moulded out of increasing condemnation that depicted those attacking policing agents as different from the IRA that had fought during the conflict. The logical implication of such reasoning was that their violence was also different from IRA violence during the conflict. Gerry Adams remarked that anti-policing militants 'are not the IRA – the IRA has left the stage'.[82] Admittedly, this discourse existed prior to the 2009 attacks. It was discernible even during the policing debate when Adams argued that 'there is only one IRA, and that's the one which fought the British for a very long time'.[83] However, the 2009 attacks amplified such criticism due to the increased need to broadcast its core message that current militants were not the IRA and that, as a result, their violence was neither acceptable nor justified. This was echoed in protests that 'the Irish Republican Army leadership and volunteers have long since declared that the war is over ... the tiny splinter groups that carry out these attacks are pursuing a militarist agenda primarily designed to justify their own existence and perpetuate their own factions'.[84] A growing sense of resentment towards those claiming *continuity* with the IRA of the past can be detected through Martin McGuinness's protest that 'I was a member of the IRA but that war is over now. The people responsible ... are clearly signalling that they want to restart that war. They do not have the right to do that'.[85]

With militants going on to kill another PSNI officer (Ronan Kerr) in April 2011 and two prison officers (David Black in November 2012 and Adrian Ismay in March 2016), this line of argument has remained constant in Sinn Féin discourse on current violence. For example, Adams told those assembled

---

[82] Quoted in 'Gerry Adams Lays Down Challenge to Killers – I'll Meet You Any Time', *An Phoblacht*, 14 April 2011.

[83] 'CIRA Says No to Adams Invitation', BBC News, 26 January 2007.

[84] Caoimhin O' Caoláin, quoted in L. Friel, 'Peace Process Under Attack', *An Phoblacht*, 12 March 2009.

[85] Quoted in L. Friel, 'Peace Process Under Attack'.

at a 2015 hunger strike commemoration in Dundalk that 'none of the many alphabet groups that now claim the proud name of the Irish Republican Army have a right to that title'.[86] According to this rationale, when the IRA stood down in July 2005 it took the justification for, and legacy of, armed struggle with it. This legacy was then passed via corporate transfer to Sinn Féin as the latter-day political inheritors of that struggle. This overarching notion of corporate transfer has also been used outside of internal memory politics to buffer against allegations of post-2005 IRA activity. Senior Sinn Féin member Bobby Storey dismissed media allegations of IRA culpability for the shooting of Kevin McGuigan, arguing 'the IRA is gone. The IRA is stood down, they have put their arms beyond use, they have left the stage, they're away and they are not coming back. So there is no current status of the IRA. There are no IRA members. The IRA has gone'.[87] Basically, this argument contends that any current violence, whether that is attacks on the PSNI or the work of maverick elements, cannot be the deeds of an organisation that has since retired itself.

The thrust of this narrative has percolated down from elite level to grassroots level, where former combatants have used it to frame their own understanding of current armed activity and how it differs from the armed campaign they fought. They have drawn on macro-level criticisms about the scale, absence of support for and motivation of current militant activity, many of which were, ironically enough, once levelled at their own campaign.[88] Their differentiation encompassed many strands of argument, including that current militants will never have 'the experience and the machine that the IRA were able to put together',[89] are 'a tiny minority' with 'virtually no influence in this area'[90] and are motivated by nefarious personal and 'securocrat' agendas rather than by ideology.[91] Varying degrees of empathy were, however, expressed for former comrades who had a 'genuine' difficulty with the transition. Contrasting these disaffected republicans with current militants engaged in status seeking, one interviewee noted:

---

[86] 'Sinn Féin's Gerry Adams says IRA "Has Gone Away"', BBC News, 23 August 2015: www.bbc.co.uk/news/uk-northern-ireland-politics-34033753 (accessed 23 August 2015).

[87] G. Moriarty, 'Bobby Storey: The IRA is "Stood Down" and has Left the Stage', *Irish Times,* 13 September 2015: www.irishtimes.com/news/ireland/irish-news/bobby-storey-the-ira-is-stood-down-and-has-left-stage-1.2350112 (accessed 10 November 2015).

[88] Hearty, 2016b.

[89] A, supporter of Sinn Féin policy, interview, April 2013.

[90] AD, supporter of Sinn Féin policy, interview, July 2013.

[91] B, supporter of Sinn Féin policy, interview, April 2013.

> I'll take criticism – positive criticism – from anybody who has come through it [armed struggle] and who has an issue. Of course. Absolutely. They've invested as much as anybody else and they are quite entitled to make points and criticise. But what I don't do is take criticism from people who have played no role in the conflict, who have played no role in delivering for our communities and are basically naysayers who for one reason or another find themselves in where they are at the moment. Either that's from a security agenda being put there or they feel the need to run about the community as some sort of hard man or whatever it might be. I don't know, but I take none of their criticisms for it.[92]

The upshot of this is a clear separation between the campaign fought by former combatants and current armed activity. By extension of this, then, current activity can also be seen to differ from the armed struggle carried out by the patriot dead in the past. Accordingly, current militants are seen as little more than misguided or criminal pretenders unable to lay claim and unworthy of laying claim to the legacy of 30 years of sacrifice and hard-fought armed struggle.[93]

The differentiation inherent in the Sinn Féin argument allows them not only to criticise current armed activity but to go one step further and call for the community to help the PSNI curtail it. The most emphatic manifestation of this was when Martin McGuinness labelled the killers of PSNI Constable Stephen Carroll 'traitors' to the Irish people and urged republicans to 'wholeheartedly weigh in' behind the PSNI investigation.[94] In calling for co-operation with the PSNI, McGuinness was clearly seeking to draw a succinct line between 'acceptable' and 'legitimate' armed struggle of the past and 'unacceptable' and 'illegitimate' armed activity in the present. Despite encouragement to furnish the PSNI with details relating to militant activity, 'informing' still remains a spectre of the past within the wider Irish republican community. Not only has this been conceded by the PSNI[95] but it has also been acknowledged by supporters of Sinn Féin who disagree with current militant activity.

---

[92] B, supporter of Sinn Féin policy, interview, April 2013.

[93] Hearty, 2016b.

[94] Quoted in D. McKittrick, 'The Investigation: Two Arrested as Sinn Féin Brands Gunmen "Traitors"', *Independent*, 11 March 2009: www.independent.co.uk/news/uk/crime/the-investigation-two-arrested-as-sinn-fein-brands-gunmen-traitors-1642090.html (accessed 17 May 2017).

[95] V. Kearney, 'Dissident Republicans: PSNI Say They Have Thwarted Murder Bids', BBC News, 11 March 2016: www.bbc.co.uk/news/uk-northern-ireland-35787273 (accessed 18 April 2016).

One interviewee referred to an 'inherent element' within Irish republicanism that 'it's just not what you do', but cautioned, 'that shouldn't be mistaken as support for them groupings'.[96] One 'mild sceptic' encapsulated the anomaly that such calls had for former combatants, frankly conceding that 'for me personally, I would never encourage anybody to do that against somebody that would lift a gun for Irish freedom. I just wouldn't go down that road'.[97] This sentiment validates the view proffered by one anti-policing republican who argued that for most Irish republicans 'deep down they know that being an informer is an informer regardless of what generation you are in. You know some people say, "oh everything changes". Well everything changes but some things stay the same and I think that people are well aware of what that is'.[98] Thus, despite clear indication from Sinn Féin that co-operating with the PSNI on matters relating to militant activity is now acceptable, and despite differentiating between 'acceptable' and 'unacceptable' armed struggle, it appears that the stigmatisation around informing remains prevalent in the Irish republican psyche. Moreover, a residual physical threat does remain given that militant groups have continued to kill people – primarily their own members – for alleged informing.[99]

The Sinn Féin narrative of rupture has not gone unchallenged by those engaged in or supportive of current armed activity. A counter-narrative of continuity depicting current attacks as no different from those conducted by the IRA during the conflict has emerged. The logic of this being that if attacks against policing agents in the past were justifiable then attacks in the present must be justifiable too. Present attacks are placed in a historical context of generations of armed resistance, meaning that any criticism of current attacks would equate criticism of attacks carried out by the patriot dead during past armed struggle. While Sinn Féin criticised militant attacks as the work of those out of vogue with post-conflict political development in the North of Ireland, those opposed to policing referred to them as 'the lessons of Irish history … that as long as the British Government and British occupation troops remain in Ireland there will be Irish people to oppose their presence here'.[100] This

[96] B, supporter of Sinn Féin policy, interview, April 2013.

[97] L, supporter of Sinn Féin policy, interview, June 2013.

[98] AC, critic of Sinn Féin policy, interview, November 2013.

[99] 'Man Shot in Donegal Named Locally as 27-Year-Old Andrew Burns from Strabane', *Independent*, 13 February 2008; 'Real IRA Murder Victim Kieran Doherty is Buried', BBC News, 1 March 2010: http://news.bbc.co.uk/1/hi/northern_ireland/foyle_and_west/8543145.stm (accessed 20 March 2015).

[100] Ruairi O'Bradaigh, quoted in D. Gordon, 'Republican Sinn Féin Links Soldier Murders to "British Occupation"', *Belfast Telegraph*, 9 March 2009.

reflects a 'root causes' understanding of Irish republican violence that sees it as a natural consequence of continued failure to address the core issue that birthed it in the first instance.[101] Likewise, in refusing to condemn a November 2014 mortar attack on a PSNI patrol car in Creggan, Councillor Gary Donnelly of the 32CSM likened it to past violence before noting, 'Sinn Féin have not condemned the PIRA and have representatives who carried out violence'.[102] So, although pro-policing republicans differentiate between 'acceptable' attacks on the RUC and similar but nonetheless 'unacceptable' strikes against the PSNI, anti-policing groups do not subscribe to such a skewed reading of the policing script.

For one opponent, Sinn Féin criticism of current activity is an attempt to 'jealously protect' the legacy of the armed struggle in order to fend off anyone challenging their hegemony.[103] Another dismissed the 'traitors' remark by reducing it to 'an ownership thing'.[104] Hanley notes that those who have continued armed activity after larger sections of republicanism have embraced constitutional means have always faced criticism in relation to their tactics, motives, 'war records' and level of support.[105] This was touched on by one interviewee who noted that the criticism that current militants were motivated by self gain and had not fought the 'war' was 'as old as the hills', having been fallaciously used by the pro-treaty forces during the Civil War.[106] But the counter-narrative of continuity has become more than a purely defensive rhetorical device for anti-policing republicans. It has strategic agency and purpose through its ability to challenge the Sinn Féin claim to the legacy of the armed struggle. This has seen a corporate-transfer-based argument countered by a moralistic argument premised on a 'root causes' understanding. This is particularly noticeable in the response of imprisoned republicans in Maghaberry to Sinn Féin's attempt via the 'traitors' remarks:

> To renounce the right to wage war against the British, whilst falsely claiming the name Óglaigh na hÉireann. Adams and Co. do not own the rights to the Irish Republican Army, and we can assure them that the IRA

---

[101] Blackbourn, 2009.

[102] 'Gary Donnelly: Independent Councillor Refuses to Condemn Bomb Attack on PSNI', *Derry Journal*, 4 November 2014: www.derryjournal.com/news/gary-donnelly-independent-councillor-refuses-to-condemn-bomb-attack-on-psni-1-6396244 (accessed 20 March 2015).

[103] AA, critic of Sinn Féin policy, interview, October 2013.

[104] AC, critic of Sinn Féin policy, interview, November 2013.

[105] Hanley, 2003.

[106] AA, critic of Sinn Féin policy, interview, October 2013.

> remains alive and well and will continue to bring the fight to the British invaders.[107]

Criticism of the 'traitors' remark was not confined to those supportive of armed struggle. Many interviewees who disagreed with Sinn Féin and with current armed struggle – albeit the latter being from a 'tactical' rather than a 'moral' perspective[108] – also challenged the remark. Noting an apparent hypocrisy given that Sinn Féin commemorates those who did the same in the past, one interviewee opined:

> It's a strange comment from the man because if the same act is something in the 70s it's not something else in 2013. Yeah, political circumstances change ... but it doesn't change from for a united Ireland to actively working against it, because that there is what the connotation of 'traitor' is.[109]

Moreover, whilst those who have accepted policing may 'forget' that many of the criticisms they now level at opponents were once levelled at them, this is precisely what others 'remember'. In noting the Sinn Féin attitude towards 'dissenting republicans', it was argued that:

> The people in 'harrumph house' [Stormont] were very proud in the '70s, '80s and '90s to say to the likes of you in an interview, 'Oh yes, I'm a dissenter in the pure tradition of Theobald Wolfe Tone'. But now you're a micro group. Well, when they started they only had 10 or 12 members. You've no support. They had no support. No one wants you. You know, you hear all this and it's like rewinding back to 1970/71.[110]

Evidently, then, the IRA name and legacy remain a rich resource within modern Irish republicanism. Successfully building continuity with the IRA of the past, or, conversely, successfully differentiating one's opponents from the IRA of the past enables hegemons to speak with a moral authority gleaned from those who had 'gone before' into the arena of battle. Paradoxically, it allows one lobby to differentiate between current attacks and remarkably similar attacks carried out in the past whilst simultaneously allowing the other lobby to buffer themselves from the criticism heaped on them by those

---

107 'Statement from Republican POW's, Maghaberry Jail', *Saoirse*, June 2009.

108 J, critic of Sinn Féin policy, interview, June 2013.

109 V, critic of Sinn Féin policy, interview, September 2013.

110 P, critic of Sinn Féin policy, interview, June 2013.

now endorsing policing. This is demonstrative that, as Bean remarks, the IRA name is 'a legitimating memory worth fighting over'.[111]

While simplistic competing narratives of rupture and continuity can usefully demonstrate the intricacies of internal disagreement, they nonetheless expose the insularity of Irish republicanism's views on its own violence and epitomise its failure at times to locate itself within a changed global environment.[112] To this end, the internally constructed difference/sameness axis can be usefully evaluated against external discourses proffered by the British state and the Irish–American diaspora. The events of 9/11 and the subsequent 'war on terror' has impacted more generally on global interpretations of the use of political violence.[113] Increased revulsion at the destruction and bloodshed that accompanies political violence has created an intolerance that has left current militants facing 'perhaps the most unfavourable climate ever for the physical force tradition'.[114] Irish republican political violence has not been immune to the post-9/11 rethink on the 'morality of terrorism'.[115] An interesting discourse on where it fits into this framework has emerged. Although the UK has always endured a threat of political violence in the Irish context, the modern focus on the threat of 'international terrorism' has seen the latter labelled a greater and more bloody threat than the former due to its deliberate mass targeting of civilians.[116] The implication of this would be that the IRA campaign on the British mainland was a 'lesser evil' than the current activities of jihadi fundamentalists. This conclusion has even seen a differentiation being made between both forms of violence by a decorated British Army war hero.[117] Indeed, the approach of the Blair government both rhetorically and legislatively, through the failed Northern Ireland Offences Bill, defeated in the Commons in 2005, was to differentiate clearly between the two.[118] The thrust of this differentiation is directed at historical Irish political violence and less, it seems, at current militant activity. The changing nature of anti-terror legislation suggests that any differentiation is premised only on distinguishing *past* Irish political violence, rather than current militant activity, from 'new terrorism'. The shifting

[111] Bean 2007a, 127.

[112] Hearty, 2016b.

[113] Rolston, 2006a.

[114] Tonge, 2004.

[115] Shanahan, 2009, 5.

[116] Bamford, 2004.

[117] 'IRA Not Like ISIS as Cardinal Claimed Says British Army Hero', 7 March 2015: www.irishcentral.com/news/IRA-not-like-ISIS-as-cardinal-claimed-says-British-Army-hero.html (accessed 20 March 2015).

[118] Blackbourn, 2009.

parameters of anti-terror legislation from the specific to the general means that those engaged in political violence in the Irish context are being combated under the same legislation as those involved in 'new terrorism'.[119] Moreover, MI5 'terrorism' risk assessments frequently cite threats from Irish republicans along with threats from jihadi fundamentalist groups. This is suggestive that if prevailing state discourse on 'terrorism' differentiates between Irish political violence and that of 'new terrorism' it applies only to past instances given that anti-terror legislation does not treat current Irish republican activity any differently from 'new terrorism'.

The same applies to changed attitudes among the Irish-American diaspora. Their traditional view of Irish republican violence was couched in the romanticism of a struggle for national liberation. Armed struggle enjoyed favourable interpretations in light of violent political struggle against apartheid in South Africa and against Western imperialism in Vietnam. It was interpreted and presented in simple black-and-white terms as a struggle against injustice, not only by overtly republican support groups like Noraid,[120] but also, in the early years of the conflict, by leading Irish-American politicians.[121] The events of 9/11, in tandem with the development of the peace process, heralded significant changes in attitudes towards support for and financing of Irish republican violence. After 9/11, Irish-American support moved away from armed struggle waged for a British withdrawal to favour instead full implementation of the GFA and republican commitment to constitutional politics.[122] Thus, despite there being virtually no substantive difference between the aims and methodology of current and past armed struggle, external discourses offer succour to the pro-policing argument that current militant activity is somehow different from previous armed struggle. This is unlikely, however, to register any significant change to the ideological self-justification espoused by current militants who rely on ideological purity and 'root causes' arguments to assuage any criticism, whether that be internal or external.

Analysing Irish republican memory entrepreneurship

Contestation over the patriot dead revolves around the fact that no one can categorically state how they would view contemporary political developments. There is no doubting the accuracy of this simple fact, yet it has not prevented

[119] Bamford, 2004.

[120] Cochrane, 2007a.

[121] Cochrane, 2007b.

[122] Tonge, 2004.

rival hegemons from making a deluge of claims about the patriot dead. One critic argued that to claim that the patriot dead would support current strategy 'is to take a liberty where none was granted ... it is to steal a sacrifice and put it in a place other than its rightful one'.[123] Although there is merit in this argument, there is no recognition that the same applies to arguments that they would have definitely rejected current strategy. It may appear somewhat macabre or perhaps just plain frivolous to an onlooker to claim that a dead person would view events in a particular way, yet this is essentially the crux of mnemonic contestation over the patriot dead.

To fully appreciate this point it is necessary to critically examine the role of the competing sides as 'memory entrepreneurs' and to establish why the patriot dead are invaluable in this regard. Before such an examination it is vital to acknowledge that the role of 'memory entrepreneurs' is not simply to create shared references to the past but also to regulate how the past is used and by whom it is used.[124] To a certain degree, their role is to monopolise the past in furtherance of a particular agenda. The mechanics of this becomes evident upon examination of the battle between competing 'memory entrepreneurs' within contemporary Irish republicanism.

Pro-policing memory entrepreneurship

On an obvious level, using the memory of those who engaged in armed resistance to the state and its policing agents represents a quandary for the pro-policing lobby. However, the reality remains that they had to use the patriot dead to sell their position to the grassroots. There are two reasons for this. First, the armed campaign of the past has been of such centrality to the depiction of the Sinn Féin strategy as another 'step' along the winding road to victory that it cannot be suddenly dropped. If 'memory entrepreneurs' do not use the memory of past armed struggle and the patriot dead the only other option is to 'forget' it. The centrality of this memory to keeping the grassroots on board and the more general importance of the patriot dead to the wider Irish republican collective largely precludes Sinn Féin from enforcing an 'overt silence' that 'forgets' this 'difficult past'.[125] Rather than 'forget' the armed struggle, Sinn Féin engages in memory entrepreneurship through a process highlighted by Griffin and Bollen whereby the past is used in a way that relates to the questions and challenges faced by the collective in the present.[126] The courage of the dead in the past is

---

123 McIntyre, 2008b, 113.

124 Abou-Assi, 2011.

125 Vinitzky-Seroussi and Tegger, 2010.

126 Griffin and Bollen, 2009.

passed on to those critically engaging with policing. The armed struggle of the dead against policing agents becomes the political struggle of those critically engaging with policing. This reflects how the image of the dead and what they died 'for' changes in tandem with the political needs of elites.[127] During the conflict, the memory of 'men of war' was needed to rally support for the cause, but post-conflict this need transforms into the need to convey the patriot dead as visionaries with the foresight that the fighting would eventually give way to politics.[128]

Secondly, if Sinn Féin does not 'remember' the patriot dead this essentially forfeits a powerful political resource to their rivals. If rivals seize the mantle of the past uncontested they can unilaterally speak with a mandate from the dead. This mandate has echoed for hundreds of years and echoes most voluminously at grassroots level. 'Memory entrepreneurs' therefore 'remember' not simply so as to prevent 'forgetting' but also for the hegemonic purpose of keeping a powerful resource from rivals.[129]

Anti-policing memory entrepreneurship

The anti-policing lobby, for their part, are constrained by having to share the 'contested space' of the past with Sinn Féin. By necessity they have to use the same martyrs, the same armed struggle and the same past as Sinn Féin. The campaign of anti-policing militarists has not reached the level of IRA violence prior to the ceasefires. They do not have a rich tapestry of martyrs who died post-ceasefire that they can call upon to sanctify their current campaign. Anti-policing 'memory entrepreneurs' are constrained by the fact that, as argued by Majstorovic, emotional symbols and heroes that form the basis of collective memory cannot be created out of nothing and must have some basis in the experienced past.[130] In the absence of a tailor-made hero that suits a current agenda unquestioningly, 'memory entrepreneurs' are forced to write older collective heroes into the collective memory in a way that adheres to their current political agenda. For example, the African American civil rights movement had to rely on the memory of Abraham Lincoln before the memory of Martin Luther King and Malcolm X became available to them.[131] Rather than being able to utilise the memory of those who definitely died in opposition to the GFA and policing (i.e. someone killed on 'active service'

[127] Schwartz, 1997.

[128] Hearty, 2017.

[129] Abou-Assi, 2011.

[130] Majstorovic, 1997.

[131] Sandage, 1993.

post-GFA and post-policing), they are forced into a mnemonic battle with Sinn Féin over what it is that the patriot dead of past armed struggle fought and died for. Interestingly, opponents of policing have begun commemorating deceased veteran republicans who had 'fought the war' and opposed the current Sinn Féin strategy.[132] With this comes the implicit assumption that these critics of Sinn Féin who have plugged the martyr gap had a mandate from the patriot dead they had fought alongside. However, the prominent role in Sinn Féin commemoration bestowed upon former combatants who were active, arrested or imprisoned with the venerated dead[133] demonstrates that implications of support by association cut both ways. If Irish republican memory entrepreneurs cannot proffer an unquestioning and irrefutable endorsement of current strategies from the patriot dead, they can invoke the blessing of what is seemingly the next best thing – their comrades in arms and/or their families.

In this context, memory contestation is not over what happened per se – no one contests that there was an armed struggle– but over the *meaning* of what happened in the past. As Hodgkin and Radstone articulate, 'contestation, then, is very often not conflicting accounts of what actually happened in the past so much as the question of who are or what is entitled to speak for that past in the present'.[134] Essentially, the memory of the dead becomes reduced to the fact that 'the dead are supposed to have died for the same reason as what the survivors think that they have died for'.[135] In such an ambiguous environment clarity vanishes as contestation thrives. If memory politics is, as Boyarin defines it,[136] 'rhetoric about the past mobilised for political purposes', then memory contestation between competing Irish republican 'memory entrepreneurs' can be regarded as an apposite microcosm to examine intra-communal memory politics more generally.

---

[132] 'Commemoration Honours "Forgotten" Volunteer', *Examiner,* 26 June 2012; 'Commemoration for Volunteer Kevin "Kiddo" Murray', *Sovereign Nation* (January/February 2007).

[133] 'Anniversary Marked in Queen's and UCD', *An Phoblacht,* 13 March 2008; 'Oglach Seamus McElwain 25th Anniversary Commemoration', 14 April 2011: http://ograshinnfein.blogspot.co.uk/2011/04/oglach-seamus-mcelwain-25th-anniversary.html (accessed 6 August 2014); 'Camloch Hunger Striker Remembered on 30th Anniversary of his Death', *Examiner,* 17 May 2011.

[134] Hodgkin and Radstone, 2003, 9.

[135] Kattago, 2009.

[136] Boyarin, 1994.

Conclusion

The patriot dead were at the heart of the memory politics that underpinned the Irish republican debate on policing. Being a venerated sect within the Irish republican constituency, their memory was heavily drawn upon by 'memory entrepreneurs' on both sides of the debate. Pro-policing republicans claimed that the patriot dead had fought the hard battle that paved the way for the struggle to be continued through peaceful means, whilst their anti-policing counterparts claimed that endorsing policing was siding with the very forces that sent these women and men to their graves. Commemorative events quickly took on increased political meaning, as they became battlegrounds for competing elites to 'sell' their position to grassroots supporters and to build that all-important link with those who had made the ultimate sacrifice in pursuit of the republican ideal of a sovereign Irish republic. They also became the ideal ground to identify with the families and comrades of the patriot dead, thus sealing their approval for current positions. The prominence of the patriot dead in the wider policing debate reflects not only their importance within Irish republicanism, but also the general importance that war dead have to political elites and hegemons across the globe. Although it is impossible to state with any clarity how the patriot dead would view events that transpired after their deaths, this has not stopped elites from attempting to do so, whether this be through the building of new narratives that link present political developments with past armed struggle or through overlooking the vastly differing political contexts in existence today as opposed to when those past sacrifices were made. What remains constant, however, is the overarching premise of sacrifice that competing Irish republican narratives converge on. While these are collectively celebrated in performative and ritualistic commemorations of the martyred dead, they can also underpin prevailing narratives of victimhood and suffering at the hands of the state that pose challenges for post-conflict 'moving on' agendas. This matter is examined in the following chapter.

Chapter 5

Transition, 'Never Again' and 'Moving On'

Introduction

This chapter critically examines how individual and collective memories of human rights abuses impacted on Irish republicans during the policing debate. In doing so, it examines the value that 'remembering' past abuses has for those constructing a politicised 'never again' mantra out of past experiences. This has seen increasing emphasis placed on accountability mechanisms and a belief that 'critical engagement' can prevent the repetition of past abuse through republican involvement in these bodies. Although this notion has been contested by Irish republican critics who continue to reject policing, those who have embraced 'critical engagement' have frontloaded aspects of accountability and human rights protection that stand in contrast to the policing of the past. In the absence of wholesale 'forgetting' of past human rights abuse, the chapter examines how individuals 'move on' in the aftermath of such abuse to engage in a new 'working relationship' with policing agents. Examination then turns to the issue of truth recovery. This leads to a more general discussion on perceptions of 'victimhood' within transitional Northern Ireland, where 'official' conflict narratives have largely excluded the Irish republican policing experience.

Human rights abuses

Conflicts are characterised by human rights abuses perpetrated by all parties involved. The North of Ireland was no exception. When examining the memory of past harm, one must remain cognisant of the fact that while Irish republicans suffered human rights abuses they also inflicted them. As such, they represent the collective 'victim–perpetrator'.[1] Given that conflict narratives silence 'in-group' wrongdoing, the memories recounted in this chapter generally lack reciprocity of Irish republican human rights abuses beyond a general acceptance of collective wrongdoing on a somewhat abstract level. This is premised largely on the fallibility of the combatant and the fact that all 'sides' commit wrongs during 'war'. The 'memory of perpetrators', on the other hand, means British state human rights violations are amplified in individual and collective accounts. The master narrative constructed through interview data is largely inward-looking in terms of recognition of suffering rather than commission of harms. This is not to diminish the gravity of human rights violations foisted upon Irish republicans by the state; these were manifold and of considerable severity.[2] Despite state prevarication and denial, international and domestic court rulings against the state in relation to the right to life, the treatment of detainees, interrogation centres and interrogation practices moved republican grievances beyond mere allegation.[3] Such abuse was not confined to certain individuals or locations or temporal limits but became the collective republican policing experience. This reflects the collectivised nature of Kitsonian counter-insurgency that believed polluting the 'water' through collective punishment and wide-scale human rights abuses would defeat the 'fish'. When recounting individual experiences of brutality during interrogation, house raids and daily harassment, interviewees were able to locate these within the collective experience by referencing similar experiences of family and friends. Personal narratives become subsumed into the collective past, as the fabrics of autobiographical and collective memory become interwoven in what Brockmeier labels the 'manifold layers' of memory.[4] This interaction reveals how memory is 'knowledge about oneself' both as an individual and as a member of the collective.[5] The 'intricate and recursive connection' between the autobiographical and collective means that while personal memories of human rights violations are 'embodied' in the individual, they are 'embedded' in the larger social context of collective experience.[6] When human rights violations

---

[1] Hearty, 2014.

[2] Human Rights Watch, 1992; Amnesty International, 1978.

[3] For rulings on these matters, see *McCann* v. *UK* (1995) 21 EHRR 97; *Jordan* v. *UK* (2003) 37 EHRR 2; *Kelly and others* v. *United Kingdom* (ECtHR, App. 30054/96, Judgment of 4 May 2001); *Ireland* v. *UK* (1978) 2 EHRR 25; *R.* v. *Brophy* [1980] 4 NIJB 66 (CC); *R.* v. *Flynn and Leonard* [1972] May NIJB 112, 131.

[4] Brockmeier, 2002.

[5] Assmann, 2008, 114.

[6] Van Dijck, 2006.

are remembered, they are thus 'remembered' as an individual sufferer and a member of the suffering collective.

In ethno-nationalist conflict, suffering transcends the individual level to become a group matter,[7] allowing 'suspect community' policing to naturally tie individual memories of police abuse to widespread human rights abuse experienced by the collective. Narratives of suffering can thus become collectively relevant. An instructive example of a narrative of collective suffering is lynching narratives related by the African American collective in the 'deep South' where the localised nature of memory helps the individual to 'remember' as part of a localised group.[8] In the North of Ireland, the locality of memory can also influence how and what the individual 'remembers', with Eilish Rooney highlighting the interaction between her personal memories of the conflict and localised events in West Belfast.[9] This localisation of memory bridges the gap between individual and familial memories and those of the wider collective. It is particularly notable when individuals 'remember' as members of a community that has experienced exceptionally high levels of violence, as in Ardoyne,[10] or as members of a minority community in a certain area, as in the case of border Protestants.[11] When narrating past suffering, the collective terms 'we' and 'us' replace the individual 'I' and 'me'.[12]

In an environment of collectivised suffering the physical manifestations of what Nora calls 'sites of memory' take on added importance.[13] This is especially so if the site is readily identifiable with collective suffering. Sites synonymous with torture, disappearance and murder such as the Higher School of Mechanics of the Navy (ESMA) in Argentina[14] and Villa Grimaldi in Chile[15] can themselves assume mnemonic agency. For Irish republicans, Long Kesh prison[16] and Castlereagh and Gough barracks interrogation centres have assumed a similar centrality in collective memory. These sites were mentioned by different interviewees when discussing memories of human rights abuse in a way that contextualised their own experiences within the confines of those of

7 Bar-Tal, 2003.

8 Rogers, 1999.

9 Rooney, 2000.

10 Ardoyne Commemoration Project, 2002.

11 Patterson, 2010.

12 Pennebaker and Gonzales, 2009, 191.

13 Nora, 1989.

14 Davis, 2013.

15 Hite, Collins and Joignant, 2013.

16 Aguiar, 2015.

the wider collective. Consider the following account of one interviewee's 'first-hand experience' of a detention centre:

> I got hit over the head ... with a Yellow Pages book – which sounds sort of funny, but if you're in a sitting position and you're 16 years of age and a guy in his late forties, 6' 2", heavily built, comes flying at you with an implement like that – across the back of the head, kicks to the shins, sleep deprivation, lack of food, lack of water and lack of washing facilities. Locked up, sort of, in between, as they call interview sessions. So, I mean it was brutal but not as brutal as some that went before or came after me.[17]

What is immediately discernible is that not only does the interviewee 'remember' their ordeal in sufficient detail but easily places it into a wider experience of those who suffered the same treatment before and after they did. The assertion that this was 'not as brutal' as that experienced by those that 'went before or came after' is borne out by interview data from other interviewees who recalled more severe brutalisation.

When examining wide-scale harassment in retrospect, it is difficult to fathom the enormity of how it became an accepted part of daily life. Living in an environment where this defined rather than disrupted everyday life represents a tense existence. Whilst some interviewees reflected on traumatic experiences, others retrospectively examined the 'black humour' in past experiences. The recalcitrance that birthed this 'black humour' was seen as a means of survival in an otherwise difficult environment:

> It was maybe more for your own sanity when you think of it now. It was a kind of a mechanism you put in there, you know, to keep yourself safe. If you didn't laugh at it you could have been swinging from the trees, really, because to put it into context today, there was nothing humorous about guns, you know, held at gun point, you know the threats of being killed, the threats of being brought to Gough barracks for seven days' detainment.[18]

The prevalence of memories of human rights abuse and the ease with which they are recalled in remarkable detail demonstrates that these memories have not been 'forgotten'. Indeed, the fundamental question is not if they are 'remembered' but rather if it is even possible to 'forget' them. This poses the further problem of the impact they have on 'moving on' processes. It is simply

---

[17] P, critic of Sinn Féin policy, interview, June 2013.

[18] AB, critic of Sinn Féin policy, interview, October 2013.

natural that memories of human rights abuse should be 'remembered', even if more mundane memories have been 'forgotten'. Some memories are 'remembered' precisely because of the impact they had on a person's life and their sense of identity.[19] The memories of human rights abuse related by interviewees were not only traumatic on a personal level – considering that many took place at a young age – but also at the collective level in that they fed into their identity as the 'other' in a state that deemed them 'fair game' for repressive policing. The impact such traumatic incidents had at the individual level is seen in the fact that they are 'inscribed and re-inscribed into everyday narratives'.[20] Likewise, for collectives that have endured the horrors of conflict, there is no luxury of determining whether to 'remember' or not – remembering is a reality not a choice.[21] So, while 'forgiveness' and 'moving on' may be subject to human control, 'forgetting' is not.[22] At the individual level and at the collective level, memories of policing continue to revolve around the 'memory of offence' – defined as memories of past injustice that 'refuse to let the past go'.[23]

Interview data demonstrates just how pressing the 'memory of offence' remains at the individual level. Referring to a traumatic episode of prolonged torture they endured during interrogation, one interviewee effortlessly listed off the names of the RUC officers involved before concluding that 'even though that's a long, long time ago I'll still remember their names to the day I die'. Evaluating the difficulty this created in terms of accepting policing at the personal level, they argued, 'I don't think anybody should look at me and say, "well he's a man of the past that man", because I definitely wouldn't be. I wouldn't want anybody to experience what I experienced'.[24] In recalling an exceptionally harrowing event they had witnessed, another interviewee said that they could 'still see' the 'hatred' on the faces of the RUC personnel involved. Accepting that people like this might still be involved in policing was 'difficult' for the interviewee.[25] When it comes to individual memories of policing, Sartre's aphorism, that 'our victims know us by their scars and their chains, and it is this that makes their evidence irrefutable', rings true.[26]

Evidently, then, 'memories of offence' remain prevalent at the individual level. It is logical that this becomes an obstacle to 'moving on' with policing.

---

[19] Gaskell and Wright, 1997, 177.

[20] Edkins, 2003, 15.

[21] Lundy and McGovern, 2008b, 32.

[22] Amadiume and An-Na'im, 2000, 7.

[23] Bevernage, 2010.

[24] L, supporter of Sinn Féin policy, interview, June 2013.

[25] U, supporter of Sinn Féin policy, interview, August 2013.

[26] Sartre, 1967, 12.

The latter interviewee captured this difficulty, conceding that although one may come 'intellectually' to accept that endorsing policing 'needs to happen', it does not lessen how one has 'emotional' memories of policing.[27] If such 'emotional' memories cannot be 'forgotten' how does one who has suffered at the individual and collective level attempt to 'move on'?

'Moving on'

Prior to examining the 'moving on' process that some Irish republicans have embarked on, it is necessary to firstly examine what that term means. In transitional justice lexicon 'moving on' refers to the process of societal movement from violent conflict to peaceful co-existence to eventual reconciliation.[28] This creates an environment of 'positive peace' which is more than the mere absence of violent conflict ('negative peace').[29] Examples of this conventional 'moving on' include the 'rainbow nation' of South Africa (residual difficulty aside),[30] Chile[31] and Colombia,[32] where survivors, victims, former combatants and perpetrators live side by side. Of course, just because the process has happened – or is happening – does not lessen the inherent difficulty of it.

It would be disingenuous to suggest that this type of 'moving on' has characterised Irish republican engagement with policing. Structural and political factors preclude this. First, Northern Ireland remains segregated along ethno-nationalist lines – particularly so in working-class localities where resources are scarce and contested rather than 'shared' as in more-affluent 'mixed' areas.[33] Consequently, former RUC officers do not live in working-class neighbourhoods populated by former republican combatants. Instead of enjoying 'positive peace', the glass ceiling stops at 'negative peace'. This represents 'moving on' from violent conflict into an environment of 'not war not peace'.[34] This leads neatly to the second factor, which is that the dynamic of conflict in the six counties and those conflicts witnessing a fuller 'moving on' process vary markedly. In South Africa and Chile, the crux of the matter was the nature of those states rather than the existence of those states. In the

---

27 U, supporter of Sinn Féin policy, interview, August 2013.

28 Buckley-Zistel, 2009.

29 Galtung, 1967.

30 Meskell, 2010.

31 Hite and Collins, 2009.

32 Prieto, 2012.

33 Shirlow, 2012.

34 Sluka, 2009.

six counties, from the republican perspective, the issue was the very existence of the Northern Ireland state. Thus, despite accepting the GFA and endorsing policing the Irish republican objective remains dismantling that state in the long term. In such a context, one can question if a more conventional form of 'moving on' is at all possible. Interviewees who endorse policing pointed out that this endorsement was tempered largely by the fact that it serves their ideological goal of dismantling the state and by the general socio-economic reality that their community 'needs' a police force. Memory is fused with strategy, meaning that endorsement is 'critical' and 'strategic' rather than one of wholesale acceptance. When reference is made to Irish republicans 'moving on' with policing it is not movement in a 'positive peace' sense, but rather in a 'negative peace' sense from historical hostility into a new 'working relationship' – or, as McEvoy and Shirlow label it, 'moving out of conflict'.[35]

However, the fact that this is 'moving into' a new 'working relationship' rather than 'moving on' with former enemies per se does not lessen personal difficulty. Many interviewees who have accepted policing at the macro level struggle to accept it personally at the individual level. Even limited 'moving on', such as entering into a new 'working relationship', entails engagement with former enemies responsible for wrongs inflicted on the collective and individual levels. As outlined above, these wrongs are never 'forgotten'; thus, those who enter the new 'working relationship' must find a way of dealing with them.

Dealing with such a difficult past is – in the words of those who have endorsed policing – to think 'strategically' about the issue. This involves thinking in collective terms rather than individualising the issue and mirrors a similar thought process adopted by pro-policing interviewees in relation to ideology. 'Strategic' and 'critical' seemed to operate as much-used bywords for subverting individual difficulty to the 'common good'. The process of not individualising the issue entails concentrating on the future collective 'end goal' rather than on the difficult personal past. Elaborating on the tension between 'remembering' past abuse and 'moving on' in order to suit ideological and community needs, one interviewee argued:

> I understand people having an issue with policing. I have issues with policing. I'll always have issues with policing. There isn't a time or a day that you're not looking at elements of stuff that's going on within the issue of policing and not remembering back to what they're about. But ... you need to be understanding your own politics and what you're about. If you

[35] McEvoy and Shirlow, 2009.

> don't have a strategy then you'll always sit in the house and criticise, but if you've a clear strategy and understanding of what's required, where you want to be, then you know what has to happen. And some of that is hard.[36]

Not everyone has been able to relegate past personal experiences to a secondary position. Referring to the 'difficult debates' and 'difficult conversations' involving such people, one interviewee conceded that 'some people just didn't buy into it and still don't. I understand that. I respect that. These people have suffered, you know, and maybe just can't get over that. Maybe time will help that'.[37] For those struggling to see past individual memories of suffering, even buying into a critical or strategic 'working relationship' is difficult; there is friction instead of interaction between autobiographical memory and collective memory, while difficult personal pasts and a narrative of wider strategic thinking repel rather than intertwine. The violence of the past is, after all, 'highly personalised' in autobiographical memory, making it prone to dissonance with macro-level 'moving on' discourses[38] – whether premised on reconciliation or strategic thinking.

Those who have 'moved into' a new 'working relationship' have married their own perception of 'moving on' with their ideological view of policing being a vehicle to reach ideological goals. They have 'moved into' 'critical engagement' after accepting that engagement would be 'critical' and 'strategic', thus subverting any difficulty they had on a personal level to the fact that a *critical* engagement was premised on the provision of 'proper' policing, whilst a *strategic* engagement represented another means of progressively dismantling the Northern Ireland state. This nonetheless involves engaging with people they were once trying to kill and vice versa. This has not precluded former combatants 'moving on' to engage on a professional level even if there is little bonhomie on an interpersonal level. This entails acceptance of the 'others'' past without repudiating one's own past, to allow community 'needs' to be met in the present. Elaborating on this balancing act, one former combatant commented:

> The district commander for this area, you know, I know his background. He knows my background. But that's it. You know, you have to park that and get on with the job, or else you don't park it and then we just become bogged down in recrimination and all of that, and you know you're certainly going nowhere.[39]

---

36 B, supporter of Sinn Féin policy, interview, April 2013.

37 I, supporter of Sinn Féin policy, interview, May 2013.

38 Buckley-Zistel, 2013, 140.

39 AD, supporter of Sinn Féin policy, interview, July 2013.

If residual difficulty at the interpersonal level nevertheless persists, it is likely to be mutual, with the above interviewee opining, 'I'm in no doubt that some of the people I speak to you know they would have reasons to not want to necessarily sit in a pub with me having a pint'. The emphasis on not 'having a pint' with former enemies mirrors a wider pattern noted by Shirlow and McEvoy whereby engagement with former enemies is largely limited to areas of mutual concern, such as tackling interface violence or lobbying on former prisoner rights, rather than on an informal social basis.[40] The fact this represents 'moving on' with a purpose enabled those who have taken the step into engaging with policing to approach the issue in a manner similar to other post-conflict engagements with the prison administration, the British government, Unionism and loyalists.

The above should not suggest that there has been *no* reappraisal of attitudes at the interpersonal level. Some interviewees reported something of a thawing in their initial attitudes towards the policing agents they were now interacting with. Whilst this was gradual and tentative, it was nonetheless progress at the interpersonal level:

> I remember my first engagement with the PSNI and there was some there who just sat growling at us, yawning, shaking their heads, hanging back in their seats. They were so rude and arrogant it was unbelievable ... One of them who was particularly nasty at the beginning of the day came over to me at the end of the day and he says, 'Well, I suppose my attitude's changed a bit'. He says, 'But I'm willing to listen'. And I said to him – here's me to him – 'Well, that's good, that's movement'. And here's me, 'I'm willing to listen too'. Here's me, 'But if you ever see me in [place] don't talk to me', because I wasn't ready to move that further either. And neither was he.[41]

Thus, even though the personal animosity had lessened and there was a willingness 'to listen', the interviewee and the PSNI officer had yet to reach the position of 'moving on' to converse openly outside the realms of policing oversight bodies. Although the republican engagement remains 'critical' and 'strategic' and although 'moving into' a new 'working relationship' has not seen the type of 'moving on' seen elsewhere, there has nonetheless been some reappraisal at the interpersonal level. While they may not be reconciled – and one can question if there can ever be reconciliation when republicans and policing never enjoyed conciliation in the first place – both parties are certainly

---

[40] Shirlow and McEvoy, 2008.

[41] G, supporter of Sinn Féin policy, interview, May 2013.

interacting in a new manner. To this end, one former combatant admitted, 'I never thought that I would see the day I'd be sitting in the room with police and having a civil conversation. You know, instead of "no comment" as in Castlereagh'.[42]

Never again

For Irish republicans who have 'moved into' the new 'working relationship' with policing, one way of dealing with past abuses was to find a positive rather than destructive use for such memories. In doing so, the notions of 'remembering' and revenge are logically decoupled.[43] To this end, a 'never again' mantra was constructed around memories of past human rights abuse. The basic crux of the 'never again' mantra is that transitioning societies should not 'forget' difficult pasts for the sake of present or future political expedience.[44] The moral obligation to 'remember' past wrongdoing supersedes any self-serving 'forgetting'.[45] Memory assumes a positive rather than a destructive role in transitioning societies by contributing to future change,[46] hopefully through creating a new culture of human rights that precludes repetition of past wrongs. If past human rights violations are not 'remembered', they will not have been learnt from.[47] The premise of this argument expands beyond the Northern Ireland context and is evident in transitioning societies as diverse as Latin America, South Africa and Rwanda.[48] While these transitions may be diverse and have experienced considerably different scales and forms of harm, what remains constant is the inherent usability of memory and the penchant of collectives for using it in this way.

Engaging memory of past abuses

The centrality of the 'never again' mantra to the Sinn Féin discourse mirrors its heavy emphasis on bringing accountability to policing. As well as representing ideological advancement towards reunification, Sinn Féin argued that 'critical engagement' would allow republicans to 'put manners' on the

[42] F, supporter of Sinn Féin policy, interview, May 2013.

[43] Assmann, 2008, 219.

[44] Crocker, 1999.

[45] Andrews, 2003.

[46] Lundy and McGovern, 2008c.

[47] Streich, 2002.

[48] Lemarchand, 2008; Hamber, 2007.

PSNI.[49] 'Putting manners' on the PSNI would involve entering policing oversight bodies to ensure that past human rights violations do not occur again. One republican at the time of the debate argued that 'republicans inside the North's policing institutions will ensure that never again will citizens' lives be endangered by those empowered to protect them'.[50] Another argued that policing was a 'challenging issue' precisely because 'we don't want anyone, ever again to experience the type of political policing we have had'.[51] In a mnemonically charged plea for support for the Ard Fheis motion, one senior republican told delegates that:

> There are many in this hall who have suffered either directly or indirectly from the unaccountable, partisan political policing of the past. I personally know how sore those wounds are and I know how they can grip us like a vice, trapping us to forever live in the past. Our pain is real and we have felt it but I ask each and every delegate here today to think and act strategically to ensure that never again do our communities suffer from unaccountable, partisan, political policing.[52]

Rather than trying to enforce 'forgetting' of this problematic past, Sinn Féin showcased it as a reason why republicans should accept endorsement. With the wider collective and individuals failing to 'forget' past abuses, the value of 'remembering' them, so their logic ran, lay in making sure they are consigned to the past.

The 'never again' mantra gained increasing traction at grassroots level. Several interviewees who now engage with policing recognise that whilst they have not 'forgotten' past abuse, they can use the memory of such abuse within oversight bodies to ensure it is not repeated. That this is difficult is not contested but personal difficulty is offset against the collective benefit of guarding against future repetition. Evaluating the tension between this personal difficulty and the benefits of effecting change from within one interviewee commented:

---

[49] Gerry Adams, quoted in 'CIRA Says No to Adams Invitation', BBC News, 26 January 2007.

[50] J. Gibney, 'First Step to Accountable Policing is Support', *Irish News*, 25 January 2007.

[51] Catriona Ruane, quoted in E. O'Dwyer, 'Speakers Exude Confidence and Stress Need for Unity', *An Phoblacht*, 1 February 2007.

[52] S. Murray, 'Address to Extraordinary Ard Fheis', 28 January 2007: Northern Ireland Political Collection, Linenhall Library, Belfast.

> There's hundreds and thousands of families and activists who could easily sit back and say, 'There's not a chance of me taking on or supporting this issue of policing because of my experience'. I don't think there is one republican family in the occupied six counties at that stage couldn't have done that. Every family could've done that. All of us have those levels of experience from harassment to particular deaths within the family as a result of the RUC in collusion with the loyalists. But that wasn't what we were about. We're about bringing about change, we're about tackling the issues very much head on and that meant going in and making the changes that need to be made.[53]

Another interviewee who sits on an oversight body similarly opined:

> I know people have an awful lot of memories ... I don't think you automatically have to forget your memories. I really don't think people have to forget the collusion and the murders and the beatings and the torture of people you know, because that's what makes us all what we are, you know. But I think if you're involved in community at all you have to use that. You have to use that to change it and to make it better, and while I would still remember a lot of those things – and there's things that I'll never forget from my personal family never mind the wider community – I think we have to keep moving forward to strive for a better police force. And that's what it's about, you know.[54]

Those who have 'moved into' a new 'working relationship' with policing agents thus subscribe to Brown's notion of 'memory as warning' whereby 'remembering' past abuses can preclude future repetition.[55]

Challenging the mantra

Simply saying 'never again' does not in itself automatically preclude past abuse reoccurring. The growth of genocide in the twentieth century is testament to this. The horrors of the Turkish genocide of the Armenians did not stop the horrors of the Holocaust, which in turn failed to prevent later genocide in Rwanda.[56] Likewise, recent conflicts in Africa can be traced back to colonialism and the slave trade, which questions why the memory of slaughter during

[53] B, supporter of Sinn Féin policy, interview, April 2013.

[54] G, supporter of Sinn Féin policy, interview, May 2013.

[55] Brown, 2013.

[56] Hirsch, 1995, 2.

colonialism did not stop similar slaughter following decolonisation.[57] Instead, it is imperative that contentious issues are identified openly, frankly discussed and appropriate preventative measures put in place to avoid repetition. 'Remembering to prevent' strategies only have enforceability if they are accompanied by a bureaucratic system of accountability capable of discouraging repetition through increased sanctions for human rights violations.[58] Whether taking seats on policing accountability bodies represents Sinn Féin lip service to or practical implementation of the 'never again' aspiration remains an issue of contention.

For those who have embraced the new 'working relationship', their very presence on policing bodies means they can implement their 'never again' mantra in real terms. The fact that one can enter a body that was once opposed and effect reform is not in itself a preposterous notion. Werner Fischer the former East German 'dissident' was tasked with disbanding the Stasi.[59] Moreover, former ANC operatives entered the policing institutions in South Africa to effect reform – something 'critical engagers' argue they can emulate.[60] This is contrasted with the impunity of the past, where the Police Authority of Northern Ireland (PANI) was toothless in holding the RUC to account for human rights violations. O'Rawe argues that rather than holding the RUC to account, the PANI construed its role as defending the force in the face of criticism.[61] To all intents and purposes, claims of policing abuse were essentially investigated by the RUC themselves.[62] This is contrasted with the current accountability mechanisms where republicans – according to those undertaking 'critical engagement' – can effectively force the PSNI to 'account themselves to us'.[63] The success of republicans in doing this is evident in the fact that, 'they are more uncomfortable being there than I am'[64] and that it is a 'new arrangement that I'd say they're a lot more unhappy with than we are'.[65] A strong emphasis on accountability continues to pervade the Sinn Féin narrative: they objected to allowing the National Crime Agency (NCA) to operate in Northern Ireland as

[57] Soyinka, 2000, 25.

[58] de Brito, Aguilar and Gonzalez-Enriquez, 2001, 14.

[59] Andrews, 2003.

[60] D. Doherty, 'A View from South Africa: ANC Fighter Turned Police Chief Robert McBride Visits Derry', *An Phoblacht*, 24 June 2004; P. O Faolaín, 'Policing Debate Part of Broader Strategic Plan', *An Phoblacht*, 18 January 2007.

[61] O'Rawe, 2008, 121.

[62] Committee on the Administration of Justice, 1982.

[63] H, supporter of Sinn Féin policy, interview, May 2013.

[64] F, supporter of Sinn Féin policy, interview, May 2013.

[65] H, supporter of Sinn Féin policy, interview, May 2013.

an unaccountable 'arresting arm' for MI5,[66] while, perhaps somewhat symbolically rather than substantively, they withdrew from the selection process to appoint the PSNI Deputy Chief Constable in September 2014 because the 'compromised' process lacked 'absolute transparency'.[67]

Whilst not doubting the sincerity of their belief that they are now holding the PSNI to account, the claims of those sitting on oversight bodies need to be assessed in a wider memory politics context. The memory of past RUC impunity becomes a paradigmatic example of a 'usable past' that is adaptable for a broader political agenda. A problematic past is juxtaposed with a preferential present arrangement, allowing memory to act as a legitimating factor for current positions.[68] This occurs in a wider transitional context where a 'zero sum' lens means any meaningful Irish republican input into running the state apparatus is seen as a republican gain at the expense of the traditional Unionist hegemony.[69] While this may enable those participating in 'critical engagement' to feel vindication, critics remaining 'outside' policing take a different view. They rely on their lived experience with the PSNI rather than first-hand experience of 'critical engagement' to colour their current views of policing.

This becomes problematic as their lived experience of and interaction with policing has been characterised by post-Patten 'political policing'. In such a context, it is simply logical that one will question the validity of any 'never again' mantra by likening current experiences with the PSNI to past encounters with the RUC. Drawing the distinction between the theory of the pro-policing argument and the practical limitations of it, one interviewee opined:

> See, that kind of thinking, right, I don't disagree with that kind of thinking whereby if you have a memory and you go into something with that there memory you try and stop it, right, but that doesn't happen. The accountability structures are set up in such a manner whereby it can't happen.

[66] Raymond McCartney, quoted in 'SDLP Move Undermined the Good Friday Agreement – McCartney', *Derry Sinn Féin*, 5 February 2015: www.derrysinnfein.ie/sdlp-move-undermined-the-good-friday-agreement-mccartney-2/ (accessed 1 May 2015).

[67] 'Senior Police Post: Policing Board Rejects Sinn Féin Criticism', BBC News, 15 September 2014: www.bbc.co.uk/news/uk-northern-ireland-29204482 (accessed 1 May 2015).

[68] Bodnar, 1992.

[69] Evans and Tonge, 2013.

> I mean, operational policing is still decided by the Chief Constable, so if that's the rationale for going in they went into the wrong structure.[70]

For critics, the flaws inherent in the accountability mechanisms themselves become replicated in Sinn Féin accountability claims. These concerns should not be dismissed out of hand. 'National security' – long used to justify draconian policing measures and hugely problematic where reform and accountability are concerned[71] – remains a 'reserved' policing and justice matter. Despite various accountability bodies existing in Northern Ireland, a regressive transfer of such powers outward means control over this historically problematic issue resides with intelligence agencies in Whitehall. The accountability remit of the NIPB does not extend to 'the most high-risk area of covert policing', creating 'a serious gap in the accountability framework'.[72] This reflects a more global, post-9/11, 'war on terror' trend whereby society is increasingly being asked to entrust democracy to intelligence agencies at the expense of transparency.[73] Citing 'national security' considerations therefore remains a means of making issues requiring significant scrutiny 'off limits'. One critic dismissed the accountability bodies as 'meaningless talking shops', on the basis that:

> Accountability doesn't lie within the wrestlings of the few people who sit around the policing partnership boards, and the great and the good from the community that are allowed or invited to sit on them and get paid again £3,000 of the taxpayers' money to sit and waste time talking shite, basically. Because they're not really hitting these hard issues ... It's silly stuff, maybe speeding, and young fellas revving their cars at night. You know, I'm not seeing the big difference here or the value or the merits.[74]

Failure to see the 'big difference' can be attributed to the fact that 'national security' remains the premise for the 'political policing' of those 'left behind' and also to the PSNI's ability to refuse to answer any question because of the security situation. This contradicts the Patten vision of open and accountable policing where matters are disclosed in the public interest and not withheld in the 'police interest'.[75] The problem has filtered down from the macro level of the NIPB to the local level, where reform has moved local accountability bodies

70 V, critic of Sinn Féin policy, interview, September 2013.
71 Tomlinson, 2012; Committee on the Administration of Justice, 2003.
72 Beyers, 2013, 90.
73 Hillyard, 2002.
74 AB, critic of Sinn Féin policy, interview, October 2013.
75 Ellison, 2007.

away from the Patten vision by burdening them with a 'heavily restricted remit' through a role that is consultative rather than critical.[76] Moreover, whilst the creation of the Office of the Police Ombudsman of Northern Ireland (OPONI) has been much lauded,[77] the ever-increasing activities of MI5 remain outside its remit.

With MI5 afforded an increasing role in tackling the militant threat (and with the PSNI increasingly working in tandem with MI5 on this front),[78] concerns over accountability intensify. First, members of the PSNI that should in theory be accountable to Northern Ireland accountability bodies are increasingly operating in a system that is *not* regulated by these bodies. Secondly, fundamental shortcomings in the regulation of Covert Human Intelligence Sources (CHIS) under the Regulation of Investigatory Powers Act (RIPA) (2000) means that 'the potential for abuses and corruption in the system remains'.[79] This has led to the increased targeting of republicans for recruitment by the 'intelligence services'[80] and to cases like the prolonged administrative detention of Martin Corey from April 2010 to January 2014 on 'intelligence'-based evidence not disclosed in court or to his defence team.[81] Likewise, in March 2016, RNU member Tony Taylor had his licence revoked by the British secretary of state, as he was returned to jail without being charged, questioned or afforded legal representation.[82] More menacingly, in the 'Craigavon 2' case (John Paul Wooton and Brendan McConville jailed for the killing of PSNI constable Stephen Carroll amidst a catalogue of concerns about the safety of their conviction), the 'intelligence services' embarked on a brazen campaign of subterfuge that included: deliberately deleting data from a tracking device, arresting and subsequently attempting to pressure a defence witness into retracting his statement and implicating a defence solicitor, trying to plant incriminating evidence in McConville's prison cell and spying on a defence witness and defence lawyers.[83]

---

[76] Beyers, 2013.

[77] Bayley, 2008.

[78] Gilmore, 2009.

[79] Hirsch, 2001.

[80] Committee on the Administration of Justice, 2012b.

[81] 'JWI Case Assessment Martin Corey', Justice Watch Ireland, 2013: www.justice-watchireland.com/?page_id=14 (accessed 7 March 2014).

[82] 'Secretary of State Revokes Prison Licence of Derry Republican', *Derry Journal*, 11 March 2016: www.derryjournal.com/news/secretary-of-state-revokes-prison-licence-of-derry-republican-1-7269765 (accessed 19 April 2016).

[83] 'Case Facts, Synopsis & Court transcripts', Justice for the Craigavon 2, 2013: http://justiceforthecraigavontwo.com/facts-of-their-case/ (accessed 7 March 2014).

This activity asks fundamental questions of accountability bodies and challenges the basis of the 'never again' mantra by providing an outlet for current activity by the 'intelligence services' and PSNI to be linked with that which created problems in the past. This creates a sense of continuity regarding MI5 that is problematic for Sinn Féin on two fronts: on an accountability front given the resistance to change and accountability exercised by intelligence agencies[84] and on a memory politics front where republicans have long memories of MI5 activity that has been to their detriment.[85] More fundamentally, it exposes how the accountability mechanisms were designed to regulate an idealised, rather than the actual, post-GFA reality, meaning that the shortcomings seen above are silenced in the public discourse on post-Patten police accountability.[86] According to one anti-policing republican, the breadth of the 'national security' rider means that Sinn Féin has falsely conflated what is at very best only a limited degree of scrutiny over-policing with actual accountability that might be enforced through sanctions against the most problematic intelligence elements.[87] Had the unmet Patten recommendations on covert policing oversight been adopted the landscape might be different.

The cumulative effect of this is that critics not only question the validity of the 'never again' mantra but also question the role of those espousing the mantra from within policing oversight bodies. Contrasting the Sinn Féin accountability claims with their own lived experience, one interviewee concluded:

> I think it is delusional on their part that they think they can put manners onto the PSNI. It's been clear that they haven't. They've no real power over the PSNI. Harassment and human rights violations are occurring every day but as long as their organisation is intact, they see no threat from the state, they're not getting their doors knocked in, they're not being harassed, then they can delude themselves that they have put manners on the PSNI.[88]

Central to the anti-policing discourse is the notion that Sinn Féin had cocooned their own support base from 'political policing' whilst ignoring or being complicit in that inflicted on intra-communal rivals. Although it is impossible to substantiate such claims, what is known is that similar claims

84 Rolston, 2002.
85 Horgan, 2013, 157.
86 Topping, 2015, 165.
87 Catney, 2007, 32.
88 X, critic of Sinn Féin policy, interview, October 2013.

have been made against the ANC,[89] against Yasser Arafat in Palestine[90] and against Fine Gael and Fianna Fáil in the past.[91] Regardless of the accuracy or inaccuracy of such claims it is clear that the *perception* is enough to colour current views of policing and the role of 'former comrades' on accountability bodies. This perception of Sinn Féin involvement in 'political policing' fits neatly with a critical counter-narrative of their assimilation into the system they set out to oppose. Highlighting the disparity between a PSNI apology for raiding the home of a Sinn Féin official in Derry[92] and a raid on their own home, one interviewee commented:

> I don't know the last time I got an apology for my house being raided and they found nothing, no charges and I'm intimidated and I'm losing a day's pay and I'm possibly going to be sacked. They are outraged – utterly outraged – when anybody dare go to the home of one of their members ... So to their grassroots they're doing a great job of holding the police to account but they are cherry picking what cases they're holding to account and it seems to be when it comes to their own members that's all they're interested in. They haven't intervened in any other case that I'm aware of.[93]

Whilst those sitting on accountability mechanisms may see the merits of 'critical engagement', the above accounts demonstrate that what those who continue to be 'politically policed' see is a situation where 'former comrades' are at best powerless to prevent this kind of activity or at worst actively complicit in it. Hence the assertion that Sinn Féin 'must carry the responsibility of every act carried out against the republican community because that is what they signed up to in their acceptance of British policing in Ireland'.[94] Sinn Féin representatives on accountability mechanisms are seen not as human rights defenders but as a modern permutation of the 'Broy harriers' threading a well-worn path of using 'political policing' to repress dissent amongst 'former comrades'.[95] Given

---

89 Mattes, 2002.

90 Lia, 1999.

91 Hanley, 2003.

92 'Sinn Féin Criticise Police Raid on Derry Mayor's Home', BBC News, 13 July 2012: http://www.bbc.co.uk/news/uk-northern-ireland-foyle-west-18826243 (accessed 3 January 2014).

93 AC, critic of Sinn Féin policy, interview, November 2013.

94 'Gibney's Comments Contemptible', *Sovereign Nation* (February/March 2014).

95 'Provos to Join British Police', *Saoirse*, 188 (December 2002); ''Charlie Kerrins Commemorated in Tralee', *Saoirse*, 273 (January 2010).

the propensity for this throughout Irish history,[96] such an accusation is not only mnemonically charged but also fits into an overarching counter-narrative of Sinn Féin's complete assimilation into the state. Unsurprisingly, those sitting on accountability bodies reject this accusation. They argue that while they have taken the cases of their intra-communal rivals to public prominence and addressed them via accountability mechanisms, critics have taken the easy option of criticising Sinn Féin from their 'comfort zone' of non-engagement.[97] An interesting counter-allegation is that those claiming to be at the receiving end of 'political policing' are not the victims of a 'securocrat agenda' but rather a product of it.[98] This reinforces the narrative outlined in the previous chapter whereby those opposing Sinn Féin are motivated by nefarious personal and British agendas rather than genuine ideological commitment.

The cumulative effect either way is that high-profile post-critical engagement cases of 'political policing' – Martin Corey, the 'Craigavon 2' and Stephen Murney[99] (subjected to 'internment by remand' before the dropping of charges) – were, according to one sceptic, 'reality therapy' that accountability mechanisms did not operate as Sinn Féin suggested.[100] For Éirígí, the conclusion to be drawn is that 'despite all of the talk of "accountability" and "transfer of powers" the PSNI remains firmly under the control of the British government'.[101] This made policing oversight bodies in Northern Ireland 'mechanisms of unaccountability'.[102]

Truth recovery

Within the Irish republican constituency there are differing views on how past human rights violations by the state should be addressed. Whilst views are highly individualised – interviewees stated they were speaking for themselves and not for others – they coalesce around the traditional tension between

[96] Hanley, 2003.

[97] AD, supporter of Sinn Féin policy, interview, July 2013.

[98] B, supporter of Sinn Féin policy, interview, April 2013.

[99] 'Éirígí Press Officer Stephen Murney Cleared of Terrorism Charges', BBC News, 21 February 2014: www.bbc.co.uk/news/uk-northern-ireland-26328297 (accessed 7 March 2014).

[100] Q, critic of Sinn Féin policy, interview, July 2013.

[101] 'Imperialism – Ireland and Britain', Éirígí, 2007: https://web.archive.org/web/20140826184807/www.eirigi.org/campaigns/imperialism_paper.html (originally accessed 12 December 2013).

[102] 'The Mechanisms of Unaccountability', *Poblacht na nOibrithe*, 2012, 4.

'truth' and 'justice'. Before examining individual views on the matter, it is necessary to examine how the issue was framed during the policing debate.

Pushing for truth recovery

In accordance with a political script framed by accountability, 'critical engagement' was portrayed as being in furtherance of truth recovery. Rather than seeking answers from outside policing bodies, it was suggested that republicans could more effectively source answers from within. The rationale for this being that 'only by engaging with them can we more quickly uncover evidence of the collusion we know existed between the RUC and Unionist paramilitaries'.[103] The potential for the move to advance truth recovery was not lost on one victim who told Ard Fheis delegates, 'I want you to support the motion today but I want you to do so in the context of giving practical support to the various support groups, victims and families working to expose collusion and campaigning for the abolition of plastic bullets'.[104] This theme was revisited by Adams in his closing remarks, when he announced that campaigns for truth recovery 'have entered a new phase of activity'.[105] These assertions all fit neatly with a pro-policing script of increased accountability, yet they overlook certain practical impediments. Chief amongst these are the fact that attempts at unearthing the truth from within have been undermined in the past[106] – and this will continue[107] – as well as the fact that a black-and-white paper trail of such matters is unlikely ever to have existed. Indications are that avoiding a paper trial was a deliberate tactic used by state agencies.[108] Admittedly, there is reciprocity of the lack of a palpable paper trial when it comes to the transgressions of non-state actors, where corporate memory (essentially the cumulative information that individual members of a since defunct organisation agree to offer) can instead be tactically used to 'deal with the past'. These practical difficulties have not lessened the republican appetite for truth recovery.

Despite undergoing almost two decades of transition, Northern Ireland has yet to experience any overarching truth-recovery process. While comprehensive

[103] L. McKeown, 'Out from Behind the Doors', *An Phoblacht*, 25 January 2007.

[104] Seamus Finucane, quoted in E. O'Dwyer, 'Speakers Exude Confidence and Stress Need for Unity', *An Phoblacht*, 1 February 2007.

[105] Quoted in 'The Higher They Build Their Barriers the Stronger We Become', *An Phoblacht*, 1 February 2007.

[106] Stalker, 1988.

[107] Popkin and Bhuta, 1999.

[108] Committee on the Administration of Justice, 2015.

proposals were outlined in the Haas/O'Sullivan document and the later Stormont House Agreement (SHA), these have yet to be implemented. The 'A Fresh Start' agreement of November 2015 avoided the 'dealing with the past' quagmire altogether. The continued absence of a comprehensive truth-recovery process is a product of how the matter was initially approached. The GFA adopted a certain degree of 'forgetting' at the macro-level in order to prevent divisive issues like policing and 'dealing with the past' scuppering any prospective deal.[109] These issues were delegated to various commissions to be resolved outside the process of negotiating the GFA. However, the work of these bodies was not without shortcomings. Whilst a body was established to address the issue of victimhood, the subsequent Bloomfield Report largely refused to acknowledge the victims of state violence.[110] Likewise, the Patten Report may have 'inevitably reflected' on the human rights abuse committed by the RUC, but it failed to provide an in-depth investigation or to establish any mechanisms to deal with RUC personnel implicated in human rights violations.[111] For the majority of those who suffered at the hands of state actors, their experiences have been omitted from the official 'dealing with the past' agenda. That this would create an appetite for truth recovery is unsurprising. Lack of official acknowledgement only fuels grassroots victim–survivor mobilisation and memory projects when past human rights abuse is not addressed during transition.[112]

The accountability gap

The failure to acknowledge, much less punish, killings by state actors created and sustained 'an enormous accountability gap'.[113] An opportunity to rectify this lacuna followed the *Jordan* ruling, where the state was held to be in breach of its procedural Article 2 obligations to effectively investigate killings by state agents. The British government subsequently unveiled a 'package of measures' purportedly dedicated to satisfying this obligation. The establishment of the specialist Historical Enquiries Team (HET) police unit to investigate unsolved 'cold cases' was one such measure.[114] The HET remit was to 'reopen and review' 2,568 unsolved conflict cases (there were 3,268 unsolved cases in total but cases involving the RUC were given to OPONI to

109 Slater, 2000, 3.
110 Lundy and McGovern, 2007.
111 Lundy and McGovern, 2008b.
112 Kent, 2011; Kaiser, 2002.
113 Ní Aolaín, 2002.
114 Lundy, 2011.

investigate).[115] However, it degenerated into farce, lurking from one controversy to another before it was euthanised in 2014 amidst an official discourse of police resource restraints rather than a more accurate admission of systematic failure. Throughout its turbulent existence the HET had its approach to cases involving state actors declared illegal by Her Majesty's Inspectorate of the Constabulary (HMIC),[116] had the NIPB declare it had no confidence in the HET leadership[117] and saw victims group Relatives for Justice eventually advise its members to disengage from HET investigations.[118] From start to finish it had forfeited its remit to determine the legality of state killings, to concentrate instead on 'controlling the emergence of damaging truths'.[119] The most comprehensive critique of the HET has been conducted by Patricia Lundy. Her in-depth research revealed a catalogue of 'anomalies and inconsistencies' in cases involving state actors, including: the 'pragmatic approach' of interviewing state actors as witnesses rather than suspects under caution, the failure to verify their claims of illness and extensive pre-interview disclosure.[120] The cumulative effect of this was that cases involving state actors were being treated less robustly than those involving non-state actors. Indeed, one Victims Commissioner conceded that state actors had been given 'favourable treatment'.[121] This seems to have been official HET policy given that their guidelines invoked a 'rule of law' narrative on the conflict to differentiate explicitly between state and non-state violence.[122] Concerns were also raised over the potential involvement of former RUC Special Branch personnel in historical investigations of past RUC wrongdoing.[123] This not only replicated the impunity inherent in old investigations but also proved detrimental to confidence that the past will be 'dealt with' impartially by the state. These concerns were vindicated in a damning HMIC report.[124] They were also implicitly vindicated through the Haass/O'Sullivan proposals, which suggested scrapping the HET and removing cases from the Ombudsman

115 Aiken, 2013, 128.

116 Rolston, 2014b.

117 Lundy and Rolston, 2016.

118 Aiken, 2013, 131.

119 Lundy and Rolston, 2016.

120 Lundy, 2013.

121 Patricia McBride, quoted in 'HET Enquiries Team Must be Even-Handed: Victims Commissioner', BBC News, 4 April 2012: www.bbc.co.uk/news/uk-northern-ireland-17608644 (accessed 4 April 2012).

122 Committee on the Administration of Justice, 2015.

123 Committee on the Administration of Justice, 2013a.

124 Her Majesty's Inspectorate of Constabulary, 2013.

and setting up a new Historical Investigations Unit (HIU) with the ability to reinvestigate cases not satisfactorily examined by the HET.[125] Following the timely disbandment of the HET, its duties passed to the PSNI Legacy Investigation Branch in anticipation of the HIU being set up in the aftermath of the SHA arrangements for 'dealing with the past'. HMIC have, however, expressed concern that the Legacy Investigation Branch continues to lack accountability and transparency.[126]

The disbanding of the HET was welcomed by many victims – particularly, but not exclusively, victims of state violence and families of Irish republican combatants.[127] The body had in many cases conducted flawed reviews – not reinvestigations – that had merely replicated rather than remedied initial flaws and biases in the original RUC investigations.[128] Unsurprisingly, it failed abysmally to fulfil its remit to deliver Article 2 compliant investigations and to satisfy victims. Indeed, Rolston has noted that many victims felt their engagement with the body had delivered little in terms of truth, justice or accountability.[129] Moreover, Lundy and Rolston have been scathing in their criticism of the body, particularly its claim that the 'pragmatic approach' was necessary to get at the 'truth' of cases. Arguing that the body was set up as an investigatory body to satisfy Article 2 obligations, not to perform a simple truth recovery function, they conclude that 'the HET presents a disingenuous zero-sum analysis, claiming that without a pragmatic approach any chance of establishing 'the truth' will be scuppered. This implies a 'truth recovery' process and not the investigative police process which was understood to be the HET's brief'.[130] Even Nevin Aiken, who is more measured in his analysis of the body, concluded that the body was severely limited in delivering any semblance of truth and justice.[131]

---

[125] For the Haass/O'Sullivan proposals on parading, symbols and 'dealing with the past', see 'An Agreement Among the Parties of the Northern Ireland Executive on Parades, Select Commemorations, and Related Protests; Flags and Emblems; and Contending with the Past', 31 December 2013: www.northernireland.gov.uk/haass.pdf (originally accessed 10 May 2014); see www.peaceagreements.org/wggsite/downloadAgreementDocument/id/624.

[126] C. Smith, 'HMIC Concern Over Accountability of PSNI's Legacy Investigations Branch', BBC News, 24 June 2015: www.bbc.co.uk/news/uk-northern-ireland-33248848 (accessed 10 July 2015).

[127] Rolston, 2014b, 13.

[128] Lundy and Rolston, 2016.

[129] Rolston, 2014b.

[130] Lundy and Rolston, 2016.

[131] Aiken, 2013, 131.

The cumulative impact of the HET debacle was to further increase pre-existing republican misgivings about state commitment to addressing its role in the conflict. Typically cynical criticism of the HET, based on the observed reality of its performance, that arose during interviews, included its failure to pursue state actors and a more general belief that the body was compromised on the basis that the state would not fund a body that was genuinely capable of meaningfully 'challenging them'.[132] These criticisms occurred against a backdrop where both republicans and loyalists had been convicted on the basis of HET investigations.[133]

There is also a wider context beyond the HET that speaks more emphatically about state failure to 'deal with the past' through its 'package of measures'. The state has continued to obstruct inquests into state killings.[134] Even when convened it is questionable, given trends of prolonged delay, non-disclosure, inability to declare unlawful killing and the lack of impartiality of jurors, whether they are Article 2 compliant. Some examples demonstrate the magnitude of the problem. Former RUC officers were involved in the collation and redaction of evidence for an inquest into an RUC 'shoot-to-kill' case in Lurgan in 1982. Deputy Chief Constable Drew Harris claimed there was no conflict of interest or no likely adverse impact arising from this despite a considerable delay in disclosure.[135] In other cases, it has taken legal action to compel the PSNI to release necessary evidence.[136] Moreover, the inquest ruling into the deaths of republicans Dessie Grew and Martin McCaughey was legally contested by the families who were unhappy with a lack of transparency and rigour.[137] The upshot of all of this is that despite putting in place a 'package of measures' following *Jordan*, the reality remains that 'over ten

---

[132] V, critic of Sinn Féin policy, interview, September 2013.

[133] 'John Proctor Murder: Life Sentence for Seamus Kearney', BBC News, 28 November 2013: www.bbc.co.uk/news/uk-northern-ireland-25136281 (accessed 8 January 2014); 'Robert Rogers Jailed over Eileen Doherty Murder in Belfast', BBC News, 15 March 2013: www.bbc.co.uk/news/uk-northern-ireland-21797836 (accessed 8 January 2014).

[134] Committee on the Administration of Justice, 2013b.

[135] 'Police Regret Inquest Delay', *Lurgan Mail*, 23 September 2014: www.lurganmail.co.uk/news/local-news/police-regret-inquest-delay-1-6315071 (accessed 26 April 2015).

[136] Committee on the Administration of Justice, 2015, 15.

[137] 'SAS Inquest into Shooting of IRA Men Martin McCaughey and Dessie Grew was Ineffective, Court Told', *Belfast Telegraph*, 13 March 2015: www.belfasttelegraph.co.uk/news/northern-ireland/sas-inquest-into-shooting-of-ira-men-martin-mccaughey-and-dessie-grew-was-ineffective-court-told-31062736.html (accessed 26 April 2015).

years later there are still significant delays, deficiencies and obstruction of the implementation of resolution in the very cases which were subject to these judgements'.[138] The lack of state commitment to truth recovery became further evident when it allowed its insistence on holding a 'national security' veto on information disclosure to excise attempts to 'deal with the past' from 'A Fresh Start'. Victims of state violence criticised this as an attempt to blunt the potential of the mechanisms outlined in the SHA to uncover state complicity in 'countless deaths'.[139] Mary Lou McDonald of Sinn Féin was more frank in her condemnation:

> The British government has put the need to cover up for their agents, army, police and political establishment during the conflict above the rights of the families of the victims and the cause of reconciliation ... It should be remembered that these are events which in many instances happened 30 to 40 years ago and pose no threat to 'national security' in any form. This has everything to do with controlling and curtailing the disclosure of information and nothing to do with 'national security'.[140]

In an incident that broke with convention, a former British soldier was arrested and charged in relation to a legacy case in April 2015.[141] This was followed by a subsequent arrest arising from Bloody Sunday.[142] These arrests were preceded by the earlier reopening of the internee 'hooded men' torture case against the state.[143] Even here, however, there has been criticism of

---

[138] Committee on the Administration of Justice, 2015, 2.

[139] 'British Government Exposed as Anti-Agreement Rejectionist on the Past', Relatives for Justice, 17 November 2015: http://relativesforjustice.com/british-government-exposed-as-anti-agreement-rejectionists-on-the-past/ (accessed 23 November 2015).

[140] M. McDonald, 'Mary Lou McDonald on Stormont's "Fresh Start" Agreement', *An Phoblacht*, 18 November 2015: www.anphoblacht.com/contents/25493 (accessed 23 November 2015).

[141] 'John Pat Cunningham Death: Former Soldier Charged with Attempted Murder', BBC News, 25 April 2015: www.bbc.co.uk/news/uk-northern-ireland-32459312 (accessed 25 April 2015).

[142] 'Bloody Sunday: Ex-soldier arrested over Londonderry shootings', BBC News, 10 November 2015: www.bbc.co.uk/news/uk-northern-ireland-34775466 (accessed 10 November 2015).

[143] 'Hooded Men: Irish Government Bid to Reopen "Torture" Case', BBC News, 2 December 2014: www.bbc.co.uk/news/uk-northern-ireland-30296397 (accessed 22 May 2015).

governmental failure to voluntarily disclose material relevant to the case.[144] Whether this signals the end of state actor impunity is a matter of conjecture at this point. However, it can be concluded that it is, at its very best reading, an incredibly belated attempt by the state to offer some form of truth and justice to its victims.

Truth, justice and acknowledgement

While the need for truth recovery was unanimously accepted, what remained divisive was whether this should entail simply unearthing the truth or actively prosecuting former state actors. This division is not unique to Irish republicanism, but mirrors disagreement on the matter in transitioning societies more generally.[145] For some, truth recovery means disclosure of the 'truth' devoid of any prosecutorial process. According to one former combatant, it was not about 'putting torturers and killers in jail' but about getting 'the system into the dock'. Drawing on the example of South Africa, they added:

> They were able to get all these ... top notch cops and put them in the dock and even get them convicted, which is okay, which is well and good. They didn't get Apartheid into the dock. You know what I mean? They didn't get the system into the dock. All that they got were these individuals. Once the system was gone it was very hard to get someone who actually supported Apartheid.[146]

This view was shared by another former combatant who stated that the truth recovery process should entail state acknowledgement that there was a 'war' in which it had played an integral role:

> I think in terms of that, you know, 'Do you want people brought into courts and all', I think it's an acknowledgment that there was a war on here, there was a conflict on here. Republicans are up front and say, 'Yeah, we were engaged in it and probably did a lot of things that shouldn't have been done'. You want that sort of reciprocal response on their part, you know.[147]

---

144 'Hooded Men Case: Villiers Withholding Material, Says Lawyer', *Newsletter*, 6 April 2016: www.newsletter.co.uk/news/northern-ireland-news/hooded-men-case-villiers-withholding-material-says-lawyer-1-7315203 (accessed 19 April 2016).

145 Jelin, 2003.

146 A, supporter of Sinn Féin policy, interview, April 2013.

147 M, supporter of Sinn Féin policy, interview, June 2013.

One interviewee highlighted that what was most relevant to many victims was truthful answers to 'why' and 'where' and 'what for', noting that for some the belated conviction of perpetrators would make 'no difference to their life whatsoever'.[148] Disclosing the 'truth' of what 'the system' was implicated in rather than securing the 'justice' of convicting individuals is the premise of this approach to truth recovery. This Irish republican interest in unearthing the 'truth' and getting acknowledgement that there was institutional abuse of power rather than prosecuting individual perpetrators has also been discussed by Lundy and McGovern.[149]

Others take a divergent view, seeing disclosure as a precursor to fuller truth recovery that involves 'justice' via prosecution. One republican evinced a belief that while the disclosure of 'truth' would be 'words', this needed to be followed by 'action' to bring state actors to 'justice' for killing 'the very civilians that they were meant to be protecting'.[150] A former combatant used their own experience to draw the distinction between the punishment of non-state actors for their role in the conflict and the non-punishment of state actors embroiled in wrongdoing:

> I ended up in jail for it. I never complained about it. I never criticised anybody for putting me in jail ... but the question is what about all the RUC people who shot and injured and attacked and used guns on innocent people and murdered people? They never done a day in jail. Right, so there's that legacy there. There's that inequality.[151]

An interesting analysis of this 'legacy' of 'inequality' was offered by one former combatant who was not in favour of prosecutions but nonetheless noted that the socio-economic implications of having a conviction were irrelevant for most state actors. Drawing on the numerous impediments a conviction brings for former combatants, the interviewee pointed out that 'on the other side [security forces] there wasn't ... they don't have any discriminatory measures against them because they were never in court'.[152] The real-life implications of this can be seen in the Civil Service (Special Advisers) Act (Northern Ireland) 2013 that discriminates against former prisoners but has no palpable impact on former state actors.[153]

---

148 AB, critic of Sinn Féin policy, interview, November 2013.

149 Lundy and McGovern, 2007.

150 T, supporter of Sinn Féin policy, interview, August 2013.

151 S, critic of Sinn Féin policy, interview, July 2013.

152 M, supporter of Sinn Féin policy, interview, June 2013.

153 Coiste na nIarchimi, 2013, 3.

The demand for state acknowledgement that there was a 'war' in Northern Ireland has become central to the Irish republican approach to truth recovery – though not necessarily for all victims of state violence, who might only seek a simple acknowledgement in official discourses of their victimhood at the hands of the state. With the meta-conflict continuing to rage, the classification of the conflict remains contested. The Haass/O'Sullivan document recognised – albeit not necessarily agreeing – that for Irish republicans the conflict represented a 'war' fought by 'freedom fighters'. Unionists have rejected the language of war as a republican rewriting of the past,[154] choosing instead to retain the rejection of 'moral equivalence' that underpins the 'rule of law' narrative. The earlier examination of the HET demonstrates that a similar mentality defines the state view on the matter. Insistence on having the state acknowledge there was a 'war' has left Irish republicans susceptible to claims they are intent on legitimising their own version of the past.[155] Demands for truth recovery are subsequently reduced to a revisionist rewriting of the past that has seemingly duped victims groups and academics into deflecting from how the IRA were responsible for most conflict-related death by propagating their postcolonial interpretation that state structural exclusion made conflict necessary.[156] Dismissing demands for truth recovery among the wider Nationalist constituency as such has two significant flaws. First, it assumes that any such truth recovery process offers only benefit for Irish republicans without in fact conducting a more considered cost–benefit calculation. Secondly, it denies victims of state violence any semblance of agency by decontextualising their demands through reducing them to misguided 'fellow travellers'. It is worth elaborating on both these points.

State acknowledgement that there was a 'war' would indeed be rhetorically beneficial to Irish republicans. Most notably, it would support their claim to the 'victim–perpetrator' identity. After all, every side kills and gets killed in 'war'. This would help deconstruct the contrived hierarchy of perpetrators that has deemed non-state actors (especially Irish republicans) 'more guilty' perpetrators than state actors.[157] The theme of common suffering from war on a basic human level has thus entered the Sinn Féin discourse. Martin McGuinness argued that 'there needs to be an acceptance that human beings cry, die, bleed and grieve and are mourned in the same way, and that our

---

[154] M. Davenport, "Unmistakeable Taste of Freshly-Picked Cherries', BBC News, 7 January 2014: www.bbc.co.uk/news/uk-northern-ireland-25643314 (accessed 9 January 2014).

[155] Hopkins, 2015.

[156] McGrattan, 2013.

[157] Hearty, 2016a.

common humanity should acknowledge that'.[158] This has percolated through the 'uncomfortable conversations' initiative that Sinn Féin has launched as part of its endeavour to 'deal with the past' through engaging with Unionists and former state agents.[159] The initiative has seen republicans express regret for certain actions and acknowledge the pain inflicted on victims of IRA violence. Declan Kearney thus told an 'uncomfortable conversations' event:

> I am sorry for the pain experienced by the RUC family during the war, the suffering caused to the unionist section of our community, the human tragedy of the Shankill bomb being one instance of that. And equally for the pain of IRA volunteers killed in this command area here in Derry and elsewhere.[160]

Inherent in Kearney's statement, however, is a sense of common wrongdoing that flows from the associated sense of common suffering. This underpins republican approaches to their own wrongdoing that is often articulated in terms of the fallibility of the combatant or the 'they did bad things, we did bad things' discourse. The departure from the 'memory of perpetrators' therefore comes with a certain level of qualification. The memory of 'us' as perpetrator is inextricably linked in broader terms to the abiding memory of 'them' as perpetrator. Note, for example, Gerry Adams' sentiment that Charles Windsor (Prince Charles) was indeed a victim of the conflict given that the IRA killed his uncle Lord Mountbatten, but that his role as Colonel-in-Chief of the Parachute Regiment responsible for massacres in Ballymurphy and Derry also made him a victimiser.[161] On the one hand, it could be contended that this accurately reflects the reality of the victim–perpetrator phenomenon.[162] On the other

---

[158] N. McAdam, 'State Helped Perpetuate the Troubles, says McGuinness', *Belfast Telegraph*, 29 June 2015: www.belfasttelegraph.co.uk/news/northern-ireland/state-helped-perpetuate-the-troubles-says-mcguinness-31336336.html (accessed 23 November 2015).

[159] J. Hedges, '"Uncomfortable Conversations" Collection Launched in Linen Hall Library', *An Phoblacht*, 20 April 2015: www.anphoblacht.com/contents/24916 (accessed 19 April 2016).

[160] 'Sinn Féin Chairman Declan Kearney "Sorry" for All Troubles Victims', BBC News, 27 August 2015: www.bbc.co.uk/news/uk-northern-ireland-politics-34069960 (accessed 27 August 2015).

[161] Quoted in 'Prince Charles Meets Sinn Féin Leader Gerry Adams', BBC News, 19 May 2015: www.bbc.co.uk/news/uk-northern-ireland-32786393 (accessed 22 May 2015).

[162] Hearty, 2014.

hand, it could be argued that it follows the more prevalent trend in Northern Ireland of trying to mitigate 'in-group' transgressions by tying them to the perceived wrongness of 'out-group' transgressions. For Unionists, this involves exonerating the security forces through a macabre numbers game that apportions total blame to republicans on the basis that they were directly responsible for the majority of conflict-related deaths. For Irish republicans, this involves couching recognition of their own role in the conflict in a discourse of collective wrongdoing across the board.

But truth recovery would incur costs for Irish republicans too. Rhetorically, the republican response to their transgressions has been (as the daughter of informer Caroline Moreland was told): 'it was a war and that's what happens'.[163] If there is a formal admission of 'war', however, the rhetorical and legal landscape would alter. Rather than being 'things that shouldn't have been done', the less salubrious elements of the republican past, like enforced disappearance, would need assessing within the scope of the laws of armed conflict. With Irish republicans exercising extreme caution in how they have so far labelled their own transgressions,[164] a formal admission of war would introduce the spectre of war crimes into the discursive equation. This was not lost on the son of Jean McConville, who called for her killers to be tried in The Hague.[165] It is also arguable that defences based on corporate responsibility would lose their traction. Scrutiny moves beyond the gunman or bomber onto those who sanctioned or ordered such acts. Hence the son of informer Frank Hegarty called for Martin McGuinness to be questioned on what he knew about the killing.[166] More fundamentally, increased scrutiny into the state role in the 'dirty war' could unearth further state agents within the IRA. In light of the growing catalogue of revelations about the role of the British agent codenamed 'Stakeknife', this could prove to be the most 'uncomfortable conversation' of all. High-level IRA–state collusion would fail to fit any party's master narrative of the conflict. In totality then, if demands for fuller truth recovery offer post-conflict legitimacy for republicans this may come at the considerable price of the previous taken-for-granted narrative. This questions the veracity of the

---

163 'Caroline Moreland: IRA "and State" Blamed over Murder', BBC News, 10 June 2015: www.bbc.co.uk/news/uk-northern-ireland-33069102 (accessed 30 June 2015).

164 McEvoy and Conway, 2004.

165 F. O'Cionnaith, 'McConville: My Mother's Murder is a War Crime', *Irish Examiner*, 7 April 2015: www.irishexaminer.com/ireland/mcconville-my-mothers-murder-is-a-war-crime-322535.html (accessed 27 November 2015).

166 'Frank Hegarty: Martin McGuinness "Needs Questioned" Over Murder, Son Says', BBC News, 25 November 2015: www.bbc.co.uk/news/uk-northern-ireland-foyle-west-34918934 (accessed 25 November 2015).

'rewriting the past' claims; inducing a fuller truth recovery process capable of piecing together a narrative of war crimes and extensive state penetration is hardly a stroke of Sinn Féin revisionist genius.

Demands for truth recovery must also be evaluated within their broader contextual confines of the meta-conflict. As noted earlier, the meta-conflict has been characterised by attempts to diminish, challenge and deny the victimhood of victims of state violence – particularly if they are Irish republican. This 'shame avoidance' approach is epitomised by the exclusivist definition of 'innocent victim' that has failed to move beyond those killed by Irish republicans.[167] More recently, this has moved onto a legislative footing through the hierarchies of victimhood and perpetrators inherent in the Civil Service (Special Advisers) Act (Northern Ireland) 2013.[168] Denial of victimhood to those killed by the RUC in particular can be traced to the official discourse that RUC personnel killed during the conflict were not 'combatants' but simply 'innocent victims' killed by 'terrorists'. Such a view propagates false binaries of victim and perpetrator that fail to exist so neatly amidst the chaos of conflict.[169] This not only overlooks the RUC's counter-insurgency role and their implication in human rights violations, but it also creates the curious situation whereby civilians killed by plastic bullets become 'innocent victims' of other 'innocent victims'. Even if Irish republicans have tacitly accepted the victimhood of state actors killed during the IRA campaign, there has been little reciprocation of this in the official discourse on policing – although pro-state paramilitaries did express 'true and abject remorse' for the deaths of their victims.[170] To successfully recognise the victimhood of differing constituencies it is necessary to identify first with the victim, and then reconcile this with the 'otherness' of the opposing victim constituency to which they belong.[171] Preciously clinging to a 'rule of law' narrative for the purpose of the meta-conflict allows 'shame avoidance' to prevent this.

When this broader context is taken into consideration, what has been falsely labelled as joint enterprise in a rewriting of the past is more accurately an attempt to erode the 'conspiracy of silence' that has denied victimhood.[172] The agency of victims of the state is predicated not on exculpating Irish republicans of wrongdoing (even Irish republicans, after all, acknowledge their own transgressions) but on securing acknowledgement that they exist and that their

---

167 Breen-Smyth, 2007, 96.

168 Hearty, 2016a.

169 Borraine, 2000, 128.

170 Lundy and Rolston, 2016.

171 Fassin and Rechtman, 2009, 282.

172 David and Choi, 2009.

victimhood, pain and right to truth and/or justice are equal to those of victims of Irish republican violence. Continued denial of this in a transitional context will not cause the appetite for acknowledgement and redress amongst those wronged by the state to dissipate.[173] Victims of state violence in Spain[174] and Peru,[175] for example, have all persisted with long-standing campaigns for truth and justice in the face of impunity, denial and cover-up in official discourses. To somehow 'other' the victims of state violence in the North of Ireland as purely contrived, politically motivated actors is therefore a matter of illogic. Their demands for recognition, voice, truth and justice are as natural and foreseeable as those of victims of state violence elsewhere *and* those of victims of non-state actors in Northern Ireland. Accordingly, the issue is not one of rewriting the past but of trying to correct persistent imbalance on the issue of victimhood in official discourse; the hyper visibility of victims of Irish republican aggression against the invisibility of victims of state violence, the acknowledgement of victims of non-state violence against the denial of victims of state violence, and the deconstruction of hierarchies of victimhood and perpetratorship versus their political construction and maintenance. While the meta-conflict that sustains this imbalance continues, the turn to memory-politics mobilisation by victims of state violence (Irish republicans included) will be inevitable.[176]

Conclusion

Irish republican policing memory comprises a wealth of memories of human rights abuses foisted at the individual and collective levels by the RUC. Despite the passage of time and the more general movement of Northern Ireland into a process of transition, such memories have not been 'forgotten'. For some Irish republicans, individual memories remain a barrier to fuller acceptance of policing. For others, their own personal experience has been subverted to the collective need to 'move into' a new 'working relationship' with policing agents. In this new 'working relationship' they have sought to find a constructive rather than destructive use for memories of past abuses. This has seen the political construction of a 'never again' mantra by those who have accepted policing and attempts to enforce this mantra through participation on oversight bodies. However, a number of flaws in these bodies coupled with lived experience of policing since Sinn Féin acceptance have led many to question and reject

173 Immler, 2012.

174 Aguilar and Ramirez-Barat, 2014, 239.

175 Saona, 2014.

176 Lundy and McGovern, 2008a.

the premise of this mantra. For them, 'never again' means 'more of the same'. Criticisms of accountability bodies are replicated in wider criticism of the HET and attempts by the state to address its past wrongdoing. This failure, along with more general rejection of Irish republican victimhood in official discourse, has led to increased republican scrutiny of how the past is 'dealt with' and has led to increased demands within the constituency for the acknowledgement of their victimhood and of state wrongdoing. In the absence of such a happening the past human rights abuses suffered by the collective remain part of a problematic and contested conflict legacy.

Chapter 6

The PSNI and 'Community Policing'

Introduction

This chapter critically evaluates how memory interacts with police reform to frame opposing narratives of 'community policing'. Interrogating changes in police symbolism, composition and the PSNI's supposed core function in working-class republican communities, it examines how a problematic legacy continues to impact on views of 'community policing'. The 'critical engagement' narrative of 'community policing' that is framed by assertions of newness and change, and the critical counter-narrative of 'cosmetic reform' dismissing police reform as an attempt to normalise 'British' policing are both dissected. Although these narratives are intrinsically linked to ideologised views of involvement in transitional processes, this chapter looks beyond the 'black-and-white' views proffered by competing narratives to draw on the nuances of the overlapping 'grey' areas that define lived reality on the ground. Viewing this through competing lenses of *continuity* and *rupture*, it highlights where reform has successfully cultivated a new image of the PSNI and a new attitude towards 'community policing' within republican communities *and* where reform has struggled to do so. At this introductory stage, it must be noted that the generic term 'community policing' remains undefined, contested and contingent upon context.[1] Notwithstanding this, the term is used here to denote the Patten vision of 'policing with the community' whereby a co-operative community–police relationship that tackles and prevents anti-social behaviour and crime displaces a previous relationship of political hostility and suspicion.

[1] Fielding and Innes, 2006; Brogden and Nijhar, 2013, 2.

Symbolism

The Independent Commission on Policing for Northern Ireland recognised the divisive impact that the overtly Unionist ethos, culture and composition of the RUC had on police ownership in the North of Ireland.[2] Culling policing of divisive symbolism was a necessary first step in addressing the problematic legacy of police ownership. Police reform duly introduced a change of name, uniform and symbolism. Striving for inclusivity, reform made the PSNI appear overtly neutral where the RUC had been overtly Unionist. Changing the name and uniform of contested police forces has been tried elsewhere in a bid to bring previously excluded groups 'on board'. In the Basque Country, the autonomous police force was given the Basque cultural name 'Ertzaintia' along with a new uniform intended to reflect their Basque origins; these reforms did not prevent the separatist Euskadi Ta Askatasuna (ETA) from attacking the force.[3]

Reforms of this nature have an obvious aesthetic impact on policing. Policing agents have a new name, new uniform and new symbolism. Physically they look different and are known by a different name. Despite this, assertions of wholesale newness remain problematic. As the Basque case demonstrates, aesthetic reforms are not enough to convince excluded groups of the newness of reformed bodies. When memory is added to this, the overarching context becomes further complicated. Memories of past policing are not going to disappear with the sudden appearance of a new uniform or a new name.

Irish republican critics of policing reform level the charge that a uniform and name change are symptomatic of 'cosmetic reform'. Their argument contends that while these changes remove an overt sense of Unionism on an aesthetic level, they fail to change the core policing function of upholding, what is for them, an illegitimate state. Cue the assertion of one critic that 'when Patten was making the proposals of the name change, the uniform change and all the other cosmetic changes that was being done to make policing more acceptable ... the fundamentals of policing wasn't addressed'.[4] Believing the entire reform process to be 'cosmetic' rather than 'fundamental', any *rupture* with the RUC is, as per this argument, aesthetic rather than substantive. Promotion of the PSNI as a new force with a new 'community policing' function is dismissed as an attempt to normalise 'British' policing. This 'cosmetic reform' narrative is married to a wider ideological view but it can also function to present lived reality on the ground through a lens of continuity:

---

[2] Independent Commission on Policing for Northern Ireland, 1999, 14.1.

[3] O'Rawe and Moore, 1997, 225.

[4] R, critic of Sinn Féin policy, interview, July 2013.

> Where I live there is still that distrust of the police and the view that they are very much a political and paramilitary police force. You know, you could change the name of the Titanic to whatever, it's still going to sink ... for those who say, 'yes it's a new police force', well, then, the answer to that is, 'Well it's only cosmetic, it's only a name change'.[5]

Somewhat paradoxically, while these reforms have neutralised the general public image of policing without impressing Irish republicans, in the same instance they were the focal point for much of the Unionist ire at reform.[6] Despite disgruntlement on either side of the ethno-nationalist divide with these 'first stream' reforms, Topping notes that this has been where policing was most 'radically transformed'.[7] The public image of policing in Northern Ireland is now that of a young forward-looking police force.[8]

Within Irish republicanism, however, the policing debate does not hinge on symbolism, uniform or name. These are not regarded as the key signifiers of rupture or continuity. Although viewed as necessary and welcome by 'critical engagers', they remain a peripheral issue. The crux of the policing debate penetrates deeper to more substantive matters of who is wearing the new uniform and what their function is and how they conduct themselves. Examination now turns to these matters, with an interrogation of how police composition is presented by opposing narratives.

Composition

The composition of the RUC was defined by religious imbalance, with Catholic representation plummeting to 8 per cent during the conflict.[9] The task of Patten reformers was to overturn this by enticing the minority community into the policing world. If Catholic representation rose, so the logic ran, then the PSNI could not be labelled a Protestant police force. Subsequently, a 50/50 recruitment policy that matched recruit levels from the 'two communities' was adopted. As a consequence, 'just over 30 per cent' of PSNI officers now come from a 'perceived Roman Catholic background'.[10] Although not a 50/50 split, in comparative terms this is markedly more balanced than the RUC. The tactic

[5] J, critic of Sinn Féin policy, interview, June 2013.

[6] Byrne and Monaghan, 2008, 25.

[7] Topping, 2008b.

[8] Roche, 2008.

[9] Ellison and Smyth, 2000.

[10] Freedom of Information request, F-2013-04401, on file with author.

of getting excluded groups 'on board' through recruitment processes has been used outwith Northern Ireland. Notable cases are in Tamil-speaking areas of Sri Lanka to help recruit for the Sinhalese-dominated police force[11] and in Bosnia through quotas for Bosniacs, Bosnian Croats and Bosnian Serbs.[12] Quotas purportedly increased police ownership by having a common Bosnian identity displace narrower lenses of competing ethnicities.[13] The recruitment quota policy was therefore neither novel nor unique to police reform in Northern Ireland.

The level of Catholic representation within policing has evidently increased, but heralding this as an unqualified assertion of newness is misleading. As most interviewees pointed out, there were always some Catholics in the police force. What there was not, they argue, was a substantial Nationalist representation. For critics, speaking of 'Catholic' PSNI recruits was sectarianising the issue of police reform in order to give succour to 'cosmetic reform'. Concentrating on the religion of the police officer rather than their attitude and conduct – what Fielding calls police officer 'demeanour'[14] – deflected from the lack of substantive change. This was borne out in the analysis of one critic who used the memory of 'demeanour' to contextualise increased Catholic representation in the following way:

> The ratio of Roman Catholics to Protestants differs greatly ... but having said that, these are middle-class Catholics who would view the likes of myself with the same disdain and hatred that these people [RUC officers in Castlereagh] do. They are a sort of Unionist ... they're called Cormac and they are called Fíonnuala and stuff but in any dealings over the so-called change from '94 that I have had ... you're still left in no uncertain doubt, you know, that you're a piece of crap on their shoe.[15]

In addition to verifying that communicative interaction conditions attitudes towards police officers more generally,[16] this comment also reveals that in this particular localised and politicised context memory reinforces a sense of continuity rather than rupture. Remembering and likening the past

---

[11] C. Haviland, 'Ex-Tamil Tiger Rebels "Free to Join the Sri Lankan Police"', BBC News, 30 January 2012: www.bbc.co.uk/news/world-asia-16795442 (accessed 7 February 2012).

[12] Cordone, 1999.

[13] Celador, 2005.

[14] Fielding, 1989.

[15] P, critic of Sinn Féin policy, interview, June 2013.

[16] Bradford, Jackson and Stanko, 2009.

Table 6.1 District recruitment, 2007–13

Policing district	Number of recruits
A	63
B	184
C	382
D	352
E	179
F	113
G	100
H	187
n/a	146
Total	1,706

hostile 'demeanour' of Catholic RUC officers to that of Catholic PSNI officers hampers assertions of newness.

This speaks volumes about the flawed conflation of the terms 'Catholic' and 'Nationalist' – symptomatic of an erroneous 'two tribes' understanding of political division within the six counties.[17] Within the 8 per cent Catholic membership of the RUC there were likely to be few Nationalists and no republicans. A Catholic RUC officer was not necessarily a Nationalist one. O'Dochartaigh goes so far as to argue that the entire premise of policing made it practically impossible for one to simultaneously be a Nationalist and also in the RUC.[18] Brogden expands upon this observation, arguing that policing reform cannot then be premised on getting more Catholics into policing but must bring Nationalists into policing.[19]

The crux of the matter was addressed by one supporter of critical engagement who frankly admitted that while the level of Catholic representation had increased, the reality was that these recruits were still drawn from middle-class communities 'where the houses are about £500,000'.[20] Rather than representing something of a broad generalisation, this assertion *is* supported by empirical data on PSNI recruitment trends shown in Table 6.1.[21] The figures

[17] Shirlow and McGovern, 1997, 9.

[18] O'Dochartaigh, 1997.

[19] Brogden, 1995.

[20] T, supporter of Sinn Féin policy, interview, August 2013.

[21] Freedom of Information request, F-2013-04401, on file with author. The district for 146 recruits could not be determined because of overlapping postcodes. Eighty-six

in Table 6.1 highlight that Irish republican scepticism is not a misconception shaped by memory but an observation of post-reform reality.

From 2007 to 2013, 1,706 recruits applied to join the PSNI from addresses with a Northern Ireland postcode. The uptake amongst working-class Nationalist communities was negligible: only 63 recruits applied from A District (West and North Belfast) and only 100 applied from G District (Foyle, Strabane, Limavady and Magherafelt). These districts also contain some Unionist areas, so it cannot be assumed that all applicants were Nationalist or even Catholic. Yet even if this was the case, uptake remains minimal when compared with other areas. Recruitment to the PSNI remains strongest in areas where recruitment to the RUC was traditionally strong – C District (Ards, Castlereagh, Down and North Down) 382 and D District (Antrim, Carrickfergus, Lisburn and Newtownabbey) 352. These areas have considerable middle-class as well as Unionist populations. Table 6.1 suggests that Catholic PSNI recruits are for the most part being drawn from the same milieu as were Catholic RUC recruits.

Table 6.2 indicates that even following a subsequent PSNI recruitment drive in late 2013, areas with considerable working-class Nationalist populations like A District and F District still exhibit the lowest rates of PSNI recruits.[22] Table 6.3 demonstrates that, even in terms of applicants, trends in later recruitment drives are still favourable to traditional rather than new recruitment patterns.[23] Claims of newness in terms of encompassing previously excluded groups may not be as watertight as initially perceived. Even the level of Catholic PSNI recruits has fallen under scrutiny recently. Since the 50/50 recruitment policy ended in March 2011, Catholic recruitment has dipped to 17 per cent.[24] In the two post-50/50 recruitment cycles only 77 of 400 new PSNI officers were Catholic, compounding the fact that in 2014, 76 per cent of PSNI applicants who made the merit pool were from a Protestant

recruits applied from an address outside Northern Ireland. The time period 2007–13 was chosen because 2007 marked the beginning of 'critical engagement', while 2013 was the year interviews were conducted and also the year that the Freedom of Information request was submitted.

[22] Freedom of Information request, F-2015-01771, on file with author. This relates to recruitment Competition 1 that was advertised from 19 September 2013 to 11 October 2013, with appointments complete by May 2015.

[23] This relates to Competition 2, advertised from 28 May 2014 to 20 June 2014, with appointments ongoing at time of request.

[24] 'Catholic PSNI Applicant Numbers "Down"', UTV, 30 September 2015: https://web.archive.org/web/20151002003228/www.u.tv/News/2015/09/30/Catholic-PSNI-applicant-numbers-down-45963 (originally accessed 17 November 2015).

Table 6.2 District recruitment, 2013–15

Policing district	Number of recruits
A	9
B	31
C	108
D	84
E	37
F	26
G	32
H	55
n/a	19
Total	**401**

Table 6.3 District applicants, 2014

Policing district	Number of applicants
A	252
B	415
C	1,300
D	1,196
E	697
F	376
G	472
H	704
n/a	444
Total	5,856

background.[25] These recent revelations demonstrate that not only are the PSNI failing to attract working-class Nationalists but are increasingly struggling to attract Catholics in general. This clearly runs against the grain of the Patten vision of having the community policed by a force that is representative of that community.

This does not deny, however, that the PSNI's image and ethos are less Unionist and more Nationalist than the RUC's. Regarding the former, the RUC

[25] Byrne, 2015.

had strong institutional links to the Orange Order.[26] That Orange presence has dissipated. Only 1.3 per cent of PSNI members (95) are registered Orange Order members, 0.6 per cent (46) registered Royal Black Preceptory members and 0.2 per cent (19) registered Apprentice Boys, although by comparison no PSNI member is registered as a member of the Knights of Columbanus.[27] In terms of the latter, the PSNI has a GAA team[28] and delivers speeches in Irish.[29] Dependent on how far back one opts to 'remember' – memory, after all, has no universalistic time boundaries[30] – the presence of Irish speakers and GAA activists within policing can be seen as either rupture or continuity. How far back one chooses to 'remember' is necessitated by the end point one wants one's policing narrative to make – either that police reform makes the PSNI 'new' or conversely that 'cosmetic reform' means the PSNI is not 'new'. In comparison with the RUC, with a predominant Unionist make-up and ethos, a lens of rupture seems most apposite. 'Critical engagers' reinforce their narrative of newness and change by juxtaposing Nationalists within the PSNI with the absence of such people in the predominantly Unionist RUC. If, however, one opts to 'remember' pre-partition policing, a lens of continuity can be adopted. Critics point to the presence of Irish speakers and GAA activists within pre-partition policing. Contestation thus reflects the 'malleability of memory', because how one wishes to represent the PSNI depends on which way the memory of cultural Nationalism within policing is moulded – around the RUC for rupture or around the RIC for continuity.

The thread of continuity running through the cosmetic reform narrative suggests that whether PSNI officers speak Irish or involve themselves in Gaelic games is a non-issue as long as they continue to uphold an illegitimate state. To support this argument, parallels were drawn between the RIC and those partaking in Nationalist past times within the PSNI today. The former, despite their religious creed, indigenous roots and expressions of cultural Nationalism, were nonetheless a 'British' force and the same now applied to the latter:

> Someone being a Gaelic speaker, playing Gaelic football, declaring their interest for the unity of Ireland, it doesn't matter to me. They're still a

---

[26] Guelke, 2012, 61.

[27] Freedom of Information request, F-2015-00806, on file with author. Freedom of Information request, F-2015-01864, on file with author.

[28] J. Campbell, 'PSNI Lined up for Historic Croker Date with Garda', *Belfast Telegraph*, 17 November 2011.

[29] 'PSNI Officers Being Trained to Give Talks in Irish', *Belfast Telegraph*, 20 May 2009.

[30] Soyinka, 2000, 21.

> policeman donning a British policeman's hat in my country. The RIC going back to that period, you know, had many Gaelic speakers, many native Gaelic speakers and cultural Irish people.[31]

A lens of continuity suggests that cultural Nationalists within the PSNI are 'British policemen' in the same vein as the 'British policemen' in the RUC who did not share their cultural Nationalist pastimes and the 'British policemen' in the RIC that did. In an attempt to substantiate this argument, another critic cited how an RIC man shot by Dan Breen at Soloheadbeg in 1919 was from the Gaeltacht quarter of West Galway, whilst the son of the RIC man who arrested Roger Casement went on to captain Cork to an all-Ireland title decades later.[32] Critics therefore reinforce the anti-policing narrative of 'cosmetic reform' by engaging in extended memory politics that 'remembers' the role that cultural Nationalists within the RIC previously played in upholding the state and suppressing republicans.

Others questioned the extent to which speaking Irish or playing Gaelic games are even indicative of political Nationalism. For one critic, such a black-and-white reading of this blurred the lines between cultural Nationalism and political Nationalism. Even though PSNI officers may be Irish-speaking GAA members they could nonetheless be 'apolitical'.[33] There is little reason to fault this assertion as it stands as a simple matter of logic.

Those partaking in 'critical engagement' draw on their lived experience with PSNI officers to argue that the cultural Nationalism of recruits clearly demonstrates that there are people within the PSNI who would not have joined the RUC. These recruits were not motivated to join the police by sectarian enmity, thus a lens of rupture is adopted. Alluding to one Irish-speaking Gaelic footballer, an interviewee argued that they 'didn't join the PSNI to beat up Taigs'.[34] Another interviewee at the public face of 'critical engagement' drew on their personal interaction with the PSNI as evidence of a notable rupture from the RUC. Comparing recent interaction with what they 'remember' in the past, they observed that 'from talking to some of the senior PSNI people they are completely different to what my experience was in the past with the big, thick, Orange, ignorant, flippant RUC guy who just wanted to put a bullet in your head'.[35]

---

31 AC, critic of Sinn Féin policy, interview, November 2013.

32 AA, critic of Sinn Féin policy, interview, October 2013.

33 V, critic of Sinn Féin policy, interview, September 2013.

34 M, supporter of Sinn Féin policy, interview, June 2013.

35 AD, supporter of Sinn Féin policy, interview, July 2013.

According to the logic employed by those leading 'critical engagement', the fact that there are now people present within the PSNI that have no affinity with the RUC world view means that the PSNI is a 'new' entity. Memory enables a lens of rupture to view a 'new breed' of police officer not motivated by a desire to become embroiled in sectarian 'suspect community' policing but by a desire to serve their community: 'from speaking to quite a few there's ones within the PSNI have said very openly and very clearly they never would've joined the RUC because they wanted to be part of a police service not part of some type of counter-insurgency force irrespective of what title it was given'.[36] The 'critical engagement' narrative thus becomes one of change and newness: new personnel, new motivation and new function. The policing narrative is no longer framed by threat but by community service premised on providing 'proper policing' to republican communities:

> People do tackle me about, you know, being on the PCSP and stuff like that. I keep saying to them, you know, 'supporting the RUC or supporting the police force maybe is the wrong phrase'. What I'm personally supporting is our community and our community's right to a civil police force.[37]

Memory aids this narrative reframing by enabling those partaking in 'critical engagement' to 'remember' this past sense of threat and juxtapose it with the new function they see the PSNI fulfilling today. Research into attitudes within the PSNI by Avril Roulton, which found that young PSNI recruits regard the RUC outlook to be 'outdated and living in the past', gives the argument above some credence.[38] A similar observation was noted by one community activist who spoke of the willingness of younger PSNI officers to 'step outside the box' – to engage positively with communities on the ground and break away from the institutional protection the 'old school RUC' presence valued.[39] This willingness led another community activist to conclude that some within the PSNI are 'very much up for' addressing the policing issues most relevant to republican communities on the ground.[40] Although this may simply reflect more general inter-generation mentality shifts within policing, for 'critical engagers' the upshot of the above differentiation nonetheless offers vindication that there are now people within the PSNI who are motivated by a desire to serve their community. In a master narrative of community service, this

---

36 AD, supporter of Sinn Féin policy, interview, July 2013.

37 G, supporter of Sinn Féin policy, interview, May 2013.

38 Roulton, 2009.

39 C, community activist, interview, May 2013.

40 D, community activist, interview, May 2013.

warrants assertions of newness, yet in a counter-narrative of 'cosmetic reform' such claims are unfounded. What merits a deeper examination at this juncture is how performance of the PSNI 'community policing' function contributes to this debate.

'Community policing'

Previous researchers have noted the inherent difficulty in measuring attitudes towards 'community policing' within republican communities because of uncertainty over whether criticisms result from legacy issues or post-conflict concerns about rising crime and disorder.[41] There is undoubted veracity in this observation. Even in a post-Patten age of 'policing with the community',[42] republican experiences of policing are largely drawn from memories of 'suspect community' policing, counter-insurgency policing and violent 'public order' policing. These memories did not disappear because a certain number of people held up a voting card at the opportune moment one Sunday evening in Dublin. They remain internalised within the collective and individuals. This inescapably impacts on current views of the PSNI, even where 'community policing' is concerned. Another difficulty in measuring Irish republican attitudes towards 'community policing' is that the general mimics the particular, and the local mimics the global. The assertion here is that many of the criticisms made by Irish republicans mirror criticisms persistently made in criminological literature on policing more generally. Poor police performance,[43] detachment from the communities they are meant to be serving due to perceived shortcomings birthed by 'Dixon of Dock Green' misconceptions,[44] a problematic classist 'canteen culture'[45] and the blurred lines between policing confidence, consent and legitimacy[46] have all raised their head in societies elsewhere. However, how these issues are framed, interpreted and critiqued by Irish republicans have a particular local dimension. Northern Ireland is, after all, a post-reform society trying to move away from a historical 'divided-society' policing model towards one premised on 'policing with the community'. This has produced a peculiarly localised analysis of more general policing problems through the invocation

41 Ellison, Shirlow and Mulcahy, 2012; Byrne and Monaghan, 2008, 41.

42 Shearing, 2000.

43 Bradford, Jackson and Stanko, 2009.

44 Davies and Thomas, 2008.

45 Brogden, 1991.

46 Bradford, Jackson, Hough and Farrall, 2008.

of memory. If, as Ellison, Pino and Shirlow contend,[47] the most apposite point to view community–police relations is from the most difficult vantage point, this research is well placed. 'Community policing' is critiqued by those who 'remember' ineffective 'normal' policing in the past and have considerable, perhaps even unrealistic, expectations in the present.

Memory acquires a consistent importance in gauging the PSNI's 'community policing' performance. It allows current 'community policing' to be measured against what Irish republican communities 'remember' from the past. The contribution that effective 'community policing' can make to having the PSNI accepted as a 'new' force cannot be underestimated. Even after reform, excluded groups rarely accept the police nonchalantly. The 'new' police force must earn its legitimacy. Improving 'community policing' on the ground is 'a key public confidence-building measure' in this process.[48] 'Community policing' becomes a 'band aid plaster' for past legitimacy problems,[49] largely because concentration turns to the positive present rather than negative past. The apparent 'newness' of the reformed force is accentuated by contrasting it with a problematic predecessor. Groenewald and Peake argue that 'a police force that is seen to have changed its character, making a break from repressive practices of the past and working in partnership with communities from which it was historically removed has profound symbolic resonance'.[50] With memory functioning to reinforce but also challenge views of newness, the importance of this becomes magnified. With the PSNI having undergone aesthetic reform and now comprising Nationalists seeking to serve their community, the next piece of the post-reform jigsaw is actually delivering an effective service on the ground in previously excluded communities.

In trying to earn their legitimacy as a community service in republican communities, the PSNI faced the task of having to provide not merely a satisfactory service, but a service capable of ameliorating local policing experiences in light of past negative experiences.[51] Reality on the ground in republican communities suggests that the PSNI has yet to achieve this. Existing research has consistently shown that republican communities regard the PSNI as having poor response times, poor clean-up rates and a clear disinterest in policing crime.[52] The PSNI response to this criticism further problematises the matter. Byrne, Topping and Martin have noted that rather than being open

47 Ellison, Pino and Shirlow, 2013.

48 Tshwete, 2001.

49 Brogden and Nijhar, 2013, 13.

50 Groenewald and Peake, 2004.

51 Topping and Byrne, 2012b, 175.

52 Ellison, Pino and Shirlow 2013; Byrne and Monaghan, 2008, 51.

with the community about their shortcomings, the PSNI detrimentally reverts to defensive operational speak and official figures.[53] Similarly, one interviewee complained that the PSNI uses 'facts and figures' to deflect from policing shortcomings on the ground.[54] An 'Excel culture' might allow the PSNI to defend itself, but it carries little advantage in terms of local engagement.[55] Recourse to these 'facts and figures' and pleas of resource restraints are viewed by sceptical republican communities as a smokescreen for avoiding meaningful interaction that might actually solve the problem.

'Over-policing' and 'under-policing'

Facts, figures and resource restraints may hold currency at the official level but at grassroots level within republican communities they are worthless. Evaluation occurs through lived observation of 'community policing'. To this end, evaluation is conducted on a comparative basis; comparative to what was experienced in the past and comparative with what is the perception of policing in other communities. Byrne and Topping highlight the belief within working-class republican communities that middle-class and Unionist areas benefit from more normalised, community-orientated policing.[56] Concerns over differential policing coalesce around the dichotomous issues of aggressive 'over-policing' in response to relatively minor issues and 'under-policing' via failure to solve low-level issues. The contention of those on the ground is that while working-class republican communities continue to suffer from 'over-policing' and 'under-policing', middle-class and Unionist communities do not.

'Over-policing' and 'under-policing' have been historically problematic within republican communities, and more generally in historically excluded groups, like indigenous communities in Australia and black communities in South Africa.[57] Any residual manifestation of these problems will challenge assertions of newness and a community service narrative. One community activist recounted 'the police raid to end all police raids' that was mounted in their area, opining that such aggressive 'over-policing' would not happen elsewhere.[58] Aggressive 'over-policing' represents problematic continuity rather than rupture, causing a remembering of similar police aggression under 'suspect community' policing. Corroboration of this was found in the

53 Byrne, Topping and Martin, 2014, 26.

54 I, supporter of Sinn Féin policy, interview, May 2013.

55 Byrne and Monaghan, 2008, 50; Topping, 2008b.

56 Byrne and Topping, 2012b, 46.

57 Cunneen, 2001; Ruteere and Pommerolle, 2003.

58 D, community activist, interview, May 2013.

admission of one interviewee who noted, 'I know in this area people don't see much change in policing ... they still come in here very, very heavy handed to deal with some of the most simplest of issues'.[59] 'Under-policing' is problematic too, reflective not only of the transitional, post-reform context but also more generally of how failure to address 'broken windows' crime heightens fears over crime and disorder.[60] Rather than buying into a defence based on resource restraints, 'under-policing' is attributed to a disinterest in delivering effective policing for republican communities. In South Armagh, for example, this led to a high-profile community protest in February 2015 amidst local claims that the PSNI were wilfully inactive in tackling local criminality and instead blaming this on austerity-driven resource restraints.[61] The ability to draw a line of continuity between current inefficiency and past 'under-policing' is evident in the argument of one sceptic that 'from my experience and from talking to people in my community, when they have rang the police they haven't got any more joy from them than they would have got from the RUC, and that's the reality of it'.[62] Highlighting policing inefficiency in republican communities, one critic argued that in affluent communities elsewhere, 'a two- to three-minute response time would suffice and you'd be dealt with in a very polite manner and efficient manner'.[63] While there may be mitigating factors – including resource restraints and the use of 'come on' attacks by militants[64] – these have little resonance at grassroots level, where PSNI inefficiency is attributed to indifference towards providing a 'community policing' service for republican communities. Where republicans on the ground 'remember' RUC indifference towards 'community policing', this feeds a suspicion that working-class republican communities are still adversely effected by an ingrained bias through punitive measures like excessive checkpoints for motoring offences.[65] Memory therefore retains a view of policing being punitive rather than community orientated.

Besides merely stating that republican communities are dissatisfied with this apparent differential policing provision, it is worth examining why there is such dissatisfaction on the matter. A community service narrative places much

59 I, supporter of Sinn Féin policy, interview, May 2013.

60 Wilson and Kelling, 1982.

61 P. Malone, '"Border Regions Losing Faith in PSNI" – Murphy', *Newry Times*, 27 February 2015: http://newrytimes.com/2015/02/27/border-regions-losing-faith-in-psni-murphy/ (accessed 28 February 2015).

62 J, critic of Sinn Féin policy, interview, June 2013.

63 P, critic of Sinn Féin policy, interview, June 2013.

64 Frampton, 2012.

65 U, supporter of Sinn Féin policy, interview, August 2013.

emphasis on the fact that republican communities 'need' a police service to curb socio-economic ills. Republican communities are therefore acquainted with the reality that 'fair and effective policing offers opportunities and promise as opposed to threats and antagonism'.[66] The ire of republican communities emanates from the fact that they are now aware of the benefits of 'fair and effective policing', but, as lived experience recounted in the interviews suggests, they are yet to benefit from these 'promises and opportunities'. Perhaps, then, republican communities feel they are 'missing out' on the benefits they believed endorsing the PSNI would bring. One outcome of this is that the door has not yet fully shut on the practice of 'rough justice'. It was believed that the Patten vision of 'policing with the community' would replace 'punishment attacks' in republican communities.[67] However, PSNI failure to effectively tackle crime in republican communities is increasingly being met by militant attempts to garner community support by dealing with crime in the traditional manner.[68] In addition to a historical precedent for 'rough justice', the continuation of the practice can also bestow some sense of legitimacy onto militant groups. In turn, this feeds into the wider politicking of the 'hearts and minds' debate within Irish republicanism on the issue of policing. This should not detract from how Community Restorative Justice (CRJ) initiatives have helped republican communities look beyond 'rough justice'.[69] This has seen belated recognition that while 'rough justice' may have filled the policing vacuum in the short term, it was inadequate in tackling a wider societal problem that only communities working with a policing service can address. One pro-policing republican retrospectively critiqued 'rough justice', arguing that, 'people will say "Awh sure you did that years ago and this happened years ago" and whatever, but that's looking back. And did it work then? No, it didn't ... you have to find alternatives'.[70]

A deeper explanation for republican dissatisfaction with 'community policing' may be found in the expectations they now have of policing. The historical detachment of republican communities from policing obfuscated what civic policing 'means', creating a context where the 'community policing' bar might be set 'unrealistically high'.[71] This occurred against the backdrop of a 'critical engagement' narrative reframing policing from being a threat to being a community service. The narrative constructed during the policing

---

[66] Ellison, Shirlow and Mulcahy, 2012.

[67] Shearing, 2000.

[68] Topping and Byrne, 2012a; Horgan and Morrison, 2011.

[69] Eriksson, 2013, 73.

[70] G, supporter of Sinn Féin policy, interview, May 2013.

[71] Ellison, Pino and Shirlow, 2013.

debate frontloaded talk of accountability, 'community policing' and 'putting manners' on the PSNI. A staple diet of tough talk may have been sufficient to persuade sceptical communities of the 'need' for 'community policing', yet at the same time it presented a somewhat idealised view of how it would be rolled out. While the benefits of 'community policing' were engorged, cognisance of resource restraints, limited 'clean-up' rates and slow response times was conspicuous by its absence. It also completely overlooked the thrust of structuralist critiques of policing. Cocooned from the lived reality of these wider issues, republican communities would struggle to reconcile them with the expectations on which 'critical engagement' was premised. With interaction with the PSNI regarding 'normal' crime being a new experience for republican communities, it was always probable that their expectations would outweigh policing realities. In one sense, then, difficulty can be attributed to the PSNI having to impress 'awkward customers'.[72]

It must be acknowledged nonetheless that in certain cases dissatisfaction stems from actual PSNI shortcomings rather than unrealistically high expectations. A catalogue of stark PSNI failings recounted by interviewees included: the victim of a house break-in being told that the PSNI did not have the resources to attend the crime scene, with further instruction for the victim to take their door off its hinges and bring it to their local PSNI station to be tested for fingerprints there; the PSNI phoning a young woman who had previously made a complaint, not with the intention of addressing the initial complaint but to ask her either to confirm or deny reports that a dead body was lying in an alley beside her house; the failure to prevent or intervene in a fatal attack on an elderly man outside a PSNI station equipped with extensive surveillance equipment; and an excessive delay in responding to the reported theft of a handbag from a car because officers were busy investigating the death of a cat that had been killed by a neighbour's dog. The natural reaction in these cases is to 'remember' shortcomings in the past and pose the rhetorical question, 'What has changed?' Although admittedly extreme examples, these cases suggest that what Mulcahy calls 'the routinization of the unprecedented'[73] – when the bizarre becomes the normal, previously synonymous with RUC counter-insurgency policing – has now seeped into PSNI 'community policing' in working-class republican areas. Such glaring shortcomings are irreconcilable with the previously identified importance of delivering a vastly improved policing service to republican communities in order to ameliorate their views of the PSNI. In light of the shortcomings identified by interviewees above it

[72] Topping, 2008a.

[73] Mulcahy, 2013, 139.

is little wonder that republican communities believe the PSNI has 'missed the mark' on 'community policing'.[74]

Community–police relations

Competing narratives on 'community policing' utilise the memory of the historical animosity that defined interaction between republican communities and policing in the North of Ireland. On the one hand, those involved in 'critical engagement' portray tentative improvement as vindication of assertions of change and newness and the recalibration of an understanding of policing as a community service. On the other hand, critics argue that residual difficulty belies the cosmetic nature of police reform. Existing research on community–police interaction is instructive in contextualising these narratives. Byrne and Topping note that even though the 'raw political basis' for communal disengagement from policing is diminishing, detachment still remains, contrary to the 'official picture' on community–police engagement.[75] The reasons for continued detachment may not reside solely with the natural reluctance of republican communities to engage. Partial explanation may lie in the nature of post-Patten 'community policing' itself. Despite the Patten vision of 'policing with the community', community safety remains 'unfairly police orientated' because the PSNI were installed as the 'main powerbroker and agenda setter'.[76] What has transpired is the retention of a system largely based on centralised authority that stands in contrast to the Patten vision of a service that will 'police with the community'.[77] Any general communal engagement has pre-imposed limitations, meaning that even if republican communities were willing to engage with policing the scope for meaningful engagement is limited by structural factors. Topping has noted that the operational 'second stream' of Patten proposals on 'community policing' have been far from successful.[78] Greater success is dependent on the PSNI actively building 'community policing' partnerships with 'hard to reach' communities which must reciprocate rather than keeping one eye fixed on the past.[79] Topping's well-made argument is placed into context by the wider reality that endorsement and engagement at a political level are very different from grassroots engagement where developments have been much slower. Joanne Murphy labels this a

[74] Byrne and Topping, 2012, 15.
[75] Byrne and Topping, 2012, 15.
[76] Ellison and O'Rawe, 2010.
[77] Hillyard and Tomlinson, 2000.
[78] Topping, 2008b.
[79] Topping, 2008a.

'schizophrenic approach' whereby official 'buy in' is not mirrored at grassroots level.[80] Within the historically excluded group, attitudes towards the PSNI's 'community policing' function are therefore 'highly variable'.[81] The 'highly variable' nature of attitudes towards the PSNI was borne out in interview data where interviewees evaluated lived reality on the ground today with what they 'remember' from the past.

For critics constructing a narrative of 'cosmetic reform', continued hostility found a natural home with the memory of RUC hostility. Continuity in 'demeanour' again reinforces their narrative that there has been little substantive change in terms of attitudes towards republican communities. Referencing an exchange (with the father of a PSNI officer stationed in a republican community) that highlighted a continued 'us' and 'them' attitude within policing towards republican communities, one critic noted:

> I was talking to a guy a couple of weeks ago ... he was saying his son was in the police. It was 'right in the heart of [area]'. You know that 'right in the heart of [area]'. Now that's what way they think. 'Right in the heart of [area]', because the son has went home to him and said the heart of [area].[82]

As further evidence of continuity of 'demeanour', the interviewee highlighted an incident in which a PSNI officer referred to residents in the same republican community as 'you people'. Another critic drew continuity with current less than cordial experiences and previous ones:

> My experience of them has not been good, just put it that way. Hasn't changed. They haven't done or said anything that's made me say, 'Oh hold on a minute'. They would say, 'Well, that's your politics dictating that', but it's not really. It's a human condition. If someone is treating you with respect, is listening to you, is treating you as a human being, then you know you are going to say, 'Well hold on a minute here. Maybe I have got this wrong. Maybe that was the bad old days', but they don't. I mean they seriously don't.[83]

These accounts indicate that, in spite of Topping's well-placed argument, for some people the natural view of policing is through one eye fixed on the past.

Where community–police relations have improved, underlying cynicism

80 Murphy, 2013, 135.

81 Ellison, Shirlow and Mulchay, 2012.

82 N, critic of Sinn Féin policy, interview, June 2013.

83 P, critic of Sinn Féin policy, interview, June 2013.

remains. Improved relations are seen as a product of a 'charm offensive' spawned by 'cosmetic reform' seeking to normalise 'British policing'. One cynic argued that the PSNI was only being superficially accepted into republican areas because funding criteria stipulating mandatory PSNI involvement in community projects leaves community groups with no other choice but to engage. Arguing that the PSNI is 'literally being forced on people' by this, the interviewee opined it was designed to ease the 'rolling out' of policing in republican communities.[84] This scepticism mirrors previously noted concerns about the impact on previously excluded communities when funding is tied to police acceptance, and also observations on how funding was previously used in a divisive politicised manner in Nationalist communities.[85] Another sceptic contended that the PSNI was engaged in 'a real hearts and minds battle' in a bid to ingratiate themselves to republican communities. This entailed funding community events in a bid to 'win over' republican communities. Citing the PSNI funding of a concert featuring Irish rebel group the Wolfe Tones during an annual community festival, they commented:

> You have to think – now I see right through it – but I mean some people might go 'Awh, sure it's grand now, it's all over; sure the police are funding the Wolfe Tones; that's okay by me you know' ... some people are susceptible to standards so if they get that there they're happy enough with how things have changed.[86]

The same community festival hosted an unprecedented event in August 2015 where Martin McGuinness and PSNI Chief Constable George Hamilton shared a platform to discuss 'dealing with the past' and improving 'community policing' in front of a largely republican audience.[87] From the scepticism above, it appears that such improved community–police relations are not necessarily viewed favourably. For critics, this type of interaction merely normalises 'British policing' rather than signifying genuine *rupture* with past policing. Not only does this reinforce their master narrative on 'cosmetic reform' and the 'normalisation' of 'British policing', it also has an obvious resonance with the claims that republicans used to make in relation

---

[84] K, critic of Sinn Féin policy, interview, June 2013.

[85] Topping, 2008a; Rolston, 2012, 482; Bean, 1995.

[86] V, critic of Sinn Féin policy, interview, September 2013.

[87] B. Rowan, 'Martin McGuinness and George Hamilton Debate: Meeting of Minds Good for the Future', *Belfast Telegraph*, 10 August 2015: www.belfasttelegraph.co.uk/opinion/debateni/brian-rowan/martin-mcguinness-and-george-hamilton-debate-meeting-of-minds-good-for-the-future-31438633.html (accessed 19 August 2015).

to road safety presentations made by the RUC in Nationalist schools. More notably, it reflects the 'iron fist in the velvet glove' structuralist critique of 'community policing' that sees it as a calculated effort to gain access to and influence within communities with legitimacy problems through seemingly benign community-oriented activity.[88]

Those involved in 'critical engagement' use their lived experience of improved community–police relations to construct a sense of rupture that feeds into their 'community policing' narrative of newness and change. Where positive community–police relations have started to take root, this is seen as evidence of movement away from viewing policing as a threat to viewing it as a community service. One interviewee who had previously recalled the hostility towards the RUC in their area noted that policing on the ground was now being seen as less threatening and in terms of being a community service:

> Every year there is an increase in numbers phoning the police. There is a different attitude and there's a lot of people like even in [area], you know, who do. We were slagging the cops; they were saying about the 'tea houses' they have around [area]. You know, the people invite them in for tea and all the rest. And those houses do exist.[89]

Police officers visiting houses in republican communities for tea rather than to raid them certainly conveys a sense of communities viewing policing in terms of being a community service rather than a threat. Another supporter of 'critical engagement' used the memory of RUC violence in republican communities to demonstrate how policing was no longer premised on threat. Recounting a conversation they had that highlighted this, they argued:

> I remember about six months ago being in this taxi ... and the guy was telling me this story ... he was saying about these young ones in [area] and they were talking about 'And they're as bad as the RUC. They stopped the other night and they were giving off to us about something'. And your man says, 'They're as bad as the RUC? Wait to I tell you about the RUC. You used to be standing, they'd pull up in the jeeps, they just jumped out battered the living daylights out of you. Threw you in the jeeps, battered the living daylights out of you, and then dumped you somewhere in the city'. They'd say to you, 'The PSNI pulled up and got out and spoke to you. Argued with you or something?' Just get real ... There's no comparison even given any

[88] McLaughlin, 2007, 66.

[89] G, supporter of Sinn Féin policy, interview, May 2013.

> sort of abuse that cops still do and cops being cops will do, but to compare it with the RUC.[90]

Tacit acceptance of this is detectable in the concession of one critic that 'there is a change in the way that the PSNI deal with people. You know you would have to be silly not to see that. You're not going into a police station anymore and getting ten bells knocked out of you when you're being interviewed. That's a reality'. Despite conceding this, the interviewee did not view it as a rupture with the past given that when it comes to 'their aggression, their lies, their set ups I don't think anything has changed'.[91]

Active co-operation

In promoting a narrative of community service those leading 'critical engagement' stress that increasing numbers of people within republican communities are contacting the PSNI on matters of 'normal' crime. To this end, one interviewee spoke of 'a complete and utter sea change' whereby people within republican communities are now 'more helpful' and 'more willing' to contact the PSNI. Elaborating on this change in mindset, the interviewee opined, 'The political element I think is no longer as overt or as in their face. They're confidence now is about will the wee drug dealer in the street who they provide information on be arrested and be put in jail. And that's where people measure their success'.[92] Likewise, another interviewee pointed out that people in their area had 'no problem' contacting the PSNI on 'ordinary crime issues'. Despite this change in outlook the PSNI response did little to instil confidence because:

> I don't know how many people have said to me there's no point ringing the police. They don't respond; if they do it's two days later ... that's what sticks in people's minds. You hear that more than 'I was robbed last night and I was really impressed with the service I got'.[93]

While the link between unsatisfactory victim–police contact and low confidence is certainly not unique to the PSNI,[94] what is crucial is the overarching post-reform, post-'critical engagement' environment it occurs in. In such a

---

[90] M, supporter of Sinn Féin policy, interview, June 2013.

[91] AC, critic of Sinn Féin policy, interview, November 2013.

[92] B, supporter of Sinn Féin policy, interview, April 2013.

[93] I, supporter of Sinn Féin policy, interview, May 2013.

[94] Bradford, Jackson and Stanko, 2009.

context, as Byrne, Topping and Martin note,[95] confidence is an operational matter 'to be lived and experienced on the ground'. Operational shortcomings create a problematic thread of 'under-policing' *continuity* that runs through any 'community service' narrative.

Despite some reported increase of contact on 'normal crime', empirical research indicates that contacting the PSNI remains an option of 'last resort' for some.[96] A tendency to contact community groups or local republicans as had been the case prior to 'critical engagement' still persists.[97] This has been used by critics to assert that the fallacy of 'cosmetic reform' is being exposed by lack of change on the ground:

> I can't say I've noticed a massive shift in attitude of the public towards support for the PSNI just because Sinn Féin says that they now support the PSNI. You know it would be wrong to say elements of the community don't use the PSNI. You know elements of the community do but elements of the community also used the RUC ... I see just as many cases of criminality and that being referred to republicans as in the past.[98]

This comment interestingly exposes a 'silence' in relation to how some people in republican communities did report 'normal' crime to the RUC. Other interviewees who touched on this suggested it resulted from the necessity to do so for insurance claims. Contextualising the matter within these confines, one critic noted, 'It's like everything else. People are trapped. Republicans have never – from 1916 – have never accepted the police but they phone the cops if they get their house broke into if they need to get a claim or compensation either directly or indirectly paid up'.[99] Critics therefore draw continuity *with* this by arguing that any increased level of contact between republican communities and the PSNI today is attributable to the same grounds of practicality rather than any change of outlook to recognise the PSNI as a new community service. Highlighting the reality of this, one opponent of policing outlined that if they were burgled:

> I would ring the police and that is because they ... are the people who will give me a crime reference number for my insurance. I think though if it was something relatively minor, that maybe in a normal society you would ring

95 Byrne, Topping and Martin, 2014a, 25.
96 Topping and Byrne, 2012a.
97 Ellison, Pino and Shirlow, 2013.
98 O, critic of Sinn Féin policy, interview, June 2013.
99 N, critic of Sinn Féin policy, interview, June 2013.

> the police about, probably not. I think people do think twice about ringing the police if I'm being realistic.[100]

The fact that republican communities still approach community groups and republicans is also observed by community activists. One community activist conceded that people in their area 'don't see the PSNI as a service like the ambulance or nurse or doctor'.[101] Instead, they still approach community groups, former republican prisoners or Sinn Féin activists who then have to direct them on to the PSNI. It is worth identifying why people contact local community or republican activists rather than the PSNI. An obvious factor is the lack of confidence that has been created not only by historical detachment but also by continued 'under-policing'. Commenting on this, a community activist stated that where people in their locality have engaged with the PSNI they have been discouraged from doing so again due to the fact they 'never get the right response' in terms of follow up and results.[102]

A more fundamental cause is the lack of local people in policing structures. An obvious caveat to this is that prolonged detachment from policing has somewhat blinded republican communities to the fact that police officers in general do not patrol their own areas. 'Community policing' everywhere involves some degree of 'policing strangers by strangers'.[103] This does not detract, however, from the fact that there is no openly identifiable local police presence – whether that is a local from working-class republican communities patrolling their own area or simply being visible in the PSNI even if based elsewhere. Nor is 'community policing' in these communities fronted by those from a similar socio-political background. Not only are locals not patrolling their own area but they are not patrolling other areas either, largely because, to all intents and purposes, there is no visible existence of such officers in the PSNI. This creates an overarching disconnect between the PSNI and working-class Irish republican communities. Even if 'community policing' officers elsewhere are geographically and socially unfamiliar with the community they are assigned to in the first instance, they can nonetheless develop a sense of being part of that community over time.[104] Empirical evidence of the continued apprehension among Irish republican communities suggests this can hardly apply to PSNI officers. The implication of this for community–police engagement is obvious, with Gordon noting that how representative a

---

[100] AC, critic of Sinn Féin policy, interview November 2013.

[101] D, community activist, interview, May 2013.

[102] E, community activist, interview, May 2013.

[103] Brogden, 1991.

[104] Davies and Thomas, 2008.

reformed police force is of the community it is tasked with serving is a 'critical barometer' for how engaged that community will ultimately become.[105] Given the above, it is therefore unsurprising that a degree of disconnect remains between working-class republican communities and PSNI officers who are still viewed as 'outsiders'.

Outsiders

State policing in republican communities has traditionally been performed by heavily armed 'outsiders'. Even Catholic RUC officers were, as one interviewee articulated, 'as foreign as the guys from Birmingham or wherever whenever they came on my streets'.[106] Although a 'community policing' narrative has recast PSNI officers as community servants rather than armed invaders, the view on the ground of policing agents as 'outsiders' remains. Illustrating this point, one interviewee noted that, 'Whenever I went to [holding centre] in 1975 there was cops from Newtownards and there was cops from Bangor and there was cops from Portadown and there was cops from all Unionist places in the North. What's changed?'[107] The ability to 'remember' past 'outsiders' and liken them to the PSNI is problematic for any 'community policing' narrative as there is clear incongruence between the notions of 'outsider' and community servant. Rather than reinforcing assertions of newness or change, memory serves to construct continuity between RUC 'outsiders' and PSNI 'outsiders'. If a rupture can be drawn with the RUC on the basis that, as the 'critical engagement' narrative contends, the PSNI function is to serve the community, similarly then continuity can be derived from the fact that the PSNI is still not an integral part of republican communities. One community activist touched upon this when admitting that within republican communities PSNI officers are 'not liked' and 'not respected' because they are not 'of the community or from the community'.[108] This admission is telling for the importance it places upon being 'of' or 'from' the community. Republicans, as the quintessential 'other' in the Northern Ireland state, have traditionally relied on their own community rather than the state. In the face of threatened and real violence from the 'other' and the state, 'community' became a source of collective safety and strength.[109] Local problems were largely solved by the local community without any outside interference. The prevalence of 'rough justice' meted out

[105] Gordon, 2008.

[106] A, supporter of Sinn Féin policy, interview, April 2013.

[107] L, supporter of Sinn Féin policy, interview, June 2013.

[108] D, community activist, interview, May 2013.

[109] Zurawski, 2004.

by republicans to petty criminals is testament to this.[110] Even as violent conflict subsided, republican communities continued empowering themselves from within rather than relying on the state.[111] With PSNI officers being 'outsiders' – both literally and metaphorically – 'community policing' runs contrary to the long-established grain of internalised 'self-help'. A continued detachment from and general failure to build 'community policing' rapport with these 'outsiders' results.

Illustrating the extent to which the 'outsider' perception feeds a continued disconnect, one republican in favour of 'critical engagement' conceded:

> Like there's a community police officer in this area. I don't see her. She's not part of this community. Does she know the needs of the community? I'm not sure. You know, so it's all right having these nice titles, and these public meetings take place and there's a presentation and this word 'community police officer' is available, but then no one in the community knows who she is. It's a contradiction in itself.[112]

A similar sentiment was evinced by another interviewee who noted that despite endorsing 'critical engagement' they had little affinity with the PSNI 'community policing' officers assigned to their area:

> I've no idea who the top police officer is in [area]. I don't know what time [area] police station opens to, you know, because there isn't anybody there that you know and trust. It's just a name, it's just a face, whereas if there would have been people brought in from the local community then, yeah, I think it would have been easier and the transition would have been much more smooth.[113]

Even if not overtly Unionist, PSNI officers remain 'outsiders' in the sense that they are not local. The prevalence of this parochialism leads some to question how a PSNI lacking local knowledge and trust can deliver for a community they are not part of. What merits further examination at this juncture is why policing in republican communities remains the task of 'outsiders' rather than young locals eager to serve their community.

An obvious deterrent to anyone considering joining the PSNI is the threat to their safety from militant republicans. Targeting PSNI recruits from within

---

110 McEvoy and Mika, 2001; Knox, 2002.

111 Bruce, 2004.

112 G, supporter of Sinn Féin policy, interview, May 2013.

113 T, supporter of Sinn Féin policy, interview, August 2013.

Nationalist communities is not only easier in terms of intelligence work and access but also helps to distance the PSNI from these communities. This targeting strategy was initially designed to undermine the 50/50 recruitment policy.[114] Both PSNI officers killed so far by militants (Stephen Carroll and Ronan Kerr) were Catholic. Many Catholic PSNI officers have relocated in order to avoid a similar fate. At least 78 PSNI officers have done so since the Sinn Féin endorsement.[115] More recently, militants have even taken to targeting PSNI recruitment events in a concerted bid to dampen their appeal to prospective recruits within the Nationalist community.[116] As a matter of logic, one could deduce that the persistent level of threat and the likelihood of becoming an 'outsider' to some extent dissuades prospective PSNI recruits in republican communities.

The impact of the militant threat on PSNI recruitment in republican communities was openly acknowledged by interviewees. One interviewee argued that whilst in relative terms it may have been 'more dangerous back then' to be a member of the RUC, refined targeting by militants meant that in comparative terms joining the PSNI was 'still very dangerous for young republicans'.[117] This view was shared by supporters of 'critical engagement' who expressed the same concern for the well-being of prospective recruits from republican communities. Such concern has two discernible benefits: it reinforces assertions of change and newness that underpin the 'community policing' narrative and it differentiates between past and current republican violence for the benefit of internal politicking over the legacy of past armed struggle. It was also shared by opponents, who expressed a similar belief that the job was 'still very dangerous'. The latter used the continuity inherent between current republican violence and past republican violence to reinforce their narrative that 'cosmetic reform' was not enough to fool republicans into subscribing to the normalisation of 'British' policing. One critic referred to the killing of Stephen Carroll as a 'wake-up call' that serving in the PSNI was 'still a dangerous job to be in'. Elaborating further, the interviewee asked, 'Is £24,000 a year enough to put your life on the line?' before concluding,

---

[114] Perry, 2011.

[115] It is worth noting a general decline in this pattern more recently. In 2007, 10 PSNI officers relocated, 17 in 2008, 15 in 2009, 15 in 2010, 8 in 2011, 9 in 2012 and 4 in 2013. Figures contained in Freedom of Information request, F-2014-00285, on file with author.

[116] S. McKinney, 'Elaborate Hoax at Derry Hotel Was Real Bomb – PSNI', *Irish News*, 12 October 2015: www.irishnews.com/news/2015/10/12/news/elaborate-hoax-at-derry-hotel-was-real-bomb---psni-290560/ (accessed 17 November 2015).

[117] T, supporter of Sinn Féin policy, interview, August 2013.

'I don't think so.'[118] The belief that successful militant attacks might function as a 'wake-up call' was also present in the views of another republican. Opining that 'everybody knows the name now, Ronan Kerr', the interviewee concluded that threat of a similar attack 'could be a reason not to do it'. This remark was qualified by the argument that whilst threat of attack was no doubt a reason, other 'underlying fundamental reasons' should not be discounted.[119]

The latter observation is worth drawing out. The threat of attack is undoubtedly a reason but that does not necessarily make it the reason. Accepting that it is the reason automatically discounts other factors, and replicates the shortcomings of previous state narratives on 'hidden support' examined earlier in the book. The current PSNI fatality rate from militant activity stands at two. Whilst anachronistic in a society increasingly depicted as 'moving on' and having solved the policing 'problem', the fatality rate is nonetheless unremarkable and far removed from that previously incurred by the RUC. Moreover, an examination of the PSNI 'roll of honour' reveals that those killed by militant republicans represent only a fraction of those killed during PSNI duty – statistically speaking, road traffic accidents represent a greater source of PSNI loss of life.[120] Contextualising the militant threat strengthens the assertion that it offers only a partial explanation for lack of recruitment in republican communities as *a* reason rather than total explanation as *the* reason.

While Horgan rightly identifies an increase in militant activity post-critical engagement,[121] the reality remains that even this increased level is not on a par with pre-GFA violence. Tonge estimates that current militant activity is at 12 per cent of the IRA campaign during the 1980s and 30 per cent of the rate in the 1990s.[122] Current militant activity therefore does not match 'the range and tempo of the PIRA campaign'.[123] Even if some causality is accorded to the increased targeting of Catholics, the threat of violence to PSNI members is evidently not as omnipresent as it was for members of the RUC. As a logical follow-on, the threat of violence can only provide, at best, the same level of explanation for lack of republican PSNI recruits as it did for lack of RUC recruits. That increased level of threat was *not* the sole reason for the lack of Nationalist recruits in the RUC. This is suggestive that threat of attack

[118] AC, critic of Sinn Féin policy, interview, November 2013.

[119] V, critic of Sinn Féin policy, interview, September 2013.

[120] Figures obtained from www.policememorial.org.uk/index.php?page=psni (accessed 28 March 2014).

[121] Horgan, 2013.

[122] Tonge, 2014a.

[123] International Monitoring Commission, 2010.

today provides only a *limited* explanation for the absence of PSNI recruits from republican communities. Further explanation may be found in the wider impact the threat has beyond consideration of the mere physicality of it. A newspaper article penned by a PSNI officer based in a border area highlighted as much, with the officer relating a daily routine that consists of a two-hour drive to work, getting 'down on my hands and my knees in all weathers' to check under their car for viable devices and restrictions on where to shop and eat lunch while on work breaks.[124]

Another contributory factor is the prolonged detachment that followed Patten reform. In the initial absence of any tentative movement towards working with the PSNI, for the first five years of the force's existence, republican communities continued to work in liaison with community groups outside the ambit of policing agencies. The most successful endeavour during this period was the growth of CRJ schemes.[125] Providing a non-punitive local solution to local problems and fronted by local people, the schemes gained considerable traction in republican communities.[126] The schemes – which were *not* designed to supplant the formal state system[127] – used statutory agencies like Social Services as referral services in light of legitimacy problems with policing.[128] More recently, CRJ has developed an 'active and ongoing' partnership with a range of statutory bodies including the PSNI.[129] CRJ has received criticism within the wider Irish republican constituency, with opponents of Sinn Féin arguing that they represent an extension of Sinn Féin hegemony[130] – a claim CRJ rejects.[131] Key to the grassroots success and credibility of CRJ schemes was the involvement of former combatants and republican activists. As Jarman notes, factors such as political affiliation, local residency and former combatant status give credibility to those involved in community-based initiatives in republican

---

[124] 'Frontier Life Still a Lonely One for Cops' *Belfast Telegraph*, Belfast, 1 July 2014.

[125] Mika and McEvoy, 2001.

[126] McEvoy and Eriksson, 2007, 321.

[127] McEvoy and Eriksson, 2008.

[128] Eriksson, 2013.

[129] Community Restorative Justice, 'Working Partnerships': https://web.archive.org/web/20140912114452/http://crji.ie/about/working-partnerships/ (originally accessed 17 July 2014).

[130] 'What We Have We Hold – INLA': www.redactionarchive.org/2012/03/news-april-2001.html (accessed 17 July 2014); 'GARC – Yet More Demonisation', *Ardoyne Republican*, 4 August 2012: https://web.archive.org/web/20140718162409/http://ardoynerepublican.blogspot.co.uk/2012_07_29_archive.html (originally accessed 17 July 2014).

[131] Eriksson, 2013.

districts.[132] The success of such schemes is often attributable to the 'social capital' of former prisoners and community activists leading them.[133] This is in stark contrast to the fact that PSNI officers enjoy little trust within republican communities because they are not 'of' or 'from' the community. One may infer that had this 'social capital' been used to bring republican communities towards the PSNI during its infancy rather than towards community initiatives the gap between these communities and the PSNI would have lessened.

In order to draw out the nuances of the above argument it is necessary to look to reform processes elsewhere. This is not to make simplistic like-for-like comparisons or to deny the particularised challenges posed by each localised context. Such an examination instead provides an overview of how the problem of prolonged detachment has been addressed outwith Northern Ireland. In El Salvador (former Farabundo Martí National Liberation Front (FMNL) combatants),[134] South Africa (ANC personnel),[135] post-Oslo Accord Palestine (Palestinian Liberation Organisation (PLO) activists)[136] and Namibia,[137] those formerly opposed to state security structures were integrated into reformed police forces. Without denying the specificities of each reform process, it is discernible that allowing former combatants into reformed police forces helps previously excluded communities place trust in such forces. If those previously seen as communal defenders are admitted into the new police force, barriers of trust and local familiarity erode. These remain considerable barriers in republican communities. One reason for this is that police reform in Northern Ireland failed to assimilate former combatants into reformed policing structures. Former combatants were debarred from joining the PSNI and also debarred from being independent members of District Policing Partnerships and the NIPB.[138] These prohibitions formed part of a concerted effort to curb any input that former combatants might have on 'community policing'.[139] This was part of a wider problem whereby the state was intent on keeping policing a 'top-down' issue steered by the state rather than by the community.[140] This 'defensive formalism' limited the impact that traditionally estranged yet strong communities could have, by keeping policing and justice a state matter

---

132 Jarman, 2006.

133 Jarman, 2009.

134 Stanley, 1999.

135 Rauch, 2000, 123.

136 Mubarak, 2000, 117.

137 Metsola, 2009, 116.

138 Hillyard and Tomlinson, 2000.

139 Jarman, 2006.

140 Ellison and O'Rawe, 2010.

controlled by statutory bodies.[141] It is likely that another calculation in prohibiting former combatants was how the move could assuage Unionism in light of disquiet over symbolism and the 50/50 recruitment policy. Admitting former combatants would have increased Unionist disillusionment with police reform and bolstered the growing strength of anti-GFA elements within that constituency. A 'zero sum' approach kept Unionism on board by excluding former combatants. Moreover, there was also considerable resistance in the initial Patten era among RUC members to the idea of former IRA and INLA members being integrated into the PSNI.[142]

As a consequence, the 'social capital' of former combatants was not utilised to bring people from republican communities into the PSNI during the crucial early phases of the force's existence. Instead, it was invested in community groups and schemes within republican communities. Rather than bridging the relationship gap post-reform, this strengthened detachment from policing. That republican communities still remain aloof to PSNI 'outsiders', still approach local republicans to deal with local issues and have not yet enlisted in the PSNI following 'critical engagement', are glaringly evident symptoms of this. One former combatant at the cold face of 'critical engagement' argued that the difficulties in getting young republicans into the PSNI would have been lessened had former combatants been given a more hands-on role in post-Patten policing. Stating that they had 'no doubt' that former combatants would have been willing to utilise their 'skills, contacts, experience', they argued that such involvement would have been 'a step in the right direction' that would have made getting people from republican communities into the PSNI 'much easier'. The interviewee acknowledged that this would have presented a 'big difficulty' for Unionists but such a difficulty was 'no bigger a difficulty' than getting republican recruits into the PSNI.[143]

Although a 'community policing' narrative frontloads the notion of policing now being a community service, it remains clear that at grassroots level this has not produced open acceptance of people within working-class republican communities joining the PSNI. Enlisting in policing remains something of a 'taboo' within such communities. This not only hampers assertions of newness but also begs the question of how the complaint that the PSNI are 'outsiders' with no local knowledge can be resolved without movement away from this taboo. One republican stated that individuals who had merely 'talked about applying' in their area were 'given the worst end of people's tongues'. The salience of this point is that the interviewee lived in a 'big Provisional Sinn

[141] McEvoy and Eriksson, 2008.

[142] Murphy, 2013, 59.

[143] AD, supporter of Sinn Féin policy, interview, July 2013.

Féin supporting' area, yet the notion of locals enlisting in the PSNI remained anathema to most.[144] The fact that joining the PSNI remains 'taboo' has led others to question to what extent the PSNI is being accepted as a community service at grassroots level. Alluding to the 'ill feeling' created by a local joining the PSNI, one republican asked:

> Can Matt Baggot [then PSNI Chief Constable] tell me – if he tells me this whole situation in [area], 'Yes, we've won the hearts and minds of people', then can he explain to me why nobody has come out of [area] to put their hands up in the wide open air and say, 'Listen I want to join your police force Matt'?[145]

This identifiable failure to 'put their hands up in the wide open air' reveals the untenable paradoxical situation Nationalist PSNI recruits are faced with. They are told to be open and proud of their role so as to increase uptake and support in their own communities, yet on the other hand they are advised not to be too open about it and to exercise caution for the sake of their safety and peace of mind in light of a militant threat and communal antagonism.[146]

In light of the fact that there is a threat to their safety that impacts heavily on their daily life, there is no local person of influence they can identify with, and that they would have to deal with a certain level of communal negativity, it is little wonder that there is little appetite among young people from working-class republican communities for joining the PSNI.

Future developments

Examination of 'community policing' has thus far been confined to a lens turned towards the past and present. The likelihood of the landscape changing further in the future is, however, an interesting topic of debate (albeit one premised largely on conjecture) with which to conclude this chapter. On one level, personal opinions simply mirror master-narrative positions. To this end, one critic opined:

> I cannot see anybody from [area] getting into the car in the morning with his big iron on his hip and his RUC/PSNI hat under his arm and his wee white short sleeved shirt, you know what I mean. You know, if you walk like a duck, talk like a duck, you are a duck and that's how they're seen in those

[144] AC, critic of Sinn Féin policy, interview, November 2013.

[145] L, supporter of Sinn Féin policy, interview, June 2013.

[146] Murphy, 2013, 148.

> communities. You know, if you're a cop, you're a cop, you're a cop. Doesn't matter that your wee uniform has changed and that you're less aggressive looking.[147]

On the other hand, there was sufficient fluidity for personal views to depart from master-narrative positions. For example, one supporter of 'critical engagement' felt that a 'cultural thing' within republican communities invariably precludes wholesale acceptance of locals in the PSNI.[148] Likewise, one critic espoused a belief that it is an inevitability, given the concerted effort by the church, cultural Nationalism and politicians to have the PSNI become an 'accepted part' of the wider community.[149]

Those wishing to see local republicans in the PSNI may be heartened by the fact that some former combatants now have no ideological opposition to their relatives joining the PSNI. They did express concern for the safety of relatives – only natural on a human level – but evinced a belief that they would be joining for the 'right reasons' of wanting to serve their community. This view not only reinforces a narrative of policing as a community service but also encapsulates the enormity of the sense of rupture subscribed to by these former combatants. It is apt to conclude the examination of republican views of 'community policing' with the following remark from one former combatant:

> If any relative of mine said they wanted to join the PSNI I wouldn't have a problem with it at all. I made the decision and I made the transition through a process of analysis on what is best for taking us forward and bringing our people forward and the best was to transform the PSNI ... so why would I bake a cake and not want anybody to eat it? It wouldn't make sense.[150]

Conclusion

Memory underpins competing narratives on 'community policing'. At the collective level, it can be usefully moulded to bolster wider master-narrative positions, yet at the individual level it provides contextualisation for and evaluation of change within policing or the lack thereof. When constructing a narrative of 'community policing' it juxtaposes current policing with 'suspect community' policing to sustain assertions of change in relation to

---

147 W, critic of Sinn Féin policy, interview, September 2013.

148 U, supporter of Sinn Féin policy, interview, August 2013.

149 Q, critic of Sinn Féin policy, interview, July 2013.

150 H, supporter of Sinn Féin policy, interview, May 2013.

composition and function. This engineers a sense of *rupture* from the RUC whereby memory distinguishes the 'new' from the 'old'. This narrative of a more inclusive community service cannot be divorced, however, from a more general progressive republican narrative of equality-based transformation of every aspect of the 'Orange' state.

Memory functions, however, as a double-edged sword. It can challenge as well as reinforce assertions of newness. This has given rise to a narrative of 'cosmetic reform' that uses residual difficulty on the ground in republican communities to draw continuity with past policing problems. It has been sustained by a natural drawing of continuity between past and current patterns of 'over-policing' and 'under-policing', general reticence in contacting the police force and the persistence of a view that PSNI officers are 'outsiders'. Assertions of newness become strained by the fact that, despite some obvious improvements, reality on the ground does not adhere neatly to the 'critical engagement' narrative of 'community policing'. Rather than representing a *rupture* with the past, this lived reality is tied seamlessly with past experiences in republican communities and is seen as a continuity of older problems. The willingness of former combatants to accept relatives joining the PSNI is optimistically suggestive that scope for tentative emergence out of the current 'stand-offish' mentality does exist. The realisation of the latter would certainly strengthen assertions of PSNI newness within working-class republican communities. Until then, however, any assertion that the PSNI is a new community service will be challenged by lived reality in republican communities.

Chapter 7

The PSNI and 'Political Policing'

Introduction

Establishing the overarching contexts of institutional crossover and heightened usage of 'anti-terror' legislation within which competing 'political policing' narratives are fashioned, this chapter conducts a thematic examination of how these opposing narratives are framed. The 'critical engagement' narrative is premised on the notion of rupture and assertions of change. It comprises themes such as disaggregating the policing monolith, proactively fighting the 'roll back' and of police reform being a component of an ongoing process of wider equality-based transformation. Although this narrative uses memory to draw a boundary between present and past policing, there is nonetheless an element of fluidity in its use of memory that blurs the lines of any neat separation by importing critical agitation from prior republican memory to frame current strategic interaction. Conversely, the narrative of opponents is again premised on continuity, and encompasses themes such as the continued abuse of 'anti-terror' legislation, the retention of RUC 'political policing' methods and the refined targeting of Irish republicans by the PSNI. In order to construct this narrative, critics use memory to draw a line of continuity between their current lived experience of the PSNI and previous individual and collective experiences with the RUC. They construct this narrative through ideological appeals with a basis in deeper cultural memory that is more conducive to their master-narrative position and through adoption of wider human rights discourse in a global post-9/11 climate.

Institutional crossover

Competing narratives are not constructed in an apolitical vacuum but against a politicised backdrop of contestation over police reform. Given that these narratives are built on assertions or denials of change, it is unsurprising that

Table 7.1 Institutional crossover

PSNI section/duty/rank	Total number in section/ duty/rank	Number of former RUC personnel	Level of institutional crossover (percentage)
Chief Inspector or above	60	53	88%
C3 Intelligence Branch	658	502	76%
Serious Crime Branch	432	259	60%
Task Support Group	419	213	51%
Community Policing Officers	815	328	40%

institutional crossover underpins them. More fundamentally, this reflects the reality of police reform in Northern Ireland, in that while many within the RUC availed themselves of the Patten 'golden handshake' many others transferred into the PSNI. This is problematic because, as seen with reform processes elsewhere, those forces exhibiting crossover from discredited successor forces become susceptible to claims of being tainted by the old.[1] While the nature of the conflict and policing problems in the North of Ireland and the political climate that spawned reform may differ from other cases, police reform here has not been immune from such criticism.

To draw out the relevance of this, a brief examination of institutional crossover levels should suffice. Table 7.1 indicates extensive institutional crossover from the RUC to the PSNI more than a decade after Patten.[2] This has been most concentrated at senior command level, but also in historically problematic branches dealing with intelligence, serious crime and public disorder. As seen above, former RUC members outnumber those recruited as PSNI members in these branches. Even within 'community policing' – considered the preserve of the 'new breed' of PSNI officer – there is a hardly negligible 40 per cent crossover rate. A rehiring debacle, whereby former RUC personnel were rehired under the guise of 'civilian staff', has further problematised this matter. Figures from 2012 revealed that of the 399 Grafton associate staff hired by the PSNI, 304 were former RUC personnel who had supposedly left policing since 1 January 2001.[3] Epidemic re-entry of this nature further strains

[1] Malan, 1999.

[2] Based on Freedom of Information request F-2013-04401, on file with the author.

[3] G. Kelly, 'In the New Beginning to Policing, There is No Place for an Old Boy's Network', *An Phoblacht*, March 2012.

any assertions of newness. Considering the magnitude of crossover, it is little surprise that Evans and Tonge found that 18 per cent of Nationalists believed the PSNI to be 'very similar' to the RUC, a contention perhaps strengthened by the fact that, as highlighted in the previous chapter, recruitment to the PSNI remains highest in areas where RUC recruitment was traditionally strong.[4]

It is not the mere presence of this crossover element that causes concern but also their potential to frustrate reform and to exert a negative influence on new recruits. These observations are not necessarily exclusive to the PSNI: internal resistance to any police reform is 'only natural and to be expected'.[5] While such resistance should be anticipated,[6] the more concerning outworking is that, as highlighted by Hillyard and Tomlinson,[7] crossover elements have a 'material interest' in preserving a culture of 'political policing'. In the specific North of Ireland context, this is troublesome given that crossover has been strongest in branches historically associated with human rights violations and the 'dirty war'. If those formerly engaged in wrongful policing are admitted into reformed forces there is, as Stanley and Call note,[8] the likelihood that they will attempt to preserve an old institutional culture tolerant of wrongful practices directed at those deemed the enemy. One senior Sinn Féin official thus attacked 'the in-house cabal of reactionaries still motivated by an unchanged wartime mentality'.[9]

At this juncture it is worth examining how institutional crossover has intertwined with memory to shape views of police reform at grassroots level. Its impact can be seen on two levels: the abstract level and the personal level. The former sees crossover interpreted at a generalised level, while the latter sees it interpreted through examples where crossover has been personalised. An example of the former is a concession by one endorser of 'critical engagement' that the policing void created by the Patten 'golden handshake' arrangement was filled by 'bastards with the same mentality and same background'.[10] High-profile examples of the latter include current Chief Constable George Hamilton and, more notably, Deputy Chief Constable Drew Harris, who previously worked in the hugely controversial RUC intelligence field.[11] Perhaps

[4] Evans and Tonge, 2012.

[5] O'Neill, 2005.

[6] Wulf, 2004.

[7] Hillyard and Tomlinson, 2000.

[8] Stanley and Call, 2008, 307.

[9] D. Kearney, 'Standing Up to the Dark Side of Policing', *An Phoblacht*, January 2012.

[10] U, supporter of Sinn Féin policy, interview, August 2013.

[11] B. Rowan, 'Profile: Drew Harris of the PSNI', *Belfast Telegraph*, 20 September 2014:

the most problematic instance of crossover for Nationalists was, as Murphy notes,[12] then RUC Chief Constable Ronnie Flanagan retaining his position to automatically become the first Chief Constable of the PSNI in November 2001. The ability of crossover to create a difficult sense of *continuity* at the personal level is evident in how one interviewee 'remembered' the roles that two PSNI officers central to the promotion of the new policing image were said to have played in contentious episodes while they were RUC officers during the conflict (one through a prominent role in recruitment drives, the other through involvement with the PSNI GAA set-up).[13] When individuals crossed over from the old to the new they took problematic pasts with them, and with this the suspicions of republicans who 'remember'. Accordingly, then, whether on the abstract or personal level, memory impedes claims of newness when intertwined with institutional crossover. Having drawn out the institutional reform backdrop to the policing debate, this chapter now turns to a thematic examination of how this sense of continuity and the previously established sense of rupture have shaped master narratives on 'political policing'.

'Critical engagement', 'rupture' and 'political policing'

Disaggregating the monolith

Although 'critical engagement' is intrinsically built on assertions of newness and change, there is, by the same token, a surprisingly frank acknowledgement of institutional crossover. This results from the fact that the prominence of the problem through coverage of the rehiring scandal means it cannot be denied, that lived experience of interaction with former RUC officers is a post-conflict reality and that as early as 1996 Sinn Féin recognised the inevitability of institutional crossover in any process of reform.[14] Drawing on a wider narrative of republican involvement in the transition being based on the maxims of pragmatism, negotiation and progression towards an ideological end goal, reform is framed as a process of negotiation and pragmatism in the face of any side to the conflict having failed to secure a clear victory. In framing the

www.belfasttelegraph.co.uk/life/features/profile-drew-harris-of-the-psni-30600926.html (accessed 25 August 2015).

12 Murphy, 2013, 105.

13 Z, critic of Sinn Féin policy, interview, October 2013.

14 J. Gibney, 'Address to 1996 Ard Fheis': Northern Ireland Political Collection, Linenhall Library, Belfast.

narrative as such, the republican aspiration for 'a root and branch clean out of that apparatus'[15] is juxtaposed with the post-conflict reform reality that this was 'never going to happen'.[16] Reform required 'compromise' and 'negotiation' rather than simply expelling all RUC personnel from reformed institutions.[17]

Despite accepting that there is institutional crossover, those partaking in 'critical engagement' are keen to stress a *rupture* with the RUC as a policing monolith. This occurs through accounts that differentiate between the 'new breed' of the PSNI and the RUC 'old guard'. The rupture between those labelled 'RUC' and those labelled 'PSNI' becomes further apparent in a disaggregation of the policing monolith into *good community policing* and *bad political policing*. Through disaggregation, those championing 'critical engagement' separate the 'new breed' of PSNI officer intent on serving their community from the RUC 'old guard' intent on retaining 'political policing'. Their critical support is given to those involved in 'good' policing, while they continue to oppose those exercising 'bad' policing. The most pronounced disaggregation of the policing monolith followed the arrest of Gerry Adams in April 2014. The move was declared an attempt to 'settle old scores' by 'an embittered rump of the old RUC'.[18] Upon his release Adams described the episode as the work of the 'old guard using the old methods'.[19] Sinn Féin reaffirmed their commitment to 'critical engagement' with policing and their willingness to work with the 'reformers' within the PSNI who were at odds with the 'dark side' within the force.[20] Similar sound bites followed the arrest of Sinn Féin's Northern chairperson Bobby Storey in September 2015, following the shooting of Kevin McGuigan the previous month.[21] Storey, who was never actually confronted during extensive questioning sessions with any evidence to justify his arrest, was 'personally livid' and politically

---

[15] L, supporter of Sinn Féin policy, interview, June 2013.

[16] I, supporter of Sinn Féin policy, interview, May 2013.

[17] AD, supporter of Sinn Féin policy, interview, July 2013.

[18] Martin McGuinness, cited in 'Gerry Adams Arrest: Attempt to "Settle Old Scores"', BBC News, 3 May 2014: www.bbc.co.uk/news/uk-northern-ireland-27268739 (accessed 5 May 2014).

[19] D. McKittrick and P. Apps, 'Gerry Adams Slams "Malicious and Sinister" Arrest Over 1972 Murder of Jean McConville', *Independent*, 4 May 2014.

[20] 'Gerry Adams Arrest: Sinn Féin Claims "Dark Side" to NI Police', BBC News, 1 May 2014: www.bbc.co.uk/news/uk-northern-ireland-27244878 (accessed 5 May 2014).

[21] M. Moloney, 'Gerry Adams "Seriously Concerned" by PSNI Arrest of Sinn Féin Chairperson for North', *An Phoblacht*, 9 September 2015: www.anphoblacht.com/contents/25339 (accessed 20 May 2017).

outraged by his 'unlawful detention' but would not allow the malign work of 'opponents of the Peace Process' to impede his continued support for policing.[22]

Disaggregation is also detectable in the accounts of those actively involved in 'critical engagement'. Having lived experience of the 'new breed' of PSNI officer that differs drastically from their lived experience under the RUC, interviewees construct a narrative of rupture between such PSNI officers and the 'securocrats' adhering to the RUC 'war mentality'. This can be seen in the terminology used; the 'new breed' is referred to as 'the PSNI' while the 'old guard' remain 'the RUC'. The deliberate avoidance of labelling all PSNI personnel with the RUC tag sustains broader disaggregation. When discussing 'political policing' interviewees referred to 'some' within the PSNI or 'elements' within policing rather than the PSNI as a whole. Thus, while the narrative acknowledges that an 'old guard' exists it nonetheless suggests that they are an outdated minority that are not representative of the entire PSNI. As a consequence of this, they should be separated from the 'new breed' with genuine aspirations to serve their communities. The positivity of this motivation, as seen in the 'community policing' narrative examined previously, was heralded as a sign of change within policing. Conversely, what earmarks the 'securocrats' is the retention of an RUC 'war mentality' intent on 'settling old scores'.

Consider the following acknowledgement of institutional crossover:

> The people who were involved in the early stages of the PSNI were the old guard, were the Special Branch, were the securocrats, were the real dominant Unionist sort ... they obviously came into the PSNI. And, yes, there is elements within the PSNI that hold that view, some of them still within the higher echelons.

Expanding on the 'securocrat' motivation, the interviewee continued:

> Their focus wasn't about trying to draw republicans in on the issue of policing. Their focus was about trying to keep republicans completely away from the issue of policing. That republicans would have absolutely no say in how the six counties were policed, would have absolutely no say in delivering complaints and how they were addressed, would have absolutely no

[22] J. Hedges, 'Exclusive – Bobby Storey After his Arrest, Still Totally Committed to Peace Process', *An Phoblacht*, 13 September 2015: www.anphoblacht.com/contents/25344 (accessed 10 November 2015).

> role in going to the Ombudman's or Ombudsperson's office and bringing issues and asking for accountability or asking for answers.[23]

Disaggregation of the policing monolith means that the presence of the 'old guard' with a 'war mentality' does not detract from assertions of newness or change. Even if institutional crossover is acknowledged, disaggregation allows a 'political policing' narrative to be constructed in a manner that does not necessarily contradict the essence of the 'community policing' narrative. A problematic minority, so the logic runs, cannot be taken as embodying the values of post-Patten policing in its entirety. This is evident in the remarks of one partaker of 'critical engagement':

> There is still an element of that old RUC and I see it still quite often. I'm a community activist and I'm a member of [area] PCSP and I would still see that wee, small element, but the police force here has changed radically. And anybody that says it hasn't changed, they're wrong.[24]

An arena of struggle

With the PSNI comprising the *new* in favour of change and the old obstructive of change, 'critical engagement' has been increasingly referred to as the 'new arena of struggle'.[25] As with all sites of struggle, then, this necessitates an effective strategy. The following extensive account of one former combatant actively involved in 'critical engagement' is instructive of how critically engaging republicans construct their narrative in terms of having a proactive strategy in this 'new arena of struggle'. Conceding that there remained a 'massive issue' with covert policing and with people within the PSNI who 'shouldn't be there', the interviewee argued:

> We can do one of two things; we can either ignore it, but it will definitely not go away it will just get worse, or else we can confront it. And the people that sit on the sidelines taking the sort of easy position in their own comfort zones will never change anything. In fact, what they'll do is they'll reinforce what they claim to completely oppose.

The issue is presented as a 'good versus evil' battle being played out within

---

23 B, supporter of Sinn Féin policy, interview, April 2013.

24 G, supporter of Sinn Féin policy, interview, May 2013.

25 'Adams Seeks Police Stance Backing', BBC News, 20 January 2007: http://news.bbc.co.uk/1/hi/northern_ireland/6281805.stm (accessed 23 May 2017).

policing between the new who favour reform and the old who want to obstruct reform. It is the critical engager role to empower the new and thwart the old:

> There's elements within the PSNI as well who also want to see reform, they want to see a proper service, you know, and it's really important that we empower those people by working along with them, because if we don't, the ones that want things to roll back, you know, you're just giving them an open opportunity to do that.

A narrative of strategic thinking in a 'new arena of struggle' correlates with the broader argument during the debate that policing would be a 'battle a day' for republicans seeking to 'put manners' on regressive policing elements. This shaped the interviewee's recollection of the 2006–07 debate and the practical application of it today:

> I went to all the policing debates and I went to the Special Ard Fheis and it was never said that this was going to be a case where we could dictate what the PSNI could do or what they couldn't do. We said from the very outset this was a critical engagement and again people have to understand what people meant by that.[26]

'Critical engagement' is seemingly not simply about endorsing policing but also about using 'strategy' to combat regressive elements in the 'new arena of struggle'. Premised on strategic interaction with policing, it becomes a combative type of reform that adheres to an overarching political strategy. The use of the terminology 'new arena of struggle' reflects not only how the discourse is framed by those partaking in 'critical engagement' as being strategic, but also how this allows them to draw on the memory of previous republican struggle. Although the 'critical engagement' narrative creates a separation between the new and the old, the importance of having an effective 'strategy' to fight opponents in the 'new arena of struggle' allows a certain degree of critical agitation from prior republican memory to be imported into the 'critical engagement' narrative. Given the continued presence of 'securocrats' within policing, the critical engager task is to use 'strategy' to combat such opponents:

> There are elements within the system who are ... still attempting to gain little victories against people like me and against the general direction of the political project ... All that we can do is attempt to build a bulwark

[26] AD, supporter of Sinn Féin policy, interview, July 2013.

> against them type of activities. If you catch them, you know, in a new dispensation when you're going to hopefully make them accountable ... they're not going to go away.[27]

> When you're involved in a transitional period coming out of a colonial conflict there's always hiccups, there's always difficulties, there's always battles. You know, while we have a strategy you have to be rest assured your opponents have a strategy as well, and part of their strategy is to roll back as much as they possibly can of any gains that we have made.[28]

In addition to having a certain rhetorical value, a narrative of using strategic interaction to defeat opponents reflects the peculiarities of the post-reform context critical engagers find themselves in. Although keen to liken their endorsement to that of ANC engagement with post-reform policing in South Africa, a glaring oversight of this is that Irish republicans have not had the extensive access to the policing apparatus's most problematic branches as did the ANC. Not only were former combatants debarred from joining the PSNI but what Patten called the 'force within a force'[29] transferred en masse from the RUC into the PSNI. This crossover is itself compounded by the fact that the shortcomings of the accountability mechanisms prevent their remit from encompassing the more problematic activities of those 'rolling back' reform. Nor is this helped by the fact that MI5 was handed the lead role in the problematic area of 'national security' – and critical engagers frankly acknowledge the extreme difficulty in anyone, Sinn Féin or otherwise, managing to hold MI5 to account.[30] This creates a paradox whereby those involved in 'critical engagement' champion a 'community policing' narrative that frontloads the notion of policing being a community service worthy of support while simultaneously having a 'political policing' narrative of 'critical engagement' being a 'battle a day' in trying to prevent an 'old guard' concerted 'roll back' of reform.

Rhetorically disaggregating the policing monolith and engaging a narrative of strategically fighting the 'roll back' does not, however, detract from the impact on the ground of 'political policing'. Where the PSNI is seen to unfairly target republicans a 'remembering' of past 'political policing' materialises. At grassroots level this can arise from minor issues, one example cited being the arrest of a former prisoner for a minor motoring offence while on their way to

[27] A, supporter of Sinn Féin policy, interview April 2013.

[28] AD, supporter of Sinn Féin policy, interview, July 2013.

[29] Independent Commission on Policing for Northern Ireland, 1999, para 12.10.

[30] A, supporter of Sinn Féin policy, interview, April 2013.

partake in one of the first post-Sinn Féin endorsement meetings in a republican area – something that temporarily stalled improvements in community–police relations.[31] A more general example was a mobilisation in West Belfast in response to the 'upswing' in PSNI targeting of hurlers and camogs for possession of an 'offensive weapon'.[32] High-profile cases of 'political policing' also impact at grassroots level. One community activist noted that macro-level events can have the unhelpful effect of driving people at grassroots level back into their 'comfort zones'. Where this happens, people are more reticent than before about re-emerging out of these 'comfort zones'.[33] This difficulty vindicates Nelid's observation that any new-found confidence historically detached collectives place in reformed policing bodies can be 'eroded rapidly' when past problems are mirrored in post-reform policing.[34]

The cumulative effect of all of the above is that the onset of 'critical engagement' did not make policing 'a settled issue' but merely marked the beginning of a long and difficult depoliticising process that is 'still ongoing'.[35] The magnitude of the process, and its ongoing nature, means that all the cultural and structural factors that cultivate 'political policing' 'doesn't change overnight'.[36] 'Critical engagement' being an ongoing process enables progress already attained to be juxtaposed with the need for further advances to be made. To this end assertions like, 'We dismantled the RUC. As much as we may not claim it because there is no sense in annoying people but it's self-evident that the RUC isn't here today',[37] are tempered by similar recognition that 'There is still a terrible lot needs to happen'.[38] Despite this recognition, an underlying theme of rupture remains detectable and is framed by a wider narrative of republicans having dismantled the 'Orange state' to change the political landscape in the six counties irrevocably.

Couching itself in wider terms of equality-based transformation of the 'Orange state', this again creates scope for pre-transition Northern Ireland to be invoked as part of a 'usable past' whereby even if policing today remains problematic on certain levels it is better than the 'suspect community' policing

---

[31] I, supporter of Sinn Féin policy, interview, May 2013.

[32] J. Hedges and P. Whelan, 'PSNI Clash with Hurlers Opposed by Young Republicans', *An Phoblacht*, 10 March 2014: www.anphoblacht.com/contents/23832 (accessed 23 July 2014).

[33] D, community activist, interview, May 2013.

[34] Nelid, 2001.

[35] AD, supporter of Sinn Féin policy, interview, July 2013.

[36] M, supporter of Sinn Féin policy, interview, June 2013.

[37] H, supporter of Sinn Féin policy, interview, May 2013.

[38] F, supporter of Sinn Féin policy, interview, May 2013.

of the past. Again, a preferable, yet nonetheless imperfect, present is compared with a difficult past in a way framed by rupture:

> There is no doubt there is people within the PSNI who are former RUC would like to see things rolled back. There's no doubt about people within Unionism would like to see things rolled back. You know it was their force. But I think there's a wee bit of naivety in that because things are never going to go back to the way they were. It's just never going to happen. You're never going to have a one-party Unionist regime running the North.[39]

The 'critical engagement' narrative on 'political policing' therefore invokes several strands of the 'progressive republican' master narrative, including themes of progression, equality-based reform and disempowering opponents. Premised on the notion of *rupture* with the past, the narrative contends that while policing is certainly not flawless – and there is acknowledgement that nowhere in the world can flawless policing be found – it is nonetheless more community orientated and less politicised than the 'suspect community' policing they 'remember'.

Anti-policing rejection of disaggregation

If the 'critical engagement' narrative uses disaggregation of the policing monolith to engineer a sense of rupture, then the anti-policing narrative rejects disaggregation in order to engineer a sense of continuity. This rejection is ideological but also organisational. The ideological dimension – mirroring a 'cosmetic reform' narrative – is that no distinction can be made between a community police officer and a political police officer. The core policing function in upholding an illegitimate state makes all policing, regardless of how it is labelled, inherently political. Continuity in the core function enables an ideological rebuke that 'the PSNI is the political policing of today. It was the RUC prior to the name change. It was the RIC prior to that. There is absolutely no difference whatsoever'.[40]

The organisational dimension contends that those involved in 'community policing' have to take orders from 'the wire pullers'.[41] This allows 'political policing' to control 'community policing'. Such a view subscribes to the structuralist view of policing whereby policing of every hue is ultimately state coercion. The practical outworking of this is that any given PSNI officer 'one

[39] AD, supporter of Sinn Féin policy, interview, July 2013.
[40] R, critic of Sinn Féin policy, interview, July 2013.
[41] X, critic of Sinn Féin policy, interview, October 2013.

day could be sorting out a domestic dispute but the next day actively maybe arresting a political protestor'.[42] This critique also draws on the enhanced role of MI5. 'Community policing' PSNI officers thus become the front line in MI5-led 'political policing' by harassing 'names that come down on a list':

> I've been told that they come from the intelligence services sector, you know, and I'm led to think, obviously, MI5. Now the names that are on that list are handed into [area], and I'm told by the Super down there they don't question those names ... they take it as read, right. So your community police officer on the ground, they know the name, 'whatever, de de da, there he is', and they're driving after him and it's the whole Justice and Security stop and search, humiliation tactics out on the road, you know; all that carry on.[43]

Difference in views seemingly hinges on lived interaction with post-reform policing. Those endorsing 'critical engagement' have come into contact with the 'new breed' of PSNI officer and detect a willingness to serve their communities. 'Critical engagement' has opened up a post-conflict platform for interaction with a different kind of police officer from that encountered in the past. Those outside this ambit have no such interaction. Interaction is largely limited to continuing negative experiences with problematic branches that remain predominantly Unionist and tainted by institutional crossover. It is only natural in the face of continuing negative experiences to 'remember' similar past experiences with the RUC. From this perspective, the new PSNI is seen to be operating in the same way as the old RUC did. Rather than have memory recast current lived experience as a combative type of reform, current lived experience is tied to an ideologised memory whereby rejection of 'British policing' reinforces a narrative of continued police repression.

The anti-policing narrative of 'continuity' in 'political policing'

Building on from a narrative of 'cosmetic reform' that challenges assertions of change, the anti-policing narrative uses current lived experience to construct a sense of continuity with past 'political policing' by drawing on the abuse of 'anti-terror' legislation, the retention of RUC 'political policing' methods and the refined targeting of Irish republicans. It is worth highlighting the

---

[42] AC, critic of Sinn Féin policy, interview, November 2013.

[43] AB, critic of Sinn Féin policy, interview, October 2013.

type of memories and lived experiences drawn upon to construct this continuity. Interviewees recounted past and present cases of abuse under 'stop and search' provisions, violence and/or sectarianism during house raids and arrest, the monitoring, harassment and physical assault of those attending political pickets and prominent miscarriages of justice. Interestingly, these are the same memories that are invoked by those in support of 'critical engagement' to engender a sense of rupture through their narrative that policing is now a community service. Perhaps it is worth highlighting why these particular memories proliferate throughout dichotomous policing narratives. At the individual level, it reflects how autobiographical memory – which primarily concerns individual experiences rather than master-narrative positions[44] – ties current lived experience to past personal experiences. These experiences are 'remembered' due to the impact they had, thus they provide a lens through which current lived experience is interpreted and reform processes evaluated - whether this be a likening of current and past experiences or a differentiation between them. At the collective level, these memories reinforce dominant master-narrative positions. For supporters of 'critical engagement' these memories support assertions of newness and change given that from their current lived reality they are reflective of a problematic past rather than present. Likewise, while such experiences are reflective of the current lived experience of those 'left behind', they also reinforce a central narrative plank that 'cosmetic reform' has not changed the nature or function of policing.

The anti-policing narrative is constructed within a dualistic framework that draws heavily on external factors through human rights discourse in a post-9/11 context but also draws heavily on memory that is ideologised and localised. At particular times the narrative is insular and contextually specific to anti-policing Irish republicans yet at other junctures it has wider relevance. It draws on historical lived experience of 'anti-terror' legislation to provide context for current experiences, yet these can also be placed in a globalised 'War on Terror' context. In an insightful critique of attempts to 'normalise' policing and security in post-GFA Northern Ireland, Jessie Blackbourn highlights how the challenges of the global and the local most neatly converge on the matter of 'anti-terror' legislation.[45] Accordingly, it is worth turning our initial attention to this.

[44] Schuman and Corning, 2014.

[45] Blackbourn, 2015.

The abuse of 'anti-terror' legislation

The events of 9/11 provoked a global move away from a 'rule of law' model towards using an 'extraordinary measures' model to tackle 'terrorism',[46] mainly via increased global passage and usage of 'emergency' and 'anti-terror' legislation.[47] However, there is nothing new about the application of such legislation in an Irish context. 'Emergency' legislation involving special courts and detention without trial has existed there from as early as 1761.[48] A genealogy of emergency 'anti-terror' legislation spanning from the 1883 Explosive Substances Act to the more recent Justice and Security (Northern Ireland) Act 2007 duly emerged. On the one hand, justification is grounded in the belief that the state must tackle security threats proactively.[49] On the other hand, there remains the fact that in a Northern Ireland context such legislation has been historically problematic. The thread of continuity running through this conundrum is notable in the likening of past 'stop and search' by the RUC using 'suspect community' policing with those experienced under current 'anti-terror' provisions used by the PSNI. Showing contextualisation of a current incident of 'political policing' against their previous experiences under the RUC, one interviewee argued:

> Stops and searches at that time could have been anything from the minimum of ten minutes to three hours. And the legislation they used at that time was no different to the repressive legislation that we see today with the Justice and Security stop and search ... today in 2013, you know, 20 and 30 years on, I'm after meeting a very hateful, nasty bunch from [area]. You know, people who are coming into what they call the jurisdiction under nobody's authority but some other faceless person from [area] and they can throw out whatever legislation at younger people.[50]

Current difficulties over detention without trial and 'stop and search' mirror previous difficulties under the Prevention of Terrorism Act (1974) and the Emergency Provisions Act (1973).[51] Thus, despite police reform and the GFA, similarity with a historical 'anti-terror' context and the encroachment of a global 'anti-terror' context means that the current climate of Northern Ireland

46 Guelke, 2012, 36.
47 Brysk, 2007.
48 Landman, 2007, 80.
49 Dyzenhaus, 2008, 42.
50 AB, critic of Sinn Féin policy, interview, October 2013.
51 Hillyard, 1988; Walsh, 1983; McVeigh, 1994.

'remains highly susceptible' to human rights violations.[52] The global context has become more pressing, with Gearty arguing that the sheer scope of 'anti-terror' legislation now at the disposal of the state has transformed the 'War on Terror' into the 'War on human rights'.[53] 'Stop and search' and 'internment by remand' are indeed common complaints among anti-policing Irish republicans but they are merely localised variants of the global 'War on Terror' zeal that has birthed, as Lucy Bond lists,[54] black site prisons, extraordinary rendition, enhanced interrogation techniques and secretive military commission trials.

The convergence of the local and global becomes apparent upon examination of the two most offending legislative provisions: the Terrorism Act (2000) (TACT) and the Justice and Security (Northern Ireland) Act 2007 (JSA). The former is a UK-wide legislative provision enacted to tackle all forms of 'terrorism', while the latter is a provision tailored to the threat of 'spoiler' violence in post-GFA Northern Ireland. Unlike previous and subsequent 'anti-terror' legislation, TACT was more considered and less of a knee-jerk reaction to a specific event,[55] making its enormous encroachment on human rights all the more menacing. Both acts contain 'stop and search' provisions that are prone to misuse and abuse. Under section 43 (1) TACT the security forces may stop and search persons and vehicles based on 'reasonable suspicion'.[56] A similar provision that was based on police 'authorisation' in section 44 was subsequently held to be illegal and in contravention of Article 8 rights.[57] Section 47A subsequently amended section 44 powers whereby an 'authorisation' for 'stop and search' must be necessary to prevent an attack rather than simply being expedient to preventing 'terrorism',[58] although a police officer retains the power to stop and search any vehicle or person without 'individual

[52] Wartchow, 2005.

[53] Gearty, 2005.

[54] Bond, 2015, 137.

[55] Blackbourn, 2009.

[56] Section 43 (1) TACT reads: 'A constable may stop and search a person whom he reasonably suspects to be a terrorist to discover whether he has in his possession anything which may constitute evidence that he is a terrorist'. Section 43 (2) continues: 'A constable may search a person arrested under section 41 to discover whether he has in his possession anything which may constitute evidence that he is a terrorist.'

[57] *Gillan and Quinton* v. *The United Kingdom* (Application 4158/05) (2010) 50 EHRR 45.

[58] Section 47A (TACT) states that a senior police officer may give authorisation if the officer 'reasonably suspects that an act of terrorism will take place; and reasonably considers that the authorisation is necessary to prevent such an act; [and that] the specified area(s) or place(s) [in the authorisation are] no greater than is necessary to

reasonable suspicion' where it is premised on searching for evidence that the person is a 'terrorist' or that the vehicle is being used for the 'purposes of terrorism'.[59] Section 21 JSA allows for a police officer to stop and question an individual to ascertain their identity and movements.[60] There is no 'reasonable suspicion' requirement attached to this power.[61] Section 24 JSA permits powers of stop and search for 'unlawful munitions and transmitters'.[62] The flaws of JSA 'stop and search' powers were exposed by a court ruling that they were unlawful in the absence of a Code of Practice preventing arbitrary abuse.[63] The PSNI has, however, been able to use TACT and JSA interchangeably in light of these unfavourable legal rulings.[64]

Concerns over 'anti-terror' legislation cannot, however, be confined to 'stop and search' powers. More fundamental problems exist. For example, the offence of 'glorifying terrorism' can become a 'dangerous process' that blurs the contours between 'the expression of views seen as unacceptable and offensive to mainstream opinion in the UK with the perpetration of acts of violence'.[65] Moreover, as Hodgson and Tadros have argued,[66] the enormous breadth of 'anti-terror' provisions can essentially 'make a terrorist out of nothing'. With 'extremism' superseding 'terrorism' as the evil that must be tackled, these problems will only inflame rather than dissipate. Because 'extremism' is defined in an imprecise manner that encompasses non-violent 'vocal or active opposition to fundamental British values',[67] the scope for misapplication seems limitless. Not only are non-violent political opponents of the state at risk from 'counter-extremism' provisions in the Counter-Terrorism and Security Act 2015, but religious and cultural organisations could find themselves similarly

prevent such an act; and the duration of the authorisation is no longer than is necessary to prevent such an act.'

[59] Committee on the Administration of Justice, 2012a, 21.

[60] Section 21 JSA reads: '(1) A member of Her Majesty's forces on duty or a constable may stop a person for so long as is necessary to question him to ascertain his identity and movements. (2) A member of Her Majesty's forces on duty may stop a person for so long as is necessary to question him to ascertain – (a) what he knows about a recent explosion or another recent incident endangering life; (b) what he knows about a person killed or injured in a recent explosion or incident.'

[61] Committee on the Administration of Justice, 2012a, 22.

[62] Committee on the Administration of Justice, 2012a, 23.

[63] Re Fox, McNulty and Canning [2013] NICA 19.

[64] Blackbourn, 2015, 148.

[65] Guelke, 2007.

[66] Hodgson and Tadros, 2009.

[67] Her Majesty's Government, 2015, 6.

threatened.[68] The cumulative effect of this, in a localised context, is that while Northern Ireland has always witnessed the pitfalls of wide-ranging 'anti-terror' legislation, the provisions birthed in a post-9/11 context are not only more expansive but also more permanent in nature than many of the 'temporary' Northern Ireland-specific provisions of the past – something that flies in the face of the GFA commitment to 'the removal of emergency powers in Northern Ireland' and 'as early a return as possible to normal security arrangements'.[69] Blackbourn goes further in her analysis of this, arguing that the only token by which policing and security seems more normalised in Northern Ireland is not that the GFA normalisation vision has been realised but because wide-ranging 'anti-terror' provisions have become the norm elsewhere.[70]

Theoretical concerns are concretised by the practical outworkings of such provisions. The anti-policing narrative has been built around the misuse of 'stop and search' that targets legitimate political opponents of the post-GFA state. It is constructed from lived reality of 'stop and search' as a 'disruption tactic'.[71] Defence of this 'disruption tactic' is grounded in the fact that it is apparently 'intelligence led', although it has not been ascertained whether said 'intelligence' targets someone on the basis of involvement in unlawful activity or because of legitimate political activity. The matter is further obfuscated when one considers that in the North of Ireland there is a historical record of using 'intelligence' to target 'politically unpopular individuals'[72] and of 'fair enquiry' use of 'stop and search' happening to 'degenerate into deliberate harassment'.[73] The lack of successful convictions flowing from 'stop and search' operations strengthens these assertions.[74] Furthermore, cases raised in the interview process spoke to the truth of this observation. In one case the heavily pregnant partner and infant child of a political activist were forced to stand in heavy rain while the activist was subjected to a 'stop and search'.[75] In

[68] 'Cameron's Extremism Orders "Could Criminalise Traditional Christian Teaching"', *Daily Telegraph*, 15 June 2015: www.telegraph.co.uk/news/religion/11671547/Camerons-extremism-orders-could-criminalise-traditional-Christian-teaching.html (accessed 28 August 2015).

[69] 'The Agreement: Agreement Reached in the Multi-Party Negotiations' (Good Friday Agreement), Belfast, 10 April 1998, 25: http://cain.ulst.ac.uk/events/peace/docs/agreement.htm.

[70] Blackbourn, 2015, 183.

[71] Committee on the Administration of Justice, 2012a, 25.

[72] Hirsch, 2001.

[73] Committee on the Administration of Justice, 1995.

[74] Northern Ireland Policing Board, 2013, 34.

[75] Z, critic of Sinn Féin policy, interview, October 2013.

another case the partner of a republican prisoner was subjected to a section 24 JSA search shortly after returning from a prison visit.[76] It is difficult in either case to identify how practical application met the specified aims of 'anti-terror' provisions; subjecting a heavily pregnant female and infant to a 'stop and search' in heavy rain is hardly tackling the militant threat, while an individual returning from a prison visit is highly unlikely to have explosives or transmitters on their person. The cases above point towards 'stop and search' being used as a means of harassment rather than being used to disrupt militant activity.

With Northern Ireland yet to move beyond ethno-nationalist residential segregation, a geographical breakdown of 'stop and search' figures serves as a 'proxy indicator' of any differential application on the ground.[77] CAJ note that there is an undeniably heavier usage of JSA 'stop and search' provisions in republican communities like West Belfast, Foyle and Strabane than in more Unionist-dominated areas like East Belfast, Carrickfergus and Antrim.[78] The skewed use of 'anti-terror' provisions has led CAJ to conclude that there are currently two 'policing regimes', as 'dissident republicans' are policed in a way revanchist loyalist elements are not.[79] The deleterious impact this has on policing 'buy in' among previously excluded Irish republican communities is obvious. The NIPB has conceded that despite amendments the operation of TACT and JSA continues to raise 'significant and warranted concerns' within the communities affected by them.[80] Likewise, CAJ has argued that the misuse of 'stop and search' is seen as targeting 'some working-class Nationalist communities at a time when precisely those who have not recognised the police as a legitimate body are being asked to do so'.[81]

The 'cosmetic reform' narrative extends beyond the misuse of 'stop and search' powers to assert more generally that provisions purportedly designed to tackle the militant threat are being used to curtail legitimate political opposition to the Northern Ireland transition – claims with significant historical resonance.[82] Within the confines of this argument one republican offered the following synopsis:

---

[76] V, critic of Sinn Féin policy, interview, September 2013.

[77] Committee on the Administration of Justice, 2012a, 26.

[78] Committee on the Administration of Justice, 2012a, 26.

[79] Committee on the Administration of Justice, 2012b, 67.

[80] Northern Ireland Policing Board, 2013, 12.

[81] Committee on the Administration of Justice, 2012, 74.

[82] Hillyard, 1988; Boyle, Hadden and Hillyard, 1980: Boyle, Hadden and Hillyard, 1980; McVeigh, 1994.

> The person who is on the trigger end of an AK-47 becomes the person that all of this emergency legislation and secretive type policing is about, right? But if you make the decision a month later, because there isn't anybody pulling the trigger of an AK-47 – well, do you see the ones who are actually talking in terms of sedition: they could be next year's finger person on the trigger of an AK-47. So let's do something about them now rather than waiting until next year. What you can do, then, is you can very easily go from looking to investigate someone for something you think they've done to investigating someone because of the potential you think they possess.

This led the republican to observe not a rupture whereby policing now represents a community service but 'the line of continuity between the way in which policing was done in the early '70s and the way in which policing is now being done in this century'.[83]

Rather than summarily dismissing this assertion as an anti-policing gripe, it is worth examining it – increasingly so given the recent turn towards 'counter-extremism'. As with similar concerns in the past, the temptation to dismiss them as the contrived work of the disgruntled should be resisted. Nor should critique of 'anti-terror' legislation be misrepresented as condoning the activity it purports to prevent.

Several interviewees evinced a belief that they were targeted by 'political policing' on the basis of their legitimate political opposition to the transition rather than any involvement in 'spoiler' violence. Acknowledging their political opposition to the status quo in the North of Ireland, one interviewee argued:

> Yes, I'm in [political party]. Yes, I'm a political activist. Yes, I advocate peaceful and dignified opposition to British rule in Ireland. Is that not a legitimate aspect of the Good Friday Agreement? Of course it is. So why does the police target people like me? Why do they mistreat me? Why do they mistreat my family? Why do they prevent me from asserting my rights in a political nature?[84]

Perhaps more insightful are the following extensive comments of another political activist who referred to 'political policing' as 'just a normal everyday thing of being a political activist', before elaborating that 'you have to expect your door being knocked in. You have to expect being arrested and harassed, but that's just a part of the job I suppose'. Noting that their first-hand

[83] Y, critic of Sinn Féin policy, interview, October 2013.

[84] S, critic of Sinn Féin policy, interview, July 2013.

experience of 'political policing' began 'when I became involved with politics and joined a political party', this is interpreted through what was witnessed in the past:

> Personally, when I was younger, the RUC never directly affected me. But now the PSNI is. Like, they're harassing me, they're harassing my friends, they're kicking people's doors in, they're putting comrades in jail for nothing ... So, in my experience of the PSNI, I think that they are just the same as the RUC, from looking at the RUC. Not from my own experiences of the RUC – but from looking at the RUC and what they were, to now the PSNI. It's unchanged and I would have that same view looking at the PSNI now as what the RUC would've been.[85]

Interestingly, this account highlights the interaction between autobiographical and collective memory. Although there is an inability to 'remember' human rights abuse by the RUC in their autobiographical memory, the interviewee draws on the collective memory of human rights abuse to frame their current lived experience. This provides the interviewee with an outlet to frame their current lived experience of 'political policing' with past collective experiences and to locate these experiences within the confines of the anti-policing master narrative of 'cosmetic reform'. Individual experiences become rooted to both collective experiences in the past and collective experiences in the present in a manner that draws a line of continuity between them.

According to the above accounts, those targeted under 'anti-terror' legislation were pursued on the basis of legitimate political opposition to policing. This speaks to the flaws of 'anti-terror' legislation more widely but also to the specific post-GFA political context in Northern Ireland that has seen a flawed categorisation of all those opposed to the GFA and/or policing under the 'dissident' tag. The propensity for using this 'catch-all' tag falsely conflates someone who is shooting at the PSNI with someone who has a legitimate non-violent opposition to policing. This myopic view is demonstrably erroneous. Primarily, it overlooks the existence of what Horgan and Morrison call 'non-violent dissident Republicans' 'who have demonstrated their dissidence through political activity and other non-violent methods'.[86] Secondly, it wrongly presupposes that any opposition within the Irish republican constituency to the Sinn Féin brand of pro-GFA 'mainstream' republicanism is somehow illegitimate. The reality is, as pointed out by Morrison, that:

---

85 X, critic of Sinn Féin policy, interview, October 2013.

86 Horgan and Morrison, 2011.

> There is clearly nothing wrong with disagreeing with the direction taken, and decisions made, by the Sinn Féin leadership. It actually promotes democratic voice within republican and nationalist communities. It allows for these communities to question direction. However, it is when this dissidence is manifested in violent, threatening and paramilitary activity that there is a real problem to deal with.[87]

Local government elections in 2014 revealed the existence of and appetite for legitimate political opposition to policing and to Sinn Féin, with a number of anti-policing candidates duly securing seats.[88]

Militants who actively target the PSNI may legitimately expect to be targeted under 'anti-terror' provisions. This is, after all, part of the rough and tumble that comes with involvement in political violence. Legitimate political activists adhering to non-violent opposition, despite the earlier assertion that it is 'part of the job', should not. The pitfalls that come with ignoring this reality in favour of carte blanche use of 'anti-terror' legislation against anybody opposing the status quo are obvious. First, it impinges on freedom of political thought – a freedom enshrined not only in international human rights law[89] but also in the GFA.[90] If 'political policing' is used to curtail the legitimate expression of opposition to the GFA, the self-contained right to 'free political thought' becomes reduced to a right to 'free political agreement' with the GFA. Secondly, targeting legitimate political groups under 'anti-terror' legislation will not reduce the militant threat. Instead, it only closes off 'an alternative venue' for those wishing to express

87 Morrison, 2013, 2.

88 'Independent Republican' candidates successfully elected in the 2014 local government elections were Barry Monteith, Bernice Swift, Padraig McShane and Davy Hyland. Gary Donnelly (32CSM) and Paul Gallagher (IRSP) were also elected on an 'Independent Republican' ticket. Another 'Independent Republican' candidate Dee Fennell narrowly missed out on a seat in the Old Park ward of North Belfast. RNU and Éirígí also ran candidates in North and West Belfast.

89 Convention for the Protection of Human Rights and Fundamental Freedoms (European Convention on Human Rights, as amended) Art. 9 (1) enshrines the freedom of thought, conscience and religion, and reads: 'Everyone has the right to freedom of thought, conscience and religion; this right includes freedom to change his religion or belief and freedom, either alone or in community with others and in public or private, to manifest his religion or belief, in worship, teaching, practice and observance.'

90 'The Agreement: Agreement Reached in the Multi-Party Negotiations' (Good Friday Agreement), Belfast, 10 April 1998, 20.

their political opposition in a peaceful way.[91] Failure to appreciate this in post-GFA Northern Ireland has led to legitimate political opponents of the GFA becoming the 'enemy other' as much as have those involved in 'spoiler' violence.[92] This has become central to the 'political policing' narrative of those 'left behind', where perceptions of continuity with past 'political policing' have enabled the persistence of a view that policing continues to represent a threat rather than a community service.

In portraying policing as a continued political threat, the anti-policing narrative has expanded beyond ideological opposition to 'British policing' to instrumentalise a discourse of human rights. This resonates with Sinn Féin's previous use of human rights discourse in the 1990s.[93] On one level, adopting a discourse of human rights can usefully reinforce dominant narrative positions – human rights abusers are, after all, the antithesis of community servants – but on another level they can take root more generally to alter political outlooks.[94] This is articulated through opposition to legislation like JSA and TACT that is premised on human rights considerations rather than regurgitation of an ideological position. Opposition to covert policing, the abuse of 'emergency legislation' and 'internment by remand' becomes more legalistic, human rights orientated and places greater emphasis on procedural 'foul play'. This dimension has been reinforced by the length of time between trial and sentencing and by the lack of successful convictions against those remanded and charged under 'anti-terror' legislation.[95]

This is particularly notable in criticism of high-profile cases. Consider the following commentary on the (then ongoing) Martin Corey case:

> He is supposed to be up in court at the end of September for a parole hearing. He was supposed to be every 12 months brought before a parole hearing and he hasn't had one in 24 months. Now how is that a new dispensation? How is that human rights and civil liberties being processed through this new Good Friday Agreement when you have a man in jail there 63 years of age for three and a half years?[96]

A similar observation was made in relation to the detention of (since acquitted) Éirígí activist Stephen Murney:

---

[91] Horgan and Morrison, 2011.

[92] Whiting, 2012.

[93] Bean, 2007a.

[94] McEvoy, 2000.

[95] Horgan, 2013, 160.

[96] W, critic of Sinn Féin policy, interview, September 2013.

> They still won't say Stephen Murney was a member of a bona fide political party and he had stuff in his house. I'm the [position] of [political party]. My fucking house is coming down with stuff. What are they going to do? Put me in Maghaberry beside Stephen Murney? For what? Being a member of a registered political party? ... Is that not part of your democratic human rights and so-called freedom in a democratic society to be a member of a political party?[97]

So although there is inescapable ideological opposition to 'British policing' among critics, opposition is also predicated on rejection of 'political policing' that involves 'the manipulation of the judicial system in order to put opponents of the state behind bars by any means necessary'.[98] This de-ideologised strand of the narrative again draws sustenance from the wider post-9/11 climate:

> The state in Ireland, Britain, the US and most Western states in recent times have enacted laws in order to outlaw even a whiff of political dissent. They usually call them offences against the state, anti-terrorism legislation, the patriot act and so on, and they do their best to put political activists and, CIA built, mass terrorists under the same category.[99]

This therefore means 'when you look into it ... it's never about Martin Corey. It's the legislation that they want accepted here' – legislation that was effectively 'internment by another name'.[100] Likewise, while the 'Craigavon 2' case may have its own particular concerns, the wider relevance of the case lies in 'the battery of additional powers that are always sitting there', that are initially used against 'dissident republicans' but can extend to 'dissident lawyers, the week after it could be dissident journalists, the week after that it could be dissident thinkers'.[101]

The salience of the above is that critics not only have a historical political backdrop to frame their grievances within but can also adopt a wider 'War on Terror' context to frame opposition to policing within a human rights discourse rather than an ideological one. Where opposition premised on the latter questions the legitimacy of policing, that predicated on the former questions how policing operates. As a consequence of locating itself in transitional 'legitimacy politics' and a wider 'War on Terror' context, Irish republican

---

[97] P, critic of Sinn Féin policy, interview, June 2013.

[98] O, critic of Sinn Féin policy, interview, June 2013.

[99] 'Republican Socialist Youth Movement', *Starry Plough*, Easter 2007.

[100] W, critic of Sinn Féin policy, interview, September 2013.

[101] Y, critic of Sinn Féin policy, interview, October 2013.

criticism of 'political policing' possesses a malleability allowing it to be highly ideologised on the one hand, yet grounded in human rights considerations on the other hand.

The 'PSNI/RUC'

The crux of the 'cosmetic reform' counter-narrative is a sense of *continuity* assuming nothing of substance has changed within post-Patten policing. A key means of reinforcing this has been referring to the PSNI as the 'PSNI/RUC' or continuing to refer to them as simply 'the RUC'. Current experiences become an extension of generations of 'political policing', meaning that:

> prior to 1969 policing in the North of Ireland was miserable. After 1969 it was also miserable. From the earliest days of policing in Ireland it has been discriminatory, it's been draconian, it's been oppressive, it's been militarised, it's been political. Nothing has changed since 2007.[102]

Given the historical backdrop to 'political policing' and that the central plank of the anti-policing narrative is one stressing continuity rather than rupture, it seems natural that those currently experiencing 'political policing' would liken such experiences to those experienced under the RUC. Just as those promoting a 'critical engagement' narrative of 'community policing' use their lived experience of policing to support assertions of newness and change, those opposed to policing use lived experience to challenge such assertions by using a lens of continuity to view current 'political policing'. A narrative must necessarily gravitate towards the end point it wishes to make.[103] This means that critics use their lived experience of current 'political policing' to draw direct parallels with what they 'remember' RUC tactics and the RUC mentality to be. One critic made a blatant assertion of *continuity* with RUC tactics by opining that 'the PSNI are determined to remain a political police force. They are determined to hold on to the old tactics of the RUC'.[104] Another noted, 'there's still the same political policing goes on' even though since 'critical engagement' the PSNI has 'probably got better at it, probably more professional in their approach'. Continuity, however, is grounded in the outworking that, 'if we call a protest out here tomorrow I guarantee the police would be up and down harassing us, videotaping us etc. for their own

102 S, critic of Sinn Féin policy, interview, July 2013.

103 Davis, 2002, 14.

104 O, critic of Sinn Féin policy, interview, June 2013.

nefarious purposes. That's exactly the same thing the RUC did, you know, so there is no real difference'.[105]

In addition to reinforcing master-narrative positions, memory can also contextualise lived reality by providing a reference point for what those subjected to 'political policing' see unfolding around them. One former combatant, who had previously recounted how dawn raids on their family home politicised them in their youth, drew a parallel with what they witnessed developing in their own children. Drawing continuity not only in the aggression and sectarianism experienced during a recent arrest but also in the politicising effect it had, the interviewee commented:

> I told the cops in the Land Rover that 'You have made a serious mistake' – not by arresting me – made a serious mistake in that now my kids are going to grow up hating the cops because they seen their Da getting handcuffed and dragged out of his own home in a pair of boxer shorts with nothing else on and threw into a Land Rover and held for a number of hours and no explanation given. What he said to me was, 'I don't give a fuck, you're nothing but a Fenian bastard'. So, as far as I was concerned, the PSNI were not much different to the RUC in that context. My kids now will not talk to them, will not engage them, will not speak to them, will not look anywhere near them. They see them as oppressive, and that's not my fault. That's their fault.[106]

The ability of 'political policing' to have the effect described above is not new.[107]

Interviewees use autobiographical memory to 'remember' in a way that feeds into a collective memory of past 'political policing' *and* a master narrative of 'cosmetic reform'. These experiences become located not only in a collective memory of 'political policing' under the RUC but also in the current lived experience of PSNI 'political policing' endured by those 'left behind'. This entails a juxtaposition of what is observed on the ground with the PSNI today and what is 'remembered' of RUC 'political policing':

> I like to believe and consider myself as a professional and somebody who is open minded. So, regardless of the hateful experience I as an individual and my entire family and neighbours had, I like to think that I can separate that, you know, and look at any individual on any level. That said, the current

[105] J, critic of Sinn Féin policy, interview, June 2013.

[106] S, critic of Sinn Féin policy, interview, July 2013.

[107] McVeigh, 1994, 101.

> PSNI in my opinion – informed opinion and experience – are not doing anything much differently than the old RUC did in the past.[108]

A similar thread of *continuity* based on comparative lived experience runs through the assessment of another republican that:

> My experience of the PSNI is – how can I say it – of no difference between the RUC to put it in better terms. The characteristics, the attitude and the central task of the PSNI is identical to that of the RUC ... I fail to see any difference between the RUC and the PSNI.[109]

This is the flip side of how those engaged in 'critical engagement' use memory to promote a 'community policing' narrative. If memory is used in the 'community policing' narrative to frame policing as a community service on the basis that change in composition and mentality represent a *rupture* from the RUC, then the 'political policing' narrative uses memory to retain the framing of policing as a threat on the basis of continuity *w*ith RUC attitudes and tactics. In drawing a mnemonic line of continuity, the implication of the 'political policing' narrative is that if the RUC was a threat to republican communities then the PSNI that acts in the same manner and has the same attitude must, as a matter of simple logic, also be a threat. Drawing a comparison based on lived experience as a republican activist under the RUC and current lived experience as a republican activist under the PSNI, one republican commented:

> Sinn Féin in the mid '80s – we were out there confronting policing and we were stopped on a regular basis and we were harassed and we were arrested. We've had false accusations put against us. We were dragged in front of local magistrates' courts and we were given criminal convictions. All part of the criminalisation process for republicans. That's still going on. It's just not as large because the republican base is fragmented and it's easier for them to handpick or target individuals for this type of treatment.[110]

The assertion that a 'fragmented' republican base has led to the refined targeting of 'political policing' has entered the anti-policing narrative more generally, thus it is worth drawing out.

---

[108] AB, critic of Sinn Féin policy, interview, October 2013.

[109] O, critic of Sinn Féin policy, interview, June 2013.

[110] R, critic of Sinn Féin policy, interview, July 2013.

Targeted minority

While the anti-policing narrative is built on the premise that the substance of 'political policing' has not changed, there is implicit recognition that the scope has. Considering that master narratives need a basis in observed reality to gain credence,[111] the anti-policing narrative reflects movement away from indiscriminate RUC 'suspect community' policing to 'political policing' that now specifically targets republican activists. Feeding into wider narratives of 'cosmetic reform' and the normalisation of 'British policing', the 'political policing' narrative becomes one of refined targeting rather than any meaningful change. This is not to suggest that aspects of policing at a wider level do not remain problematic in republican communities. After all, policing in republican districts remains somewhat reactive and is still notably militarised.[112] Although certainly *more* normalised, a continuing emphasis on 'anti-terror' policing and public order policing means that it is yet to become entirely 'normal' in any visible sense.[113] Consequently, even supporters of 'critical engagement' readily concede that:

> Any police that drive about in armoured cars and carry sub-machine guns – it's very hard to see them as your ordinary Bobby on the beat that you can go up and ask a question to or that you can feel totally secure with. You still see when they're in shopping centres and they're carrying guns, you still feel a wee bit uneasy because you remember back to what things were like before, and I think to a certain extent that hasn't changed.[114]

As a result of this, Topping and Byrne have concluded that the 'community policing' and 'counter-terrorist' strategies of the PSNI 'have become mutually exclusive policing tasks'.[115]

Notwithstanding this, house raids, vehicle checkpoints and 'stop and search' are no longer the defining characteristics of policing for most within republican communities – something 'critical engagers' use to support assertions of change. Anti-policing republicans have been forced to accommodate this lived reality into their policing narrative by acknowledging a refinement of 'political policing' to concentrate more rigorously on republican activists rather than the wider community. The following is an insightful synopsis of

---

[111] Benford and Snow, 2000.

[112] Topping and Byrne, 2012b, 163.

[113] Topping, 2015, 150.

[114] T, supporter of Sinn Féin policy, interview, August 2013.

[115] Topping and Byrne, 2012b, 163.

the difference in scope between RUC 'suspect community' policing and PSNI 'political policing':

> If you look historically, right: the '30s, '40s, '50s they can intern a small republican group. That resolves the issue. The '60s again. Late '60s there's an explosion of republicanism and you have to use this here widespread approach because you don't know. '70s, '80s and '90s the same. Even up to the early 2000s and then the splits occur and you can sort of pick off group by group and go 'right, there's a small protest, that's who is involved', and start all over again to build intelligence up and target those people rather than targeting the community at large.[116]

Continuity is nonetheless found through the assertion that Irish republicans – regardless of their numerical strength – have *always* been politically policed. This entails a remembering of previous generations when Irish republicanism was numerically weak. This also permeated the views of another republican who noted that 'I always compare now to the '40s and '50s when you had small groupings of people dotted up and around the country'. The interviewee felt that the absence of a mass movement today 'certainly does make their job [political policing] easier because there's less of us to deal with'.[117]

Just as anti-policing republicans 'remember' pre-conflict eras to dismiss an argument that cultural Nationalism represents change in policing, they similarly 'remember' a collectively inherited, rather than personally experienced, memory of previous eras when Irish republican activists were a persecuted minority, to dismiss the argument that policing is now a community service rather than a threat. Where the latter phase of conflict does not provide a neat fit with their narrative end point, they 'remember' previous eras that do. Anti-policing republicans are therefore able to reach further back in time to frame their current narrative and contextualise current lived experience. This represents a strategic reach into collective and cultural memory when experienced forms of memory are insufficient. They draw on the memory of 'political policing' that is 'remembered' yet not experienced. With the identity of victimhood capable of being drawn down from previous generations,[118] anti-policing republicans utilise the identity of the targeted minority to frame their narrative of 'political policing' in a post-Patten environment. This prevents what Jensen refers to as the post-reform

[116] V, critic of Sinn Féin policy, interview, September 2013.
[117] AC, critic of Sinn Féin policy, interview, November 2013.
[118] Assman and Shortt, 2012.

'invisibilisation' of police wrongs that often seeks to reinforce the image of the 'new' police and the image of the 'new' post-conflict state.[119] Extended remembering that 'remembers' beyond 1969 feeds into over-arching themes of the anti-policing narrative such as ideological purity, 'cosmetic reform', policing remaining 'political' rather than community orientated and the assimilation of 'former comrades' into the state leading to increasingly invisibilised 'political policing' of Irish republican dissenters within the post-GFA state.

This has found its way into the commemorative culture of the purist RSF, where older collective heroes killed by 'former comrades' in the Free State establishment are commemorated.[120] These heroes, though few in number, are eulogised as the embodiment of ideological purity sent to their death by corruptible 'former comrades' doing the dirty work of the foreign enemy.[121] In addition to being a powerful resource for mobilising in collective remembrance, this memory can also be mapped onto the present-day context. The implication being that like the collective heroes of yesteryear, the present-day persecuted few – imprisoned and politically policed Irish republicans – are today derided and marginalised by 'former comrades' siding with the jailer. This has seen increased importance afforded to republican prisoners and their protests in the anti-policing discourse. This is drawn on to undermine claims of post-GFA normality by highlighting the continued repression and imprisonment of Irish republicans who disagree with Sinn Féin.[122] The ability of prison protest to achieve such an end was not lost on the prisoners themselves:

> The refusal of Republican prisoners to be broken, our challenges to the Jail regime and the mobilisation of our comrades on the outside are obviously proving to be a challenge to the normalisation narrative. The colossal response from the DUP, NIPS/POA and the PSNI, along with the puppet master engineering of MI5, stands testament to that. We also await the responses of Sinn Féin and the SDLP to this matter given their knowledge of the context of our struggle and the involvement of their new and 'Civic Police Force' in propping up the unaccountable repressive Maghaberry regime ... the new tactic of political prosecution against RPPs [Republican Political Prisoners] will not silence us. Our resolve today is as strong as

[119] Jensen, 2009, 76.

[120] 'Liam Mellows remembered in Wexford', *Saoirse*, December 2013.

[121] 'Charlie Kerrins commemorated in Tralee', *Saoirse*, December 2013.

[122] Whiting, 2015.

> that of Republican prisoners who resisted criminalisation in the H Blocks, Crumlin Road and Armagh Gaol.[123]

Notable too, is the placing of current prison protests against the backdrop of previous protests, something aided by the fact that recent protests have mirrored the tactics previously used in the past.[124] A discourse challenging criminalisation attempts by 'former comrades' assimilated into the state underlines this but also reverts again to the dominant theme of 'true' republicans being persecuted by those since corrupted:

> Previous attempts by the Brits and their puppets to criminalise us was met with the necessary resistance and this is still the case today ... we are Prisoners of War and we will continue to oppose all attempts to criminalise us. In today's struggle we are being labelled as traitors and worse by Martin McGuinness and his colleagues, and by the continuation of the Brit black propaganda machine. This is an old British tactic formulated in London by MI5, and ably assisted in their work by our former comrades led by Gerry Adams. We are not the traitors. The former Republicans who sit in the bastion of Unionism and administer British rule are the real traitors to Ireland and her dead generations.[125]

An unmistakeable ideological dimension persists whereby the prisoners are 'proof of the dedication of men and women to the full freedom of Ireland'.[126] However, it has also drawn from human rights discourse too. This demands 'an end to the vile, degrading and abusive practice of strip-searching'[127] and protests at 'the physical and mental torture and the ongoing human rights abuses faced by Republican prisoners on a daily basis'.[128] It is therefore not only that Irish republicans are captive in 'England's Maghaberry Prison' that is wrong as an ideological matter, but the fact that they are forced to endure strip searches that are 'close to rape' that is also wrong as a human rights matter.[129]

---

[123] 'Statement from Roe 4 Republican Political Prisoners Maghaberry', 20 March 2015: http://107cowgate.com/2015/03/20/statement-from-roe-4-republican-political-prisoners-maghaberry/ (accessed 24 August 2015).

[124] Whiting, 2015.

[125] 'Statement from Republican POWs, Maghaberry Jail', *Saoirse*, June 2009.

[126] 'Easter Statement from the Leadership of the Republican Movement', *Saoirse Nua*, Spring 2013.

[127] 'Maghaberry', *Poblacht na nOibrithe*, 2012.

[128] 'Campaign Stepped up in Scotland', *Sovereign Nation*, February/March 2014.

[129] 'Legacy of 1916 Rising Under Attack', *Saoirse*, August 2014.

Despite the cumulative effects of 'political policing', anti-policing republicans remain defiant that it will not defeat or deter them. In fact, they assert that it will only strengthen their resolve. Such reasoning draws on the observed realities of 'repression-mobilisation' theory,[130] and seemingly relies on much-cited 'cyclic' phases of Irish history for validation. Accordingly, current 'political policing' will fail to defeat radical Irish republicanism and will only regenerate an environment conducive to conflict. In reaching such a conclusion, one critic of policing suggested a replaying of history whereby post-Patten 'political policing' was creating the context for 'round two' of conflict:

> People are being smoke-screened and being told smoke and mirrors, told lies, told half truths, threatened with, 'Well you go down that road and you know what's going to happen'. But Irish republicans have been going down that road for 900 years. Imprisonment and death does not deter them.[131]

Conclusion

Narratives on 'political policing' are inescapably reflective of competing master narratives on the wider issue of policing in the North of Ireland. Intertwining memory with current lived reality, they are used to reinforce the 'end point' of competing master narratives – either to make or challenge assertions of newness and change, so as to engineer a sense of rupture or continuity with the policing of the past. 'Critical engagers' draw on the matter to reinforce a narrative of strategic interaction with post-reform policing being 'a battle a day' in the 'new arena of struggle'. Disaggregating the policing monolith into the new and the old, their task is empowering the new and thwarting the old intent on rolling back reform. This feeds back into a wider narrative of ongoing 'progressive republican' equality-based transformation of the Northern Ireland state. Anti-policing critics, however, juxtapose their current experiences with autobiographical and collective memories of 'political policing' to draw a line of continuity between past and current policing problems in republican communities. Autobiographical and collective memories of past 'suspect community' policing provide the lens through which current 'political policing' is viewed, portrayed and interpreted. Where present-day policing is seen to be biased, oppressive and predicated on the wrongful direction of 'anti-terror' legislation against those partaking in legitimate political opposition to the GFA, opponents

---

130 Campbell and Connolly, 2003.

131 P, critic of Sinn Féin policy, interview, June 2013.

of policing find a natural home for these lived experiences in a catalogue of verisimilar episodes from the past. While demonstrating an ability to be highly ideologised and distinctly localised on the one hand, the anti-policing narrative has also adopted wider human rights discourse and changing global contexts on the other hand too. In this capacity, memory functions not as a bar for measuring the success of reform in making policing a community service to republican communities but rather as one measuring the lack of success of policing reform in making policing seem less threatening. The malleability of 'political policing' memory means that in as much as it has been used by 'critical engagers' to make assertions of newness and change that recast strategic interaction as combative reform, it has simultaneously been used by their critics to challenge these by asserting that policing remains a 'political' threat to Irish republicans who oppose the political status quo in post-GFA Northern Ireland.

Conclusion

This book set out to critically examine the role of memory in the Irish republican debate on policing. In doing so, it addressed the interlocking research questions of what role memory plays in the debate and how it performs this role. The conclusions reached herein have been drawn from an in-depth case study conducted across a broad spectrum of opinion within contemporary Irish republicanism. Drawing on the interaction between autobiographical memory and collective memory, this book highlights how memory helped condition attitudes towards policing during the 2006–07 debate and that, in conjunction with lived reality since then, it continues to condition views of policing in the six counties. Interestingly, this interaction in itself illustrates how any examination of the role of memory in the Irish republican policing debate should not be restrictively confined to memory politics. It is only by looking beyond specifically political usage of memory that a fuller appreciation of its role in the debate can be attained. To this end, it must be recognised that the role of memory in the debate is not restricted to hegemonic memory politicking but is central to how individuals interpret transitional processes too. Hence, as Susanne Buckley-Zistel has argued, while memory is adaptable for competing political discourses it is also 'highly personalised' for those with lived experience of the violent past.[1]

Irish republican policing memory is multifaceted. It operates in different ways on different levels for different ends. The 'malleability of memory' means that memory, even if remaining substantively constant for the most part, is capable of being moulded to suit whatever context it needs to function in. In terms of what role memory plays, it has been both an enhancer of and an impediment to the transitional process in Northern Ireland – particularly so if one subscribes to a 'thick' version of transitional justice that expands beyond the 'thin' legalistic notion of punishing past wrongs via the courtroom.[2]

[1] Buckley-Zistel, 2013, 140.

[2] McEvoy 2008; Buckley-Zistel, 2013, 134.

In order fully to appreciate this point, it is instructive to reiterate how transitional justice scholars have conceptualised transition in the six counties; it represents movement from a state that was beset by political violence and human rights abuse into one characterised by consociational power sharing and other reforms that have removed the worst excesses (but not every instance) of political violence and human rights abuses. This has not seen society or opposing political entities forsake conflicting ideological aspirations but it has unarguably led to the forging of new 'working relationships' with 'former enemies' that are designed to prevent the recurrence of conflict and human rights abuses. Memory has been at the core of accommodating these new peace-building engagements even though it has also been at the heart of competing efforts to politically define the past by transforming the old 'propaganda war' into a new post-conflict 'war by other means'. An examination of how it performs these roles reveals a moulding of memory through competing notions of *memory as continuity* that likens the present to the past and *memory as rupture* that differentiates between the present and the past. The consequences of using memory in the Irish republican policing debate are acceptance of police reform that aids 'moving on' processes and, conversely, continued rejection of police reform that frustrates these processes. Irish republican policing memory, in being malleable and multifaceted, operates on three contextual levels:

- the conventional level – reflecting how the Irish republican constituency faces the same challenges that all collectives undergoing the process of transition face;
- the inter-communal level – reflecting how Irish republican memory acts as counter-memory in meta-conflict memory politics;
- the intra-communal level – reflecting how memory has come to be politically contested within rather than between ethno-nationalist collectives.

It is the role that memory performs in the last context that is most markedly political, thus it is here that the academic understanding of memory politics in the Northern Ireland transition moves beyond a restrictive study reducing it to dissonance between Orange and Green master narratives. This new insight into internal memory politics, however, should not detract from how memory functions on the other levels. Before elaborating on intra-communal memory contestation, the role of memory at the conventional and inter-communal levels must be sufficiently summarised.

Memory at the conventional level

The Irish republican community, like any other collective emerging from prolonged conflict, is undergoing the arduous process of 'dealing with the past'. At the individual and collective levels, memory underpins this process. A cursory glance evidences how Irish republican memory facilitates 'remembering' that performs conventional roles like preventing 'forgetting' in order to benefit future generations[3] and commemorating collective and individual loss.[4] Admittedly, these functions are in no way endemic to the Irish republican debate on policing, yet neither are they alien to it. It is through operating at the conventional level that partial explanation can be found for wider transitional justice phenomena – such as a never-again mantra, demands for truth recovery and increased emphasis on human rights and post-conflict accountability – coming to bear on the debate. This reiterates how the Irish republican policing debate cannot be detached from the transitional context in which it plays out. The debate is shaped not only by highly charged internal memory politics but also by an external transitional process. This means that the role that memory plays in transitional contexts more generally will undoubtedly come to influence the debate. The implication of this is that while Irish republican policing memory operates at the conventional level through demands for truth recovery, increased accountability etc. it is also adaptable to political strategy.

A snapshot of memory's role at the conventional level should not be taken as the totality of its role in the policing debate. If it were, the more elaborate uses tailored to localised specificities of the transitional context of the North of Ireland would be overlooked. Acknowledging the operation of memory at the conventional level provides an insight into the importance of 'remembering' for the individual and collective trying to 'deal with the past' yet it fails to appreciate the political usage of that past. Limiting an understanding to the conventional level makes Irish republican memory appear benign by divesting it of political value. This masks the (counter)hegemonic power memory holds during transitional processes. The 'remembering' process seen in the policing debate may be reflective of the conventional role memory plays in transition but at the same time it *cannot* be regarded as an entirely apolitical process stemming from an entirely apolitical need to 'remember'. Accordingly, when evaluating the role of memory in the debate one must navigate between over-politicising its role by restricting this to a memory politics examination that overlooks conventional uses, on the one hand, and the danger of depoliticising it entirely, on the other hand.

---

[3] Brown, 2011.

[4] Waldorf, 2010.

Memory at the inter-communal level

The political value of Irish republican memory becomes obvious when evaluated at the inter-communal level. This involves mnemonic contestation between ethno-nationalist blocs that reflects traditional tension between competing Orange and Green master narratives. At this level, Irish republican memory is located within a contested realm of memory politics defined first by the long-term absence of any truth recovery process and secondly by continued delay in implementing 'dealing with the past' processes contained in recent political deals. In the absence of any process that might birth a 'shared narrative' reflecting the conflict experiences of all 'sides', Irish republican memory is a case par excellence of counter-memory. As such, it serves to counter the silencing of Irish republican experiences in official state, Unionist and RUC narratives. The counter-narrative progresses beyond an attempt to have experiences recognised to feed into wider meta-conflict memory politics over who is to 'blame' for the death and destruction of the conflict. The political value of Irish republican memory in this context is inextricably linked to the value of victimhood claims that can challenge or reinforce attribution of collective guilt.[5] Irish republican memory becomes a memory politics statement that Irish republicans were not exclusively to blame for the conflict nor were they immune from the misery of it. In doing so, it challenges the construction of dubious hierarchies of victimhood and fundamentally challenges traditional understandings of victimhood that are premised on an illogical dichotomy between victimhood and perpetratorship.

Leading on from this latter point, Irish republican memory has highlighted the role of the RUC and other state agencies in systematic human rights abuse that stretched well beyond direct responsibility for conflict-related death to encompass brutalisation of detainees, violence meted out in the jails and the daily intrusion into the lives of the 'suspect community'. Given the extent of state human rights abuse and the continued impact of its legacy, it is evident that any 'dealing with the past' process must adequately address the issue. This necessitates acceptance that wrongdoing was not confined to the political violence of the dubiously, if politically convenient, labelled 'terrorist'. The first step in this process is confronting, and then ultimately dismantling, politicised hierarchies of victimhood and perpetratorship that seek to fallaciously exonerate the British state for the destructive role it played in the conflict.[6] On the other hand, critics have been (perhaps too) quick to equate such

[5] McEvoy and McConnachie, 2012.

[6] Hearty, 2016a.

calls with an Irish republican 'rewriting' of the past that legitimates their political violence by attacking the conduct of the state.[7] There is, for sure, meta-conflict currency in highlighting state wrongdoing. However, dismissing the non-hierarchal approach to 'dealing with the past' in its entirety on this basis only replicates the pitfalls of over-politicising the role of memory at the expense of recognising its other functions. While Irish republican demands for truth, justice, accountability and victim recognition can indeed be politicised through pursuing a meta-conflict agenda, at the same time they represent the natural yearnings of those emerging from a prolonged conflict that had a deleterious impact at both the individual and collective levels. As observations made of transitions elsewhere testify to, when victimhood is denied in official discourse, those silenced and overlooked will mobilise to assert their counter-memory.[8] Irish republicans are no different from other collectives undergoing the process of transition in this regard.

This is not to foolhardily imply that the Irish republican policing counter-narrative is not itself exclusivist. It is a conflict narrative, and conflict narratives are by their very nature selective. This means that just as the interviewees in this case study can fault the state, Unionist and RUC narratives for overlooking the Irish republican policing experience, so too can those who have articulated these narratives elsewhere similarly fault the Irish republican counter-narrative for its 'silences'. The inherent mnemonic selectivity caused by reliance on the 'memory of perpetrators' in opposing policing narratives justifies this mutual criticism.

In terms of the wider Northern Ireland transition, Irish republican memory at the inter-communal level can be seen to perform conflicting roles as both an impediment to and an enhancer of transition. By feeding into contested memory politics in the continued absence of any overarching process to 'deal with the past', it may be seen as an obvious impediment to further transition by becoming 'war by other means' in the meta-conflict. Disagreement over the past is locked in to existing master narratives favourable to 'us' and critical of 'them'. However, it is the very absence of any overarching process to 'deal with the past' that may paradoxically endow Irish republican memory with a certain redemptive quality that transforms it into an enhancer of transition. In the absence of a 'shared narrative' in the North of Ireland, Irish republican memory can contribute to a broader understanding of past conflict and the underlying reasons for that conflict.[9] Chapter 2 certainly suggests that such potential exists, whether that be through attempts to engage with former RUC officers

[7] McGrattan, 2013; Hopkins, 2015.

[8] Jelin, 2007; Kent, 2011.

[9] Hearty, 2014.

in order to provide them with the Irish republican perspective on policing, the willingness 'to listen' to the experiences of the 'other' or belated acceptance of the reality that a tradition of 'policing families' within Unionism means not every RUC officer was motivated by sectarian enmity. Even if such engagements only birth an acknowledgement of the 'other' perspective that is decidedly 'thin', the implication is, nonetheless, that it can help reduce the scope for the recurrence of violence and provide a deeper understanding of the past that aids 'moving on' processes. That Irish republicans would seek to use memory in this way correlates with the more prevalent peace-builder role former combatants across the board in the North of Ireland have enthusiastically embraced.[10]

Memory at the intra-communal level

Memory being contested within, as well as between, ethno-nationalist collectives, irrevocably dispels the notion that memory politics in transitioning Northern Ireland can be neatly reduced to flawed 'two tribes' interpretations. Although this may be the most easily understood manifestation, the 'dealing with the past' process must acknowledge that contestation stretches beyond Orange and Green binaries to include contestation premised on the binaries of having 'moved on' with or being 'left behind' by transition. A fuller understanding of hidden discourses in transitional justice and peace processing can only be attained by looking beyond dominant master narratives and engaging with the narrative of those 'left behind'. By doing so, this case study has shown how hidden discourses can be identified, how they are framed, how they are constructed and how they are circulated. In transcending the strict parameters of memory politics, there is recognition that while these processes are consciously undertaken by those wishing to 'spoil' transition, they also help to frame understandings of missing out on the 'peace dividend' at the individual level and, as such, can frame lived experience of the transition.

That memory politics contestation can manifest at the intra-communal level provides an insight into the interaction between memory and ideology and memory and reform processes during periods of transition. Interaction in both cases can be understood through the competing notions of *memory as continuity* and *memory as rupture*. Given that memory has an ability to contextualise and give political meaning to the exigencies of the present by providing reference to the past, it is perhaps merely foreseeable that it would manifest through these lenses. Additionally, given that memory is malleable and context

[10] Shirlow and McEvoy, 2008.

specific, it is equally foreseeable that political disagreement within the Irish republican constituency would force competing hegemons to interchangeably adopt these competing lenses dependent on the particular challenges memory politics posed at any given point.

Memory and ideology

By interacting with ideology, memory subjects transitional processes to interpretation through long-held belief systems. This compares positions currently adopted with positions held in the past. Such a comparison creates political claims of what is ideologically sound and what is ideologically flawed. Ideology can therefore facilitate as well as restrict concessionary moves in transitional processes. To this end, it assumes a bipolar ability both to enhance and impede transition. In order fully to demonstrate this point, it is worth reverting to the competing lenses of continuity and rupture. Where memory interacts with ideology to create the 'progressive republican' reading of 'critical engagement' it functions as *memory as continuity.* 'Critical engagement' is mapped into a wider process whereby the destruction of the 'Orange state' by equality-based reform from within is the natural continuity of 'armed struggle'. Memory and strategy become inextricably linked to the extent that transitional strategy is framed by the understanding that it is the continuation of past armed struggle by other means. This can help the individual 'make sense' of the transitional process, as evidenced by the expression of narratives mapping a progression from 'rebel' to 'revolutionary'. However, it can also be utilised for memory politics purposes by elites at the collective level via the 'extension of struggle' narrative. The result of both is that former combatants once militarily opposed to policing agents now 'critically engage' with them yet feel no ideological betrayal. As 'progressive republicans', they are now pursuing the same end goal albeit by different means. Memory, when inextricably linked to strategy in this way, can be simultaneously regarded as an enhancer to transition and an impediment to transition. As an impediment, memory contributes to the entrenching of dichotomous ideological goals and political positions that impose a 'negative peace' limitation on 'moving on' processes. By drawing a line of continuity with a process designed effectively to remove the Northern Ireland state, memory only facilitates peaceful coexistence alongside rather than any ideological renegotiation with former enemies. However, the importance of *memory as continuity* in bringing into being a peaceful coexistence of this kind should not be overlooked. It is the reassurance that one has not 'sold out' on long-held principles and ideological end goals provided by this sense of continuity that creates scope to pursue them through non-violent means. The ability to constructively engage with former enemies via a means other than sustained political violence makes it an enhancer to transition.

Interaction between ideology and memory can also be an impediment to transition by hardening absolutist positions. In accordance with a 'constitutional nationalist' reading of the transition, *memory as rupture* depicts 'critical engagement' as a departure from long-held ideological goals. 'Critical engagement' becomes the continuity of previous failed 'reform from within' projects, rather than the continuation of past struggle by other means. *Memory as rupture* becomes an impediment to transition by hardening absolutist positions through a value-laden understanding that precludes the compromise necessary for a 'working relationship' with former enemies. As is the case with *memory as continuity* seen above, this can help rationalise the transitional process at the individual level, yet it is also politically expedient for those wishing to 'spoil' transition. This hardening of absolutist positions may manifest itself in residual armed activity but it is also given expression through legitimate non-violent political opposition.

It has become glaringly evident that any examination of ideological opposition to the transition within Irish republicanism cannot be reduced to a flawed understanding that opponents are 'conflict junkies'. The multitude of views proffered throughout this case study demonstrates that there is a spectrum of attitudes towards current armed activity, ranging from outright rejection to firm support. Not everyone who opposes the GFA, transition or policing should be automatically assumed to be in favour of 'spoiler' violence. In fact, some non-violent political opponents argue that sporadic armed activity only serves to curtail the expression of legitimate political criticism.[11] Irish republican opposition to the transition cannot, then, be examined through a simplistic 'war or peace' approach. It must comprise fuller examination of non-violent leftist and class-based critiques if the true extent of disenfranchisement with the transition within the constituency is to be grasped. Although these dimensions have always been prevalent in academic coverage of Protestant/Unionist/Loyalist disillusionment with the Northern Ireland transition,[12] it has only been more recently that academic coverage of Irish republican opposition has ventured beyond examination of militant groups. Admittedly, this case study does not conduct an exhaustive Irish republican critique of the transition and policing that is leftist or class based, but in acknowledging that such critiques do exist and that they remain neglected, it has moved current academic understanding further beyond an erroneous 'war versus peace' dichotomy.

[11] Q, critic of Sinn Féin policy, interview, July 2013.

[12] Lundy and McGovern, 2008a; Shirlow, 2012.

Memory and reform processes

This case study offers an original empirical insight into how police reform is interpreted and presented through the medium of memory among two key constituencies: those who resisted the state policing apparatus in the past but who now endorse it, and those who continue to resist it. Such an in-depth interrogation of how memory underpins individual interpretation of police reform and how it shapes the master narratives of competing hegemons provides a deeper insight into how memory politics can enhance or impede transition through enabling or disabling previously excluded groups to 'buy into' reformed institutions.

Competing lenses of continuity and rupture are again the most apposite for examining this interaction. *Memory as rupture* can enhance transition through assertions of newness and change in a post-reform environment. These assertions seek to differentiate between present policing in a post-reform, transitional context and pre-reform policing during past violent conflict. This provides a neat, if simplistic, separation of the 'old' from the 'new' by juxtaposing lived experience of the PSNI with lived experience of the RUC. This enhances transition by creating scope for new 'working relationships' to be built with the 'new breed' of policing agent, as well as allowing constructive post-conflict engagement predicated on community 'needs' with those once considered the enemy. The interaction of *memory as rupture* and police reform has generated a 'community policing' narrative whereby policing has been framed as a community service rather than a political threat.

A further manifestation of memory as an impediment to transition is found in the line of continuity drawn between current policing problems in Irish republican communities and those encountered in the past. *Memory as continuity* possesses a negative capacity that challenges the assertions of newness and change inherent in *memory as rupture*. It impedes transition by preventing any differentiation between pre-reform policing and post-reform policing. This shapes current attitudes towards policing by linking rather than separating current and past 'political policing', current and past 'over-policing' and current and past 'under-policing'. Rather than nourishing post-conflict 'working relationships' with former enemies, *memory as continuity* sustains residual suspicion towards policing 'outsiders'. This has been reinforced by shortcomings that are perhaps a foreseeable product of all reform processes, such as institutional crossover and the retention of a 'canteen culture'. However, it is also reflective of more substantive localised problems with the police reform process, such as the 'rehiring' debacle and the impotence of local accountability mechanisms on a seemingly infinite list of 'national security' matters. Like much else, this demonstrates the convergence of general globalised policing problems with problems that are specific to the transitional context of the North of Ireland.

Memory as continuity therefore assumes a duality of purpose; it contextualises what the individual perceives to be change – or lack thereof – following 'critical engagement', and it is also used to underpin competing master narratives on the issue within Irish republicanism. The applicability of the latter is evident first in the 'new arena of struggle' narrative that 'critical engagers' have adopted in relation to the RUC 'old guard', and secondly in the 'cosmetic reform' narrative where anti-policing republicans mirror post-Patten experiences of 'political policing' in past collective and individual experiences of the RUC. In drawing this issue out in Chapter 7, this book demonstrates that, contrary to official discourse, the policing problem has not been 'solved' following 'critical engagement'. Although there is an unprecedented level of acceptance of policing in the North of Ireland, there remain considerable legitimacy problems borne out of the past in some republican communities. Moreover, aspects that are commonly misconstrued as symptoms of the 'policing legacy' – the misapplication of 'anti-terror' legislation and 'political policing' – still plague post-Patten policing. One could legitimately question whether these issues can be effectively addressed as a legacy issue when they remain all too familiar during transition. Examining these issues has prevented post-'critical engagement' invisibility of continuing policing problems, and has provided the impetus, and indeed highlighted the need, for a more expansive and robust critique of how political opposition to the transition in the six counties is policed.

Intra-communal memory politics during transition

Memory politics is a key component of the hegemonic battle between drivers of transition and 'spoilers' of transition within the wider Irish republican community. Although memory is used at the individual and collective levels to 'make sense' of transition, at the political level it is deliberately used as a political resource by competing hegemons. Competing actors within Irish republicanism assume the role of 'memory entrepreneurs' that monopolise the past to promote their current agendas. This has seen the past used to shore up the electoral mandate of those driving transition and to plug a legitimacy gap for those 'spoilers' who do not have or do not seek such a mandate.

Sinn Féin has adopted an 'extension of struggle' narrative that uses *memory as continuity* to portray their strategy of working the transition as a natural post-conflict pursuit of the ideological goals sought during the armed struggle. The strategies (or lack thereof) of opponents are dismissed as futile militancy, an ignorance of revolutionary political change and the malign work of British 'securocrats'. They are no different from any other political elite in the sense that they strive to build continuity between the past and their present strategy at the expense of their rivals' claim to that same past. In this context, intra-communal memory contestation becomes about 'owning' rather than understanding the past. It is less about making sense of the transition and more concerned with making a fit between current and past positions. The importance of making the past fit the present is evident through the effort they expend in laying claim to the patriot dead and the legacy of the IRA's armed campaign. The necessity of this has been heightened by two closely connected factors: increased movement away from the traditionalist stance leaving them susceptible to claims of 'sell out' and, flowing from this, the emergence of new political and militant 'spoiler' groups within the constituency to level such accusations.

These groups use memory to impede transition by challenging the Sinn Féin claim to the past. This is achieved through a dual process of presenting their positions and strategies – political and/or military – as the continuity of the orthodox Irish republican position and strategy, and through portraying Sinn Féin strategy as a rupture from this. This has seen 'spoiler' groups utilise republican commemorative culture to challenge the Sinn Féin claim to the patriot dead and the retention of Sinn Féin's previous rhetorical positions on the inevitability of Irish republican resistance as long as occupation continues. For those of a less militant hue, there has been a reversion to a radical leftist form of Irish republicanism that Sinn Féin (in the North of Ireland at least) has increasingly moved away from. Inasmuch as memory is a shield for the drivers of transition, it too can be seen as a sword for 'spoilers' who use it to mobilise in opposition to transitional processes, to critique processes of transition and to compete with intra-communal rivals driving the process of transition.

It is precisely because memory is malleable that it simultaneously functions on differing levels through the mediums of *memory as continuity* and *memory as rupture* both to impede and enhance transition. The constant interchange between these typologies demonstrates that memory is contingent upon the context in which it is being used, the purpose for which it is being used and the actor by which it is being used. This accounts for the nuances of how it is used in the inter-communal and the intra-communal contexts, how it is used to own the past and to understand the past, how it is used by the individuals at grassroots level and by elites at the collective level. Irish republican memory has shown memory to be dependent on an amalgam of these variables, with the memory of the same past used for very different purposes and ends.

The malleability of Irish republican memory is compounded by the fact that it exists in a transitional context that necessitates more steps into the relative unknown. The paradox is that when faced with a venture into the unknown, the tendency of Irish republicanism is to look backwards for guidance. This reveals its Janus-like nature: it looks forward in indefinite anticipation of the certain future day of self-determination but it simultaneously surveys the long and unrelenting road already traversed in search of that day. Therein lies the crux of the mnemonic debate within modern Irish republicanism. That debate can best be understood not as contestation over what happened in the past but as contestation over what that past now 'means' in a political climate that has changed dramatically both internally and externally. Contestation is reduced not to issues of what Irish republicans sought in the past or what they seek in the future (arcane disagreements over the particular relevance of socialism aside), but to marked differences in current strategies purporting to work towards the common, historical goal of national self-determination.

At the time of writing, the centenary year of the Easter Rising has drawn to a close. How and when the sovereign (and socialist) Irish Republic declared by Pádraig Mac Piarais in 1916 will come to be realised remains more uncertain than ever before. The broader Irish republican constituency is more fractured than it has ever been at any time since 1916, while opposing strategies for attaining the vision of 1916 remain limited by their own inherent shortcomings. Sinn Féin's electoral performances in the centenary year failed to live up to expectations – their vote dropped in the assembly elections by 2.9 per cent (the biggest drop by any major party), causing their hopes of being the largest political party in the six counties to dissipate, while an impressive rise in the vote in the 26 counties was not enough to see them enter government or become the largest opposition party there. Previous notions of driving forward the agenda for Irish unity while being in government in both jurisdictions post the 1916 centenary year have, for the time being at least, come to pass. Likewise, securing a border poll on Irish unity as per the provisions of the GFA has proven problematic almost 20 years after the accord was signed. In the aftermath of 'Brexit' – a considerable political game-changer by all accounts – both Theresa Villiers and her successor James Brokenshire have ruled out holding a border poll.[13] In light of this, Sinn Féin efforts in the closing stages of the centenary year were diverted into opposing a 'hard border' post-Brexit rather than challenging the

[13] 'EU Referendum: Theresa Villiers Rules Out Sinn Féin's Border Poll Call', BBC News, 24 June 2016: www.bbc.co.uk/news/uk-northern-ireland-36622120 (accessed 12 October 2016); 'Northern Ireland EU Dream DESTROYED: James Brokenshire Says NO Referendum after Brexit', *Express*, 20 July 2016: www.express.co.uk/news/politics/691435/Politics-James-Brokenshire-no-Northern-Ireland-EU-referedum-Brexit (accessed 12 October 2016).

border itself.[14] Perhaps these structural limitations are a reminder of the reality that being able to reform the Orange state out of existence under the terms of the GFA is not the same thing as being able to reform British involvement in Ireland out of existence.[15] Early 2017 has, somewhat paradoxically, brought more uncertainty yet renewed vigour for Sinn Féin and its 'progressive republican' project. Amidst the scandal caused by a Renewable Heating Incentive (RHI) scheme, Martin McGuinness (since deceased) resigned as Deputy First Minister, attributing his decision to Arlene Foster's refusal to accommodate an inquiry into the RHI affair and, more notably, to DUP intransigence on equality matters. Consequently, the Stormont assembly the party had invested so much in collapsed and fresh elections were held in March 2017. This election saw the party reassert its traditional dominance in West Belfast while also moving further ahead of the SDLP in South Down (also going on to take both it and Foyle off the SDLP in the June 2017 general election), increase its share of the vote by nearly 4 per cent and come within 1,200 votes and a single assembly seat of the DUP – a monumental reversal of the fortunes seen at the polls less than a year previously when it was stung by a PBP-driven protest vote against Tory cuts. The loss of a Unionist majority at Stormont for the first time ever has emboldened their discourse about dismantling the 'Orange state', given their renewed calls for a post-Brexit border poll some added bite and reaffirmed its election pledge that there will be no return to the pre-collapse 'status quo'. On the one hand, this could be the defenders of equality-agenda republicanism further flexing their 'ethnic tribune' muscle while still high on electoral success directly attributable to doing just that but, on the other hand, their pledge begs the question of how the GFA institutions long championed as a stepping stone to unity can actually aid the strategic advancement of that objective if they are now, by the party's own admission, failing to deliver as initially envisaged when 'critical engagement' began. Sinn Féin was led into these elections by Michelle O'Neill after McGuinness retired from elected politics due to ill health. Many have seen this move as the harbinger of a generational transition within the upper echelons of the party. If the 'progressive republican' blueprint devised by the Adams leadership does eventually come to fruition (and that admittedly is a huge 'if') it seems increasingly likely that it will not be at the political helm when it does so.

For their part, the critics of Sinn Féin strategy hardly set the world alight in the centenary year either. Despite predictions that the centenary year would

[14] 'Anti-Brexit Protests Held at Six Locations on the Border', BBC News, 8 October 2016: www.bbc.co.uk/news/uk-northern-ireland-37595774 (accessed 12 October 2016).

[15] Catney, 2007, 30.

be used as a launching pad for a more protracted military campaign,[16] at the time of writing there is little evidence to suggest this was the case. While militant activity has certainly grown in recent years,[17] this has still fallen considerably short of matching the intensity of the Provisional campaign and, more fundamentally, there is little suggestion as to how it can deliver where the Provisional campaign did not – or for that matter how it can deliver where Sinn Féin's reform from within strategy cannot. Politically, opponents of Sinn Féin, like Éirígí and RNU, have not managed to use the patriotic fervour of the centenary year to mount a serious electoral challenge to the Sinn Féin hegemony. Granted, anti-policing candidates did previously win a number of local council seats, but disaffection with the Stormont administration largely translated itself into votes for PBP in the 2016 assembly elections. Perhaps 'mild sceptics' had a point when they argued that whatever its shortcomings the Sinn Féin strategy should not be rejected by republicans in the absence of a viable alternative.[18] In the centenary year, Saoradh put itself forward as this alternative. Whether it is in fact the magic bullet that anti-GFA republicans have long sought cannot be determined yet given its infancy. What is certain is that the task facing the party in challenging Sinn Féin hegemony is sizeable. It chose not to contest the March election.

Evidently, then, even if the end goal for Irish republicans is crystal clear, the waters of how to attain it remain muddied. Memory has provided reassurance and comfort, perhaps even inspiration, but it has not produced consensus. Splits and departures too numerous to recite have created a plethora of actors claiming to possess the unerring blueprint to achieve the as of yet unattained holy grail. For these hegemons, a rich tradition of struggle and sacrifice is an immeasurably valuable political resource worth contesting. Given that memory is integral to hegemonic claims of ownership over the past during periods of contested transition, the intra-communal memory politicking of Irish republicans certainly seems more inevitable than it does remarkable.

[16] Morrison, 2013.

[17] Morrison, 2016b.

[18] Ó hAdhmaill, 2007, 35.

References

Elsa Abou-Assi, 'Collective Memory and Management of the Past: The Entrepreneurs of Civil War Memory in Post-war Lebanon', *International Social Science Journal*, 61.202 (2011), pp. 399–409.

Gerry Adams, *Free Ireland: Towards a Lasting Peace* (Dingle: Brandon Books, 1986).

—— 'Address to Sinn Féin Ard Fheis', 29 March 2003: www.sinnfein.ie/contents/312 (accessed 20 February 2013).

'Adams Apologises to Volunteer's Families', *Derry Journal*, 26 January 2007.

'Adams Seeks Police Stance Backing', BBC News, 20 January 2007: http://news.bbc.co.uk/1/hi/northern_ireland/6281805.stm (accessed 23 May 2017).

'The Agreement: Agreement Reached in the Multi-Party Negotiations' (Good Friday Agreement), Belfast, 10 April 1998, 25: http://cain.ulst.ac.uk/events/peace/docs/agreement.htm.

'An Agreement Among the Parties of the Northern Ireland Executive on Parades, Select Commemorations, and Related Protests; Flags and Emblems; and Contending with the Past', 31 December 2013: www.northernireland.gov.uk/haass.pdf (originally accessed 10 May 2014); see www.peaceagreements.org/wggsite/downloadAgreementDocument/id/624.

Laura Aguiar, 'Back to Those Walls: The Women's Memory of the Maze and Long Kesh Prison in Northern Ireland', *Memory Studies*, 8.2 (2015), pp. 227–41.

P. Aguilar and C. Ramirez-Barat, 'Amnesty and Reparations without Truth or Justice in Spain', in N. Wouters (ed.), *Transitional Justice and Memory in Europe (1945–2013)* (Cambridge: Intersentia, 2014), pp. 199–257.

Nevin T. Aiken, *Identity, Reconciliation and Transitional Justice: Overcoming Intractability in Divided Societies* (Oxford: Routledge, 2013).

Stan L. Albrecht and Miles Green, 'Attitudes Towards the Police and the Larger Attitude Complex: Implications for Police-Community Relationships', *Criminology*, 15.1 (1977), pp. 67–86.

Derek H. Alderman, 'Street Names and the Scaling of Memory: The Politics of Commemorating Martin Luther King Jr Within the African American Community', *Area*, 35.2 (2003), pp. 163–73.

Rogelio Alonso, 'The Modernization in Irish Republican Thinking Toward the Utility of Violence', *Studies in Conflict & Terrorism*, 24.2 (2001), pp. 131–44.
—— *The IRA and Armed Struggle* (London: Routledge, 2007).
I. Amadiume, and A. An-Na'im, 'Introduction: Facing Truth, Voicing Justice', in I. Amadiume, and A. An-Na'im (eds), *The Politics of Memory: Truth, Healing and Social Justice* (London: Zed Books, 2000), pp. 1–19.
Amnesty International, 'Report of an Amnesty International Mission to Northern Ireland (28th Nov 1977–6th Dec 1977)' (London: Amnesty International, 1978).
—— *Political Killings in Northern Ireland* (London: Amnesty International, 1994).
Benedict Anderson, *Imagined Communities* (London: Verso, 2006).
Brendan Anderson and Joe Cahill, *Joe Cahill: A Life in the IRA* (Dublin: O'Brien Press, 2002).
Martina Anderson, 'Address to Sinn Féin Ard Fheis', 19 February 2006: www.sinnfein.ie/contents/6077 (accessed 20 February 2013).
Molly Andrews, 'Grand National Narratives and the Project of Truth Commissions: A Comparative Analysis', *Media, Culture & Society*, 25.1 (2003), pp. 45–65.
'Anniversary Marked in Queen's and UCD', *An Phoblacht*, 13 March 2008.
'Anti-Brexit Protests Held at Six Locations on the Border', BBC News, 8 October 2016: www.bbc.co.uk/news/uk-northern-ireland-37595774 (accessed 12 October 2016).
Ardoyne Commemoration Project, *Ardoyne: The Untold Truth* (Belfast: Beyond the Pale, 2002).
'"Armed Struggle is Over" – INLA', BBC News, 11 October 2009: http://news.bbc.co.uk/1/hi/northern_ireland/8301241.stm (accessed 6 October 2015).
Elizabeth A. Armstrong and Suzanna M. Crage, 'Movements and Memory: The Making of the Stonewall Myth', *American Sociological Review*, 71.5 (2006), pp. 724–51.
P. Arthur, 'Conflict, Memory and Reconciliation', in M. Elliot (ed.), *The Long Road to Peace in Northern Ireland*, 2nd edn (Liverpool: Liverpool University Press, 2007).
A. Assman, 'Memory, Individual and Collective', in R. E. Godwin and C. Tilly (eds), *The Oxford Handbook of Contextual Political Analysis* (Oxford: Oxford University Press, 2006), pp. 210–24.
—— 'To Remember or to Forget: Which Way Out of a Shared History of Violence?', in A. Assman and L. Shortt (eds), *Memory and Political Change* (Basingstoke: Palgrave Macmillan, 2012), pp. 53–71.
J. Assmann, 'Communicative and Cultural Memory', in A. Erll and A. Nunning (eds), *Cultural Memory Studies: An International and Interdisciplinary Handbook* (Berlin: Walter de Gruyter, 2008).
'Attempts to Recruit an Informer', *Sceal*, 87 (31 March 1988).

'B-Specials No Change', *United Irishman*, October 1969.

Bradley Bamford, 'The United Kingdom's "War Against Terrorism"', *Terrorism and Political Violence*, 16.4 (2004), pp. 737–56.

D. Bar-Tal, 'Collective Memory of Physical Violence: Its Contribution to the Culture of Violence', in E. Cairns and M. D. Roe (eds), *The Role of Memory in Ethnic Conflict* (Basingstoke: Palgrave Macmillan 2003), pp. 77–93.

'The Barricades are Down – but the People Have Risen', *Tatler*, 25 (1971).

David H. Bayley, 'Post-Conflict Police Reform: Is Northern Ireland a Model?', *Policing*, 2.2 (2008), pp. 233–40.

Kevin Bean, 'The New Departure? Recent Developments in Republican Strategy and Ideology', *Irish Studies Review*, 3.10 (1995), pp. 2–6.

—— *The New Politics of Sinn Féin* (Liverpool: Liverpool University Press, 2007a).

—— 'Defining Republicanism: Shifting Discourses of New Nationalism and Post-Republicanism', in M. Elliot (ed.), *The Long Road to Peace in Northern Ireland*, 2nd edn (Liverpool: Liverpool University Press, 2007b), pp. 133–46.

—— '"New Dissidents are but Old Provisional's Writ Large"? The Dynamics of Dissident Republicanism in the New Northern Ireland', *Political Quarterly*, 83.2 (2012), pp. 210–18.

—— 'Endings and Beginnings? Republicanism Since 1994', *Studies in Conflict & Terrorism*, 37.9 (2014), pp. 720–32.

Kevin Bean and Mark Hayes, 'Sinn Féin and the New Republicanism in Ireland: Electoral Progress, Political Stasis and Ideological Failure', *Radical History Review*, 104 (2009), pp. 126–42.

'The Belfast Agreement' (Belfast: Northern Ireland Office, 1998): https://www.gov.uk/government/publications/the-belfast-agreement (accessed 27 May 2017).

'Belfast's "Battle of St Matthew's" Remembered', *An Phoblacht*, 1 July 2014: www.anphoblacht.com/contents/24150 (accessed 7 August 2014).

Christine Bell, *Peace Agreements and Human Rights* (Oxford: Oxford University Press, 2003).

Christine Bell, Colm Campbell and Fionnuala Ní Aolaín, 'Justice Discourses in Transition', *Social & Legal Studies*, 13.3 (2004), pp. 305–28.

Robert D. Benford and David A. Snow, 'Framing Processes and Social Movements: An Overview and Assessment', *Annual Review of Sociology*, 26 (2000), pp. 611–39.

D. Bernsten and A. Bohn, 'Cultural Life Scripts and Individual Life Stories', in P. Boyer and J. V. Wertsch (eds), *Memory in Mind and Culture* (Cambridge: Cambridge University Press, 2009), pp. 62–82.

Berber Bevernage, 'Writing the Past Out of the Present: History and the Politics of Time in Transitional Justice', *History Workshop Journal*, 69.1 (2010), pp. 111–31.

Paul Bew and Henry Patterson, *The British State and the Ulster Crisis: From Wilson to Thatcher* (London: Verso, 1985).

M. Beyers, 'Policing Accountability', in Committee on the Administration of Justice, *Mapping the Rollback? Human Rights Provisions of the Belfast/Good Friday Agreement 15 Years on* (Belfast: Committee on the Administration of Justice, 2013).

Jessie Blackbourn, 'International Terrorism and Counterterrorist Legislation: The Case Study of Post 9/11 Northern Ireland', *Terrorism and Political Violence*, 21.1 (2009), pp. 133–54.

—— *Anti-Terrorism Law and Normalising Northern Ireland* (Abingdon: Routledge, 2015).

'Blame Britain', *United Irishman*, September 1969.

'Bloody Sunday: Ex-Soldier Arrested Over Londonderry Shootings', BBC News, 10 November 2015: www.bbc.co.uk/news/uk-northern-ireland-34775466 (accessed 10 November 2015).

John Bodnar, *Re-making America: Public Memory, Commemoration and Patriotism in the Twentieth Century* (Princeton, NJ: Princeton University Press, 1992).

Lucy Bond, *Frames of Memory After 9/11: Culture, Criticism, Politics and Law* (Basingstoke: Palgrave Macmillan, 2015).

Alex Borraine, *A Country Unmasked: Inside South Africa's Truth and Reconciliation Commission* (Oxford: Oxford University Press, 2000).

Owen Bowcott, 'The 76-Year-Old Dissident Taking on Sinn Féin', *Guardian*, 1 March 2007: www.theguardian.com/politics/2007/mar/01/uk.northernireland1 (accessed 17 May 2017).

Timothy Bowman, *Carson's Army: The Ulster Volunteer Force 1910–22* (Manchester: Manchester University Press, 2012).

James Bowyer Bell, *The Secret Army: The IRA*, 3rd edn (Piscataway, NJ: Transaction, 1997).

J. Boyarin, 'Space, Time and the Politics of Memory', in J. Boyarin (ed.), *Remapping Memory: The Politics of Time Space* (Minneapolis: University of Minnesota Press, 1994).

Kevin Boyle, Tom Hadden and Paddy Hillyard, *Ten Years on in Northern Ireland: The Legal Control of Political Violence* (London: Cobden Trust, 1980).

Ben Bradford, Jonathan Jackson and Elizabeth A. Stanko, 'Contact and Confidence: Revisiting the Impact of Public Encounters with the Police', *Policing & Society*, 19.1 (2009), pp. 20–46.

Ben Bradford, Jonathan Jackson, M. Hough and S. Farrall, 'Trust and Confidence in Criminal Justice: A Review of the British Research Literature', in A. Jokinen, E. Ruuskanen, M. Yordanova, D. Markov and M. Ilcheba (eds), *Review of Need: Indications of Public Confidence in Criminal Justice for Policy Assessment* (Bristol: Polity Press, 2008).

Séamus Breathnach, *The Irish Police: From Earliest Times to the Present Day* (Dublin: Anvil, 1974).

Suzanne Breen, 'Sinn Féin Told to Stay Away from South's Grave', *Sunday Tribune*, 31 December 2006.

M. Breen-Smyth, 'Remembering in Northern Ireland: Victims, Perpetrators and Hierarchies of Pain and Responsibility', in B. Hamber (ed.), *Past Imperfect: Dealing with the Past in Northern Ireland and Societies in Transition* (Derry: INCORE, 1999).

—— *Truth Recovery and Justice after Conflict: Managing Violent Pasts* (London: Routledge, 2007).

John D. Brewer and Bernadette Hayes, 'Victimhood and Attitudes towards Dealing with the Legacy of a Violent Past: Northern Ireland as a Case Study', *British Journal of Politics & International Relations*, 17.3 (2015), pp. 512–30.

John D. Brewer and Kathleen Magee, *Inside the RUC: Routine Policing in a Divided Society* (Oxford: Clarendon Press, 1991).

'British Government Exposed as Anti-Agreement Rejectionist on the Past', Relatives for Justice, 17 November 2015: http://relativesforjustice.com/british-government-exposed-as-anti-agreement-rejectionists-on-the-past/ (accessed 23 November 2015). 'Brits Out', *The Freedom Fighter*, 4 (December 1976).

Jens Brockmeier, 'Introduction: Searching for Cultural Memory', *Culture and Psychology*, 8.1 (2002), pp. 5–14.

Mike Brogden, *The Police: Autonomy and Consent* (London: Academic Press, 1982).

—— *On the Mersey Beat* (Oxford: Oxford University Press, 1991).

—— 'An Agenda for Post-Troubles Policing in Northern Ireland: The South African Precedent', *Liverpool Law Review*, 17.1 (1995), pp. 3–27.

Mike Brogden and Preeti Nijhar, *Community Policing: National and International Models and Approaches* (Abingdon: Routledge, 2013).

Kris Brown, '"Ancestry of Resistance"; The Political Use of Commemoration by Ulster Loyalists and Irish Republicans in a Post Conflict Setting', *Transitional Justice Institute Research Paper*, No. 09-09-5 (2009a), pp. 1–47.

—— '"Recipe for Disaster?" Trust, Memory and Space in a Post Conflict City: A Case Study of the Tri-Service Home Coming Parade in Belfast 2008', *Round Table*, 98.403 (2009b), pp. 427–38.

—— 'Rights and Victims, Martyrs and Memories: The European Court of Human Rights and Political Transition in Northern Ireland', in A. Buyse and M. Hamilton (eds), *Transitional Jurisprudence and the ECHR; Justice, Politics and Rights* (Cambridge: Cambridge University Press, 2011), pp. 52–80.

—— 'Commemoration as Symbolic Reparation: New Narratives or Spaces of Conflict?', *Human Rights Review*, 14.3 (2013), pp. 273–89.

K. Brown and E. Viggiani, 'Performing Provisionalism: Republican Commemorative Practice as Political Performance', in L. Fitzpatrick (ed.), *Performing Violence in Contemporary Ireland* (Dublin: Carysfort Press, 2010), pp. 225–48.

Steve Bruce, *The Edge of the Union: The Ulster Loyalist Political Vision* (Oxford: Oxford University Press, 1994).

—— 'Turf War and Peace: Loyalist Paramilitaries Since 1994', *Terrorism and Political Violence*, 16.3 (2004), pp. 501–21.

R. Bryant, 'The Fractures of a Struggle: Remembering and Forgetting Erenkoy', in Y. Papadakis and R. Bryant (eds), *Cyprus and the Politics of Memory: History, Community and Conflict* (London: I. B. Tauris, 2012), pp. 168–94.

Colm Bryce, 'Back to Armed Struggle? The Dissidents Analysed', *Irish Marxist Review*, 2.5 (2013), pp. 25–45.

A. Brysk, 'Human Rights and National Insecurity', in A. Brysk and G. Shafir (eds), *National Insecurity and Human Rights: Democracies Debate Counterterrorism* (Los Angeles: University of California Press, 2007), pp. 1–13.

Susanne Buckley-Zistel, 'Connecting Transitional Justice and Development', International Conference on 'The Contribution of Civil Society and Victim Participation in Transitional Justice Processes', Marburg, 2 December 2009: https://web.archive.org/web/20160528125934/www.victim-participation.org/files/Buckley-Zistel.pdf (originally accessed 31 July 2014).

—— 'Between Pragmatism, Coercion and Fear: Chosen Amnesia after the Rwandan Genocide', in A. Assmann and L. Shortt (eds), *Memory and Political Change* (Basingstoke: Palgrave Macmillan, 2012), pp. 72–88.

—— *Conflict Transformation and Social Change in Uganda: Remembering after Violence* (Basingstoke: Palgrave Macmillan, 2013).

Frank Burton, *The Politics of Legitimacy: Struggles in a Belfast Community* (London: Kegan Paul, 1978).

Johnny Byrne, 'Arresting this Slide in Catholic Officers Crucial if Faith in Police is Not to Suffer', *Belfast Telegraph*, 23 October 2015: www.belfasttelegraph.co.uk/opinion/news-analysis/arresting-this-slide-in-catholic-officers-crucial-if-faith-in-police-is-not-to-suffer-34132654.html (accessed 17 November 2015).

Johnny Byrne and John Topping, *Community Safety: A Decade of Development, Delivery, Challenge and Change in Northern Ireland* (Belfast: Belfast Conflict Research Consortium, 2012).

Johnny Byrne and Linda Monaghan, *Policing Loyalist and Republican Communities: Understanding Key Issues for Local Communities and the PSNI* (Belfast: Institute for Conflict Research, 2008).

Johnny Byrne, John Topping and Richard Martin, 'The Influence that Politicians, Community Leaders and the Media Have on Confidence in the Police in Northern Ireland' (Belfast: Northern Ireland Policing Board, 2014).

'Call to Ulster Protestants', *Republican News*, 13 July 1974.

'Cameron's Extremism Orders "Could Criminalise Traditional Christian Teaching"', *Daily Telegraph*, 15 June 2015: www.telegraph.co.uk/news/religion/11671547/Camerons-extremism-orders-could-criminalise-traditional-Christian-teaching.html (accessed 28 August 2015).

'Camloch Hunger Striker Remembered on 30th Anniversary of his Death', *Examiner*, 17 May 2011.

'Campaign Stepped up in Scotland', *Sovereign Nation*, February/March 2014.

Colm Campbell and Fionnuala Ní Aoláin, 'The Paradox of Transition in Liberal Democracies', *Human Rights Quarterly*, 27.1 (2005), pp. 172–213.

Colm Campbell and Ita Connolly, 'A Model for the "War against Terrorism"? Military Intervention in Northern Ireland and the 1970 Falls Curfew', *Journal of Law and Society*, 30.3 (2003), pp. 341–75.

Duncan Campbell, 'The Army's Secret Opinion', *New Statesman*, 13 July 1979.

John Campbell, 'PSNI Lined up for Historic Croker Date with Garda', *Belfast Telegraph*, 17 November 2011.

'Caroline Moreland: IRA "and State" Blamed over Murder', BBC News, 10 June 2015: www.bbc.co.uk/news/uk-northern-ireland-33069102 (accessed 30 June 2015).

'Case Facts, Synopsis and Court Transcripts', Justice for the Craigavon Two (2013): https://jftc2.com/facts-of-their-case/ (accessed 17 May 2017).

'Catholic PSNI Applicant Numbers "Down"', UTV, 30 September 2015: https://web.archive.org/web/20151002003228/www.u.tv/News/2015/09/30/Catholic-PSNI-applicant-numbers-down-45963 (originally accessed 17 November 2015).

T. Catney, 'Don't Sell the Future Short', in C. Ó Brolcháin (ed.), *The Politics of Policing* (Belfast: James Connolly Debating Society, 2007), pp. 30–33.

Gemma C. Celador, 'Police Reform: Peace Building Through "Democratic Policing"?', *International Peacekeeping*, 12.3 (2005), pp. 364–76.

'Charlie Kerrins Commemorated in Tralee', *Saoirse*, 273 (January 2010).

Kathy Charmaz, 'Premises, Principles and Practices in Qualitative Research: Revisiting the Foundations', *Qualitative Health Research*, 14.7 (2004), pp. 976–93.

'CIRA Says No to Adams Invitation', BBC News, 26 January 2007: http://news.bbc.co.uk/1/hi/northern_ireland/6301051.stm (accessed 23 April 2012).

'Civil War Britain's Aim', *United Irishman*, October 1969.

S. Cobb, 'A Narrative Perspective on Mediation: Towards the Materialization of the "Storyteller" Metaphor', in J. P. Folgner and S. T. Jones (eds), *New Directions in Mediation: Communication Research and Perspectives* (London: SAGE, 1994), pp. 49–63.

Feargal Cochrane, 'Civil Society beyond the State: The Impact of Diaspora Communities on Peace Building', *General Media Journal: Mediterranean Edition*, 2.2 (2007a), pp. 19–29.

—— 'Irish-America, the End of the IRA's Armed Struggle and the Utility of "Soft Power"', *Journal of Peace Research*, 44.2 (2007b), pp. 215–31.

Mark Cochrane, 'Security Force Collusion in Northern Ireland 1969–99: Substance or Symbolism', *Studies in Conflict & Terrorism*, 36.1 (2013), pp. 77–97.

Coiste na nIarchimi, 'Submission to the Panel of Parties of the NI Executive, also known as "The Haass Talks", on Dealing with the Past, on behalf of the Executive Committee and Members of Coiste na nIarchimi' (Belfast: Coiste na nIarchimi, 2013).

'Collaborators', *Sceal*, 28 (15 January 1987).

R. V. Comerford, 'Republicans and Democracy in Modern Irish Politics', in F. McGarry (ed.), *Republicanism in Modern Ireland* (Dublin: University College Dublin Press, 2003).

'Commemoration for Volunteer Kevin "Kiddo" Murray', *Sovereign Nation* (January/February 2007).

'Commemoration Honours "Forgotten" Volunteer', *Examiner*, 26 June 2012.

'Comment', *Sceal*, 8 (7 August 1986).

Committee on the Administration of Justice, 'Complaints Against the Police', Working Party Report No. 3 (Belfast: Committee on the Administration of Justice, 1982).

—— *No Emergency, No Emergency Law* (Belfast: Committee on the Administration of Justice, 1995).

—— 'Questions and Issues on the Devolution of Justice and Policing Functions' (Belfast: Committee on the Administration of Justice, 2003).

—— 'Still Part of Life Here? A Report on the Use and Misuse of Stop and Search/Question Powers in Northern Ireland' (Belfast: Committee on the Administration of Justice, 2012a).

—— 'The Policing You Don't See: Covert Policing and the Accountability Gap Five Years on FROM the Transfer of "National Security" Primacy to MI5' (Belfast: Committee on the Administration of Justice, 2012b).

—— 'CAJ's Submission to the Northern Ireland Policing Board Working Group on the PSNI, Historical Enquiries Team (HET)', Submission No. S420 (Belfast: Committee on the Administration of Justice, 2013a).

—— 'Submission to the Committee of Ministers from the Committee on the Administration of Justice (CAJ) in relation to the Supervision of Cases Concerning the Action of the Security Forces in Northern Ireland', Submission No. S421 (Belfast: Committee on the Administration of Justice, 2013b).

—— 'The Apparatus of Impunity? Human Rights Violations and the Northern Ireland Conflict: A Narrative of Official Limitations on Post-Agreement Investigative Mechanisms' (Belfast: Committee on the Administration of Justice, 2015).

Edmund Compton, 'Report of the Committee of Enquiry into Allegations Against the Security Forces of Physical Brutality in Northern Ireland Arising Out of Events on the 9th August 1971', Cmnd 4823 (London: HMSO, 1971).

Alon Confino, 'Collective Memory and Cultural History: Problems of Method', *American Historical Review*, 102.5 (1999), pp. 1386–403.

Paul Connerton, *How Societies Remember* (Cambridge: Cambridge University Press, 1989).

—— *How Modernity Forgets* (Cambridge: Cambridge University Press, 2009).

Brian Conway, 'Active Remembering, Selective Forgetting and Collective Identity: The Case of Bloody Sunday', *Identity: An International Journal of Theory and Research*, 3.4 (2003), pp. 305–23.

Claudio Cordone, 'Police Reform and Human Rights Investigations: The Experience of the UN Mission in Bosnia and Herzegovina', *International Peacekeeping*, 6.4 (1999), pp. 191–209.

Colin Coulter, 'Under Which Constituitional Arrangement Would You Still Prefer to be Unemployed? Neoliberalism, the Peace Process and the Politics of Class in Northern Ireland', *Studies in Conflict & Terrorism*, 37.9 (2014), pp. 763–76.

Susan A. Crane, 'Writing the Individual Back into Collective Memory', *American Historical Review*, 102.5 (1997), pp. 1372–85.

'Crime and Punishment', *Strabane Republican*, 1972.

David A. Crocker, 'Reckoning with Past Wrongs: A Normative Framework', *Ethics & International affairs*, 13 (1999), pp. 43–64.

Gerald Cromer, 'Tales From the Underground', *Journal of Aggression, Maltreatment and Trauma*, 9.1–2 (2004), pp. 45–55.

Chris Cunneen, *Conflict, Politics and Crime: Aboriginal Communities and the Police* (Sydney: Allen & Unwin, 2001).

Mark Davenport, 'Unmistakeable Taste of Freshly-Picked Cherries', BBC News, 7 January 2014: www.bbc.co.uk/news/uk-northern-ireland-25643314 (accessed 9 January 2014).

Roman David and Susanne Y. Choi, 'Getting Even or Getting Equal? Retributive Desires and Transitional Justice', *Political Psychology*, 30.2 (2009), pp. 161–92.

Annette Davies and Robyn Thomas, 'Dixon of Dock Green Got Shot! Policing, Identity Work and Organizational Change', *Public Administration*, 86.3 (2008), pp. 627–42.

Coreen Davis, *State Terrorism and Post-Transitional Justice in Argentina: An Analysis of Mega Cause I Trial* (Basingstoke: Palgrave Macmillan, 2013).

J. E. Davis, 'Narrative and Social Movements: The Power of Stories', in J. E. Davis (ed.), *Stories of Change: Narrative and Social Movements* (New York: University of New York Press, 2002).

Ciarán de Baroid, *Ballymurphy and the Irish War*, 2nd edn (London: Pluto Press, 2000).

A. de Brito, P. Aguilar and C. Gonzalez-Enriquez, 'Introduction' in A. de Brito, P. Aguilar and C. Gonzalez-Enriquez (eds), *The Politics of Memory: Transitional Justice in Democratizing Societies* (Oxford: Oxford University Press, 2001), pp. 1–39.

G. Demirici, 'The Question of Turkey: Contested, Forgotten and Remembered Memories', in A. Hol, D. Siegel and C. Brants (eds), *Transitional Justice: Images and Memories* (Farnham: Ashgate, 2013), pp. 15–32.

'Derry's Story', *United Irishman*, November 1969.

Michaela DeSoucey, Jo-Ellen Pozner, Corey Fields, Kerry Dobransky and Gary A. Fine, 'Memory and Sacrifice: An Embodied Theory of Martyrdom', *Cultural Sociology*, 2.1 (2008), pp. 99–121.

P. Devine-Wright, 'A Theoretical Overview of Memory and Conflict', in E. Cairns and M. D. Roe (eds), *The Role of Memory in Ethnic Conflict* (Basingstoke: Palgrave Macmillan, 2003), pp. 9–33.

Bernadette Devlin-McAliskey, 'Left Behind by Good Friday', *Jacobin*, 21 (2016): https://www.jacobinmag.com/2016/04/bernadette-devlin-interview-derry-civil-rights-troubles-good-friday/ (accessed 2 May 2016).

Anna Di Lellio and Stephanie Schwander-Sievers, 'The Legendary Commander: The Construction of an Albanian Master Narrative in Post-war Kosovo', *Nations and Nationalism*, 12.3 (2006), pp. 513–29.

B. Dickson and R. Osborne, 'Equality and Human Rights since the Agreement', in P. Carmichael and Others (eds), *Devolution and Constitutional Change in Northern Ireland* (Manchester: Manchester University Press, 2007), pp. 152–66.

'Disband the RUC/PSNI', *Saoirse*, 238 (February 2007).

'Dissidents Roar "No, No, No" to SF Policing Plans', *Derry Journal*, 19 January 2007.

Paul Dixon, *Northern Ireland: The Politics of War and Peace*, 2nd edn (Basingstoke: Palgrave Macmillan, 2008).

—— 'An Honourable Deception and Quest: The Labour Government, the Good Friday Agreement and the Northern Ireland Peace Process', *British Politics*, 8.2 (2013), pp. 108–37.

D. Doherty, 'A View from South Africa: ANC Fighter Turned Police Chief Robert McBride Visits Derry', *An Phoblacht*, 24 June 2004.

A. Dolan, 'An Army of Our Fenian Dead: Republicanism, Monuments and Commemoration', in F. McGarry (ed.), *Republicanism in Modern Ireland* (Dublin: University College Dublin Press, 2003).

Ron Dudai, 'Informers and the Transition in Northern Ireland', *British Journal of Criminology*, 52.1 (2012), pp. 32–54.

D. Dyzenhaus, 'The Compulsion of Legality', in V. Ramraj (ed.), *Emergencies and the Limits of Legality* (Cambridge: Cambridge University Press, 2008).

'Easter Statement from Republican POW's Maghaberry Jail', *Saoirse*, 241 (May 2012).

'Easter Statement from the Leadership of the Republican Movement', *Saoirse Nua*, Spring 2013.

'Editorial', *An tÓglách*, 3 (December 1967).

Jenny Edkins, *Trauma and the Memory of Politics* (Cambridge: Cambridge University Press, 2003).

Aaron Edwards and Cillian McGrattan, 'Terroristic Narratives: On the (Re) Invention of Peace in Northern Ireland', *Terrorism and Political Violence*, 23.3 (2011), pp. 357–76.

Éirígí (2008) 'Different Name Same Aim': https://web.archive.org/web/20131112052000/www.eirigi.org/pdfs/campaigns/PSNI_Leaflet.pdf (originally accessed 7 March 2014).

'Éirígí Press Officer Stephen Murney Cleared of Terrorism Charges', BBC News, 21 February 2014: www.bbc.co.uk/news/uk-northern-ireland-26328297 (accessed 7 March 2014).

Graham Ellison, 'A Blueprint for Democratic Policing Anywhere in the World? Police Reform, Political Transition and Conflict Resolution in Northern Ireland', *Police Quarterly*, 10.3 (2007), pp. 243–69.

Graham Ellison and Aoghan Mulcahy, 'Policing and Social Conflict in Northern Ireland', *Policing and Society*, 11.3–4 (2001), pp. 243–58.

Graham Ellison and Greg Martin, 'Policing, Collective Action and Social Movement Theory: The Case of the Northern Ireland Civil Rights Campaign', *British Journal of Sociology*, 51.4 (2000), pp. 681–99.

Graham Ellison and Jim Smyth, *The Crowned Harp: Policing Northern Ireland* (London: Pluto Press, 2000).

Graham Ellison and Mary O'Rawe, 'Security Governance in Transition: The Compartmentalizing, Crowding Out and Corralling of Policing and Security in Northern Ireland', *Theoretical Criminology*, 14.1 (2010), pp. 31–57.

Graham Ellison, Nathan W. Pino and Peter Shirlow, 'Assessing the Determinants of Public Confidence in the Police: A Case Study of a Post-Conflict Community in Northern Ireland', *Criminology and Criminal Justice*, 13.5 (2013), pp. 552–76.

Graham Ellison, Peter Shirlow and Aoghan Mulcahy, 'Responsible Participation, Community Engagement and Policing in Transitional Societies: Lessons from a Local Crime Survey in Northern Ireland', *Howard Journal of Criminal Justice*, 51.5 (2012), pp. 488–502.

Jon Elster, *Closing the Books: Transitional Justice in Historical Perspective* (Cambridge: Cambridge University Press, 2004).

—— 'Justice, Truth, Peace', *Nomos*, 51 (2012), pp. 78–97.

Richard English, *Irish Freedom: The History of Nationalism in Ireland* (London: Macmillan, 2006).

Anna Eriksson, *Justice in Transition: Community Restorative Justice in Northern Ireland* (London: Routledge, 2013).

'EU Referendum: Theresa Villiers Rules Out Sinn Féin's Border Poll Call', BBC News, 24 June 2016: www.bbc.co.uk/news/uk-northern-ireland-36622120 (accessed 12 October 2016).

Jocelyn Evans and Jon Tonge, 'Menace Without Mandate? Is There Any Sympathy for Dissident Irish Republicanism in Northern Ireland', *Terrorism and Political Violence*, 24.1 (2012), pp. 61–78.

——— 'From Abstention to Enthusiasm: Sinn Féin, Nationalist Electors and Support for Devolved Power-Sharing in Northern Ireland', *Irish Political Studies*, 28.1 (2013), pp. 39–57.

'Extract from Presidential Address by Gerry Adams, then President of Sinn Féin, on the Issue of Abstentionism (Resolution 162), Sinn Féin Ard Fheis, Dublin (1 November 1986)': www.cain.ulst.ac.uk/issues/politics/docs/sf/ga011186.htm (accessed 7 August 2014).

Roger Faligot, *Britain's Military Strategy in Ireland: The Kitson Experiment* (London: Zed, 1983).

Frantz Fanon, *The Wretched of the Earth* (Harmondsworth: Penguin, 1967).

——— *A Dying Colonialism* (Harmondsworth: Penguin, 1970).

Michael Farrell, *Northern Ireland: The Orange State* (London: Pluto Press, 1976).

——— *Arming the Protestants: The Formation of the Ulster Special Constabulary and the Royal Ulster Constabulary 1920–27* (London: Pluto Press, 1983).

Didier Fassin and Richard Rechtman, *The Empire of Trauma: An Inquiry into the Condition of Victimhood* (Princeton, NJ: Princeton University Press, 2009).

Dennis Faul and Raymond Murray, *The RUC: The Black and Blue Book* (Dublin: Abbey, 1975).

Allen Feldman, *Formations of Violence: The Narrative of the Body and Political Terror in Northern Ireland* (Chicago: University of Chicago Press, 1991).

Nigel Fielding, 'Constraints on the Practice of Community Policing', in R. Morgan and D. Smith (eds), *Coming to Terms with Policing* (London: Routledge, 1989), pp. 49–63.

Nigel Fielding and Martin Innes, 'Reassurance Policing, Community Policing and Measuring Police Performance', *Policing & Society*, 16.2 (2006), pp. 127–45.

'Final Warning', *Sceal*, 81 (18 February 1988).

D. Fitzpatrick, 'Commemoration in the Irish Free State: A Chronicle of Embarrassment', in I. McBride (ed.), *History and Memory in Modern Ireland* (Cambridge: Cambridge University Press, 2001), pp. 184–203.

'Forkhill Barracks Mortared', *An Phoblacht*, 20 November 1986.

'Forums', *Iris*, 10 (July 1985).

'A Fresh Start: The Stormont Agreement and Implementation Plan' (London: HMSO, 2015).

Martyn Frampton, *The Long March; The Political Strategy of Sinn Féin 1981–2007* (Basingstoke: Palgrave Macmillan, 2009).

——— *Legion of the Rearguard: Dissident Irish Republicanism* (Dublin: Irish Academic Press, 2011).

——— 'Dissident Irish Republican Violence: A Resurgent Threat?', *Political Quarterly*, 83.2 (2012), pp. 227–37.

'Frank Hegarty: Martin McGuinness "Needs Questioned" Over Murder, Son Says', BBC News, 25 November 2015: www.bbc.co.uk/news/uk-northern-ireland-foyle-west-34918934 (accessed 25 November 2015).

'Fraternisers Beware', *Armalite*, 3 (9 June 1973).

'"Fresh Start" Represents the State's History of Failure', Republican Network for Unity, 19 November 2015: https://web.archive.org/web/20151123225626/www.republicanunity.org/fresh-start-represents-six-countys-history-of-failure/ (originally accessed 14 December 2015).

Laura Friel, 'Peace Process Under Attack', *An Phoblacht*, 12 March 2009.

'Frontier Life Still a Lonely One for Cops' *Belfast Telegraph*, 1 July 2014.

Victoria J. Gallagher, 'Memory and Reconciliation in the Birmingham Civil Rights Institute', *Rhetoric & Public Affairs*, 2.2 (1999), pp. 303–20.

Johan Galtung, *Theories of Peace: A Synthetic Approach to Peace Thinking* (Oslo: International Peace Research Institute, 1967).

'GARC – Yet More Demonisation', *Ardoyne Republican*, 4 August 2012: https://web.archive.org/web/20140718162409/http://ardoynerepublican.blogspot.co.uk/2012_07_29_archive.html (originally accessed 17 July 2014).

John Garry and Neil Matthews, 'Prince Charles Handshake Shows the Modernisation of Sinn Féin', *The Conversation*, 21 May 2015: https://theconversation.com/prince-charles-handshake-shows-the-modernisation-of-sinn-fein-42152 (accessed 4 September 2015).

T. Garvin, 'An Irish Republican Tradition?', in I. Honohan (ed.), *Republicanism in Ireland: Confronting Theories and Traditions* (Manchester: Manchester University Press, 2008).

'Gary Donnelly: Independent Councillor Refuses to Condemn Bomb Attack on PSNI', *Derry Journal*, 4 November 2014: www.derryjournal.com/news/gary-donnelly-independent-councillor-refuses-to-condemn-bomb-attack-on-psni-1-6396244 (accessed 20 March 2015).

G. D. Gaskell and D. B. Wright, 'Group Differences in Memory for a Political Event', in J. W. Pennebaker and others (eds), *Collective Memory of Political Events: Social Psychological Perspectives* (Mahwah, NJ: Lawrence Erlbaum Associates, 1997).

Conor Gearty, '11 September 2001, Counter-terrorism and the Human Rights Act', *Journal of Law and Society*, 32.1 (2005), pp. 18–33.

'Gerry Adams Arrest: Attempt to "Settle Old Scores"', BBC News, 3 May 2014: www.bbc.co.uk/news/uk-northern-ireland-27268739 (accessed 5 May 2014).

'Gerry Adams Arrest: Sinn Féin Claims "Dark Side" to NI Police', BBC News, 1 May 2014: www.bbc.co.uk/news/uk-northern-ireland-27244878 (accessed 5 May 2014).

'Gerry Adams Lays Down Challenge to Killers – I'll Meet You Any Time', *An Phoblacht*, 14 April 2011.

Jim Gibney, 'Address to Ard Fheis', 24 March 1996: Northern Ireland Political Collection, Linenhall Library, Belfast.

—— 'First Step to Accountable Policing is Support', *Irish News*, 25 January 2007.

'Gibney's Comments Contemptible', *Sovereign Nation* (February/March 2014).

Margaret Gilmore, 'No Way Back? Examining the Background and Response to the Rise of Dissident Terrorist Activity in Northern Ireland', *RUSI Journal*, 154.2 (2009), pp. 50–55.

Ben Gook, 'Being There is Everything', *Memory Studies*, 4.1 (2011), pp. 13–22.

David Gordon, 'Republican Sinn Féin Links Soldier Murders to "British Occupation"', *Belfast Telegraph*, 9 March 2009.

Jane Gordon, 'Post-Conflict Transformation: The Process of Institutional Legitimation of the Police in Northern Ireland', *Ethnopolitics*, 7.1 (2008), pp. 137–57.

Brian Graham and Yvonne Whelan, 'The Legacies of the Dead: Commemorating the Troubles in Northern Ireland', *Environmental and Planning D: Society and Space*, 25.3 (2007), pp. 476–95.

William Graham, 'McGuinness Admits Sinn Féin is Playing for "Big Stakes" on Policing', *Irish News*, 16 January 2007.

Susan-Mary Grant, 'Raising the Dead: War, Memory, and American National Identity', *Nations and Nationalism*, 11.4 (2005), pp. 509–29.

R. L. Green, 'Ancestral Dreams: Reliving the Pat, Recreating the Future', in D. E. Eber and A. G. Neal (eds), *Memory and Representation: Constructed Truths and Competing Realities* (Bowling Green, Ohio: Bowling Green State University Popular Press, 2001).

Larry J. Griffin and Kenneth A. Bollen, 'What Do These Memories Do? Civil Rights Remembrance and Racial Attitudes', *American Sociological Review*, 74.4 (2009), pp. 594–614.

Hesta Groenewald and Gordon Peake, *Police Reform Through Community-Based Policing: Philosophy and Guidelines for Implementation* (New York: International Peace Academy, 2004).

Adrian Guelke, 'The Northern Ireland Peace Process and the War against Terrorism: Conflicting Conceptions?', *Government and Opposition*, 42.3 (2007), pp. 272–91.

—— *Politics in Deeply Divided Societies* (Cambridge: Polity Press, 2012).

Clare Hackett and Bill Rolston, 'The Burden of Memory: Victims, Storytelling and Resistance in Northern Ireland', *Memory Studies*, 2.3 (2009), pp. 355–76.

Maurice Halbwachs and Lewis A. Coser, *On Collective Memory* (Chicago: University of Chicago Press, 1992).

Frank Haldemann, 'A Different Kind of Justice: Transitional Justice as Recognition', Global Fellows Forum, NYU School of Law, 7 February 2006: http://www.law.nyu.edu/sites/default/files/upload_documents/haldemannpaper.pdf (accessed 17 May 2017).

Brandon Hamber, *Transforming Societies after Political Violence: Truth, Reconciliation and Mental Health* (New York: Springer, 2007).

Brandon Hamber and Roger A. Wilson, 'Symbolic Closure Through Memory, Reparation and Revenge in Post-Conflict Societies', *Journal of Human Rights*, 1.1 (2002), pp. 35–53.

Brian Hanley, 'The Rhetoric of Republican Legitimacy', in F. McGarry (ed.), *Republicanism in Modern Ireland* (Dublin: University College Dublin Press, 2003).

—— *The IRA: A Documentary History 1916–2005* (Dublin: Gill & Macmillan, 2010).

Brian Hanley and Scott Miller, *The Lost Revolution: The Story of the Official IRA and the Workers' Party* (London: Penguin, 2010).

Jerry Harris, 'Bolivia and Venezuela: The Democratic Dialectic in New Revolutionary Movements', *Race & Class*, 49.1 (2007), pp. 1–24.

Badi Hasisi and Ron Weitzer, 'Police Relations with Arabs and Jews in Israel', *British Journal of Criminology*, 47.5 (2007), pp. 728–45.

David Hassan, 'The Gaelic Athletic Association, Rule 21 and Police Reform in Northern Ireland', *Journal of Sport & Social Issues*, 29.1 (2005), pp. 60–78.

Chris Haviland, 'Ex-Tamil Tiger Rebels "Free to Join the Sri Lankan Police"', BBC News, 30 January 2012: www.bbc.co.uk/news/world-asia-16795442 (accessed 7 February 2012).

M. Hayes, 'Building Cross-Community Support for Policing', in J. Doyle (ed.), *Policing the Narrow Ground: Lessons from the Transformation of Policing in Northern Ireland* (Dublin: Royal Irish Academy, 2010), pp. 59–67.

Katy Hayward and Milena Komarova, 'The Limits of Local Accommodation: Why Contentious Events Remain Prone to Conflict in Northern Ireland', *Studies in Conflict & Terrorism*, 37.9 (2014), pp. 777–91.

Kevin Hearty, 'A Shared Narrative? A Case Study of the Contested Legacy of Policing in the North of Ireland', *British Journal of Criminology*, 54.6 (2014), pp. 1047–66.

—— 'Legislating Hierarchies of Victimhood and Perpetrators: The Civil Service (Special Advisers) Act (Northern Ireland) 2013 and the Meta-Conflict', *Social & Legal Studies*, 25.3 (2016a), pp. 333–53.

—— 'From "Former Comrades" to "Near Enemy": The Narrative Template of "Armed Struggle" and Conflicting Discourses on Violent Dissident Irish Republican Activity (VDR)', *Critical Studies on Terrorism*, 9 (2016b), pp. 269–91.

—— 'How the "Suspect Community" Became "Critical Engagers": The (Re) Framing of the Irish Republican Narrative on Policing in Northern Ireland', *Irish Political Studies* (2016c), pp. 1–22.

—— 'The Malleability of Memory and Irish Republican Memory Entrepreneurship: A Case Study of the "Loughgall Martyrs"', *Ethnopolitics* 16.2 (2017), pp. 126–44.

John Hedges, '"Uncomfortable Conversations" Collection Launched in Linen Hall Library', *An Phoblacht*, 20 April 2015: www.anphoblacht.com/contents/24916 (accessed 19 April 2016).

—— 'Exclusive – Bobby Storey After his Arrest, Still Totally Committed to Peace Process', *An Phoblacht*, 13 September 2015: www.anphoblacht.com/contents/25344 (accessed 10 November 2015).

John Hedges and Peader Whelan, 'PSNI Clash with Hurlers Opposed by Young Republicans', *An Phoblacht*, 10 March 2014: www.anphoblacht.com/contents/23832 (accessed 23 July 2014).

John R. Hepburn, 'Social Control and the Legal Order: Legitimated Repression in a Capitalist State', *Contemporary Crises*, 1.1 (1977), pp. 77–90.

Her Majesty's Government, 'Principles for Policing in Northern Ireland: A Discussion Paper Prepared by Her Majesty's Government' (London: HMSO, 1998).

—— 'Prevent Duty Guidance: Guidance for Specified Authorities in England and Wales on the Duty in the Counter-Terrorism and Security Act 2015 to Have Due Regard to the Need to Prevent People from Being Drawn into Terrorism' (London: HMSO, 2015).

Her Majesty's Inspectorate of Constabulary, 'Inspection of the Police Service of Northern Ireland Historical Enquiries Team' (London: HMIC, 2013).

'HET Enquiries Team Must be Even-Handed: Victims Commissioner', BBC News, 4 April 2012: www.bbc.co.uk/news/uk-northern-ireland-17608644 (accessed 4 April 2012).

Arthur Hezlet, *The B-Specials* (London: Pan Books, 1973).

'The Higher They Build Their Barriers the Stronger We Become', *An Phoblacht*, 1 February 2007.

Paddy Hillyard, 'Political and Social Dimensions of Emergency Law in Northern Ireland', in A. Jennings (ed.), *Justice Under Fire: The Abuse of Civil Liberties in Northern Ireland* (London: Pluto Press, 1988), pp. 191–212.

—— 'In Defence of Civil Liberties', in P. Scraton (ed.), *Beyond September 11: An Anthology of Dissent* (London: Pluto Press, 2002), pp. 107–13.

Paddy Hillyard and Janice Percy-Smith, *The Coercive State* (London: Pinter, 1988).

Paddy Hillyard and Mike Tomlinson, 'Patterns of Policing and Policing Patten', *Journal of Law and Society*, 27.3 (2000), pp. 394–415.

Cara Hirsch, 'Policing Undercover Agents in the United Kingdom: Whether the Regulation of Investigatory Powers Act Complies with Regional Human Rights Obligations', *Fordham International Law Journal*, 25.5 (2001), pp. 1282–334.

Herbert Hirsch, *Genocide and the Politics of Memory: Studying Death to Preserve Life* (Chapel Hill: University of North Carolina Press, 1995).

Katherine Hite and Cath Collins, 'Memorial Fragments, Monumental Silences and Reawakenings in 21st Century Chile', *Millennium: Journal of International Studies*, 38.2 (2009), pp. 379–400.

'Historic Day as Sinn Féin Mayor Attends Armistice Day Ceremony in Belfast', *Belfast Telegraph*, 11 November 2013: www.belfasttelegraph.co.uk/news/northern-ireland/historic-day-as-sinn-fein-mayor-attends-armistice-day-ceremony-in-belfast-29743016.html (accessed 4 September 2013).

Katherine Hite, Cath Collins and Alfredo Joignant, 'The Politics of Memory in Chile', in Cath Collins, Katherine Hite and Alfredo Joignant (eds), *The Politics of Memory in Chile: From Pinochet to Bachelet* (Boulder, Colo.: FirstForumPress, 2013).

Ali K. Hlongwane, 'Commemoration, Memory and Monuments in the Contested Language of Black Liberation: The South African Experience', *Journal of Pan African Studies*, 2.4 (2008), pp. 135–70.

Eric Hobsbawm, *The Age of Revolution 1789–1848* (London: Weidenfeld & Nicolson, 1962).

K. Hodgkin and S. Radstone, 'Contested Pasts', in K. Hodgkin and S. Radstone (eds), *Contested Pasts: The Politics of Memory* (London: Routledge, 2003), pp. 1–22.

Jackie Hodgson and Victor Tadros, 'How to Make a Terrorist Out of Nothing', *Modern Law Review*, 72.6 (2009), pp. 984–98.

I. Honohan, 'Introduction: Putting Irish Republicanism in a Wider Context', in I. Honohan (ed.), *Republicanism in Ireland: Confronting Theories and Traditions* (Manchester: Manchester University Press, 2008), pp. 1–20.

'Hooded Men Case: Villiers Withholding Material, Says Lawyer', *Newsletter*, 6 April 2016: www.newsletter.co.uk/news/northern-ireland-news/hooded-men-case-villiers-withholding-material-says-lawyer-1-7315203 (accessed 19 April 2016).

'Hooded Men: Irish Government Bid to Reopen "Torture" Case', BBC News, 2 December 2014: www.bbc.co.uk/news/uk-northern-ireland-30296397 (accessed 22 May 2015).

Stephen Hopkins, 'The Chronicles of Long Kesh: Provisional Irish Republican Memoirs and the Contested Memory of the Hunger Strikes', *Memory Studies*, 7.4 (2014), pp. 425–39.

—— 'Sinn Féin, the Past and Political Strategy: The Provisional Irish Republican Movement and the Politics of "Reconciliation"', *Irish Political Studies*, 30.1 (2015), pp. 79–97.

John Horgan, *Divided We Stand: The Strategy and Psychology of Ireland's Dissident Terrorists* (Oxford: Oxford University Press, 2013).

John Horgan and John Morrison, 'Here to Stay? The Rising Threat of Violent Dissident Republicanism in Northern Ireland', *Terrorism and Political Violence*, 23.4 (2011), pp. 642–69.

Human Rights Watch, *Children in Northern Ireland Abused by Security Forces and Paramilitaries* (New York: Human Rights Watch, 1992).

S. A. Hunt and R. D. Benford, 'Collective Identity, Solidarity and Commitment', in D. A. Snow, Sarah Anne Soule and Hanspeter Kriesi (eds), *The Blackwell Companion to Social Movements* (Oxford: Blackwell, 2004), pp. 433–57.

'Ian Paisley Criticised Over Dublin-Monaghan Bombs Comment', BBC News, 10 January 2014: www.bbc.co.uk/news/uk-northern-ireland-25673999 (accessed 28 September 2015).

Nicole L. Immler, 'Too Little Too Late? Compensation and Family Memory: Negotiating Austrias Holocaust Past', *Memory Studies*, 5.3 (2012), pp. 270–81.

'Imperialism – Ireland and Britain', Éirígí, 2007: https://web.archive.org/web/20140826184807/www.eirigi.org/campaigns/imperialism_paper.html (originally accessed 12 December 2013).

Independent Commission on Policing for Northern Ireland, 'A New Beginning: Policing in Northern Ireland: The Report of the Independent Commission on Policing for Northern Ireland' (London: HMSO, 1999).

International Lawyers Inquiry, *Shoot-to-kill? International Lawyers Inquiry into the Lethal Use of Firearms by the Security Forces in Northern Ireland* (Cork: Mercier Press, 1985).

International Monitoring Commission, 'Twenty-Fifth Report of the International Monitoring Commission' (London: HMSO, 2010).

'IRA Man's Family Accuse SF Leaders of "Dishonesty"', *Derry Journal*, 16 January 2007.

'IRA Not Like ISIS as Cardinal Claimed Says British Army Hero', 7 March 2015: www.irishcentral.com/news/IRA-not-like-ISIS-as-cardinal-claimed-says-British-Army-hero.html (accessed 20 March 2015).

Irish Republican Socialist Party, *Perspectives on the Future of Republican Socialism in Ireland* (Belfast: Irish Republican Socialist Party, 2010).

—— *Republican Socialist Programme for Ireland* (Belfast: Irish Republican Socialist Party, 2010).

Neil Jarman, 'Peace Building and Policing: The Role of Community Based Initiatives', *Shared Space*, 3 (2006), pp. 31–44.

—— 'Policing the Peace: Community-Based Peacebuilding and Political Transition', in J. Popiolkowski and N. Cull (eds), *Public Diplomacy, Cultural Interventions and the Peace Process in Northern Ireland: Track Two to Peace* (Los Angeles, Calif.: USC Center on Public Diplomacy, 2009).

James M. Jasper and Jane D. Poulsen, 'Recruiting Strangers and Friends: Moral Shocks and Social Networks in Animal Rights and Anti-Nuclear Protests', *Social Problems*, 42.4 (1995), pp. 493–512.

Elizabeth Jelin, *State Repression and the Struggles for Memory* (London: Latin America Bureau, 2003).

—— 'Public Memorialization in Perspective: Truth, Justice and Memory of Past Repression in the Southern Cone of South America', *International Journal of Transitional Justice*, 1.1 (2007), pp. 138–56.

S. Jensen, 'The Vision of the State: Audiences, Enchantments and Policing in South Africa', in A. M. Jefferson and S. Jensen (eds), *State Violence and Human Rights: State Officials in the South* (London: Routledge, 2009), pp. 60–78.

'John Proctor Murder: Life Sentence for Seamus Kearney', BBC News, 28 November 2013: www.bbc.co.uk/news/uk-northern-ireland-25136281 (accessed 8 January 2014).

'John Pat Cunningham Death: Former Soldier Charged with Attempted Murder', BBC News, 25 April 2015: www.bbc.co.uk/news/uk-northern-ireland-32459312 (accessed 25 April 2015).

'Join the RUC and See the Next World', *Freedom Fighter*, 5 (1976).

G. Jones, 'Tebbit Launches Bitter Attack on Patten's Proposals for RUC', *Daily Telegraph*, 6 October 1999.

'JWI Case Assessment Martin Corey', Justice Watch Ireland, 2013: www.justice-watchireland.com/?page_id=14 (accessed 7 March 2014).

Susana Kaiser, 'Escraches: Demonstrations, Communication and Political Memory in Post-dictatorial Argentina', *Media Culture Society*, 24.4 (2002), pp. 499–516.

Laura Kalmanowiecki, 'Origins and Applications of Political Policing in Argentina', *Latin American Perspectives*, 27.2 (2000), pp. 36–56.

Wolf Kansteiner, 'Finding Meaning in Memory: Methodological Critique of Collective Memory Studies', *History and Theory*, 41.2 (2002), pp. 179–97.

S. Karstedt, 'The Lives and Times of Sentenced Nazi War Criminals: Re-Negotiating Guilt and Innocence in Post-Nuremburg Germany 1950–1975', in A. Hol, D. Siegel and C. Brants (eds), *Transitional Justice: Images and Memories* (Farnham: Ashgate, 2013), pp. 33–50.

Siobhan Kattago, 'War Memorials and the Politics of Memory: The Soviet War Memorial in Talilinn', *Constellations*, 16.1 (2009), pp. 150–66.

Declan Kearney, 'Standing Up to the Dark Side of Policing', *An Phoblacht*, January 2012.

—— 'The Two Significant Sinn Féin and Royal Meetings Will Promote Reconciliation and Healing', *An Phoblacht*, 22 May 2015: www.anphoblacht.com/contents/25006 (accessed 4 September 2015).

Vincent Kearney, 'Dissident Republicans: PSNI Say They Have Thwarted Murder Bids', BBC News, 11 March 2016: www.bbc.co.uk/news/uk-northern-ireland-35787273 (accessed 18 April 2016).

Brian Kelly, 'Neoliberal Belfast: Disaster Ahead?', *Irish Marxist Review*, 1.2 (2012), pp. 44–59.

Gerry Kelly, 'Address to All-Ireland Conference on Policing and Justice', 14 January 2006: Northern Ireland Political Collection, Linenhall Library, Belfast.

—— 'In the New Beginning to Policing, There is No Place for an Old Boy's Network', *An Phoblacht*, March 2012.

Lia Kent, 'Local Memory Practices in East Timor: Disrupting Transitional Justice Narratives', *International Journal of Transitional Justice*, 5.3 (2011), pp. 434–55.

'Kevin McGuigan Murder: Provisional IRA Still Exists, says PSNI Chief', BBC News, 22 August 2015: www.bbc.co.uk/news/uk-northern-ireland-34026678 (accessed 24 August 2015).

'Kevin McGuigan: Reaction to PSNI's Assessment on Murder', BBC News, 20 August 2015: www.bbc.co.uk/news/uk-northern-ireland-34011551 (accessed 23 August 2015).

Laleh Khalili, *Heroes and Martyrs of Palestine: The Politics of National Commemoration* (Cambridge: Cambridge University Press, 2007).

Anatoly M. Khazanov and Stanley G. Payne, 'How to Deal with the Past', *Totalitarian Movements and Political Religions*, 9.2–3 (2008), pp. 411–31.

Colin Knox, '"See No Evil, Hear No Evil": Insidious Paramilitary Violence in Northern Ireland', *British Journal of Criminology*, 42.1 (2002), pp. 164–85.

T. Landman, 'The Continuity of Terror and Counterterror', in A. Brysk and G. Shafir (eds), *National Insecurity and Human Rights: Democracies Debate Counterterrorism* (Los Angeles: University of California Press, 2007), pp. 75–91.

Cheryl Lawther, '"Securing" the Past: Policing and the Contest over Truth in Northern Ireland', *British Journal of Criminology*, 50.3 (2010), pp. 455–73.

—— 'Unionism, Truth Recovery and the Fearful Past', *Irish Political Studies*, 26.3 (2011), pp. 361–82.

—— 'Denial, Silence and the Politics of the Past: Unpicking the Opposition to Truth Recovery in Northern Ireland', *International Journal of Transitional Justice*, 7.1 (2013), pp. 157–77.

—— *Truth, Denial and Transition: Northern Ireland and the Contested Past* (London: Routledge, 2014).

Michael Lea and Sam Greenhill, 'Fury as Adams says British Special Forces Provided Pizza Delivery Murders of Unarmed Soldiers', *Daily Mail*, 9 March 2009.

'Legacy of 1916 Rising Under Attack', *Saoirse*, August 2014.

R. Lemarchand, 'The Politics of Memory in Post-Genocide Rwanda', in P. Clark and Z. D. Kaufman (eds), *After Genocide: Transitional Justice, Post-Conflict Reconstruction and Reconciliation in Rwanda and Beyond* (London: Hurst, 2008), pp. 65–75.

'Let us Make an Honourable Agreement', *Republican News*, 13 July 1974.

Brynjar Lia, 'The Establishment of a Palestinian Police Force in the West Bank and Gaza Strip', *International Peacekeeping*, 6.4 (1999), pp. 157–70.

James H. Liu and Dennis J. Hilton, 'How the Past Weighs on the Present: Representations of History and their Role in Identity Politics', *British Journal of Social Psychology*, 44.4 (2005), pp. 537–56.

'Local Man Reveals RUC Blackmail Attempt', *Sceal*, 58 (3 September 1987).

Patricia Lundy, 'Commissioning the Past in Northern Ireland', *Review of International Affairs*, 60.1138–39 (2010), pp. 101–33.

—— 'Paradoxes and Challenges of Transitional Justice at the "Local" Level: Historical Enquiries in Northern Ireland', *Contemporary Social Science: Journal of the Academy of Social Sciences*, 6.1 (2011), pp. 89–105.

—— 'The Historical Enquiries Team Research Brief: Assessment of Historical Enquiries Team (HET) Review Processes, and Procedures in Royal Military Police Investigation Cases', in Committee on the Administration of Justice, *Mapping the Rollback? Human Rights Provisions of the Belfast/Good Friday Agreement 15 Years On* (Belfast: Committee on the Administration of Justice, 2013).

Patricia Lundy and Bill Rolston, 'Redress for Past Harms? Official Apologies in Northern Ireland', *International Journal of Human Rights*, 20.1 (2016), pp. 104–22.

Patricia Lundy and Mark McGovern, 'The Politics of Memory in Post-Conflict Northern Ireland', *Peace Review*, 13.1 (2001), pp. 27–33.

—— 'The Ethics of Silence: Action Research, Community "Truth Telling" and Post-Conflict Transition in the North of Ireland', *Action Research*, 4.1 (2006), pp. 49–64.

—— 'Attitudes Towards a Truth Commission for Northern Ireland in Relation to Party Political Affiliation', *Irish Political Studies*, 22.3 (2007), pp. 321–38.

—— 'A Trojan Horse? Unionism, Trust and Truth Telling in Northern Ireland', *International Journal of Transitional Justice*, 2.1 (2008a), pp. 42–62.

—— 'Telling Stories, Facing Truths: Memory, Justice and Post-Conflict Transition', in C. Coulter and M. Murray (eds), *Northern Ireland After the Troubles: A Society in Transition* (Manchester: Manchester University Press, 2008b), pp. 29–48.

—— 'Truth, Justice and Dealing with the Legacy of the Past in Northern Ireland 1998–2008', *Ethnopolitics*, 7.1 (2008c), pp. 177–93.

Noel McAdam, 'State Helped Perpetuate the Troubles, says McGuinness', *Belfast Telegraph*, 29 June 2015: www.belfasttelegraph.co.uk/news/northern-ireland/state-helped-perpetuate-the-troubles-says-mcguinness-31336336.html (accessed 23 November 2015).

Ian McAllister, '"The Armalite and the Ballot Box": Sinn Féin's Electoral Strategy in Northern Ireland', *Electoral Studies*, 23.1 (2004), pp. 123–42.

Chris McAuley, *Nationalist Women and the RUC* (Belfast: Sinn Féin Women's Department, 1988).

James W. McAuley, 'Unionisms Last Stand? Contemporary Unionist Politics and Identity in Northern Ireland', *Global Review of Ethnopolitics*, 3.7 (2003), pp. 60–74.

Padraig McAuliffe, 'Transitional Justice's Expanding Empire: Reasserting the Value of the Paradigmatic Transition', *Journal of Conflictology*, 2.2 (2011), pp. 32–44.

Sean Mac Brádaigh, 'Remembering the Past, Looking to the Future', *Iris* (summer 2007).

I. McBride, 'Introduction: Memory and National Identity in Modern Ireland', in I. McBride (ed.), *History and Memory in Modern Ireland* (Cambridge: Cambridge University Press, 2001), pp. 1–42.

Martin McCleery, *Operation Demetrius and its Aftermath: A New History of the Use of Internment without Trial in Northern Ireland 1971–75* (Manchester: Manchester University Press, 2015).

C. McCrudden, 'Equality and the Good Friday Agreement', in J. Ruane and J. Todd (eds), *After the Good Friday Agreement: Analysing Political Change in Northern Ireland* (Dublin: University College Dublin Press, 1999), pp. 96–121.

Oliver McDonagh, *States of Mind: A Study of Anglo-Irish Conflict 1780–1980* (London: Unwin Hyman, 1983).

Mary L. McDonald, 'Address to Extraordinary Ard Fheis', 28 January 2007: Northern Ireland Political Collection, Linenhall Library, Belfast.

—— 'Mary Lou McDonald on Stormont's "Fresh Start" Agreement', *An Phoblacht*, 18 November 2015: www.anphoblacht.com/contents/25493 (accessed 23 November 2015).

Sara McDowell, 'Armalite, Ballot Box and Memorialisation: Sinn Féin and the State in Post-Conflict Northern Ireland', *Round Table*, 96.393 (2007), pp. 725–38.

Kieran McEvoy, 'Law, Struggle and Political Transformation in Northern Ireland', *Journal of Law and Society*, 27.4 (2000), pp. 542–71.

—— 'Letting Go of Legalism: Developing a "Thicker" Version of Transitional Justice', in K. Mcevoy and L. Mcgregor (eds), *Transitional Justice from Below: Grassroots Activism and the Struggle for Change* (London: Bloomsbury, 2008), pp. 15–45.

Kieran McEvoy and A. Eriksson, 'Restorative Justice in Transition: Ownership, Leadership and "Bottom-Up" Human Rights', in D. Sullivan and L. Tift (eds), *The Handbook of Restorative Justice: A Global Perspective* (London: Routledge, 2007).

—— 'Who Owns Justice? Community, State and the Northern Ireland Transition', in J. Shapland (ed.), *Justice, Community and Civil Society* (Cullompton: Willian, 2008), pp. 157–89.

Kieran McEvoy and Harry Mika, 'Punishment, Policing and Praxis; Restorative Justice and Non-Violent Alternatives to Paramilitary Punishments in Northern Ireland', *Policing and Society: An International Journal of Research and Policy*, 11.3–4 (2001), pp. 359–82.

Kieran McEvoy and Heather Conway, 'The Dead, the Law and the Politics of the Past', *Journal of Law and Society*, 31.4 (2004), pp. 539–62.

Kieran McEvoy and Kirsten McConnachie, 'Victimology in Transitional Justice: Victimhood, Innocence and Hierarchy', *European Journal of Criminology*, 9.5 (2012). pp. 527–38.

Kieran McEvoy and Peter Shirlow, 'Re-Imagining DDR: Ex-Combatants, Leadership and Moral Agency in Conflict Transformation', *Theoretical Criminology*, 13.1 (2009), pp. 31–59.

—— 'The Northern Ireland Peace Process and "Terroristic" Narratives: A Reply to Edwards and McGrattan', *Terrorism and Political Violence*, 25.2 (2013), pp. 161–66.

F. McGarry, 'Introduction', in F. McGarry (ed.), *Republicanism in Modern Ireland* (Dublin: University College Dublin Press, 2003).

John McGarry, 'Police Reform in Northern Ireland', *Irish Political Studies*, 15.1 (2000), pp. 173–82.

John McGarry and Brendan O'Leary, *Explaining Northern Ireland* (Oxford: Blackwell, 1995).

—— 'Proving our Points on Northern Ireland (and Giving Reading Lessons to Dr Dixon)', *Irish Political Studies*, 11.1 (1996), pp. 142–54.

—— *Policing Northern Ireland: Proposals for a New Start* (Belfast: Blackstaff Press, 1999).

—— 'Consociational Theory, Northern Ireland's Conflict and its Agreement: Part 1 What Consociationalists can Learn from Northern Ireland', *Government and Opposition*, 41.1 (2006), pp. 43–63.

R. MacGinty, 'Irish Republicanism and the Peace Process: From Revolution to Reform', in M. Cox, A. Guelke and F. Stephen (eds), *A Farewell to Arms? Beyond the Good Friday Agreement*, 2nd edn (Manchester: Manchester University Press, 2006), pp. 124–38.

Mark McGovern, 'Irish Republicanism and the Potential Pitfalls of Pluralism', *Capital & Class*, 71 (2000), pp. 133–61.

—— '"The Old Days are Over": Irish Republicanism, the Peace Process and the Discourse of Equality', *Terrorism and Political Violence*, 16.3 (2004), pp. 622–45.

Sean McGowan, 'Republicanism and Policing – A Historical Context', Irish Republican Socialist Party, 13 February 2007: www.irsp.ie/Background/theory/republicanismandpolicing.html (accessed 24 April 2012).

Cillian McGrattan, *Northern Ireland 1968–2008: The Politics of Entrenchment* (Basingstoke: Palgrave Macmillan, 2010).

—— *Memory, Politics and Identity: Haunted by History* (Basingstoke: Palgrave Macmillan, 2013).

Martin McGuinness, 'Republican Strategy Now the Route Map to Irish Unity', *Iris* (summer 2007).

Gillian McIntosh, *The Force of Culture: Unionist Identities in Twentieth Century Ireland* (Cork: Cork University Press, 1999).

Anthony McIntyre, 'Modern Irish Republicanism: The Product of British State Strategies', *Irish Political Studies*, 10.1 (1995), pp. 97–122.

——— 'Chuckle Ar La, 8 May 2007', *Irish Review*, 38 (2008a), pp. 65–68.

——— *Good Friday; The Death of Irish Republicanism* (New York: Ausubo Press, 2008b).

——— 'Of Myths and Men: Dissent Within Republicanism and Loyalism', in A. Edwards and S. Bloomer (eds), *Transforming the Peace Process in Northern Ireland: From Terrorism to Democratic Politics* (Dublin: Irish Academic Press, 2008c), pp. 114–30.

——— 'The Motivation of the Irish Rebel and Resistance to the Label "Terrorist"', in M. Breen-Smyth (ed.), *The Ashgate Research Companion to Political Violence* (Farnham: Ashgate, 2012).

Feargal Mac Ionnrachtaigh, *Language, Resistance and Revival: Republican Prisoners and the Irish Language in the North of Ireland* (London: Pluto Press, 2013).

Susan McKay, 'People Did Not Die or Take Up Arms for Equality: They Did So for Freedom', *Tribune*, 24 October 2010.

Tommy McKearney, *The Provisional IRA: From Insurrection to Parliament* (London: Pluto Press, 2011).

Laurence McKeown, 'Out from Behind the Doors', *An Phoblacht*, 25 January 2007.

Seamus McKinney, 'Elaborate Hoax at Derry Hotel Was Real Bomb – PSNI', *Irish News*, 12 October 2015: www.irishnews.com/news/2015/10/12/news/elaborate-hoax-at-derry-hotel-was-real-bomb---psni-290560/ (accessed 17 November 2015).

David McKittrick, 'The Investigation: Two Arrested as Sinn Féin Brands Gunmen "Traitors"', *Independent*, 11 March 2009: www.independent.co.uk/news/uk/crime/the-investigation-two-arrested-as-sinn-fein-brands-gunmen-traitors-1642090.html (accessed 17 May 2017).

David McKittrick and Peter Apps, 'Gerry Adams Slams "Malicious and Sinister" Arrest Over 1972 Murder of Jean McConville', *Independent*, 4 May 2014.

Eugene McLaughlin, *The New Policing* (London: SAGE, 2007).

Mitchel McLaughlin and Paige Arthur, 'Redefining Republicanism: A Political Perspective and Academic Perspective', *IBIS Working Papers*, 5.5 (2001).

Fiona McLernon, Ed Cairns, Miles Hewstone and Ron Smith, 'The Development of Intergroup Forgiveness in Northern Ireland', *Journal of Social Issues*, 60.3 (2004), pp. 587–601.

Sean MacStiofáin, *Memoirs of a Revolutionary* (Edinburgh: Gordon Cremonesi, 1975).

Robbie McVeigh, *It's Part of Life Here: The Security Forces and Harassment in Northern Ireland* (Belfast: Committee on the Administration of Justice, 1994).

'Maghaberry', *Poblacht na nOibrithe*, 2012.

Agnes Maillot, *New Sinn Féin: Irish Republicanism in the Twenty First Century* (London: Routledge, 2004).

'The Main Easter Commemorations', *Irish Republican News*, 26 March 2016: http://republican-news.org/current/news/2016/03/the_main_easter_commemorations.html#.VxSPNzArLIU (accessed 18 April 2016).

Steven Majstorovic, 'Ancient Hatreds or Elite Manipulation? Memory and Politics in The Former Yugoslavia', *World Affairs*, 159.4 (1997), pp. 170–82.

'Make Sinn Féin's Betrayal the Catalyst for a Real People's Alternative!', *IRSP*, 18 November 2015: www.irsp.ie/news/?p=2039 (accessed 14 December 2015).

'Man Shot in Donegal Named Locally as 27-year-old Andrew Burns from Strabane', *Independent*, 13 February 2008.

Mark Malan, 'Peacebuilding in South Africa: Police Reform in Mozambique and South Africa', *International Peacekeeping*, 6.4 (1999), pp. 171–90.

Siniša Malešević, *Identity as Ideology: Understanding Ethnicity and Nationalism* (Basingstoke: Palgrave Macmillan, 2006).

Paul Malone, '"Border Regions Losing Faith in PSNI" – Murphy', *Newry Times*, 27 February 2015: http://newrytimes.com/2015/02/27/border-regions-losing-faith-in-psni-murphy/ (accessed 28 February 2015).

Otwin Marenin, 'Parking Tickets and Class Repression: The Concept of Policing in Critical Theories of Criminal Justice', *Contemporary Crises*, 6 (1982), pp. 241–66.

Sabine Marschall, 'Commemorating "Struggle Heroes": Constructing a Genealogy for the New South Africa', *International Journal of Heritage Studies*, 12.2 (2006), pp. 176–93.

'Martin McGuinness Opinion Piece on Deal', *Derry Sinn Féin*, 4 December 2015: www.derrysinnfein.ie/news/3530/ (accessed 14 December 2015).

Alex Maskey, 'Address to 1996 Ard Fheis': Northern Ireland Political Collection, Linenhall Library, Belfast.

Robert B. Mattes, 'South Africa: Democracy Without the People', *Journal of Democracy*, 13.1 (2002), pp. 22–36.

'The Mechanisms of Unaccountability', *Poblacht na nOibrithe*, 2012.

C. Merridale, 'War, Death and Remembrance in Soviet Russia', in J. Winter and E. Sivan (eds), *War and Remembrance in the Twentieth Century* (Cambridge: Cambridge University Press, 2000).

L. Meskell, 'Trauma Culture: Remembering and Forgetting in the New South Africa', in D. Bell (ed.), *Memory, Trauma and World Politics* (Basingstoke: Palgrave Macmillan, 2010), pp. 157–75.

L. Metsola, 'The Special Field Force and Namibian Ex-Combatant "Reintegration"', in A. M. Jefferson and S. Jensen (eds), *State Violence and Human Rights: State Officials in the South* (London: Routledge Cavendish, 2009), pp. 102–21.

Harry Mika and Kieran McEvoy, 'Restorative Justice in Conflict: Paramilitarism, Community and the Construction of Legitimacy in Northern Ireland', *Contemporary Justice Review*, 3.3 (2001), pp. 291–319.

David Mitchell, 'Cooking the Fudge: Constructive Ambiguity and the Implementation of the Northern Ireland Agreement, 1998–2007', *Irish Political Studies*, 24.3 (2009), pp. 321–36.

Nicholas Moll, 'Fragmented Memories in a Fragmented Country: Memory Competition and Political Identity-Building in Today's Bosnia and Herzegovina', *Nationalities Papers: The Journal of Nationalism and Ethnicity*, 41.6 (2013), pp. 910–35.

Ed Moloney, *Voices from the Grave: Two Men's War in Ireland* (London: Faber and Faber, 2011).

Mark Moloney, 'Gerry Adams Clarifies "Bastards" Comment – About Bigots, Homophobes and Racists', *An Phoblacht*, 25 November 2014: www.anphoblacht.com/contents/24570 (accessed 16 December 2015).

—— 'Gerry Adams "Seriously Concerned" by PSNI Arrest of Sinn Féin Chairperson for North', *An Phoblacht*, 9 September 2015: www.anphoblacht.com/contents/25339 (accessed 20 May 2017).

Gerry Moriarty, 'Ian Paisley: Power House Unionist Who Eventually Shook Hands with Nationalists', *Irish Times*, 31 December 2014: www.irishtimes.com/news/politics/ian-paisley-powerhouse-unionist-who-eventually-shook-hands-with-nationalists-1.2051277 (accessed 7 October 2016).

—— 'Bobby Storey: The IRA is "Stood Down" and has Left the Stage', *Irish Times*, 13 September 2015: www.irishtimes.com/news/ireland/irish-news/bobby-storey-the-ira-is-stood-down-and-has-left-stage-1.2350112 (accessed 10 November 2015).

J. F. Morrison, 'Why Do People Become Dissident Irish Republicans', in P. M. Currie and M. Taylor (eds), *Dissident Irish Republicanism* (New York: Continuum, 2011), pp. 17–42.

—— *The Rise and Origins of Dissident Irish Republicanism: The Role and Impact of Organizational Splits* (New York: Bloomsbury, 2013).

—— 'An Interview with Danny Morrison', *Terrorism and Political Violence*, 28.3 (2016a), pp. 620–35.

—— 'Fighting Talk: The Statements of "the IRA/New IRA"', *Terrorism and Political Violence*, 28.3 (2016b), pp. 598–619.

'Motion Passed by Sinn Féin at Extraordinary Ard Fheis on Policing, RDS, Dublin (28 January 2007)': www.cain.ulst.ac.uk/issues/politics/docs/sf/sf280107motion.htm (accessed 24 April 2012).

Ahmad Mubarak, 'Police Transformation: The Palestinian Authority Perspective', *Crime and Policing in Transitional Societies* (2000).

Aoghan Mulcahy, 'Policing History: The Official Discourse and Organisational Memory of the Royal Ulster Constabulary', *British Journal of Criminology*, 40.1 (2000), pp. 68–87.

—— *Policing Northern Ireland: Conflict, Legitimacy and Reform* (London: Routledge, 2013).

Aoghan Mulcahy and Graham Ellison, 'The Language of Policing and the Struggle for Legitimacy in Northern Ireland', *Policing and Society*, 11.3–4 (2001), pp. 383–404.

Marc Mulholland, 'Irish Republican Politics and Violence Before the Peace Process, 1968–1994', *European Review of History*, 14.3 (2007), pp. 397–421.

G. Mulvenna, 'Labour Aristocracies, Triumphalism, and Melancholy: Misconceptions of the Protestant Working-Class and Loyalist Community', in T. Burgess and G. Mulvenna (eds), *The Contested Identities of Ulster Protestants* (Basingstoke: Palgrave Macmillan, 2015), pp. 159–76.

'Murder', *The Freedom Fighter*, 7 (1977).

Joanne Murphy, *Policing for Peace in Northern Ireland: Change, Conflict and Community Confidence* (Basingstoke: Palgrave Macmillan, 2013).

D. Murray, 'Post-Accord Police Reform', in J. Darby (ed.), *Violence and Reconstruction* (Notre Dame, Ind.: University of Notre Dame Press, 2006).

Sean Murray, 'Address to Extraordinary Ard Fheis', 28 January 2007: Northern Ireland Political Collection, Linenhall Library, Belfast.

'The Nature of Strategy, Politics, Revolution and British Withdrawal', *Republican News*, 27 March 1976.

'The Necessity of Policing and the Necessity for Constitutional Change', 32 County Sovereignty Movement: www.32csm.net/p/32csm-policy-documents.html (accessed 24 April 2012).

'Neither Ó hAnluain or Sabhat Would Follow "A Path of Deceit, Duplicity and Treachery Over 20 Years"', *Saoirse*, 238 (February 2007).

Rachel Nelid, 'Democratic Police Reforms in War Torn Societies', *Conflict, Security & Development*, 1.1 (2001), pp. 21–43.

John Nelson, 'Social Memory as Ritual Practice: Commemorating Spirits of the Military Dead Yasukuni Shinto Shrine', *Journal of Asian Studies*, 62.2 (2003), pp. 443–67.

'New Patsy O'Hara Hunger Strike Mural Unveiled in Belfast', *IRSP*, 18 November 2013: www.irsp.ie/news/?p=1335 (accessed 6 August 2014).

Fionnuala Ní Aolaín, 'Truth Telling, Accountability and the Right to Life in Northern Ireland', *European Human Rights Law Review*, 5 (2002), pp. 572–90.

'NI Assembly Election: DUP Remains Largest as Assembly Count Ends', BBC News, 7 May 2016: www.bbc.co.uk/news/election-2016-northern-ireland-36234717 (accessed 12 May 2016).

Caoilfhionn Ní Dhonnabhaín, 'Motion Passed by Huge Majority', *An Phoblacht*, 1 February 2007.

Pierre Nora, 'Between Memory and History: *Les Lieux de Mémoire*', *Representations*, 26 (1989), pp. 7–24.

'No Other Law: The Politics of Policing in Occupied Ireland', 32 County Sovereignty Movement, 15 January 2007: http://indiamond6.ulib.iupui.edu:81/32CSM210107.html (accessed 17 May 2017).

'Northern Ireland EU Dream DESTROYED: James Brokenshire Says NO Referendum after Brexit', *Express*, 20 July 2016: www.express.co.uk/news/politics/691435/Politics-James-Brokenshire-no-Northern-Ireland-EU-referedum-Brexit (accessed 12 October 2016).

'Northern Ireland Executive Breached Duty Over Anti-Poverty Strategy', BBC News, 30 June 2015: www.bbc.co.uk/news/uk-northern-ireland-33326631 (accessed 30 June 2015).

Northern Ireland Office, 'Foundations for Policing' (London: HMSO, 1996).

Northern Ireland Policing Board, 'Human Rights Thematic Review on the Use of Police Powers to Stop and Search and Stop and Question under the Terrorism Act 2000 and the Justice and Security (NI) Act 2007' (Belfast: Northern Ireland Policing Board, 2013).

Northern Ireland Retired Police Officers Association, 'Written Submission by the Northern Ireland Retired Police Officers Association to Dr Richard Haass on "Dealing with the Past"' (Belfast: Northern Ireland Retired Police Officers Association, 2013): www.slideshare.net/MickFealty/nirpos-haass-submission-on-dealing-with-the-past-13-november-2013 (accessed 5 August 2014).

Sean O'Bradaigh, '40 Years of Éire Nua', *Republican Sinn Féin*: https://republicansinnfein.org/miscellaneous/rsfposition/40-years-of-eire-nua-by-sean-o-bradaigh/ (accessed 3 October 2016).

Eoin Ó Broin, *Sinn Féin and the Politics of Left Republicanism* (London: Pluto Press, 2009).

Vedran Obucina, 'A War of Myths: Creation of the Founding Myth of Kosovo Albanians', *Contemporary Issues*, 4.1 (2011), pp. 30–44.

Fíonnuala O'Cionnaith, 'McConville: My Mother's Murder is a War Crime', *Irish Examiner*, 7 April 2015: www.irishexaminer.com/ireland/mcconville-my-mothers-murder-is-a-war-crime-322535.html (accessed 27 November 2015).

S. O'Connor, *More than a Uniform* (Belfast: O'Connor Publications, 1999).

Niall O'Dochartaigh, *From Civil Rights to Armalites: Derry and the Birth of the Irish Troubles* (Cork: Cork University Press, 1997).

Malachi O'Doherty, *The Trouble with Guns: Republican Strategy and the Provisional IRA* (Belfast: Blackstaff Press, 1998).

C. O'Donnell, 'The Evolution of Irish Republicanism and the Peace Process in Northern Ireland', in A. Edwards and S. Bloomer (eds), *Transforming the Peace Process in Northern Ireland* (Dublin: Irish Academic Press, 2008).

Ella O'Dwyer, 'Speakers Exude Confidence and Stress Need for Unity', *An Phoblacht*, 1 February 2007.

Peadar O Faolaín, 'Policing Debate Part of Broader Strategic Plan', *An Phoblacht*, 18 January 2007.

Gearóid O'Faolean, 'The Ulster Defence Regiment and the Question of Catholic Recruitment, 1970–72', *Terrorism and Political Violence*, 27.5 (2015), pp. 838–56.

'Oglach Seamus McElwain 25th Anniversary Commemoration', *Ogra Shinn Féin*, 14 April 2011: http://ograshinnfein.blogspot.co.uk/2011/04/oglach-seamus-mcelwain-25th-anniversary.html (accessed 6 August 2014).

'Ógra Shinn Féin National Congress Opposes SF Policing Motion', *Ogra Shinn Féin*, 22 January 2007: www.ograshinnfein.blogspot.co.uk/2007/01/gra-shinn-fin-national-congress.html (accessed 24 April 2012).

F. Ó hAdhmaill, 'Republicans Must Remain Republican', in C. Ó Brolcháin (ed.), *The Politics of Policing* (Belfast: James Connolly Debating Society, 2007), pp. 34–39.

Brendan O'Leary and James McGarry, *The Politics of Antagonism Understanding Northern Ireland* (London: Athlone Press, 1993).

Jeffrey K. Olick, 'Collective Memory: The Two Cultures', *Sociological Theory*, 17.3 (1999), pp. 333–48.

—— 'Collective Memory: A Memoir and Prospect', *Memory Studies*, 1.1 (2008), pp. 23–29.

—— *The Politics of Regret: On Collective Memory and Historical Responsibility* (London: Routledge, 2013).

Padraig O'Malley, *Biting at the Grave: The Irish Hunger Strikes and the Politics of Despair* (Boston: Beacon Press, 1991).

'On the War Front', *Volunteer*, 19 September 1976.

William G. O'Neill, *Police Reform in Post-Conflict Societies: What We Know and What We Still Need to Know* (New York: International Peace Academy, 2005).

'An Open Debate, and a Principled Stance', *Sovereign Nation*, January/February 2007.

'Opening Address by Gerry Adams, then President of Sinn Féin (SF), to the Sinn Féin Extraordinary Ard Fheis on Policing, RDS, Dublin (28 January 2007)': http://cain.ulst.ac.uk/issues/politics/docs/sf/ga280107a.htm (accessed 10 May 2012).

M. O'Rawe, 'Policing Change: To Reform or Not to Transform', in C. Coulter and M. Murray (eds), *Northern Ireland after the Troubles: A Society in Transition* (Manchester: Manchester University Press, 2008), pp. 110–32.

Mary O'Rawe and Linda Moore, *Human Rights on Duty: Principles for Better Policing – International Lessons for Northern Ireland* (Belfast: Committee on the Administration of Justice, 1997).

Richard O'Rawe, *Blanketman: An Untold Story of the H-block Hunger Strike* (Dublin: New Island, 2005).

Nicholas O'Shaughnessy, 'Persuasion, Myth and Propaganda', *Journal of Political Marketing*, 3.3 (2004), pp. 87–103.

Mark Osiel, *Mass Atrocities, Collective Memory and the Law* (New Brunswick, NJ: Transaction, 1997).

'The Overtime Killings', *Iris*, 10 (July 1985).

D. Paez and J. H. Liu, 'Collective Memory of Conflicts', in D. Bar-Tal (ed.), *Intergroup Conflicts and their Resolution* (New York: Psychology Press, 2009), pp. 105–24.

Yiannis Papadakis, 'Greek Cypriot Narratives of History and Collective Identity: Nationalism as a Contested Process', *American Ethnologist*, 25.2 (1998), pp. 149–65.

Pat Finucane Centre, 'One Day in August: The Report of the Pat Finucane Centre into the Allegations of the Abuse of Human Rights Arising Out of the Apprentice Boys Parade in Derry City on 12th August 1995' (Derry: Pat Finucane Centre, 1995).

David Patterson, *A Legacy of Tears: 30 Years of Protestant Suffering at the Hands of Irish Republican Terrorists in South & North Armagh, 1969–1999* (Armagh: Saver Naver, 2006).

Henry Patterson, *The Politics of Illusion: Republicanism and Socialism in Modern Ireland* (London: Hutchinson Radius, 1989).

—— *Ireland Since 1939: The Persistence of Conflict* (Dublin: Penguin, 2006).

—— 'The Republican Movement and the Legacy of the Troubles', in I. Honohon (ed.), *Republicanism in Ireland: Confronting Theories and Traditions* (Manchester: Manchester University Press, 2008), pp. 147–63.

—— 'Sectarianism Revisited: The Provisional IRA Campaign in a Border Region of Northern Ireland', *Terrorism and Political Violence*, 22.3 (2010), pp. 337–56.

—— 'Beyond the Micro Group: The Dissident Republican Challenge', in P. M. Currie and M. Taylor (eds), *Dissident Irish Republicanism* (New York: Continuum International Publishing Group, 2011), pp. 65–95.

J. W. Pennebaker and A. L. Gonzales, 'Making History: Social and Psychological Processes Underlying Collective Memory', in P. Boyer and J. V. Wertsch (eds), *Memory in Mind and Culture* (Cambridge: Cambridge University Press, 2009), pp. 171–93.

Robert Perry, 'The Devolution of Policing in Northern Ireland: Politics and Reform', *Politics*, 31.3 (2011), pp. 167–78.

Sharon Pickering, *Women, Policing and Resistance in Northern Ireland* (Belfast: Beyond the Pale, 2002).

Patrick Pinkerton, 'Resisting Memory: The Politics of Memorialisation in Post-Conflict Northern Ireland', *British Journal of Politics and International Relations*, 14.1 (2012), pp. 131–52.

R. M. Pockrass, 'The Police Response to Terrorism: The Royal Ulster Constabulary', *Police Journal*, 59 (1986), p. 143.

Police Federation for Northern Ireland, *Whats in a Name? The Royal Ulster Constabulary* (Belfast: Police Federation for Northern Ireland, 1999).

'Police Regret Inquest Delay', *Lurgan Mail*, 23 September 2014: www.lurganmail.co.uk/news/local-news/police-regret-inquest-delay-1-6315071 (accessed 26 April 2015).

'Policing: Transfer of Powers Would be Advance for Struggle', *An Phoblacht*, 4 January 2007.

Francesca Polletta, '"It was like a fever ...": Narrative and Identity in Social Protest', *Social Problems*, 45.2 (1998), pp. 137–59.

Margaret Popkin and Nehal Bhuta, 'Latin American Amnesties in Comparative Perspective: Can the Past be Buried', *Ethics and International Affairs*, 13 (1999), pp. 99–122.

Juan D. Prieto, 'Together After War while the War Goes On: Victims, Ex-Combatants and Communities in Three Columbian Cities', *International Journal of Transitional Justice*, 6.3 (2012), pp. 1–22.

'Prince Charles Meets Sinn Féin Leader Gerry Adams', BBC News, 19 May 2015: www.bbc.co.uk/news/uk-northern-ireland-32786393 (accessed 22 May 2015).

'Provos to Join British Police', *Saoirse*, 188 (December 2002).

'PSNI Officers Being Trained to Give Talks in Irish', *Belfast Telegraph*, 20 May 2009.

Bob Purdie, *Politics in the Streets: The Origins of the Civil Rights Movement in Northern Ireland* (Belfast: Blackstaff, 1990).

'Quislings Publicly Thanked', *Republican News*, 27 June 1973.

Kevin Rafter, *Sinn Féin 1905–2005: In the Shadow of Gunmen* (Dublin: Gill & Macmillan, 2005).

F. Raimundo and A. Costa Pinto, 'From Ruptured Transition to Politics of Silence: The Case of Portugal', in N. Wouters (ed.), *Transitional Justice and Memory in Europe (1945–2013)* (Cambridge: Intersentia, 2014), pp. 173–98.

Janine Rauch, 'Police Reform and South Africa's Transition', in *Crime and Policing in Transitional Societies*, Proceedings of conference held at Jan Smuts House, University of the Witwatersrand, Johannesburg, 30 August–1 September 2000 (South African Institute of International Affairs, 2001): www.kas.de/wf/doc/kas_4865-1522-2-30.pdf?040622164853 (accessed 17 May 2017).

'Real IRA Murder Victim Kieran Doherty is Buried', BBC News, 1 March 2010: http://news.bbc.co.uk/1/hi/northern_ireland/foyle_and_west/8543145.stm (accessed 20 March 2015).

'Report of the Advisory Committee on Police in Northern Ireland' (Hunt Report) (London: HMSO, 1969).

'Report of the Committee of Inquiry into Police Interrogation Procedures in Northern Ireland', Cmnd 7494 (London: HMSO, 1979).

Richard Reed, 'Researching Ulster Loyalism: The Methodological Challenges of the Divisive and Sensitive Subject', *Politics*, 32.3 (2012), pp. 207–19.

Kacper E. Rekawek, *Irish Republican Terrorism and Politics: A Comparative Study of the Official and the Provisional IRA* (London: Routledge, 2011).

Relatives for Justice, *Collusion* (Belfast: Relatives for Justice, 1993).

'Remembering the Burning of Bombay Street', *An Phoblacht*, 19 August 2004.
J. Renner and A. Spencer, 'Bringing Transitional Justice to Terrorism Research', in I. Tellidis and H. Toros (eds), *Researching Terrorism, Peace and Conflict Studies: Interaction, Synthesis and Opposition* (Abingdon: Routledge, 2015), pp. 64–80.
Republican Network for Unity, *Standing Outside the 'Peace Process': A Revolutionary Republican Analysis of the Irish Pacification Process by the Republican Network for Unity* (Belfast: Republican Network for Unity, 2010).
—— *Revolutionary Republicanism: National Liberation, Socialism, International Solidarity* (Belfast: Republican Network for Unity, 2013).
'Republican Socialist Youth Movement', *Starry Plough*, Easter 2007.
Ann Rigney, 'Divided Pasts: A Premature Memorial and the Dynamics of Collective Remembrance', *Memory Studies*, 1.1 (2008), pp. 89–97.
'The Road to Peace, Freedom and Justice', *Waterside Republican Newssheet*, 3 (April 1989).
'Robert Rogers Jailed over Eileen Doherty Murder in Belfast', BBC News, 15 March 2013: www.bbc.co.uk/news/uk-northern-ireland-21797836 (accessed 8 January 2014).
Rosellen Roche, 'Still the 'Brutes in the Suits'? Continuing Perceptions of the Police in Northern Ireland', *Irish Journal of Anthropology*, 11.1 (2008), pp. 42–49.
Kim Lacy Rogers, 'Lynching Stories: Family and Community Memory in the Mississippi Delta', in Kim Lacy Rogers, Selma Leydesdorff and Graham Dawson (eds), *Trauma and Life Stories: International Perspectives* (London: Routledge, 1999).
Bill Rolston, *Unfinished Business: State Killings and the Quest for Truth* (Belfast: Beyond the Pale, 2000).
—— 'Resistance and Terror: Lessons from Ireland', in P. Scraton (ed.), *Beyond September 11: An Anthology of Dissent* (London: Pluto Press, 2002), pp. 59–66.
—— '"An Effective Mask for Terror": Democracy, Death Squads and Northern Ireland', *Crime, Law and Social Change*, 44.2 (2006a), pp. 181–203.
—— 'Dealing with the Past: Pro-State Paramilitaries, Truth and Transition in Northern Ireland', *Human Rights Quarterly*, 28.3 (2006b), pp. 652–75.
—— 'Trying to Reach the Future through the Past: Murals and Memory in Northern Ireland', *Crime, Media, Culture*, 6.3 (2010), pp. 285–307.
—— *Children of the Revolution: The Lives of Sons and Daughters of Activists in Northern Ireland* (Derry: Guildhall Press, 2011).
—— 'The State's Role in the Management and Resolution of Violent Conflict: Learning from Northern Ireland?', in M. Breen-Smyth (ed.), *The Ashgate Research Companion to Political Violence* (Farnham: Ashgate, 2012).
—— 'Messages of Allegiance and Defiance: The Murals of Gaza', *Race & Class*, 55.4 (2014a), pp. 40–64.

—— 'Satisfaction with the HET: Relatives' Views' (2014b): http://relativesforjustice.com/wp-content/uploads/2014/01/HET-research-Relatives-Views-by-Prof-Bill-Rolston.pdf (accessed 11 October 2016).

E. Rooney, 'Learning to Remember and Remembering to Forget: Beloved from Belfast', in L. Pearce (ed.), *Devolving Identities: Feminist Readings in Home and Belonging* (Farnham: Ashgate, 2000), pp. 215–34.

Richard Rose, *Governing without Consensus: An Irish Perspective* (London: Faber & Faber, 1971).

F. Stuart Ross, 'Between Party and Movement: Sinn Féin and the Popular Movement against Criminalisation, 1976–82', *Irish Political Studies*, 21.3 (2006), pp. 337–54.

Marc H. Ross, *Cultural Contestation in Ethnic, Conflict* (Cambridge: Cambridge University Press, 2007).

Avril Roulton, 'Policing Reforms in Northern Ireland: An Examination of Alienation Experienced by Former Royal Ulster Constabulary Officers as a Result of the Report of the Independent Commission on Policing', PhD thesis, University of Ulster, 2009.

Brian Rowan, 'Martin McGuinness and George Hamilton Debate: Meeting of Minds Good for the Future', *Belfast Telegraph*, 10 August 2015: www.belfasttelegraph.co.uk/opinion/debateni/brian-rowan/martin-mcguinness-and-george-hamilton-debate-meeting-of-minds-good-for-the-future-31438633.html (accessed 19 August 2015).

—— 'Profile: Drew Harris of the PSNI', *Belfast Telegraph*, 20 September 2014: www.belfasttelegraph.co.uk/life/features/profile-drew-harris-of-the-psni-30600926.html (accessed 25 August 2015).

'RSF: Leading the Struggle', *Saoirse*, 237 (January 2007).

Joseph Ruane and Jennifer Todd, *The Dynamics of Conflict in Northern Ireland: Power, Conflict and Emancipation* (Cambridge: Cambridge University Press, 1996).

RUC GC Foundation, *Royal Ulster Constabulary George Cross Garden* (Kesh: RUC Publications, 2003).

Gerry Ruddy, 'Ireland: Some Thoughts on the Policing Issue', *Plough*, 3:40 (12 December 2006).

Mutuma Ruteere and Marie-Emmanuelle Pommerolle, 'Democratizing Security or Decentralizing Repression? The Ambiguities of Community Policing in Kenya', *African Affairs*, 102.409 (2003), pp. 587–604.

Chris Ryder, *The RUC: A Force Under Fire* (London: Methuen, 1989).

V. Salvi, 'The Slogan "Complete Memory": A Reactive (Re)-Signification of the Memory of the Disappeared in Argentina', in F. Lessa and V. Druliolle (eds), *The Memory of State Terrorism in the Southern Cone: Argentina, Chile and Uruguay* (New York: Palgrave Macmillan, 2011), pp. 43–61.

Scott A. Sandage, 'A Marble House Divided: The Lincoln Memorial, the Civil Rights Movement, and the Politics of Memory, 1939–1963', *Journal of American History*, 80.1 (1993), pp. 135–67.

Andrew Sanders, *Inside the IRA: Dissident Republicans and the War for Legitimacy* (Edinburgh: Edinburgh University Press, 2011).

Margarita Saona, *Memory Matters in Transitional Peru* (Basingstoke: Palgrave Macmillan, 2014).

Jean-Paul Sartre, 'Preface' to F. Fanon, *The Wretched of the Earth* (Harmondsworth: Penguin, 1967).

'SAS Inquest into Shooting of IRA Men Martin McCaughey and Dessie Grew was Ineffective, Court Told', *Belfast Telegraph*, 13 March 2015: www.belfasttelegraph.co.uk/news/northern-ireland/sas-inquest-into-shooting-of-ira-men-martin-mccaughey-and-dessie-grew-was-ineffective-court-told-31062736.html (accessed 26 April 2015).

'Save the RUC', *Daily Telegraph*, 28 September 1999.

Scarman Report, 'Government of Northern Ireland Violence and Civil Disturbances in Northern Ireland 1969, Report of Tribunal of Inquiry' (London: HMSO, 1972).

Howard Schuman and Amy Corning, 'Collective Memory and Autobiographical Memory: Similar but Not the Same', *Memory Studies*, 7.2 (2014), pp. 146–60.

Barry Schwartz, 'Memory as a Cultural System: Abraham Lincoln in World War II', *American Sociological Review*, 61.5 (1996), pp. 908–27.

—— 'Collective Memory and History: How Abraham Lincoln became a Symbol of Racial Equality', *Sociological Quarterly*, 38.3 (1997), pp. 469–96.

Barry Schwartz, Yael Zerubavel and Bernice M. Barnett, 'The Recovery of Masada: A Study in Collective Memory', *Sociological Quarterly*, 27.2 (1986), pp. 147–64.

Phil Scraton, *The State of the Police* (London: Pluto, 1985).

—— *Power, Conflict and Criminalisation* (London: Routledge, 2007).

'SDLP Move Undermined the Good Friday Agreement – McCartney', *Derry Sinn Féin*, 5 February 2015: www.derrysinnfein.ie/sdlp-move-undermined-the-good-friday-agreement-mccartney-2/ (accessed 1 May 2015).

'Seamus Harvey 30th Anniversary', *An Phoblacht*, 25 January 2007.

'Sean Sabhat 50th Anniversary Marked in Limerick', *Saoirse*, 237 (January 2007).

'Secretary of State Revokes Prison Licence of Derry Republican', *Derry Journal*, 11 March 2016: www.derryjournal.com/news/secretary-of-state-revokes-prison-licence-of-derry-republican-1-7269765 (accessed 19 April 2016).

Martin Seliger, 'Fundamental and Operative Ideology: The Two Principal Dimensions to Political Argumentation', *Policy Sciences*, 1.1 (1970), pp. 325–38.

'Senior Police Post: Policing Board Rejects Sinn Féin Criticism', BBC News, 15 September 2014: www.bbc.co.uk/news/uk-northern-ireland-29204482 (accessed 1 May 2015).

'SF Policing Board Nominees Named', BBC News, 23 April 2007: http://news.bbc.co.uk/1/hi/northern_ireland/6581857.stm (accessed 7 August 2014).

'SF to Meet with Families of "Fallen Comrades"', *Derry Journal*, 19 January 2007.

Tim Shanahan, *The Provisional Irish Republican Army and the Morality of Terrorism* (Edinburgh: Edinburgh University Press, 2009).

'Sharing Power with DUP a "Shameful Act"', *Saoirse*, 240 (April 2007).

Clifford Shearing, '"A New Beginning" for Policing', *Journal of Law and Society*, 27.3 (2000), pp. 386–93.

Peter Shirlow, 'Ethno-Sectarianism and the Reproduction of Fear in Belfast', *Capital & Class*, 27.2 (2003a), pp. 77–93.

—— '"Who Fears to Speak": Fear, Mobility and Ethno-Sectarianism in the Two "Ardoynes"', *Global Review of Ethnopolitics*, 3.1 (2003b), pp. 76–91.

—— 'Sympathies, Apathies and Antipathies: The Falls-Shankill Divide', *Irish Geography*, 41.3 (2008), pp. 337–40.

—— *The End of Ulster Loyalism?* (Manchester: Manchester University Press, 2012).

Peter Shirlow and Kieran McEvoy, *Beyond the Wire: Former Prisoners and Conflict Transformation in Northern Ireland* (London: Pluto Press, 2008).

Peter Shirlow and Mark McGovern, 'Introduction: Who are "the People" Unionism, Protestantism and Loyalism in Northern Ireland', in Peter Shirlow and Mark McGovern (eds), *Who are 'The People'? Unionism, Protestantism and Loyalism in Northern Ireland* (London: Pluto Press, 1997), pp. 1–15.

Peter Shirlow, Jonathan Tonge, James McAuley and Catherine McGlynn, *Abandoning Historical Conflict? Former Political Prisoners and Reconciliation in Northern Ireland* (Manchester: Manchester University Press, 2010).

Kirk Simpson, 'Voices Silenced, Voices Rediscovered: Victims of Violence and the Reclamation of Language in Transitional Justice Societies', *International Journal of Law in Context*, 3.2 (2007), pp. 89–103.

—— *Unionist Voices and the Politics of Remembering the Past in Northern Ireland* (Basingstoke: Palgrave Macmillan, 2009).

'Sinn Féin Chairman Declan Kearney "Sorry" for All Troubles Victims', BBC News, 27 August 2015: www.bbc.co.uk/news/uk-northern-ireland-politics-34069960 (accessed 27 August 2015).

'Sinn Féin Criticise Police Raid on Derry Mayor's Home', BBC News, 13 July 2012: http://www.bbc.co.uk/news/uk-northern-ireland-foyle-west-18826243 (accessed 3 January 2014).

'Sinn Féin's Gerry Adams says IRA "Has Gone Away"', BBC News, 23 August 2015: www.bbc.co.uk/news/uk-northern-ireland-politics-34033753 (accessed 23 August 2015).

'Sinn Féin Responds to Patten', *An Phoblacht*, 2 December 1999.

Sinn Féin, 'Éire Nua: The Social and Economic Programme of Sinn Féin' (Dublin: Sinn Féin, 1971).

—— *Moving Beyond Sectarian Policing in Newry* (Newry: Sinn Féin, 1995).

—— 'Submission to the Review of Parades', 1996: Northern Ireland Political Collection, Linenhall Library, Belfast.

—— 'Policing: A New Beginning? Amendments to Bring the Police Bill into line with the Patten Report' (Belfast: Sinn Féin, 2000).

—— 'A New Beginning to Policing: Response to the Revised Implementation Plan on Policing' (Belfast: Sinn Féin, 2001).

—— '"Wag the Dog": British Securocrats are a Threat to the Peace Process' (Belfast: Sinn Féin, 2002).

—— 'Who Sanctioned Britain's Death Squad? Time for Truth' (Belfast: Sinn Féin, 2003).

—— 'A New Beginning to Policing' (Belfast: Sinn Féin, 2007).

E. Slater, 'Introduction', in E. Slater and M. Peillon (eds), *Memories of the Present: A Sociological Chronicle of Ireland, 1997–1998* (Dublin: Institute of Public Administration, 2000).

Jeff A. Sluka, *Hearts and Minds, Water and Fish: The IRA and INLA in a Northern Irish Ghetto* (Greenwich, Conn.: JAI Press, 1989).

—— 'In the Shadow of the Gun: "Not-War-Not-Peace" and the Future of Conflict in Northern Ireland', *Critique of Anthropology*, 29.3 (2009), pp. 279–99.

—— 'Staying Alive While Conducting Primary Research: Fieldwork on Political Violence', in M. Breen-Smyth (ed.), *The Ashgate Companion to Political Violence* (Farnham: Ashgate, 2012).

Anthony D. Smith, 'Culture, Community and Territory: The Politics of Ethnicity and Nationalism', *International Affairs*, 72.3 (1996), pp. 445–58.

Chris Smith, 'HMIC Concern Over Accountability of PSNI's Legacy Investigations Branch', BBC News, 24 June 2015: www.bbc.co.uk/news/uk-northern-ireland-33248848 (accessed 10 July 2015).

Robbie Smith, 'The not so Irish News', *Iris*, 10 (July 1985).

William B. Smith, *The British State and the Northern Ireland Crisis 1969–73: From Violence to Power Sharing* (Washington, DC: United States Institute of Peace Press, 2011).

Jim Smyth, 'Symbolic Power and Police Legitimacy: The Royal Ulster Constabulary', *Crime, Law & Social Change*, 38.3 (2002), pp. 295–310.

—— 'The Road to God Knows Where: Understanding Irish Republicanism', *Capital & Class*, 29.2 (2005), pp. 135–58.

W. Soyinka, 'Memory, Truth and Healing', in I. Amadiume and A. An-Na'im (eds), *The Politics of Memory: Truth, Healing and Social Justice* (London: Zed Books, 2000), pp. 20–37.

'Speech by Gerry Adams, then President of Sinn Féin, at an Event to Commemorate Seán Sabhat and Feargal Ó hAnnluain, County Fermanagh,

1 January 2007': http://cain.ulst.ac.uk/issues/politics/docs/sf/ga010107.htm (accessed 10 May 2012).

'Speech by Gerry Kelly, then Sinn Féin Justice and Policing Spokesperson (SF), Delivering the Policing Report to the Sinn Féin Extraordinary Ard Fheis on Policing, RDS, Dublin (28 January 2007)': http://cain.ulst.ac.uk/issues/politics/docs/sf/gk280107.htm (accessed 10 May 2012).

Lyn Spillman and Brian Conway, 'Text, Bodies and the Memory of Bloody Sunday', *Symbolic Interaction*, 30.1 (2007), pp. 79–103.

John Stalker, *Stalker* (London: Harrap, 1988).

E. Stanley, 'The Political Economy of Transitional Justice in Timor-Leste', in K. McEvoy and L. McGregor (eds), *Transitional Justice from Below: Grassroots Activism and the Struggle for Change* (Oxford: Hart Publishing, 2008), pp. 167–87.

William Stanley, 'Building New Police Forces in El Salvador and Guatemala: Learning and Counter-Learning', *International Peacekeeping*, 6.4 (1999), pp. 113–34.

William Stanley and C. Call, 'Military and Police Reform after Civil Wars', in J. Darby and R. MacGinty (eds), *Contemporary Peacemaking: Conflict, Peace Processes and Post-War Reconstruction*, 2nd edn (Basingstoke: Palgrave Macmillan, 2008), pp. 300–12.

'Statement from Republican POWs, Maghaberry Jail', *Saoirse*, June 2009.

'Statement from Roe 4 Republican Political Prisoners Maghaberry', 20 March 2015: http://107cowgate.com/2015/03/20/statement-from-roe-4-republican-political-prisoners-maghaberry/ (accessed 24 August 2015).

Gregory W. Streich, 'Is there a Right to Forget? Historical Injustices, Race, Memory and Identity', *New Political Science*, 24.4 (2002), pp. 525–42.

'Sustained Guerrilla Campaign', *Iris*, 5 (Easter 1991).

Malcolm Sutton, *Bear in Mind These Dead: An Index of Deaths from the Conflict in Ireland 1969–2001*, 2nd edn (Belfast: Beyond the Pale, 2001).

'Tasks', *An tÓglách*, 1967.

Ruti Teitel, *Transitional Justice* (Oxford: Oxford University Press, 2000).

'Ten-Point Summary: Spoil Your Vote and Spoil It Early', *Republican News*, 27 June 1973.

'Text of Irish Republican Army (IRA) Statement on the Ending of the Armed Campaign (28 July 2005)': http://cain.ulst.ac.uk/othelem/organ/ira/ira280705.htm (accessed 10 March 2014).

'Thanks for Support', *Freedom Fighter*, 5 (January 1977).

Chris Thornton, 'Adams Backs PSNI as He Honours IRA Men', *Belfast Telegraph*, 2 January 2007.

Mike Tomlinson, 'From Counter-Terrorism to Criminal Justice: Transformation or Business as Usual', *Howard Journal of Criminal Justice*, 51.5 (2012), pp. 442–57.

Jon Tonge, 'They Haven't Gone Away You Know: Irish Republican "Dissidents" and "Armed Struggle"', *Terrorism and Political Violence,* 16.3 (2004), pp. 671–93.

—— 'Sinn Féin and "New Republicanism" in Belfast', *Space and Polity,* 10.2 (2006), pp. 135–47.

—— 'Nationalist Convergence? The Evolution of Sinn Féin and SDLP Politics', in A. Edwards and S. Bloomer (eds), *Transforming the Peace Process in Northern Ireland: From Terrorism to Democratic Politics* (Dublin: Irish Academic Press, 2008), pp. 59–67.

—— 'Republican Paramilitaries and the Peace Process', in B. Barton and P. Roche (eds), *The Northern Ireland Question: The Peace Process and the Belfast Agreement* (Basingstoke: Palgrave Macmillan, 2009), pp. 165–80.

—— 'An Enduring Tradition or the Last Gasp of Physical Force Republicanism? Dissident Republican Violence in Northern Ireland', in P. M. Currie and M. Taylor (eds), *Dissident Irish Republicanism* (New York: Continuum International Publishing Group, 2011), pp. 97–118.

—— 'No-one Likes Us; We Don't Care: "Dissident" Irish Republicans and Mandates', *Political Quarterly,* 83.2 (2012), pp. 219–26.

—— 'A Campaign Without End? "Dissident" Republican Violence in Northern Ireland', *Political Insight,* 5.1 (2014a), pp. 14–17.

—— *Comparative Peace Processes* (Cambridge: Polity Press, 2014b).

Jon Tonge, Peter Shirlow and James W. McAuley, 'So Why Did the Guns Fall Silent? How Interplay, not Stalemate Explains the Northern Ireland Peace Process', *Irish Political Studies,* 26.1 (2011), pp. 1–18.

John Topping 'Community Policing in Northern Ireland: A Resistance Narrative', *Policing & Society,* 18.4 (2008a), pp. 377–96.

—— 'Diversifying from Within: Community Policing and the Governance of Security in Northern Ireland', *British Journal of Criminology,* 48.6 (2008b), pp. 778–97.

—— 'Accountability, Policing and the Police Service of Northern Ireland: Local Practice Global Standards?', in S. Lister and M. Rowe (eds), *Accountability of Policing* (Abingdon: Routledge, 2015), pp. 150–71.

John Topping and Jonny Byrne, 'Paramilitary Punishments in Belfast: Policing Beneath the Peace', *Behavioural Sciences of Terrorism and Political Aggression,* 4.1 (2012a), pp. 41–59.

—— 'Policing, Terrorism and the Conundrum of "Community": A Northern Ireland Perspective', in B. Spalek (ed.), *Counter-Terrorism: Community-Based Approaches to Preventing Terror Crime* (Basingstoke: Palgrave Macmillan, 2012b), pp. 157–80.

Anna L. Tota, 'Homeless Memories: How Societies Forget their Past', *Studies in Communication Sciences,* 1.2 (2001), pp. 193–214.

'Total Collaboration with British Rule', *Soairse,* 238 (February 2007).

Steve Tshwete, 'South Africa: Crime and Policing in Transition', *Crime and Policing in Transitional Societies*, 30 (2001), pp. 27–28.

José Van Dijck, 'Record and Hold: Popular Music between Personal and Collective Memory', *Critical Studies in Media Communication*, 23.5 (2006), pp. 357–74.

Michael Van Tengen Page and M. L. R. Smith, 'War by Other Means: The Problem of Political Control in Irish Republican Strategy', *Armed Forces & Society*, 27.1 (2000), pp. 79–104.

Vered Vinitzky-Seroussi and Chana Teeger, 'Unpacking the Unspoken: Silence in Collective Memory and Forgetting', *Social Forces*, 88.3 (2010), pp. 1103–22.

Vamik D. Volkan, *Blood Lines: From Ethnic to Ethnic Terrorism* (Bolder, Colo.: Westview Press, 1997).

L. Waldorf, 'Like Jews Waiting for Jesus: Posthumous Justice in Post-Genocide Rwanda', in R. Shaw and L. Waldorf (eds), *Localising Transitional Justice: Interventions and Priorities After Mass Violence* (Stanford, Calif.: Stanford University Press, 2010), pp. 183–202.

Graham Walker, *A History of the Ulster Unionist Party: Protest, Pragmatism and Pessimism* (Manchester: Manchester University Press, 2004).

Dermot Walsh, *The Use and Abuse of Emergency Legislation in Northern Ireland* (London: The Cobden Trust, 1983).

—— *The Irish Police* (Dublin: Sweet & Maxwell, 1998).

Lynn Wartchow, 'Civil and Human Rights Violations in Northern Ireland: Effects and Shortcomings of the Good Friday Agreement in Guaranteeing Protections', *Northwestern Journal of International Human Rights*, 3.1 (2005), pp. 1–18.

'"We are Determined to Create an Ireland of Equals" – South Armagh Annual Volunteers Day 2014', *Newry Armagh Sinn Féin*, 23 June 2014: http://newryarmaghsinnfein.com/determined-create-ireland-equals-south-armagh-annual-volunteers-day-2014/ (accessed 7 August 2014).

Ron Weitzer, *Policing under Fire: Ethnic Conflict and Police–Community Relations in Northern Ireland* (New York: State University of New York Press, 1995).

'Welcome to West Belfast, Poverty Capital of the Six Counties', *Éirígí*, 15 September 2015: https://web.archive.org/web/20160312145124/http://eirigi.org/2015/09/15/welcome-to-west-belfast-poverty-capital-of-the-six-counties/ (originally accessed 14 December 2015).

James V. Wertsch, *Voices of Collective Remembering* (Cambridge: Cambridge University Press, 2002).

—— 'Collective Memory', in P. Boyer and J. V. Wertsch (eds), *Memory in Mind and Culture* (Cambridge: Cambridge University Press, 2009), pp. 117–37.

'What We Have We Hold – INLA': www.redactionarchive.org/2012/03/news-april-2001.html (accessed 17 July 2014).

Peader Whelan, 'Lurgan Republicans under Intense British Military Intelligence Surveillance as Loyalist Death Squad Struck', *An Phoblacht*, April 2012.

'Where Were the Republicans', *United Irishman,* October 1969.
'Whither Civil Rights?', *United Irishman,* December 1969.
Sophie A. Whiting, '"The Discourse of Defence": "Dissident" Irish Republican Newspapers and the "Propaganda War"', *Terrorism and Political Violence,* 24.3 (2012), pp. 483–503.
—— *Spoiling the Peace? The Threat of Dissident Republicans to Peace in Northern Ireland* (Manchester: Manchester University Press, 2015).
—— 'Mainstream Revolutionaries: Sinn Féin as a "Normal" Political Party?', *Terrorism and Political Violence,* 28.3 (2016), pp. 541–60.
J. Whyte, 'How Much Discrimination Was There Under the Unionist Regime, 1921–68?', in T. Gallagher and J. O'Connell (eds), *Contemporary Irish Studies* (Manchester: Manchester University Press, 1983), pp. 1–35.
Rick Wilford and Robin Wilson, *Northern Ireland Devolution Monitoring Report* (Belfast: Devolution Monitoring Programme, 2007).
James Q. Wilson and George L. Kelling, 'Broken Windows', *Atlantic Monthly,* 249.3 (1982), pp. 29–38.
Stefan Wolff, *Ethnic Conflict: A Global Perspective* (Oxford: Oxford University Press, 2006).
Joanne Wright, *Terrorist Propaganda: The Red Army Faction and the Provisional IRA 1968–86* (London: Macmillan, 1991).
Herbert Wulf, *Security Sector Reform in Developing and Transitional Countries* (Berlin: Berghof Research Centre for Constructive Conflict Management, 2004).
Connla Young, 'New "Revolutionary" Republican Party Saoradh Launched', *Irish News,* 26 September 2016: www.irishnews.com/news/politicalnews/2016/09/26/news/new-revolutionary-republican-party-saoradh-launched-708613/ (accessed 4 October 2016).
Eli Zaretsky, 'Collective Memory and Narrative: A Response to Etkind', *Constellations,* 16.1 (2009), pp. 201–04.
Eviatar Zerubavel, 'Social Memories: Steps to a Sociology of the Past', *Qualitative Sociology,* 19.3 (1996), pp. 283–99.
Nils Zurawski, '"I Know Where You Live!": Aspects of Watching, Surveillance and Social Control in a Conflict Zone (Northern Ireland)', *Surveillance and Society,* 2.4 (2004), pp. 498–512.

Index

Printed and bound by CPI Group (UK) Ltd, Croydon, CR0 4YY

13/09/2026

14961098-0008